The Creative Society – and the price Americans paid for it

The Creative Society is the first history to look at modern America through the eyes of its emerging ranks of professional experts including lawyers, scientists, doctors, administrators, business managers, teachers, policy specialists, and urban planners. Covering the period from the 1890s to the early twenty-first century, Louis Galambos examines the history that shaped professionals and, in turn, their role in shaping modern America. He considers the roles of education, anti-Semitism, racism, and elitism in shaping and defining the professional cadre and examines how matters of gender, race, and ethnicity determined whether women, African Americans, and immigrants from Europe, Asia, Latin America, and the Middle East were admitted to the professional ranks. He also discusses the role professionals played in urbanizing the United States, keeping the economy efficient and innovative, showing the government how to provide the people a greater measure of security and equity, and guiding the world's leading industrial power in coping with its complex, frequently dangerous foreign relations.

Louis Galambos is Professor of History at Johns Hopkins University, where he also serves as Editor of the Papers of Dwight David Eisenhower and Co-Director of The Institute for Applied Economics, Global Health, and the Study of Business Enterprise. He is the author of numerous books on modern institutional development in America, the rise of the bureaucratic state, and the evolution of the professions, most recently *Medicine, Science, and Merck* (with Roy Vagelos, 2002). He is coeditor of two Cambridge University Press series and has received widespread recognition for his development of the "organizational synthesis" of modern U.S. history.

"Louis Galambos delivers a dazzling history of the modern United States as formed by its managers, scientists, diplomats, planners, and lawyers. The hopeful message is that, more often than not, American expertise and innovation will save the day."

    – Jay Hancock, economics columnist, *The Baltimore Sun*

The Creative Society – and the price Americans paid for it is a bold, provocative, and compelling reinterpretation of perennial dilemmas in American society written by a historian at the top of his game. Louis Galambos brings his 'organizational synthesis' to life by evoking the experiences that animated the new professionals – in education, business, government, foreign policy, and urban life – who have made America work since the 1890s. This is history at its best: thoughtful, captivating, witty, and wise. Everyone who reads *The Creative Society* will gain a new understanding of key crises in American history – and novel insights to make sense of the challenges we face today."

    – Jeffrey L. Sturchio, Senior Partner at RabinMartin, former president and CEO of Global Health Council

"Louis Galambos is equally adept as storyteller and historian. Witty, readable, illuminating, and sometimes highly personal, this is a history book with the drama of a novel. Professor Galambos charts twentieth-century American development in four broad areas – urbanization, innovation, economic security, and internationalism – and weaves throughout these concurrent narratives an astonishing array of detail. His cast of characters is America's self-proclaimed and educated professionals. Lawyers, economists, nurses, urban planners, mining engineers, teachers, and even military strategists act out a historical pageant that boasts winners and losers. Most vividly, Galambos stirs his own family story into the mix. His small-town Ohio clan of bustling Hungarian emigrants shares the stage with prominent twentieth-century figures like Emma Goldman, George Marshall, and Robert Moses. And in a masterstroke of history writing, he invites us, his readers, to enhance his storytelling with reflections on our own American experience."

    – Mary Yeager and John Lithgow, Los Angeles, California

The Creative Society
– and the price Americans paid for it

LOUIS GALAMBOS
The Johns Hopkins University

CAMBRIDGE
UNIVERSITY PRESS

CAMBRIDGE UNIVERSITY PRESS
Cambridge, New York, Melbourne, Madrid, Cape Town,
Singapore, São Paulo, Delhi, Tokyo, Mexico City

Cambridge University Press
32 Avenue of the Americas, New York, NY 10013-2473, USA

www.cambridge.org
Information on this title: www.cambridge.org/9781107600997

First published 2012

Printed in the United States of America

A catalog record for this publication is available from the British Library.

Library of Congress Cataloging in Publication data
Galambos, Louis.
The creative society – and the price Americans paid for it / Louis Galambos.
p.   cm.
Includes bibliographical references and index.
ISBN 978-1-107-01317-9 (hardback) – ISBN 978-1-107-60099-7 (paperback)
1. Creative ability in business – United States – History.   2. Professional
employees – United States – History.   I. Title.
HD53.G357   2011
331.7′10973–dc23   2011026271

ISBN 978-1-107-01317-9 Hardback
ISBN 978-1-107-60099-7 Paperback

To my four wonderful daughters, Denise, Jennifer, Katherine, and Emma

Contents

Preface

If you are reading this book, you are probably a professional or a wannabe professional in training. Training and practice in the professions require literacy and, to some extent, the curiosity that might encourage you to buy or borrow a book of essays on "The Creative Society."[1] Odds are you live and work in a city or suburb. If you have a job right now, you probably get paid by a relatively large organization and most of your income – like mine – comes to you in the form of regular paychecks. If even a few of these guesses are accurate, you should keep reading because you're the central subject of this history.

How could that be true? History, we were told in school, has always been shaped by presidents and prime ministers, by generals and dictators, by the people who make it into the headlines of newspapers, the TV news, and the blogs. If you don't believe that, just borrow your daughter or son's history text and skim through the index. You'll recognize many of the names even though it may take you a while to remember exactly what they did or when they did it.

The Creative Society looks at history from a different angle and comes to different conclusions about the American experience and the people who did the most to shape it in the twentieth and twenty-first centuries. That's where you come in. Or to be more precise, people like you, who practiced a profession and created new ideas that helped America cope

---

[1] Reaching for a counterslogan to President Johnson's Great Society, Ronald Reagan announced in the 1960s his quest for a Creative Society. My own quest is for a new historical paradigm, and I am not running for office.

with some of the major problems it faced in the twentieth century – and still faces today. Many of those professionals didn't produce entirely new ideas but instead negotiated the compromises that enabled the society to move on to the next big problem. That too is a creative process, but we usually only notice it when it doesn't work. Then the media grinds out heroes and villains. We worry. But we usually don't do anything because we leave most of those problems in the hands of the experts, the professionals.

Not all of the nation's major problems were solved with equal skill, and this book also looks into failure: institutional failure, personal failure, and intellectual failure.[2] That's why the subtitle guides you to "the price Americans paid" for their brand of creativity. We'll look into that "price" and try to get a handle on who paid and how much they paid for the choices the society made. Even great success comes with a price tag. Some paid more dearly than others, especially those who paid with their lives. I apologize for bringing up these negative themes, especially given that your professional ideology, like mine, gives overwhelming emphasis to success.[3] The American story is supposed to be a success story, and the modern professions have always been the yellow brick road to a better life. But that's not all of the American story. The history is also filled with moral struggles, collapsing policies, and bankrupt businesses. Just like the newspapers.

Don't worry, the United States is not sinking. Not right now. If it were, I'd have to use a different title. This book was conceived and most of it written before the nation's current economic crisis hit, but our financial turmoil today is a perfect example of how Americans handle and sometimes mishandle these painful situations. As the following pages should help you recall, our creative society has been challenged before.

---

[2] For an engaging account of American failure see Scott A. Sandage, *Born Losers: A History of Failure in America* (Cambridge, 2005). As the author observes (265), "Ours is an ideology of achieved identity; obligatory striving is its method, and failure and success are its outcomes. We reckon our incomes once a year but audit ourselves daily, by standards of long-forgotten origin." Sandage relates this to business, but we will find traces of this ideology sprinkled throughout the professions.

[3] Success is the central theme in Richard Florida, *The Rise of the Creative Class: And How It's Transforming Work, Leisure, Community and Everyday Life* (New York, 2002). His creative class is different than my professional experts, but our categories overlap to some extent. Florida did not write a history, but when he does venture into the past, he describes social transitions that seem painless and almost automatic. Mine are usually accompanied by pain and considerable confusion about means as well as ends. See also Richard Florida, *Cities and the Creative Class* (New York, 2005).

This history may even prepare you to deal with our future challenges at home and abroad. We'll surely have them.

The central subject of this book is how Americans tried to deal with four of those problems and how a new class of experts – the professionals – came to play a central role in all of the country's crises. The problems the experts were dealing with were very complex and very large; they were the sort of problems that are never solved quickly or completely. That's why they're so interesting.

One of the problems America had to face was learning how to cope with urban life. The cities and suburbs have been growing very rapidly since the nineteenth century, and the nation was just beginning in the twentieth century to lose its primary identification with rural and small-town life. Millions of immigrants were crowding into the cities. Viewed from the vantage point of the 1890s, it was not at all clear that the American style of helter-skelter growth would work as well as it had for the previous three centuries of our history. Nor was it clear that the cultural values and political styles inherited from an agrarian society would be suited to city life. To many Americans, the city seemed to be both intriguing and dangerous. In one regard, at least, they were right about the danger: cities were indeed dangerous to your health.[4]

The second problem involved finding new ways of keeping the U.S. economy innovative, changing to cope with new situations at home and abroad, adapting to new patterns of competition, and adopting new technologies and new types of organizations while finding and serving new markets. This was the problem that Joseph A. Schumpeter long ago pinpointed as the primary historical process in capitalist societies.[5] Capitalism evolves, Schumpeter said, through the "creative destruction" launched by entrepreneurs who destroy old forms of doing things by creating something that's new, more efficient, and more effective. We'll use some of Schumpeter's ideas. But we'll twist some of them into new shapes, reject others, and put them in a context that he wouldn't have liked.

---

[4] Some critics have suggested that the suburbs were dangerous to your intellect, if not your sanity. We explore this issue in Chapter 10.

[5] For recent developments of this theme see William J. Baumol, Robert E. Litan, and Carl J. Schramm, *Good Capitalism, Bad Capitalism and the Economics of Growth and Prosperity* (New Haven, 2007) also available at http://www.yalepresswiki.org/gcbc/ GCBC_Entire.pdf. Also see Carl J. Schramm, *The Entrepreneurial Imperative: How America's Economic Miracle Will Reshape the World (And Change Your Life)* (New York, 2006).

We will, for instance, look at innovation in public organizations and nonprofits, as well as in business and agriculture. Expertise in government and in universities, as in business, involved closing the gap that always exists between new ideas and action. In a highly organized society like the United States, this entrepreneurial gap had to be narrowed by working through institutions, all of which came to be populated with professionals just like you. In analyzing these institutions and the manner in which they impacted our history, we'll trace the distinctly American style of balancing the need for innovation against the need to balance the books. That's where the auditors creep in and organization charts start to cover the walls.

The third big problem was a result of the second industrial revolution.[6] In their rush to take advantage of the great opportunities U.S. resources offered, Americans gave little thought to the growing need for economic security in a more equitable society. Most were preoccupied with the creative side of creative destruction. Neither security nor equity was a salient political issue in the United States until near the end of the nineteenth century. Otherwise, slavery wouldn't have persisted as long as it did. Otherwise, Americans would have created a government that was as good at protecting its weakest citizens as it was at providing new opportunities to get ahead. Near the end of the nineteenth century, however, issues involving equity and security began to float up toward the top of America's political agendas in the nation and most of the states.

The fourth problem was even more complex and certainly more dangerous. No longer focused on continental expansion, the United States had to decide how it would relate to the European powers, to the nations of Asia, to Latin America, and to the Caribbean countries. America had become the world's leading industrial power and was the largest and most populous of the developed nations. The manner in which it exercised its newly acquired power was important to the rest of the world and certainly to America's citizens. It wouldn't be a simple matter to define our national security and to determine exactly how it should be defended.

---

[6] The first industrial revolution is usually associated with machine-production and water power and is dated from the late 1700s through about 1840. The second industrial revolution was driven by steam power and later electricity; the leaders were in the electrical, chemical, and electrochemical industries and in mass-production and distribution of products like automobiles. Historians usually date this development from the 1870s through the 1960s. The third industrial revolution – the information-age revolution – began about that time and continues today. It is driven by the transistor, the integrated circuit, the computer, and, more recently, the Internet and wireless communication.

As must be apparent, none of these problems lent themselves to quick solutions. Insofar as this very large, rapidly growing, highly diverse society worked out solutions, they would take decades, not months or years, to emerge. Then, the problems and American responses would both continue to evolve. Nothing, this history suggests, is permanent, including your job and maybe even your entire profession.

But we don't need to be gloomy. For the present, America is still the wealthiest, most powerful, and one of the most open nations in the world – something for which we all should be grateful. It could have been otherwise, as you'll see in the following chapters, had Americans not been creative – economically, politically, socially, and culturally.

What about the many other forms of creativity that I haven't mentioned? Are they included in this book? What about art and literature, music and architecture? Where are they? They aren't dealt with in the chapters that follow, although I believe they could easily be added to this version of America's modern history.[7] Those forms of creativity didn't generally have an impact on the four great problems at the heart of this narrative. Great art, great poetry, music, and architecture were and are extremely important, but they couldn't solve the problems that we're discussing. Professional expertise and the political and institutional leadership and brokering that would enable Americans to make use of that expertise might solve those problems. We'll see.

Along the way through more than a century of America's history, we'll meet some real people, including the author's family. I only have two excuses for using my family. First, I know them better than I know any of the other individuals who people these pages, and this enables me to capture some nuances that I might otherwise have missed. Second, four generations of the family became involved in the changes in America that I'm discussing. In researching my family, I have used the documentary record, including census materials, newspaper accounts, material now available on the World Wide Web, family memories, and my own experiences.

Many of you will see a place for your own families in this history. Mine could perhaps have avoided some of the changes I'm describing, but they didn't. Nor did I, and I mention some of the ways a society in transition shaped and reshaped my understanding of the nation's history. My family and the other individuals included became engaged in the evolution of a

---

[7] We will touch on architecture but only deal with its role in shaping responses to urban problems.

professional class and the institutions that train and support the society's experts. I don't mean to suggest that these individuals or others were typical of their ethnic group, social class, or occupation. They're in this book merely because they, like you, were caught up in this history of a changing, frequently challenged society.

The "they" in this book – the professionals – constitute a very broad and growing segment of American society. The lure of professional status and the power and income that it frequently offers have been attractive. So attractive, in fact, that they have drawn in many who have fallen short of meeting society's standards for bestowing power and prestige on a specialized occupation. I have included many, but not all, of these various groups of professionals in this history even though many of them haven't mastered the intricacies of brain surgery or quantum mechanics. Many of them can only practice within an organization (military officers, public officials, and teachers, for example), and many have important roles in history even though the theoretical aspects of their professional knowledge are limited (as is the case with business management). They nevertheless help keep the society running and their expertise has become deeply engaged with the major problems we're discussing here.[8] Throughout, I have occasionally rendered strong judgments on some of those professionals and the society's culture and institutions. I think my readers deserve those evaluations. But given that I haven't tried to prove each of these statements in a formal sense, you should read this account as an extended essay – an essay in historical interpretation.

But enough of this introduction. Let's get settled into the history by looking at some of the specific problems that existed in a specific small town in Ohio in 1931.

---

[8] If we use the U.S. Department of Labor, Bureau of Labor Statistics figures for 2006, their narrower class of "professionals and related occupations" constitutes about 20% of the work force. If we add "management, business, and financial occupations" to that figure, as I do, it jumps to more than 45 million persons, about 30% of those employed at that time in the United States. http://www.bls.gov/news.release/ecopro.to4.htm.

I

1931

If you lived in Ohio in 1931, you had plenty to worry about. The prosperity of the 1920s had given way to a depression that was grinding down the working people in small towns like Fostoria.[1] The stock market in New York had collapsed in the fall of 1929. Two years later, in the spring of 1931, when business was still in deep trouble, I was born on West Culbertson Street near the railroad tracks.[2]

The tracks that cut through the town were important because Fostoria's rail connections to Toledo and Cleveland on the north and

---

[1] In 1931, the working people I mention were almost all white. The population of Fostoria was slightly less than 13,000, and only 347 were identified as African American. That same year, nine African Americans were arrested in Alabama and charged with raping two young white women. Even though the two women had been working previously as prostitutes and the evidence was conflicting, all of the Scottsboro Boys were quickly convicted and all but one (who was thirteen years old) sentenced to death. The National Guard had to be called out to prevent a lynching before the trial. For the case and its outcome, see Dan T. Carter, *Scottsboro: A Tragedy of the American South* (Baton Rouge, Louisiana, 1969) and James R. Acker, *Scottsboro and Its Legacy* (Westport, Connecticut, 2008). It is unlikely that my father, Lou Galambos, had any sympathy for the Scottsboro Boys. At that time, he had a big black German police dog that he named "N . . . . . . "

[2] See the *Bulletin of the Department of Industrial Relations, Columbus, Ohio, Division of Labor Statistics, 1930–1937*; total employment in the state had fallen more than 17% since April of 1930. Unless otherwise indicated, all of the data included in the text and the notes in this book are drawn from the Cambridge University Press's remarkable five-volume collection of the *Historical Statistics of the United States: Earliest Times to the Present* (New York, 2006). The general editors are Richard Sutch and Susan B. Carter, and the additional editors-in-chief include Scott Sigmund Gartner, Michael R. Haines, Alan L. Olmstead, and Gavin Wright. Anthony Angiletta and Frank Smith are consulting editors on the entire project, and the developmental editor who guided the manuscripts to publication is Madeleine Adams.

Cincinnati to the south had helped make it a small manufacturing center. For a time, it appeared that the town would become a center for automobile production. But neither the Allen nor the Seneca motor companies could compete with Ford's inexpensive Model Ts. Both of the local firms went out of business.

This was a familiar story in towns like Fostoria, once a local center for buggy and wagon manufacturing. Companies came and went. Buildings were recycled. People had to find new jobs or move on. Fostoria was like the hundreds of other small communities sprinkled around the Midwest, all of which were distressed in the early 1930s by a different and more threatening kind of economic change. The depression was grinding all of the businesses and jobs in a way that only grandparents who had been alive in the 1890s had experienced.

It was hard to understand *what* was happening in the 1930s and even harder to understand *why* it was happening. Why were the businesses cutting back on their workforces? Farmers had been suffering from low prices for some years, but in the cities and towns, the 1920s had been prosperous years. Now, however, there were more and more people unemployed.[3] The stores in Fostoria were selling less. As savings began to dwindle and the number of homeless hoboes coming through on the railroads increased, the private charities that were the only source of relief were beginning to run out of money and supplies.

The local newspaper reported on the state and national leaders who were trying to explain why the prosperity of the 1920s had suddenly evaporated. Some said that the problems had all started overseas. That's what President Herbert Hoover said. He'd been very popular in Ohio in 1928, when the state gave him almost 65 percent of its votes and turned its back on the Democrat, a New York politician named Al, who was incidentally a Catholic. Hoover, whose father had been born in Ohio, was more reliable. Hoover was a Quaker who had met a payroll. He

---

[3] The *Fostoria Daily Review* was following the unemployment situation in the city and the state. That fall, there was consideration of a proposal to sell poor relief bonds (October 3, November 11 and 25), and the estimate was that about a million persons would need relief aid that winter in Ohio. As the paper reported, financier Bernard Baruch thought the nation had "disrupted the continuity of pessimism," and President Hoover agreed (November 12). But cold weather was coming, Fostoria's operating fund was short $50,000, and there was skepticism as New Year's day approached about rosy predictions that an upsurge was right around the corner (November 25; December 16 and 31). The editor suggested that God, provoked by the "money-glutted years" of the 1920s, was now handing out punishment to those who had not built their society on "the rock of brotherhood" (November 17 and 25)."

had been a very successful mining engineer, and his public service during World War I and in the Republican administrations of the 1920s had given him a rock-solid national reputation. In 1928, he seemed to be the sort of man who could understand what the people in Fostoria wanted.

By 1931, however, Hoover's explanations were starting to wear thin. It was not easy for working-class people like those in my family to understand why things happening in Britain or Germany or even stranger parts of the world were causing so much trouble in Ohio. Our family had tried to leave Europe behind. My father, Lou Galambos, was a second-generation Hungarian-American who had been raised in Toledo, Ohio, and then found both a wife and work in Fostoria. Leaving high school in his junior year, he'd become a welder, a job that put him on the shop floor in a foundry. As a welder, he was a bit above the men working with a shovel and a solid cut below the master mechanics and managers. In Fostoria, he'd met a fourth-generation German-American woman, Ruth Himburg, who was working as a secretary in his plant.[4] After a courtship eased by the interurban line between Toledo and Fostoria, they were married in 1927 and had their first child, Margaret, in the fall of 1928.

By the time I was born, Lou Galambos was scratching hard to get ahead. Looking for something better, he decided to try a different industry and a different occupation. His new choice was coal mining, and to move ahead in the machinery side of the business, he experienced an immaculate professionalization. Without returning to high school or seeking any advanced training, he became in one year a "mining engineer," just like President Hoover. At least that's what he told the Ohio Department of Health to put on my birth certificate. In this wonderful country, you could jump from the shop floor to a profession by self-assertion.[5] In the midst of a severe and worsening depression!

Even as a "mining engineer," Lou Galambos couldn't escape the country's economic collapse. He and Ruth had leaped from the frying pan into the fire. Coal mining throughout the Midwest was in sharp decline. Employment in the mines plummeted in the early 1930s, and many of the union members who had embraced mechanization in the 1920s were rewarded by losing their jobs in the 1930s.[6] For Lou Galambos,

---

4 When Ruth married Lou Galambos, he nicknamed her "Mazie," but to avoid confusion I have kept her as Ruth throughout this book.

5 My mother, Ruth, also improved her situation, lopping four years off her age. She was that much older than my father and probably was sensitive about the difference.

6 James P. Johnson, *The Politics of Soft Coal: The Bituminous Industry from World War I through the New Deal* (Urbana, 1979).

however, mechanization, like professionalization, was the road to success. Americans could afford to buy less coal, but they still needed coal. So he parlayed his mechanical skills into a new enterprise, selling and servicing coal-mining machinery. This required a great deal of moving around and some jumping from company to company, to Air Reduction Sales in Kansas City, then to St. Louis with Joy Mining Machinery. If you were on the make in this or any other business, you had to be prepared to pack up and leave, just as you had left Toledo and your father had left Hungary.

All of this moving and scratching was taking place in a nation that actually didn't have any idea what was causing the Great Depression or what to do about it. Henry Ford, the nation's most popular industrialist, urged Americans to stick with Hoover and accept his explanations of the nation's distress. The country's most distinguished academic experts in economic theory also counseled patience. Eventually, they said, the depression would bottom out. All the nation needed was "confidence" – then recovery would start in a natural, predictable way. The president's campaign managers in 1932 exuded confidence. They said his speeches were "reaching the people as never before…" They didn't reach the people in Fostoria, however, where the voters ran out of confidence in 1932 and turned against Hoover in the national election.[7]

It wasn't just Hoover who failed. This was one of the great failures of expertise in the United States. But perhaps I shouldn't be too harsh with the economists who had trouble providing convincing explanations of the depression.[8] The nation's other professionals – whether trained or self-proclaimed – weren't doing much better with some of the country's other major problems: learning, for instance, how to exercise American power in the world or how to build, control, and live in the nation's swelling urban centers.

To get a better perspective on their successes and failures, we need to look back to a previous generation, back to the 1890s. That was an era when most of America's modern professions got organized, laying institutional foundations for expertise, which are, for the most part, still

---

[7] *Los Angeles Times*, October 20, 1932, 2. *Fostoria Daily Review*, November 9, 1932, courtesy of Leonard Skonecki and Penny Justice. The vote was close: Franklin D. Roosevelt got 2,877 votes; Hoover, 2,680; and Norman Thomas, the Socialist candidate, 126.

[8] One of the economists was the distinguished Yale professor Irving Fisher. His confident prediction that stocks had reached a high and permanent level in 1929 was noted in the *Wall Street Journal*, on June 29, 2007, as a warning to "today's market titans."

with us today. That was also a decade when Americans suffered through a deep depression, tried to define their new role in world affairs, started to get serious about reforming their political institutions, worried about how best to encourage innovation and growth in business and agriculture, and grappled awkwardly with the problems of urban life.

2

Life, Death, and Learning in the Cities

In the 1890s, it wasn't easy to figure out how to improve conditions for all of those Americans squeezing into the nation's rapidly growing cities.[1] The census classified Fostoria, Ohio, as an urban community, but it was just a small town and it wasn't really growing between 1890 and 1930. In Ohio, Cincinnati was the largest city in 1890 and it was half again as large four decades later. Toledo and the state capital of Columbus more than doubled their populations in the same years, and the state's metropolis, Cleveland, had swollen to 900,000.[2]

Among the cities of the Midwest, Cleveland's growth was impressive, but Chicago was clearly the leader and the region's major transportation hub. It had shot past Philadelphia by 1930 and was the only American city other than New York with a population of more than three million. Chicago's almost unbelievable expansion and its diverse population inspired poets and historians, sociologists and novelists for many years. They've given us superb portraits of the city's spirit, accomplishments, and growing pains.

The sources of growth are easy to understand. Like the other large American cities (except one), Chicago was favored with good water

[1] The student interested in further exploring American urbanization might want to sample some of the chapters in Eric H. Monkkonen, *The Development of U.S. Cities & Towns, 1780–1980* (Berkeley, 1988) or Raymond A. Mohl, ed., *The Making of Urban America* (2nd edition, Lanham, 2006).

[2] Naomi R. Lamoreaux, Margaret Levenstein, and Kenneth L. Sokoloff, "Financing Invention during the Second Industrial Revolution: Cleveland, Ohio, 1870–1920," in Naomi R. Lamoreaux and Kenneth L. Sokoloff, eds., *Financing Innovation in the United States, 1870 to the Present* (Cambridge, 2007), 39–84.

transportation.[3] The Great Lakes traffic spurred the grain trade, and the railroads helped the city attract the livestock business from the western plains. When the city's meat-packers introduced refrigeration and opened up a new national market for dressed meat, Chicago spurted ahead of cities like Cincinnati in this important industry.[4] Opportunity and entrepreneurship were a potent combination for Chicago and other American cities, east and west.

Rapid expansion created many problems but also lots of ways to get ahead in life. That's the reason Lazlo Galambos, a Hungarian, ended up in Toledo, Ohio, on the western end of Lake Erie. He came to America in the midst of an astonishing flow of people from eastern and southern Europe. Lazlo began his American adventure working in the green gardens around Toledo, a city that already had a large Hungarian population.[5] At work he met and then married young Hazel, the daughter of two Hungarian immigrants, and worked his way up from picking onions to working metal as a molder in a local plant. Having mastered a skilled occupation, he was able to get better jobs and eventually became a foreman. He still didn't know much English, but step by step, he was playing his bit part in the American drama of progress. His three sons (the second was Lou, whom you met in the previous chapter) all played their parts by following Lazlo into metalworking in the industries of northern Ohio.

Some Midwestern urbanites were doing much better than Lazlo and his sons. The most successful ones were building great fortunes and wonderful houses on the healthy side of their cities. Yes, there was a healthy side to cities like Toledo and Chicago, a side where the wives of the Hungarian, Greek, Italian, and Polish Americans might work but couldn't afford to live. The suburbs provided homes for the growing middle class, including middle-class professionals. Most foreign-born immigrants and

---

[3] The exception is Atlanta, Georgia. There are two rivers near Atlanta: the Chattahoochee supplies water to Atlanta; and the Flint River rises near the city. But Atlanta's growth was linked to the railroad, not water transportation.

[4] Mary Yeager Kujovich, "The Refrigerator Car and the Growth of the American Dressed Beef Industry," *Business History Review*, 44 (1970), 460–82. See also the same author's "The Dynamics of Oligopoly in the Meat Packing Industry: An Historical Analysis" (Ph.D. dissertation, Johns Hopkins University, 1973). Her research provided the basis for the account in Alfred D. Chandler, Jr., *The Visible Hand: The Managerial Revolution in American Business* (Cambridge, 1977), 299–302.

[5] Thomas E. Barden and John Ahern, eds., *Hungarian American Toledo: Life and Times in Toledo's Birmingham Neighborhood* (Toledo, 2002). In addition to the right kinds of jobs and the right kinds of foods in Toledo, there were Catholic churches that were also the right kind.

African Americans were crowded into the poorer sections of the cities, around the factories. Not all of those factories were in the central business districts. But wherever they were, they attracted people like Lazlo, who got as close to work as possible. The immigrants created clusters where disease as well as crime was a problem.[6]

Staying Alive in Urban America

This was not an urban myth, although public health problems developed a mythological aspect when they were associated with the immigrants themselves rather than the conditions in which they were forced to live. Poor sewage systems bred disease in urban America, as they do from time to time in the developing world today. Poor water supplies created similar problems, as did the crowded living and working quarters that spread infections. Despite advances in handling sewage and water supplies, infection continued to be a major concern of public health authorities in all of America's largest cities, including Chicago.[7]

The reality was expressed in the bland figures collected on sickness and death. If you still lived in the countryside, say, in central or southern Illinois, rather than Chicago, you could tack a few extra years on your expected life span. If you lived in the city, you would be likely to beat the averages if you had one of those nice houses on the north side. In the crowded sections where immigrant laborers worked for hourly wages, where health care was at best spotty, where garbage pickup was sporadic, you were more likely to have tuberculosis, diphtheria, influenza, or pneumonia, none of which could be treated effectively before the 1890s.[8] It was not at all bland to have any one of those diseases.

The first of these urban killers to respond to modern medical science in America was diphtheria, and the progress in treating this disease of the

---

[6] Richard Harris and Robert Lewis, "The Geography of North American Cities and Suburbs, 1900–1950: A New Synthesis," *Journal of Urban History*, 27, 3 (March 2001): 262–92. The concepts they were revising were laid out in books such as Harlan Paul Douglass, *The Suburban Trend* (New York, a 1970 reprint of a 1925 publication), 36–37. Douglass's perspective was wonderfully optimistic: "[T]he suburbs, in spite of their limitations, are the most promising aspect of urban civilization.... They reflect the unspoiled and youthful aspect of urban civilization,... where, if at all, happiness and worthy living may be achieved, as well as material well-being."

[7] Alan M. Kraut, *Silent Travelers: Germs, Genes, and the "Immigrant Menace"* (Baltimore, 1994), 122, 143, 175, 187, 206, 210. In a 1911 report, Kraut notes, 67.3% of the public school pupils in Chicago had foreign-born fathers (226).

[8] Jane Addams had a memorable fight with municipal authority over garbage pickup.

young deserves our attention. In this case, the new medical ideas about diphtheria all came from the advanced laboratories of Europe – Germany and France, in particular. There, a new understanding of disease-causing germs was emerging. When the leading medical researchers pointed to the successes of scientific medicine, one of the therapies they described was a serum treatment effective against diphtheria. In America, private firms had drawn on advanced academic knowledge and personnel to produce the serum. They drew blood (hence serum) from horses that had been infected with the deadly germs.[9] The antibodies against the disease could be filtered out and injected into humans to give them immunity to the disease.[10]

In a few cases, public institutions produced the serum, but for the most part, this was left in the hands of companies like Mulford in Philadelphia. Mulford and other firms also produced and distributed the smallpox vaccines that were being widely used in America during these years. These early experiences led to a distinctive American blend of public, private, and nonprofit institutions that would play a central role in health care for the entire twentieth century. The successes in treating diphtheria also laid a foundation for the type of research and development that would later produce a safe, effective vaccine against the disease.[11]

While many traditional physicians were unwilling to accept the new theory that germs caused disease, the leading eastern medical schools in America responded rather quickly and positively.[12] The leaders reorganized their programs and launched a major reform movement in medical education. This is an impressive example of creativity in what was a life-or-death matter for many Americans, especially for those living in cities.

One of the leaders of reform was a professor of pathology and dean of the medical school at Johns Hopkins University in Baltimore. Given that I teach at Hopkins, you might be a bit suspicious of what I tell you about the school. But it's hard not to applaud the career of Dr. William H. Welch.

---

[9] This therapy was produced along the same lines as the serum for hog cholera mentioned in Chapter 3.

[10] Using the serum, doctors were able to cut the death rate from diphtheria in half. Louis Galambos (with Jane Eliot Sewell), *Networks of Innovation: Vaccine Development at Merck, Sharp & Dohme, and Mulford, 1895–1995* (New York, 1995), 4–20.

[11] Rob Roy MacGregor, "Corynebacterium Diphtheriae," in Gerald L. Mandell, R. Gordon Douglas, Jr., and John E. Bennett, eds., *Principles and Practice of Infectious Diseases* (New York, 1990), 1574–81.

[12] On the resistance to vaccination, see Michael Willrich, "The Mild Type," a paper presented at Johns Hopkins University, March 19, 2007.

He was raised in a family in which doctoring was the unanimous choice of a profession. His father, four of his uncles, his grandfather and great grandfather were all physicians. But at Yale University, where practical occupations in general and the sciences in particular were low on the status hierarchy, Welch turned toward classical studies for a career. He decided to make ancient Greek his life's work. Unable to get a decent job after graduation, he scraped along by teaching school for a year while he pondered his future. Not surprisingly, he then opted for the family profession and returned to Yale.

Back in New Haven, he was something of a contrarian. He launched his medical training by studying chemistry in the Sheffield Scientific School, an institution designed in part to keep modernity from infecting Yale's traditional curriculum. His decision to study chemistry would be considered normal today, but in 1872, it was an unusual choice. He was, in effect, lining up with those medical researchers who were developing new scientific concepts of disease. From there, he went to New York to study at the College of Physicians and Surgeons.[13]

Having an interest in pathology (the subdiscipline focused on disease), he headed to Germany to learn more about the latest developments in medical science. His educational tour took him to Strasbourg, Leipzig, and Breslau, and he returned to the United States with even more appreciation for laboratory research and a scientific approach to medicine. As he discovered, however, life on the profession's leading edge could be stressful. He spent years working in a tiny, ill-equipped laboratory at the Bellevue Hospital Medical College.

When Johns Hopkins hired him (1884), he at last had an opportunity to develop a modern laboratory of pathology. In his next visit to Germany, Welch was able to spend part of his time working with Robert Koch, one of the scientists whose research securely established the germ theory of disease. Returning to Baltimore, Welch taught at Johns Hopkins and pushed forward his own research.[14] He started his lectures before Hopkins even had a medical school. After getting together enough money to launch medical instruction, the school formally opened its program in 1893. Right from the start, the school adopted the highest entrance standards in the country.[15] Hopkins provided full-time positions to its teachers so

---

[13] The College of Physicians and Surgeons later became affiliated with Columbia College (which became Columbia University in 1896).

[14] On Welch's research, see Simon Flexner and James Thomas Flexner, *William Henry Welch and the Heroic Age of American Medicine* (New York, 1941), 194–98.

[15] Ibid., 58. When Welch entered medical school, the only entrance requirements were the ability to read and write.

they could spend all of their time on research and instruction. Welch guided the school through its somewhat shaky experimental phase, and by the early 1900s, Hopkins was the model institution for a professional reform movement inspired by the famous Flexner Report of 1910.[16]

With support from the Carnegie Foundation, Abraham Flexner, author of the report, surveyed the medical education available in North America. His general conclusion was that the quality of the entire system – with a few exceptions like Hopkins, Harvard, and the University of Pennsylvania – was poor and unlikely to get any better until the dangerously weak programs were weeded out. What was a weak program? Those without laboratory facilities (à la Welch), without properly trained instructors (who had studied the medical sciences, as Welch had in Germany), without opportunities for clinical work (of the sort Welch was doing). Flexner was harsh, authoritative, and right on target.[17]

Educational leaders and government officials listened and responded with reform programs in state after state. Some weak schools were improved. Others were shut down. The medical profession was beginning to close the innovation gap – the gap between theory and practice – and one result was creative destruction in the public and nonprofit sectors.[18] Like the physical frontier, this movement rolled steadily westward, depositing new deans and faculty members in school after school, wiping out poor and sometimes fraudulent programs, raising the level of medical education and, in time, of medical practice in America's cities.

Tragically, none of these individuals or institutions could protect the urban population from the great flu pandemic of 1918–1920. More than half a million Americans died from the flu and the secondary infections that frequently accompanied this viral disease.[19] Chicago, like other American cities, was hit hard, and the immigrant and African-American populations suffered severe losses.[20] It would be another quarter of a century before the medical sciences would catch up with influenza, an

---

[16] For additional detail, see ibid., and Simon Flexner, "Biographical Memoir of William Henry Welch, 1850–1934," available at http://books.nap.edu/html/biomems/wwelch .pdf.

[17] Flexner had studied with Welch and clearly expressed his admiration for his former teacher in the biography cited in the previous two notes.

[18] See the reference to Joseph A. Schumpeter's concept of creative destruction in the realm of private business in the Preface to this volume.

[19] Following World War II, the medical sciences would make great progress in understanding virology.

[20] Alfred W. Crosby, Jr., *Epidemic and Peace, 1918* (Westport, CT, 1976); Allan Chase, *Magic Shots: A Human and Scientific Account of the Long and Continuing Struggle to Eradicate Infectious Diseases by Vaccination* (New York, 1982), 196–99.

infectious disease that still creates serious problems for public health today.

Despite this setback, the combination of improved medical practices and public health measures made life in America's major cities less threatening by the end of the 1920s. In the Midwest, universities like Michigan and Minnesota, both of which had been providing first-rate medical training since the early 1900s, played crucial roles in these improvements. In 1927, they were joined by the University of Chicago, which opened a new medical school with extensive support (and some guidance) from the Rockefeller Foundation's General Education Board.

Public health innovations that were attuned to the new medical science were making themselves felt in all of the major cities. In 1909, for instance, Chicago introduced the first milk pasteurization requirement, a regulation that produced a sharp decline in infant mortality. Other cities quickly followed Chicago's lead.[21] The results of the new controls, the new medical science, and other public health measures could be seen in stunning declines in infant and maternal deaths.[22]

Planning Urban America

The improvements in healthcare and public health also provided cultural and intellectual underpinnings for a contemporary movement to harness urban growth through better city planning.[23] Urban planning, unlike medicine, was a fresh new profession in the United States. America's booming cities were fertile soil for all kinds of new professions, hundreds of which sprang up in the years between 1890 and 1930. The successful ones went through somewhat similar patterns of development: they all acquired leaders and status systems, established ideologies that proclaimed their social value, created new means of communication between their practitioners, and eventually organized their professional

---

[21]   Richard C. Meckel, *Save the Babies: American Public Health Reform and the Prevention of Infant Mortality, 1850–1929* (Baltimore, 1990), 69–91. As Meckel points out, by 1921, more than 90% of the cities with populations larger than 100,000 had most of their milk pasteurized.

[22]   "Healthier Mothers and Babies – 1900–1999," *Journal of the American Medical Association*, 282, 19 (November 17, 1999), 1807–10.

[23]   Both movements attempted to substitute professional expertise and control in urban life for America's traditional pattern of market-centered development. Both movements looked to new bureaucratic agencies with national and international cultures. Both movements gave scientific values and approaches to problem-solving significant roles in their ideologies.

institutions on a national level.[24] The urban planners followed this common path.[25]

All of this took time, however, and in the meantime, the planning in America continued to be the kind of ad hoc venture it had been since colonial times. In those early years, Philadelphia had started with a plan, as had other cities and towns, most of which adopted a simple grid for aligning their streets and properties. There were, of course, exceptions. Pierre L'Enfant, the famous French engineer, had provided a more ambitious design for the new nation's capital, and Frederick Law Olmsted later gave New York a plan for what became the city's magnificent Central Park. Olmsted went even farther in Boston, where he designed an entire system of urban green spaces.[26]

These were important breakthroughs, but for the most part, America's cities grew according to the dictates of transportation systems and businesses. Both first drew in the local residents to the center and then spewed them out to surrounding urban and suburban areas. In Chicago and elsewhere, central city congestion persuaded many entrepreneurs to look beyond the tightly packed business district for industrial sites. The workers followed, and the cities and suburbs soon became patchworks of industrial and commercial nodes linked by transportation.

The 1893 World's Columbian Exposition in Chicago spurred interest in using a formal style of planning to make this helter-skelter process more orderly. The Exposition helped launch a City Beautiful movement, an effort to make city buildings more attractive and city living more interesting. Inspired by European cities as well as the Exposition, a group of architects, landscape experts, and engineers gathered some middle- and upper-class colleagues and launched a "crusade against ugliness" in America.[27]

---

[24] Status in the professions was often vaguely defined. But normally there was a general understanding that certain kinds of professional work, certain kinds of careers, and certain institutions that trained the practitioners were more important than others.

[25] John D. Fairfield, *The Mysteries of the Great City: The Politics of Urban Design, 1877–1937* (Columbus, Ohio, 1993), chapter 4, discusses the debates over professionalization.

[26] Irving D. Fisher, *Frederick Law Olmsted and the City Planning Movement in the United States* (Ann Arbor, 1976). Keith N. Morgan, "Muskau and America: Pückler's Influence on Charles Eliot and Regional Landscape Planning in the United States," *Bulletin of the German Historical Institute*, edited by Sonja Duempelmann, Supplement 4 (2007), 67–87.

[27] William H. Wilson, "The Ideology, Aesthetics and Politics of the City Beautiful Movement," in Anthony Sutcliffe, ed., *The Rise of Modern Urban Planning, 1800–1914* (New York, 1980), 165–98. The quotation is from J. Horace McFarland, one of the apostles of city beautification (171).

There was plenty of ugliness to attack.[28] In Chicago, a small cadre of professionals and concerned business leaders joined the crusade and set out to improve their metropolis.[29] Out of their determination came Daniel Burnham's plan for Chicago (1909), an ambitious effort to bring the forces of the market and transportation technology under control.

Burnham was a successful architect whose firm had designed many of Chicago's buildings, including its skyscrapers. His company was also responsible for the famous Flatiron Building in New York, and in 1893, he led the team that planned the World's Columbian Exposition. Later, when the Merchants Club of Chicago decided to survey the city and devise a plan that would guide its growth, the businessmen looked to Burnham and Edward H. Bennett, another Chicago architect, for leadership. Three years later, they produced the 1909 Chicago Plan. "It is certain," Burnham and Bennett optimistically proclaimed, "that if the plan is really good it will commend itself to the progressive spirit of the times, and sooner or later it will be carried out."[30]

That same year, the National Conference on City Planning met for the first time in the nation's capital. By the time the United States entered World War I, the educational foundation of the new planning profession had begun to take shape. There were now readings available on the subject and university courses for training practitioners. In 1917, a national organization – in this case, the American City Planning Institute – emerged. The first incarnation of the profession's status system was completed when America's most prestigious planner, Frederick Law Olmstead, became president of the Institute.

Considerable advances were made in the 1920s.[31] Both Los Angeles and New York pushed forward with regional plans, and the federal

---

[28] Upton Sinclair's *The Jungle* (Garden City, 1906) gives vivid descriptions of the area surrounding the packing plants. The dumping grounds were full of "stinking green water" and had "a ghastly odor, of all the dead things of the universe...."

[29] Anthony Sutcliffe, *Towards the Planned City: Germany, Britain, the United States and France, 1780–1914* (New York, 1981), 106.

[30] Harold M. Mayer and Richard C. Wade (with Glen E. Holt), *Chicago: Growth of a Metropolis* (Chicago, 1969), 193–203, 274–81. As Maureen A. Flannagan, *Seeing with Their Hearts: Chicago Women and the Vision of the Good City, 1871–1933* (Princeton, 2002), makes clear, women reformers had a different vision of the good city. They wanted a livable city of homes, not a city attuned to industrial and commercial goals. They disagreed about the means as well as the ends projected by the male planners (91, 103–09, 193–201).

[31] Harlan Paul Douglass' 1925 study of *The Suburban Trend* reflected the optimism of that decade; see note 5 in this chapter. The author could discern "the permanent outlines of the scientific remaking of cities..." (272), and he looked forward to "the next Great Experiment" (327).

government attempted to introduce some order to the practice of zoning by producing a standard act for all of the states. Acceptance of the federal guidelines was voluntary, and as you might imagine, there was a great deal of variance in the resulting programs. The U.S. Supreme Court crowned these efforts by upholding zoning measures as a reasonable exercise of local authority, and the young profession applauded when Cincinnati became the first American city to endorse its city plan in 1925.

Still, planning had a long way to go in the 1920s. Cincinnati's endorsement was the first such official measure in a nation that included 288 urban places with populations over 25,000. Even among reformers, the City Beautiful movement had rather quickly yielded to a quest for the City Practical, a city that worked reasonably well.[32] The contrast between medical reform and urban reform is telling. In the case of medicine, the professional reformers could argue that they were offering life over death for all. That had a powerful appeal to a society in which average life expectancy was only 47.8 years in the early 1900s.[33] Urban reform had less to offer. It touched on public health, but that wasn't central to the reform ideology.

The opposition to medical reform was weak, both intellectually and politically, but the urban planners had to contend with powerful forces of resistance to their innovations. Real estate owners were one of the major blocks to more thoroughgoing planning, as were many of the industrial and commercial leaders who had long been shaping America's cities to suit their own economic interests.[34] Well-connected through the political parties, the opponents of significant urban reform dug in for trench warfare against plans they contended were the products of impractical advisors, including many academics.

In Chicago and most other cities, the gap between theory and practice was controlled by business leaders and their supporters in city

[32] William H. Wilson, "The Ideology, Aesthetics and Politics of the City Beautiful Movement," 186–89. As the author notes, "The later progressive infatuation with professionalism, overarching government, statistics, and immediate melioratives such as improved housing, fragmented the City Beautiful movement, replacing it with the 'city practical'" (176).

[33] By 1930, life expectancy at birth for all Americans, both sexes and all races, was 59.7 years.

[34] Raymond A. Mohl, "Shifting Patterns of American Urban Policy since 1900," in Arnold R. Hirsch and Raymond A. Mohl, eds., *Urban Policy in Twentieth-Century America* (New Brunswick, 1993), 1–7. As Mohl notes, "The American industrial city was a huge, unregulated, economic growth machine, its evolution shaped primarily by market forces that provided both the source of its strengths and the cause of its most serious problems (p. 3)."

government. As a result, Burnham's ambitious plan for Chicago generated widespread acclaim but few specific responses in the city. There were accomplishments, including Grant Park, an elevated boulevard, and the Municipal (later Navy) Pier on Lake Michigan. But the larger dimensions of planning for the entire Chicago area continued to lie in the hands of the economic interests who controlled the property and those who benefited directly from their efforts.[35]

Planning was certainly not in the hands of those new residents of Chicago who were swelling the city's slums. The Burnham plan had avoided consideration of the slums, which continued to expand following World War I. African Americans from the South were flooding into the city in search of the better life that had already brought waves of European immigrants to Chicago. Mayor William Hale Thompson tried to blend the migrants into city government, but his efforts raised racial animosities in white working-class districts where many were already upset over the increased competition for jobs. In the stockyards, in the steel mills, and in the service industries, tens of thousands of southern blacks were taking jobs that had formerly been held by European immigrants. The resulting animosities erupted in racial violence. Racial tensions had begun to mount as early as 1917 and became a full-blown urban crisis in 1919. The National Guard had to come into the city to establish order.[36] As the outbursts of violence in Chicago and other American cities suggested, the planning movement was far short of creating the orderly city life the young profession's visionaries hoped to achieve.[37] The gap between innovative professional ideas and effective urban action was still very wide.[38]

---

[35] Anthony Sutcliffe, *Towards the Planned City*, 97–98, 100–02, 106–10, 116–17. For a more optimistic evaluation of the Chicago Plan, see Mayer and Wade, *Chicago*, 276–77.

[36] James R. Grossman, *Land of Hope: Chicago, Black Southerners, and the Great Migration* (Chicago, 1989), especially 174–80. Mayer and Wade, *Chicago*, 290–91.

[37] As Anthony Sutcliffe points out, however, the efforts in Chicago had an impact on other cities, including New York. Anthony Sutcliffe, *Towards the Planned City*, 117. As late as 1917, the author notes, "planning was still a collection of ideas," and the field "had no real administrative existence" (125).

[38] See also Raymond A. Mohl and Neil Betten, "The Failure of Industrial City Planning: Gary, Indiana, 1906–1910," *Journal of the American Institute of Planners*, 38 (July 1972), 202–15. In Gary, both private and public planning failed. In 1948, the president of the American Society of Planning Officials, Charles B. Bennett, reflected on his thirty years of experience with planning: "To sum it all up, the apparently simple desires of the people who live in most of our cities have not been achieved because of a lack of simple planning; a lack of funds for essential services and physical needs due to a narrow tax

The First School Crisis

More successful by far were the urban reforms in education. In Chicago and most other American cities, the schools had long been in the hands of party politicians. The ward bosses of the late nineteenth century provided jobs to teachers and administrators who voted as they were told. In this regard, the schools were just like the garbage service. They were a source of political support and, from time to time, of contracts for construction and repairs, contracts that were a rich source of kickbacks.

In Chicago and elsewhere, the obvious limitations of this system prompted a reform movement that got underway in the 1890s and reached fruition after 1900.[39] Patronage jobs were important. But education was crucial. It was the path the second generation needed to move up, to move out of the factories and hard labor, into the middle class and maybe even into an honorable profession. Under the pressure of reform, the schools were reorganized, and the hiring of teachers shifted to a more merit-based system. Now teachers had to have achieved a certain level of education and acquired some formal knowledge of the subjects they were teaching. These changes were accompanied by the organization of the first modern bureaucratic school administrations to control funds, direct the operations of the schools, and hire and fire teachers and other administrators. The bureaucracies developed slowly and experimentally, but by the late 1920s, they had consolidated their operations and their positions in urban governments all over the United States.

In effect, these reforms made teachers and the administrators professionals for the first time.[40] They began to create their own professional organizations, means of communication, and status systems. Acquiring professional status in a male-oriented society was difficult because of the large number of women in teaching. Nurses encountered the same sort of resistance as they began their struggle to establish a professional identity. But the development of teachers colleges in higher education bolstered their position and helped raise the educational level in this

---

base; and a lack of an orderly priority program (188)." American Society of Planning Officials, *Planning 1948* (Chicago, 1948).

[39] Maureen A. Flannagan, *Seeing with Their Hearts*, charts the role of women in the ongoing reform efforts in Chicago, 32–34, 40–41, 45–46, 59, 63–70, 76, 114–17, 164–66, 169–72.

[40] This represents a significant break with most of the literature on professionalization. But as I indicated in the beginning, I am using a broad definition of professional status, and teachers fit easily into that definition, along with business managers and executives.

young profession. The state universities in the West and Midwest moved quickly to meet the demand for teacher education, followed by the University of Chicago and Columbia University. By 1910, there were more than 150 programs training teachers in U.S. colleges and universities.[41] Soon graduate-level courses and advanced degrees in teaching and school administration were being offered for the first time in America. In 1930, more than fifty institutions offered doctorate degrees in education.[42] These significant changes in both supply and demand for teachers pushed this occupation further along toward professional standing.

Teaching didn't acquire its status without some serious struggles. In many of the leading universities, graduate training in education had to fight an uphill battle against professors with deeply planted prejudices. As Harvard President Charles W. Eliot explained, "The faculty, I feel, has but slight interest or confidence in what is ordinarily called pedagogy." For many professors, the subject was merely a minor theme in the standard liberal arts curriculum, a theme so minor that it called for no separate programs, courses, or, heaven forbid, a separate department or college.

Another threat to professional status was the lure of unionization. Unions promised to increase teacher's salaries and improve their working conditions. The unions offered partnership in a movement gathering strength in America by the early 1900s, a movement with a well-defined and powerful ideology. But by opting for unions, teachers would align themselves with factory workers who were generally even further down the status ladder in American society. Already having forced their way into the middle class, teachers would affirm a blue-collar, working-class standing if they joined unions like the Chicago Teachers' Federation.[43] In effect, the teachers were being forced to decide which mattered the most – status or income, middle-class identity or power?

For a fresh young teacher like Geraldine Himburg, these choices were not difficult to make in the early 1920s. Geraldine was the first member of our family to make it into higher education and to become a professional by dint of training rather than proclamation. A combination of talent, grit, and historical circumstance accounted for this leap onto the second

[41] Christopher Lucas, *American Higher Education: A History* (New York, 2006), 233–35.
[42] Ellen Condliffe Lagemann, "Contested Terrain: A History of Education Research in the United States, 1890–1990," *Educational Researcher*, 26, 9 (December 1997), 6.
[43] In most American communities, teachers were doubtless placed in the bottom tier of the middle class, but their calling was certainly a respectable, white-collar profession. On Chicago's organization, see Maureen A. Flannagan, *Seeing with Their Hearts*, 60–3, 114–17, 139–40.

rung of the American status ladder.[44] Geraldine, who was my mother's older sister, was a bright, hardworking student who loved children, literature, and music, roughly in that order. She benefited from three historical circumstances: the high-school movement; the rapid expansion of normal schools for teacher training; and the urban reforms that replaced patronage with merit-based hiring in local schools.

Geraldine was a disciplined student who was able to continue her education because the extended, German-American family pitched in after the mother's marriage collapsed.[45] Having the mother, Carrie, and three children suddenly dumped into a small Fostoria house that already included three adults made life difficult.[46] There was never enough money or beds, and the young girls had to help by gathering coal that fell off the railroad cars along the nearby tracks. But Geraldine persisted. In 1919, wearing high-button shoes and a straw hat, she graduated Fostoria High School as valedictorian of her class.

Her academic standing made it possible for her to continue her education at the Michigan Normal School in Ypsilanti. Completing her work there in a year, she set out to teach and help support her mother.[47] Raised in a family with little money and a deep concern about status, she was true to her conservative, German-American heritage.[48] Instead of heading toward one of the state's largest cities – Cleveland, Cincinnati, or the

---

44 The first rung was occupied by Americans who had mastered a craft and had a relatively steady income. Most hardworking, first-generation – and many second-generation – immigrants made it onto this first step toward the middle class.

45 The husband and father was John Himburg, a printer, who apparently left the family and died – a suicide – in 1907. His wife, Carrie (my grandmother on the German side of the family), died in 1964. *Washington (Indiana) Democrat*, May 4, 1907. Family records.

46 The medical profession made substantial progress in these years, but the advances were not swift enough to save the life of young Kathryn Himburg, who died from an infected appendix that burst. Today, few of us have ever heard of a person dying from an infected appendix.

47 Alice Kessler-Harris, *Out to Work: A History of Wage-Earning Women in the United States* (New York, 1982), 227, 234–36, looks on teaching as a dead-end job that kept women from making it into more challenging positions in the real professions. I disagree and so too did Geraldine Himburg, who understood that she was taking a big step upward in her career.

48 Here, as elsewhere throughout this book, I am drawing on stereotypes. I am not suggesting that any of these stereotypes can be applied to all members of this or any other group of Americans. In our extended family, however, there were significant differences between the Hungarian Americans and the German Americans, differences that had cultural, social, and economic aspects. These aspects deserve a place in our history, and I believe similar characteristics may come to mind when you think about your own family background.

state capitol at Columbus – she made a conservative choice and landed a job in Middletown, which was larger than Fostoria but not by much.[49] In Middletown, about halfway between Dayton and Cincinnati, in the southwest corner of the state, Geraldine began teaching in lower school and would remain a teacher until her retirement.

For Geraldine Himburg, her job and her position in the community were both rewarding. During her initial year as a teacher, she was able to buy the first suit she had ever owned, and she marked the proud occasion with a photograph. A Methodist like her mother, she aspired to a carefully ordered life on the job and at home. In her early years, she had absorbed Germanic concepts of order and hierarchy that may have been attenuated over the generations in America but had not been entirely lost.[50] Nor were they lost to the second- and third-grade students she taught.

The social and economic struggles of labor unions were alien to her way of thinking. Nor could she endorse the ideology Samuel Gompers of the American Federation of Labor espoused: "More, More, More!" She was not opposed to guiding life with aphorisms.[51] She was also pleased to receive raises. But she was not going to strike or march around carrying a union placard to better her position in life. She preferred to set a soundly middle-class example for her students. She believed firmly in cooperation, not conflict, in the family and on the job.

Between 1890 and 1930, most teachers in the United States appear to have agreed with Geraldine rather than the union leaders. Teachers, for the most part, opted for professional standing rather than union control of their jobs. But these were choices that would be revisited by many teachers in the years ahead. The options would look different after the Great Depression eroded some of their confidence in America's economic and educational institutions.

A Little of This and a Little of That

What can we say in summing up the urban experience during these years? The bad news was the unplanned nature of the rapid growth. To some

---

[49] In 1920, the population of Fostoria was around 13,000 and of Middletown about 23,000.

[50] This is a good example of the ethnic/cultural characterizations that I mentioned in footnote 48 to this chapter.

[51] Although she did not have a man in her life, she was absolutely certain that "Clothes make the man."

extent, America's cities were being pulled apart by the expansion of new industrial and commercial nodes and by suburbanization. Each city had its own characteristics, as do all of us, but there were patterns common to most of them, patterns that stood out in the debates and political struggles taking place in Chicago. There and throughout America, the professional planners were losing their struggle with the more powerful economic and political interests that had long controlled urban development. The city planners could cite specific accomplishments, as they certainly could in Chicago. But the larger pattern of American urban evolution still involved a full measure of chaos, of growing slums, of transportation problems and urban tensions. Urban planning had yet to come of age.

The good news was that urban residents could now have longer and more pleasant lives thanks to the changes taking place in the medical sciences and public health. This was not a negligible accomplishment in a society that lagged far behind Europe in both science and urban policy. The United States was still playing catch-up in these fields of professional expertise, but the nation was steadily making progress, much to the benefit of its rapidly growing urban population.

In public education, too, there was good news. The schools and teachers had been taken out of the hands of local ward bosses. This type of reform hurt those immigrants who had been happy to trade their votes for jobs, but it certainly made for broad and deep improvements in urban education. The professionalization of teaching changed America for the better, as did the reorganization and bureaucratization of the urban school systems. High schools and normal schools throughout the country were opening a new path into teaching for women as well as men. Immigrants and their sons and daughters – including the three sons of Lazlo Galambos – were using urban education to get a foot up, and they hoped a foot closer to the middle class and the professions they associated with a better life. Even the depression of the 1930s couldn't shake the immigrant faith in education.

The professional contributions to both of these positive developments hinted at a promising future for urban America. A nation still close to farm life and the worst aspects of municipal political corruption had put up road signs pointing toward a healthier and better educated society. The changes since 1890, in a matter of just two generations, were impressive.

3

Toward a New Economy, 1890 to 1930

In 1890, a young scientist at Columbia College, Michael Pupin was just getting settled in the school's new Department of Electrical Engineering.[1] He had recently returned to New York City from Europe with a new bride and a Ph.D. in hand and was optimistic about his ability to make a success of the department despite its primitive facilities. His office and laboratory were housed in a tiny brick building that the students called a "cowshed." Even more distressing was the lack of equipment and funds. Pupin and his co-teacher had to give public lectures to raise the $300 they needed to buy additional equipment.[2]

Fortunately Pupin was used to hustling. He had first come to the United States from Serbia in 1874, armed with little more than a good secondary education and an intense drive to get ahead in his new home, New York

---

[1] Seeking additional background on the formidable transition of these years, you might want to read Robert H. Wiebe, *The Search for Order, 1877–1920* (New York, latest printing, 2000) and Glenn Porter, *The Rise of Big Business, 1860–1920* (Wheeling, IL, 3rd edition, 2006).

[2] Michael Pupin, *From Immigrant to Inventor* (New York, 1925), 279–86. The first edition of Pupin's book won a Pulitzer Prize for autobiography in 1924. Throughout this account of *The Creative Society*, I have tried to suppress my academic instinct to document fully each statement in these essays. For those who seek additional documentation, please turn to the following three bibliographical essays by Louis Galambos: "The Emerging Organizational Synthesis in Modern American History," "Technology, Political Economy, and Professionalization: Central Themes of the Organizational Synthesis," and "Recasting the Organizational Synthesis: Structure and Process in the Twentieth and Twenty-First Centuries." All three appeared, respectively, in the *Business History Review*, 44, 3 (Autumn, 1970), 279–90; 57 (Winter 1983), 471–93; and 79 (Spring 2005), 1–38.

City.[3] This was the New York of Boss Tweed, whose corrupt regime was crumbling even though his ward-level political machine would continue to dominate the city's politics for decades. Many immigrants were drawn to politics, but Pupin applied his sharp mind to languages and science and was able to enter Columbia College, where he graduated with honors in 1883. After two years studying mathematics at Cambridge, he went to Germany and completed a Ph.D. in 1889 at Berlin University. Back in New York, he would remain at Columbia, teaching electrical engineering and mathematical physics until his retirement in 1931.

Pupin's career as a research scientist, teacher, and successful inventor can be rolled around like a piece of crystal and studied from a variety of angles. Each one is interesting. At Columbia he taught several distinguished scientists, including Robert Millikan (Nobel Prize, Physics, 1923) and Irving Langmuir (Nobel Prize, Chemistry, 1932). Through his inventions, Pupin also helped the United States build up its capabilities in the sciences related to electricity, a field of central importance in the second industrial revolution.[4] It's impossible to measure in any precise way the impact of one man, even a creative one like Pupin, on the history of a nation numbering more than 63 million people in 1890 and more than 123 million by 1930.[5] But this man's career helps us appreciate the cumulative impact the flow of talent to the United States had during an era when the world's leading centers of science and technical scholarship were all in Europe. America needed the sharp minds and energy

---

[3] Pupin's mother and father could neither read nor write, but his mother encouraged him to educate himself, first at the local school and then at another school fifteen miles from his tiny town of Idvor in the Austro-Hungarian Empire. There, at Panchevo, he had his first encounters with science, with vigorous teaching, and with knowledge of a distant and interesting America. Michael Pupin, *From Immigrant to Inventor*, 1–71.

[4] The first industrial revolution began in Britain in the late eighteenth century. Machine production in the factory, using water and then steam power, sharply increased productivity, drew labor out of agriculture, and quickly supplanted home output of textiles and other manufactured goods. The second industrial revolution was another technological and organizational transformation that began in the second half of the nineteenth century and extended into the post–World War II years. Some of the leading industries were those in electrical products, chemicals, electrochemicals, and then automobiles. These were the years when mass-production and mass-distribution combined to transform the American economy.

[5] As indicated in the previous chapter's notes, all of the statistics in this book are – unless otherwise indicated – drawn from Cambridge University Press's *Historical Statistics of the United States*.

that people like Pupin had to offer.[6] Europe's loss was clearly America's gain.

The United States also gained by adding to its population the young immigrants who, like Lazlo Galambos, were less talented, less educated, and less academically inclined than Pupin. Almost 8.8 million came between 1901 and 1910, and as late as 1920, more than 400,000 came in one year.[7] Because the country had more capital and natural resources than workers to exploit them, the immigrants sustained American growth through their labor – skilled and unskilled. Their individual contributions to America's progress are buried in the national statistics and thus lost to history.

We can actually recover a small part of the nation's gain in Pupin's case. He made one of his inventions just as the United States was in the midst of a significant economic transition. At the turn of the century, the country's business system was shifting from one primarily consisting of small- and medium-sized firms to one dominated by large, industrial corporations. This was a transformation that was poorly understood. It was responded to in that stumbling, clumsy manner in which most societies experience fundamental changes. Pupin's role in the history of this particular transition was twofold: first, he and others helped ease the nation toward solutions to one of the serious problems America's businesses were experiencing; second, Pupin's career clearly marked just how much further U.S. business organizations and American higher education had to go if the country was going to continue to be a world leader in the global economy. To understand how this happened, we need to look more closely at one episode in Pupin's career as an inventor.

David Meets Goliath in America

The invention that concerns us put Pupin in direct competition with the giant Bell Telephone Co. The ensuing struggle didn't take place on a level playing field. The Bell interests employed thousands of engineers and were the world leaders in developing new telephone equipment through their manufacturing branch, Western Electric. Pupin was armed with a

---

[6] The flow of talent included Albert A. Michelson, who came from the Polish region of Prussia as a child. He too became a scientist and in 1907 won for the United States its first Nobel Prize in the sciences.

[7] U.S. Department of Justice, Immigration & Naturalization Service, *1998 Statistical Yearbook*, Table 1, 19.

pencil, some paper, and his modest laboratory at Columbia University.[8] This contest was taking place long before the advent of big science in the United States, long before scientists began receiving multimillion-dollar government grants. David was taking on the corporate Goliath.[9]

Goliath had more than a casual interest in winning. The Bell patents had expired in the 1890s, leaving the company vulnerable to low-cost competitors. The interlopers had moved quickly to fill the rural markets Bell had left without telephone service. By 1900, these "independents" were moving into the cities and had taken over about half of the U.S. market. The first principle of the Bell strategy for dealing with this competition was to stress the firm's long-distance service, something the independents couldn't offer. But Bell's long-distance service wasn't very good. It worked rather well in the Northeast, where cities were close together. But as you moved west, the distances were greater, and the Bell technology simply wouldn't work. Given that the biggest city in the Midwest, Chicago, was more than 700 miles from New York City and more than 850 miles from Boston, the country's largest telephone company had a problem. Burdened with debt and struggling to convince potential customers to adopt its service, Bell's future was in doubt.

The Bell executives were not ignoring this problem. They were scurrying to improve long-distance service, and they got some help from a distinguished British scientist, James Clerk Maxwell, who provided the theoretical basis for solving Bell's problem with long-distance service. This was another good example of America's dependent status in science and technology. Maxwell's elegant equations were the basis for analyzing electrical and magnetic fields, but to use them, you had to know calculus. In fact, you had to know it very well. Today, when high schools all over the country offer calculus I and II and university math departments provide training in advanced mathematics, it wouldn't be hard for a company to find employees who could use Maxwell's equations. But it was different in 1900, when only about 6 percent of young Americans graduated from high school and most of them had studied Latin, not calculus.

---

[8] According to Pupin's account, the idea for the invention came to him when he was on vacation in Europe and didn't have the advantage of even his modest Columbia laboratory. Upon announcing his discovery to his wife, she replied: "I will believe what you say and will gladly congratulate you if you will promise that you will not be absent-minded during the rest of our trip." Michael Pupin, *From Immigrant to Inventor*, 330–32.

[9] This tale is told with exquisite detail in Neil H. Wasserman, *From Invention to Innovation: Long-Distance Telephone Transmission at the Turn of the Century* (Baltimore, 1985).

Up to this time, American innovation in telecommunications didn't depend on scientists and engineers well trained in math. Most of the inventors in the industry were "practical" men, not well-educated scientists. Many of these practical entrepreneurs had gained experience in telegraph and then moved into the fast-growing telephone business. That was a common pattern of innovation in nineteenth-century America, but it was about to change in telecommunications.

Fortunately for Bell, the company employees included some who were capable of understanding Maxwell's equations and using them to develop the invention that would make telephone service over very long distances successful.[10] The "loading coil" was the answer. Unfortunately for Bell, Michael Pupin also understood the equations and grasped the manner in which they could be used to improve the telephone. Bell applied for a patent. Pupin also applied for a patent in what was a virtual dead heat. But Pupin won by a nose in June of 1900. Much later, a distinguished historian of technology concluded that in reality, the Bell company was ahead in the race and should have been awarded the patent.[11] But Pupin won and that version of reality made the future for Bell's competitive strategy look gloomy. David had won the battle.

But of course in this modern version of the biblical story, Goliath is a corporation and corporations have eternal life. So this corporate Goliath was stunned but not dead, and the company had lawyers who nursed it through recovery by closing the entrepreneurial gap, the vital gap between invention and innovation, between expertise and authority, between ideas and power. We'll encounter this gap over and over again in our excursion through twentieth-century history. Good ideas don't matter unless they can be put into action, and some companies and some societies are especially good at that. Modern organizations are like an electric motor that runs smoothly when the plug is fitted securely into the socket. When it isn't, the motor won't work and the job won't get

---

[10] Bell's head of research commented on the company's problem in 1898: "Since I took charge of the department, connecting theoretical work and accurate measurement . . . in telephony have appeared to me of the greatest importance. Heretofore, the difficulty of securing an assistant having the exceptional training required for this exceedingly intricate work has prevented any considerable progress along these lines." Now, however, he had been able to hire George A. Campbell, who had an engineering degree from MIT, had studied theoretical physics in Europe, and would receive a Ph.D. from Harvard on the basis of his work at AT&T. Ibid., 30–33, 142, n. 1.

[11] James E. Brittain, "The Introduction of the Loading Coil: George A. Campbell and Michael I. Pupin," *Technology and Culture*, 1 (1970), 36–57.

done.[12] We'll find other examples of that kind of failure in politics, in international relations, and in urban affairs, as well as business and agriculture.

In the case of telecommunications, Dr. Pupin had the idea for the loading coil but no means of actually applying the new concept. The Bell Company had a telephone system waiting for the innovation, and the firm wisely closed that gap by buying the patent from Pupin for slightly more than a quarter of a million dollars. That was a great deal of money in 1900. But it wasn't much to pay to protect the basic strategy of a company that would, reorganized under new leadership, become the largest private firm in the world.[13]

For our history, the encounter between Pupin and AT&T is significant because it marks a time, give or take a few years, when America's largest companies were just beginning to deal with the entrepreneurial gap. They still hadn't internalized the scientific and technological capabilities that they needed to be successful over the long term. The Bell Company didn't stand alone in this regard. General Electric, the nation's great combine in electrical equipment and generation, faced similar threats from inventors who moved onto the turf GE was trying to control. GE, Bell, DuPont, and other large American firms had tremendous financial resources. They had dominant positions in their markets and could, when they ran well, achieve formidable economies of scale. In brief, they had market power and all the advantages that first-movers possess in any undertaking, including business.[14]

But this was not enough to defend their empires – which resembled political empires in many regards – unless they could learn how to become and remain innovative. What the businesses did and what American society did at this crucial turning point would play a central role in shaping the country's economic performance for more than a century. If a touch of detail in this part of the history makes your eyes glaze over (MEGO), I apologize. But the process is so important that we need to look with care at the early efforts to inspire these corporate giants to be entrepreneurial.

Questing, they experimented with a variety of strategies. In some cases, they bought the new ideas they needed, as Bell had just done with Pupin. They also tried to learn how to create and implement those ideas within

[12] You can also think of this as a spark plug that needs to be set just right to start the motor.

[13] Neil H. Wasserman, *From Invention to Innovation*, 97.

[14] Alfred D. Chandler, Jr., *Scale and Scope: The Dynamics of Industrial Capitalism* (Cambridge, 1990).

the firm, as GE and Bell and DuPont all set out to do in the early 1900s. This may sound easy to do, but in the early decades of the twentieth century, it was not at all apparent exactly how it could be done. Bell tried for a time to get contract research done at the Massachusetts Institute of Technology. Some other companies hired private research organizations. But that only closed the gap part of the way, and besides, the firms had to employ enough talented people to understand exactly what kinds of opportunities were being created in the sciences and technologies, what their companies needed, and what should be done to employ the ideas coming from outside.

Gradually, the leading companies in the electrical, the chemical, and the electrochemical industries all drifted toward creating research-and-development organizations within their firms.[15] This left them less dependent on external sources for innovative ideas. It reduced the risk that others would buy the ideas they needed or try to use them to compete. If the large firms like Bell could do this successfully, there might be no gap at all. But to be that successful they had to have people like Pupin working for them, and they quickly discovered they wouldn't be easy to find.

Higher Education in a Truly Democratic Society

The U.S. university system was not really up to the task of churning out the talented scientists and engineers business needed early in the twentieth century. The leading eastern universities had only recently begun to break away from their religious institutions and traditional humanistic curricula. The Ivy League universities were accommodating to the new needs of society gradually and unevenly. Columbia, where Pupin was teaching, was influenced favorably by its location in New York City, the nation's leading business and financial center. Columbia responded faster than Yale, Brown, or Princeton to the new demands for scientific

---

[15] Margaret B.W. Graham and Alec T. Shuldiner, *Corning and the Craft of Innovation* (New York, 2001). David A. Hounshell and John Kenly Smith, Jr., *Science and Corporate Strategy: Du Pont R&D, 1902–1980* (New York, 1988). Leonard S. Reich, *The Making of American Industrial Research: Science and Business at GE and Bell, 1876–1926* (New York, 1985). George Wise, *Willis R. Whitney, General Electric, and the Origins of U.S. Industrial Research* (New York, 1985). W. Bernard Carlson and Stuart K. Sammis, "Revolution or Evolution? The Development of Innovation and R&D at Corning" (paper presented at Johns Hopkins, 2008).

and technical expertise. Indeed during the late nineteenth century, these three stalwart Ivies had continued to look down their elite noses with some disdain on what was going on in finance and industry.[16] Harvard was somewhat more flexible as were the two nonsectarian schools, the University of Pennsylvania and the youngest of the Ivy schools, Cornell. Cornell University had the distinction of being New York's agricultural and mechanical college, so it was attuned to practical matters.

Outside of the eastern elite institutions were a handful of leading universities where technical subjects and faculty were not disdained. These included the Massachusetts Institute of Technology, Johns Hopkins University, and the University of Chicago. At Hopkins the dedication to science, professionalism, and advanced research was intense, as it was at Chicago.[17] Because both were relatively new schools, they were spared some of the debates that slowed change in the Ivy League. At MIT, the school cultivated a particular form of vocational orientation consistent with its emphasis on engineering. Whereas each of these schools responded in its own way to the mounting demand for professional expertise in America, all three were shaped by that need and all experienced some form of internal tension over their new roles in higher education.

Beyond the eastern seaboard, the state universities and agricultural and mechanical schools (A&M's) were the institutions most influenced by society's new demands for professional training. Handicapped by their lack of academic status, these schools competed by filling niches ignored by the elite schools and by training a mass of students who lacked the social backgrounds, educational qualifications, finances, and often the capabilities that might have taken them to one of the top universities.

The Midwestern and Western schools hurried into the business of training professionals. The state schools were beholden to their legislatures and relatively quick to sense what was needed in each state's economy. Often this pushed the schools into areas of training and research that seemed to have little to do with the dominant disciplines in either the arts or sciences. Home economics, for instance, found a place at Cornell

---

[16] Laurence R. Veysey's pioneering study, *The Emergence of the American University* (Chicago, 1965), is still a good guide to the controversies within American universities during the late nineteenth century. Columbia, as Veysey notes (p. 122), established separate schools for pure and applied science in 1890.

[17] Early on, Hopkins stressed pure and not applied research, but this distinction soon faded and then disappeared. Hugh Hawkins, *Pioneer: A History of the Johns Hopkins University, 1874–1899* (Ithaca, 1960).

and other schools, even though it had nothing to do with the subject then being taught in the economics departments at those universities.[18]

To the west, in states like South Dakota, there was great enthusiasm for higher education, the professions, and the economic benefits these might bestow on the local society. In fact, South Dakota had a state university and an agricultural college before it was broken out of the Dakota Territory and admitted as a state (1889). In 1882, the administration and faculty of the university were combined in the person of Dr. Ephraim M. Epstein, who had left Russia, the Jewish religion, and New York City in his wake before he found a new life and a new occupation in Vermillion, South Dakota. Competition to get the school located in Vermillion had spurred local residents to contribute land, and Dr. Epstein started preparatory classes in the local courthouse before any buildings went up. The classes had to be preparatory because none of the students had completed high school. As late as 1889, most of the students were still in the preparatory program, but the school's curriculum gradually improved, as did its faculty and students. By the early 1900s, the Board of Regents, which was convinced the school had laid a solid foundation for professional training, established schools of law, music, medicine, and engineering.[19]

In South Dakota and elsewhere in the United States, high schools experienced tremendous growth. By 1920, more than 16 percent of all seventeen-year-olds in the United States graduated from high school. Ten years later, this figure, which included women as well as men, was more than 29 percent. This was a phenomenal rate of expansion in schools that were beginning to funnel more and more of their students into higher education.[20]

---

[18] Nancy Berlage, "The Establishment of an Applied Social Science: Home Economists, Science, and Reform at Cornell University, 1870–1930," in Helen Silverberg, ed., *Gender and American Social Science: The Formative Years* (Princeton, 1998). Home economics developed a solid foundation in public education from middle schools through high schools in many states, but its position in the university system was always intellectually precarious.

[19] Wayne S. Knutson, "The University of South Dakota: A Story of Faith and Endurance," in Herbert T. Hoover, et al., eds., *From Idea to Institution: Higher Education in South Dakota* (Vermillion, SD, 1989), 13–17. The Regents launched the professional schools in the years 1901–1907.

[20] Se-Um Kim, "The Technological Origins of the High School Movement," Munich Personal RePEc Archive (October 20, 2008), MPRA Paper No. 12087, posted December 11, 2008, http://mpra.ub.uni-muenchen.de/12087. Claudia Goldin, "America's Graduation from High School: The Evolution and Spread of Secondary Schooling in the Twentieth Century," *Journal of Economic History*, 58, 2 (1998), 345–74. See also Goldin, "The

Throughout the Midwest and West, the educational base was broader than the state university. In South Dakota it also included the Dakota Agricultural College, which was founded only six years after Custer's defeat at the battle of the Little Bighorn.[21] The school's subsequent evolution was a microcosm of higher education in the West. At the "ag college," much of its instruction in the early years was also preparatory work. This took place under the leadership of "Dr." George Lilly, who, it turned out, had not graduated from college. Like Lou Galambos, Lilly, who was an educational entrepreneur by practice, was a professional by proclamation.[22]

After South Dakota became a state, the school qualified for land-grant status and was renamed the South Dakota State College of Agricultural and Mechanic Arts. In addition to instruction in agriculture and mechanical engineering, the College supported programs in electrical and civil engineering, pharmacy, general science, and, of course, home economics. After 1914, the College aligned itself with two federal efforts to improve farm productivity and vocational training, drawing resources and new programs from Washington, DC.[23]

The network of higher education in South Dakota soon spread over the entire state. Some of the schools were oriented to teacher training – as were the Black Hills State College, the Dakota State College, and Northern State College – and others were linked to important state economic activities – as was the South Dakota School of Mines and Technology. Whatever their orientation, all of the schools encountered the same problems: limited finances, poorly trained students, and a shortage of qualified faculty and administrators.[24] The state government was determined,

Human Capital Century and American Leadership: Virtues of the Past," NBER Working Paper No. W8239 (April 2001).

[21] I can save you one Google search: the battle often referred to as "Custer's Last Stand" took place in late June 1876 near the Little Bighorn River in Montana.

[22] J. Howard Kramer, *South Dakota State University: A History, 1884 to 1975* (Brookings, 1975), 19. Lilley's frontier brand of pseudo-professionalism did not hold him back permanently. He went on to become president of another college later in his career.

[23] John E. Miller, "Science, Service, and Learning in the Land Grant Tradition," in Herbert T. Hoover, et al., eds., *From Idea to Institution*, 33–43. The school's name changed first to South Dakota Agricultural College, then to South Dakota State College of Agriculture and Mechanic Arts, and finally to South Dakota State University (1964). The school is in the town of Brookings. According to Miller, the residents originally wanted to land the penitentiary, but when Sioux Falls locked up that plum, they took the school.

[24] The schools included: the Black Hills State College, which was primarily engaged in teacher training; the Dakota Normal School, which became Dakota State College; and the South Dakota School of Mines and Technology. The Northern State College was

however, not to let South Dakota fall behind its sister states. Driven by a concern for status as well as expertise, South Dakota worked hard to solve the problems of its educational institutions and create a foundation for advanced professional education.

This pattern was repeated in all of the states to the west of Philadelphia and, somewhat later, in those that were south of Baltimore. There were variations, of course. Some of these differences were important, as they were in Texas, where the land grants that provided the financial base for the university turned out to be rich in minerals. But what was most important to this history were the relatively rapid expansion of higher education, the growing numbers of students, and the professional schools the states quickly established. This massive array of universities and colleges proved the wisdom of those political leaders who had laid the foundation for this state-based system in 1862.[25]

What emerged in each state were elaborate terraced landscapes of public and private schools. This complex, multitiered system was very expensive if you totaled up the bill for the entire country.[26] It was also wasteful insofar as it brought into higher education thousands who should never have been there and received few benefits from the experience. By 1930, the United States had almost four times as many students enrolled in higher education as Great Britain, France, and Germany combined.[27] The U.S. dropout rates were high, and many of the programs seemed

created in 1899 as the Industrial Institute of South Dakota. It became the Northern Normal and Industrial School in 1901 and opened (apparently in 1902) with seven faculty and one hundred students. There were also private, church-associated schools: Yankton Academy 1881 (Congregational), Sioux Falls College 1883 (Baptist), Augustana College 1884 (Lutheran), Dakota Wesleyan University 1885 (Methodist), Wessington Springs Junior College 1887 (Free Methodists), Huron College 1898 (Presbyterian), and Freeman Junior College 1901 (Mennonites). Beneath this tier of schools were the academies that actually functioned as high schools. All of the schools had problems finding acceptable teachers and administrators, so it was not surprising that a principal of one of the teachers' schools was a compulsive and not particularly talented gambler. It was surprising, however, that he was later convicted of murder.

[25] Williamjames Hull Hoffer, *To Enlarge the Machinery of Government: Congressional Debates and the Growth of the American State, 1858–1891* (Baltimore, 2007), 1–62.

[26] Laurence R. Veysey, *The Emergence of the American University*, 265–67, asks why the "academic boom of the early nineties" took place when it did. He looks inside and outside the universities. He looks to a generation of self-made men who wanted their children to have higher social status. Vesey also points out that immigration pushed against the old Anglo-Saxon class, forcing them to look for a way of protecting their status. One needs to add to that analysis the record of unusual wealth accumulation in America and the new demands in the economy and elsewhere for well-educated professionals.

[27] Walter M. Kotschnig, *Unemployment in the Learned Professions: An International Study of Occupational and Educational Planning* (Oxford, 1937), 13 and 206. See also:

unlikely to achieve their stated objectives. A true cost/benefit analysis, if we had one, would probably show that Americans paid too much for this giant, nationwide system of higher education. In that regard, it was typically American.

Also typically American were the system's three big advantages: for one thing, it provided access to higher education to those who couldn't otherwise have improved their lives and prospects through learning. For many, it was the only source of advanced education they could afford. Almost all of these colleges and universities were public institutions that charged very low tuitions and admitted most (in some cases all) of the graduates of their state's high schools. The professional programs, which were also part of the state-based system, were not quite as all-inclusive as undergraduate education, but they were in their early years much easier to get into than those of the eastern elites. This system slowly raised the educational level of middle-class Americans and provided an escape hatch for the white children of working-class parents who were able to squeeze into the schools. Education functioned as a giant, imperfect sieve that sifted out some of the truly talented members of the society and provided them with access to advanced education in professional schools.

In South Dakota, Ernest O. Lawrence was one of the stars who was sifted out, advanced through the system, and brought to the top of his profession. He attended school in his home town of Canton, in the southeast corner of the state, along the Big Sioux River. Ernest's father and mother were second-generation Norwegians who had moved to Canton from Wisconsin, where the father, Carl, had graduated from the university. Successful in his first teaching position, Carl had become the superintendent of schools in Canton, where his son Ernest completed high school.

Money was scarce in the family, and the following year Ernest accepted a scholarship and attended St. Olaf College in the neighboring state of Minnesota. After one year, he returned to his home state and enrolled in the University of South Dakota, where he could major in one of his favorite subjects – chemistry. In Vermillion, his physics teacher discovered his brilliance and Ernest discovered the wonder of physics. It became his

Carol Dyhouse, "Family Patterns of Social Mobility through Higher Education in England in the 1930s," *Journal of Social History*, 34, 4 (Summer 2001), 817–42; and Peter Drewek, "Limits of Educational Internationalism: Foreign Students at German Universities, 1890–1930," http://www.ghi-dc.org/publications/ghipubs/bu/027/b27drewek-frame.html.

major interest by the time he graduated in 1922. He spent a year studying physics at the University of Minnesota, a year at the University of Chicago, and then jumped to Yale, where he received his Ph.D. in physics in 1925. Four years later, he invented the cyclotron, a discovery that won him a Nobel Prize in Physics in 1939, when he was just thirty-eight years old.[28]

Scientists like Lawrence – who will pop back into our history during World War II – began to close the gulf between the United States and Europe.[29] They were products of a uniquely American system of higher education that was expanding rapidly, its evolution accelerated by the society's great wealth and the diversity and intense competition that pervaded the system.

The U.S. system made reentry easy – its second major strength – for those who initially had unfortunate performances in a college or university. Like a terraced hillside catching water as it flowed to a lower level, the system caught and held people who in other societies would have been excluded from any form of higher education. Second and third opportunities were available to those who had flopped but then matured or simply learned more about coping with advanced education.[30]

From the perspective of the creative society, the third and probably the most important strength of American higher education was that it was responsive to society's immediate needs. Here, as elsewhere in this history, you can see my particular reading of modern American history and of the American style of democracy shaping my conclusions. Those "needs" were filtered through legislatures and local governments. In practice, this meant the schools were linked to each state's primary economic activities insofar as they were represented in the state legislature and the state's interest groups. In South Dakota, that dictated an emphasis on agriculture, mining, and the commerce directly associated with them. In Ohio, as in South Dakota, the practical needs of the state economy were

---

[28] Herbert Childs, *An American Genius: The Life of Ernest Orlando Lawrence* (New York, 1968). At Yale, Lawrence encountered some status hostility expressed through pointed questioning about his family. He reacted with some emotion to this kind of Eastern snobbishness (120–21).

[29] The National Research Council had established a fellowship program for this purpose, and Lawrence received one of the Council's multiyear grants. Ibid., 93. The competitive nature of the American educational system was on display in the efforts of different programs to appoint this brilliant scientist. The University of California finally won the competition.

[30] I must admit to personal bias in this case. I was one of those who flopped the first time around.

impossible to ignore. That gave an important role in Ohio's schools to accounting, as well as other forms of training for business.

Between 1890 and 1930, the U.S. combination of a state-based and private system of higher education expanded rapidly and began to provide the professionals America needed to make a successful transition to a new style of economy. This was an economy that grew primarily by finding new ways to increase efficiency and develop new goods and services. That was, after all, what people like Ernest O. Lawrence and Michael Pupin were all about.

Innovation in Business

In addition to his research, Pupin the teacher made important contributions to a society looking for new ways to innovate. As we've seen, he taught other promising scientists, including Irving Langmuir, who graduated at Columbia in 1903. Like most ardent young scientists, Langmuir followed the trail of his mentor and headed to Europe for training in the world's leading scientific centers. After he returned to the United States, he taught for a few years at the Stevens Institute of Technology and then took a job with General Electric. GE badly needed the expertise Langmuir could provide in the development of the electric lightbulb.[31] Langmuir helped GE become a more entrepreneurial company and in doing so, he and others with professional training helped America ease its way toward the new age of research-driven growth. Along a narrow front, American business was starting toward what would later be called the knowledge economy.[32]

The progress was not smooth. In even the largest and most progressive businesses, there was tension between the R&D establishment and the executives who ran the firms. For one thing, they spoke different languages and had different backgrounds. The languages and cultures of the sciences were alien to business leaders of this generation. The businessmen

---

[31] Leonard Reich, *The Making of American Industrial Research.*

[32] The knowledge economy would acquire a new theoretical growth model when Paul Romer published his first article on "Endogenous Technological Change," *Journal of Political Economy* (October 1990). The subject acquired a new empirical base when Moses Abramovitz and Paul David published "American Macroeconomic Growth in the Era of Knowledge-Based Progress: The Long-Run Perspective," in Stanley L. Engerman and Robert E. Gallman, eds., *The Cambridge Economic History of the United States, 3, The Twentieth Century* (New York, 2000), 1–92. I have benefited from reading David Warsh's engaging account of *Knowledge and the Wealth of Nations: A Story of Economic Discovery* (New York, 2006).

were justly proud of what they'd accomplished. They could point to the great success American industry had achieved without the help of Ph.D.s. By 1900, the United States was already the leading industrial nation in the world. They'd achieved success by investing wisely in machinery, raw materials, transportation, sales, and marketing operations, all of which could be expressed in standard accounting terms. When America's largest firms combined mass production with mass distribution, their leaders could calculate with a fair degree of accuracy the risks involved in those investments and the probable payout.

R&D was different: harder to measure, harder to predict. That's why most of the largest corporations had to face a specific threat before they invested heavily in research.[33] That's why they frequently looked outside of the firm – say, to MIT – for help before creating the laboratories they needed. That's why a new role, the research manager, had to be developed to guide the research being done by professional scientists and engineers and to deal directly with the company's executives. The research manager was a broker, as well as a translator, someone who could understand and evaluate what the bench scientists and engineers were doing and then explain it to the executives in a language they could understand.

The research managers frequently had to contend with bureaucratic resistance to change. Centralized and bureaucratized, the nation's largest firms had become less flexible agents of change. Business bureaucrats, like those in the public sector and in nonprofits, were armed with a potent array of procedural weapons. Each proposal could be restudied, reconsidered, and then perhaps resisted. This was a systemic business problem – and still is today. All of my professional readers have served on committees, and most of you have had encounters with the thoroughly developed bureaucratic mind. You don't need a sophisticated explanation of the bureaucratic impediments to change. You already understand the problem.

That's why the development of effective R&D took time and considerable experimentation. The first wave of change was limited to a small number of firms. Following World War I, however, the research frontier became broader and more American businesses began to close the gap between professional science and engineering and corporate investment, between invention and innovation. Still, it was a common practice

---

[33] Even when they did encounter a specific problem that called for R&D, they might quickly terminate the research organization once the problem was solved – as was the case with Standard Oil.

for large firms to buy inventions developed by individuals and smaller companies and then use the corporations' superior resources to take the resulting innovations to national and sometimes international markets.

As this suggests, small- and medium-sized enterprises didn't have to contend to the same extent with business bureaucracies. While they had high failure rates, they continued to churn out innovations as they had in the previous century. Frequently, these innovations were launched by entrepreneurs who were the firm's major source of professional knowledge and technical capability. Normally tight on working capital, these entrepreneurs often operated near the edge of disaster, taking risks that many larger and more cautious firms would avoid. What kept the American business system growing and moving through this difficult transition was the combination of these various kinds of enterprises and the growing role of technical expertise in all of them.[34]

Agricultural Improvement

Similar changes were taking place in American agriculture, where the role played by firms like GE and AT&T was played instead by governments – national and state. In all of the A&M schools, agricultural improvement received a great deal of attention. The schools became important nodes in a national network that was developed with public dollars. The goal of the network was to improve innovation and efficiency in farming.

The roots of this public network reached back into the 1870s, when the first experimental stations were created. They drew on the A&M professional training programs for personnel and for ideas about how to solve practical problems like preventing diseases in farm animals and improving crop yields. The U.S. Department of Agriculture published the results of these studies in pamphlets that were made widely available to farmers throughout the nation.[35]

Two of the professionals who contributed to the early development of this system were Lyman Briggs and Marion Dorset. Briggs was a graduate of the Michigan Agricultural College. After taking advanced work at

---

[34] See, for instance, Naomi R. Lamoreaux, Margaret Levenstein, and Kenneth L. Sokoloff, "Financing Invention during the Second Industrial Revolution: Cleveland, Ohio, 1870–1920," in Naomi R. Lamoreaux and Kenneth L. Sokoloff, eds., *Financing Innovation in the United States, 1870 to the Present* (Cambridge, 2007), 39–84.

[35] Daniel P. Carpenter, *The Forging of Bureaucratic Autonomy: Reputation, Networks, and Policy Innovation in Executive Agencies, 1862–1928* (Princeton, 2001), especially 179–289.

the University of Michigan and Johns Hopkins University, he took a position in the U.S. Department of Agriculture, where he focused most of his attention on the problems of water retention in soils.[36] A research pioneer in what became soil physics, Briggs organized the Department's biophysical laboratory (1906) and published ecological studies on water uptake by plants. Marion Dorset had a similar early career. He came out of the undergraduate program at the University of Tennessee, that state's land-grant institution, and then went on to receive an M.D. from George Washington University in St. Louis (1904). He started working for the Department of Agriculture before he finished his medical degree, and he stayed on to conduct research in the Department's Biochemic Division.

Collaborating with two colleagues doing field work in Iowa, Dorset and his coworkers produced a serum antitoxin that was effective against hog cholera.[37] While you may have never heard of this disease, it was familiar to Midwestern farmers. When the epidemics hit, as one did in 1910, farmers could easily lose most of their hogs and a good bit of their income to the disease. In farm country, professionals like Dorset and Briggs brought new ideas to an ancient occupation.

The effort to make farming more efficient and innovative encountered some of the same problems businesses were experiencing. There were deeply planted cultural barriers to change. The agricultural programs ran into a prejudice against "book farming." Most of those actually engaged in commercial farming looked on themselves as "dirt farmers." Having succeeded in bringing in crops and raising animals for markets at home and abroad, they were more attentive to the local soil and weather than they were to Department of Agriculture pamphlets.

They had some good reasons to be skeptical. The professors and book farmers were muttering about the end of the American frontier, but the dirt farmers were continuing to expand the entire agricultural sector in America. They were starting thousands of new farms in the western and southwestern United States. The style of growth that had been going on since the first colonies was continuing. Traditional techniques had worked for three centuries. Why should they be abandoned now? Most of the nation's farmers weren't eager to buy into the ideas coming out of Washington and the universities.

---

[36] On the unusual aspects and general significance of the appointments process see Daniel P. Carpenter, *The Forging of Bureaucratic Autonomy*, 191–98.

[37] This antitoxin was made by infecting animals with the disease and then using their blood (hence serum) and the antitoxins it contained to inoculate other animals.

Determined not to give up, the scientists and government officials created an even more elaborate system to take the new knowledge and techniques directly to the farm. The extension service built on the foundation provided by the A&Ms and the sciences fostered by those schools and government subsidized research. The extension service was the D in R&D for farmers.[38] Of course farmers needed money if they were going to introduce the new style of agriculture, so the government created a separate banking system – just for agriculture – to pump cash into farming through low-interest loans.

This expanded and upgraded system of higher education, research, and direct support for innovation produced some positive results. There were scattered examples of improvement: the hogs, for instance, were certainly healthier. But the progress was even slower than it was in business. The national statistics on farm productivity don't indicate that book farming was bringing about a great wave of change in dirt farming in any region of the country.

The rule was stability. Meanwhile, agricultural overproduction drove down prices in the late 1920s. This encouraged farm organizations, agricultural editors, and many dirt farmers to look to cartels rather than science for a solution to their problems. Increasingly, they called for government-controlled prices – a form of public cartel – as the only way to get farmers back to parity with industry. Parity became a loud call for equity and security. This was a call the U.S. Congress could not long ignore.

Was the New Economy Underway?

In the years between 1890 and 1930, the results of all of this institution building, private as well as public, were mixed. If there were failures – and there were many – it was not for the want of trying to be creative. It helped to have lots of money, and America was indeed a large, rich society with a great deal to invest in higher education, professional schools, research organizations, experimental programs, and innovative policies. The best of the new institutions and the best of the professionals were

---

[38] Howard Kramer, *South Dakota State University*, 60. The extension service was appropriately named: it extended the reach of the network down to the county level. The Smith-Lever Act (1914) created the service, and the College in this case was able to benefit financially. About this same time, the College reached out by experimenting for a time with correspondence courses.

making progress in business and even in agriculture, where the resistance to change was frequently fierce. The best news was that the United States was beginning to catch up with Europe in developing scientific and technical expertise.

But as late as 1930, it was still not clear whether America was going to be as successful in the twentieth century as it had been in the previous hundred years. Mired in a deep and growing depression, Americans had every reason to be worried about the future of their farms and businesses. It's little wonder that they looked to the federal government at that time for help in dealing with the nation's economic crisis.

4

State Crafting – American Style

Whether Americans lived on a farm or in a city, they had long been the least-governed people in the developed world. State and local governments did their best to fill this void.[1] But insofar as modernization in Europe involved the creation of national administrative states – that is, a national government with a formidable bureaucracy – the United States was still premodern as late as the 1890s and apparently enjoying its unique brand of political innocence. Of course this bliss didn't last. During the next four decades, the country struggled to create new forms of national governance consistent with the needs of a very large, urban, industrial society.[2]

In a rapidly expanding democracy with fluid class boundaries and an economy experiencing alternating surges of growth and depression, state building was at best a haphazard undertaking. The profession that played

---

[1] Here I am running against the historical reinterpretations provided by two distinguished scholars, Brian Balogh and William J. Novak. Balogh's recent, path-breaking study concludes that the United States had *A Government Out of Sight: The Mystery of National Authority in Nineteenth-Century America* (New York, 2009). Novak follows a similar line of reasoning in "Long Live the Myth of the Weak State?" in the *American Historical Review*, 115 (2010), 792–800. But as late as 1890, total government revenue (federal, state, and local) was still only 6.4% of America's GNP. In 1902, local government revenues and debts (used largely for infrastructure) exceeded those of the national government. My position appears to be challenged, but not outdated.

[2] If you develop a hunger for more history of the progressive years in U.S. politics, you should sample some of the chapters in Meg Jacobs, William J. Novak, and Julian E. Zelizer, eds., *The Democratic Experiment: New Directions in American Political History* (Princeton, 2003). The essays by Michael Willrich and Brian Balogh will be of particular interest.

the leading role in that bitterly contested and bruising process was the law. Party politicians, reformers, the clergy, bureaucratic entrepreneurs within government, even economists, sociologists, philosophers, and an occasional historian made proposals.[3] As would the representatives of the myriad interest groups eager to shape every political decision. Business would, of course, have its say.[4] But it would largely be lawyers who would craft the compromises essential to an American democratic society. The lawyers dominated the entrepreneurial gap in politics.[5] Like young parents trying to shop with their children in tow, the lawyers usually had more help than they wanted. But their profession was accustomed to conflict, hardened to defeat, and strategically positioned to shape the emerging American administrative state.

What was that strategic position? Not all of America's legislators were lawyers, but many were – at all levels of government. All seven of the nation's presidents between 1890 and 1930 had studied or practiced law, and the executive branches of the federal and state governments were filled with lawyers, many of whom were staff to the line officers, the presidents and governors. In theory and usually in practice, the staff provided advice and technical assistance to the "principals" who actually wielded the power and made the crucial decisions in their administrations. But as any staff member and even some principals will tell you, the staff frequently sets the agenda and has a significant impact on the ensuing policy choices.

In the third branch of government, the judiciary, lawyers were in complete control in the states and in Washington, DC. So we'll start by looking at the judiciary and trying to determine how and to what effect their power was exercised. We'll need to ferret out the legal profession's impact on some of the significant state-building efforts of the years 1890 through 1930.

---

[3] The bureaucratic entrepreneurs are analyzed with great insight in Daniel P. Carpenter, *The Forging of Bureaucratic Autonomy: Reputations, Networks, and Policy Innovation in Executive Agencies, 1862–1928* (Princeton, 2001).

[4] New experts would emerge out of the "organizational diversity, political uncertainty, and journalistic ambiguity" of the era. One of the political innovations of the progressive years would be "an emergent field of self-described publicity 'experts.'" Adam Sheingate, "Progressive Publicity and the Origins of Political Consulting," in *Building a Business of Politics: The Origins and Development of Political Consulting in the United States* (Mss courtesy of the author).

[5] I said we would return to this idea – that is, the gap between ideas and practice – and extend it far beyond the entrepreneurship usually studied only in histories of business. Here, I am applying the concept to innovation in politics.

During these four decades, the legal profession was remaking itself, as well as many of America's most important public institutions. Legal training had traditionally been an individual exercise. You read law, normally in a lawyer's library, and when you were sufficiently read, you presented yourself to the bar. But in the late nineteenth and early twentieth centuries, the law schools were taking over the process of converting a literate citizen into a professional lawyer. Symbolizing the transition was the appointment in 1877 of the first graduate of a modern law program to the Supreme Court. Justice John Marshall Harlan joined a court that was deeply engaged with America's early efforts at state building.

Learning by Doing in the Crafting of the Regulatory State

One of these efforts involved new state and federal regulations. Many of these measures touched on economic activities, but others addressed the realms of political and social behavior. One of the major problems – and the first major difficulty confronted at the federal level – involved regulating America's railroads. This proved to be a difficult problem to solve.

It's almost impossible today to imagine the vital role the railroads played in the nation's life in the 1890s, before the age of the automobile and truck. For farmers, merchants, and manufacturers, the rates the railroads charged and the services they provided were matters of deep concern. Passengers also made frequent use of the rails, but the real problems involved commodities that were bulky, heavy, and trading on narrow margins. With products like coal and wheat, changes in rates or services could easily make the difference between a profit and loss, between success and bankruptcy for a business or a farm in Kansas or Illinois.

It was not obvious what could be done to ensure that all those millions of people who were dependent on the rail lines would receive fair service at a fair rate. In Fostoria, Ohio, as we saw in Chapter 1, the rail connections were the economic blood vessels of the city. They sustained the commerce and industry of Fostoria and its counterparts throughout the Midwest. For all of them, equity was a problem. There was widespread concern about rates that were unfair because they favored some shippers and some localities. Competition was supposed to ensure equity. But many cases, competition didn't seem to be working, and Americans let their legislators know about their concerns.

As was often the case, Americans looked to Britain – still the Mother Country in many regards – for ideas. There they discovered the policy of control by an independent regulatory agency, an approach that seemed to be useful in this case.[6] So when Illinois set out to create a new program of railroad regulation, the state focused on a concept that had already been tried and vetted in Britain. When the proposal passed through the state legislature, it received a stamp of approval from a cadre of Illinois lawyers. But then, the new agency came under the purview of a U.S. Supreme Court that included a strong-minded lawyer named Stephen J. Field.[7]

Field, the son of a New England Congregational minister, had read law and then practiced for a time with his distinguished brother, David Dudley Field.[8] Attracted to California by the gold rush, young Stephen traveled first to San Francisco and then to the tiny settlement of Marysville, California. Elected as the town's judicial official, later the justice of the peace, he worked to establish order in a disorderly, gold-feverish locale.[9] In a setting where men were often more likely to settle their differences with guns rather than law, Field, who later served in the state legislature, was successful. He was manifestly headed to places more important than Marysville. On his way to the top, this determined lawyer left the church of his father and became an Episcopalian, a choice that seems to have involved a seamless blend between religious practice and a concern for status. Elected to the state Supreme Court, Field established a solid reputation for practicality and the defense of property rights, positions that helped ease him into an appointment to the nation's senior court in 1863.

By the time the Supreme Court began to review the state efforts to control railroad rates, Field had become a staunch opponent of the regulation of business activities. He wanted a narrow definition of the public interest and was suspicious of reform policies that extended beyond what he understood to be the limits set by the Constitution. He was convinced

---

[6] Stephen Skowronek, *Building a New American State: The Expansion of National Administrative Capacities, 1877–1920* (New York, 1982), 134–35.

[7] Brian Balogh, *A Government Out of Sight*, 315–51.

[8] Daun Van Ee, *David Dudley Field and the Reconstruction of the Law* (New York, 1986). The older brother was an extremely successful and wealthy attorney, who led the movement for the codification of the laws of New York State.

[9] Carl Brent Swisher, *Stephen J. Field: Craftsman of the Law* (Washington, 1930) outlines Field's life and major accomplishments. As Swisher observes, Field "seems never to have doubted his own wisdom in the selection and interpretation of fundamental principles" (16–17).

that the property of corporations, like that of individuals, was protected by the Constitution and in particular by the Fourteenth Amendment.[10] Gradually, Field and Justice Brewer moved the Supreme Court toward their negative position on the regulatory state.[11] Justice Harlan, by contrast, spoke for moderation.

Two decisions in particular had a decisive impact on railroad regulation. One, in 1886, moved the most important aspects of regulation from the states to the federal government – where they needed to be.[12] Congress promptly responded in 1887 by creating the Interstate Commerce Commission to perform that function at the national level. The second decision, which came just as Field was retiring from the Court in 1897, stripped the Interstate Commerce Commission of the right to fix future railroad rates. Congress thought it had given the Commission that right in 1887, having prohibited rates that were unjust or unreasonable. But the Court decided otherwise.[13]

What are we to make of these judicial interventions in the process of molding a regulatory system? Decisions such as these persuaded historian Richard McCloskey to tar the legal profession of that era: "To the native conservative bias of lawyers," McCloskey said, "the Gilded Age superadded a procapitalist prejudice that was extreme even for the nineteenth century."[14] I disagree. The first decision clearly had the effect of speeding up the process of state building at the federal level. Although the second slowed that process by slightly more than a decade, it did so at a time when it was still unclear to the regulators, the legislators, and the courts exactly how the new federal system was working. Everyone was learning by doing, a process that inevitably involved steps sideways and backward as well as forward.

This governmental learning process had begun even before the ICC was in full operation. President Grover Cleveland had to decide who could guide the Commission through this process and all five of his choices were, as you might have guessed, lawyers. The Chairman of the Commission

[10] Ibid., 252–56.
[11] Ibid., 384–95. For perceptive discussions of the Waite and Fuller Courts, see Peter Charles Hoffer, Williamjames Hull Hoffer, and N.E.H. Hull, *The Supreme Court: An Essential History* (Lawrence, Kansas, 2007), 131–90. See also Robert Green McCloskey, *American Conservatism in the Age of Enterprise* (Cambridge, 1951), 72–126.
[12] *Wabash, St. Louis and Pacific Railway Company v. Illinois*, 118 U.S. 557.
[13] *Interstate Commerce Commission v. Cincinnati, N.O. & T. P.*, 167 U.S. 479.
[14] Robert Green McCloskey, *American Conservatism in the Age of Enterprise*, 75.

was Thomas M. Cooley, who had served as a Michigan Supreme Court Justice, first Dean of the University of Michigan's School of Law, and a receiver for the bankrupt Wabash Railroad.[15]

Cooley and his colleagues understood the industry they were trying to regulate, but they found it difficult to develop a regulatory approach adequate to the task. The new law told the Commissioners what to do but not how to do it. They had to find a way to give some substance to the bill's aim of producing rates and services that were "reasonable and just." Being lawyers, they adopted a case-by-case, rate-by-rate approach to the regulation problem.[16] But then they discovered that the average case was taking four years to settle and the courts were striking down almost all of the decisions that were making their way into the hands of the judiciary.[17] The 1897 decision of the Court was a climax to this initial stage of learning by doing.

Why was the learning taking so long? For one thing, railroad rates and finances were unbelievably confusing. For another, two branches of the U.S. government were trying to work out an entirely new relationship, one in which professional expertise would have a special new position, an independent position in our politics.[18] Like many business executives who wanted high-powered R&D departments but found it difficult to manage scientists, the courts were finding it hard to handle this new form of expertise in political economy. The ICC might be an independent agency, but the Supreme Court was making it clear that the agency was not independent from the judiciary.

---

[15] Cooley was joined by William R. Morrison, who had practiced law in Illinois since 1855; Augustus Schoonmaker, who had been a member of the New York Bar since 1853; Aldace F. Walker, who had practiced law in New York City and his home state of Vermont; and Walter L. Bragg, who practiced law in Alabama and had been the first president of the state's Railroad Commission. Walker went on to use his acquired knowledge of the industry as president of the Atchison, Topeka and Santa Fe Railway Company. Richard D. Stone, *The Interstate Commerce Commission and the Railroad Industry: A History of Regulatory Policy* (New York, 1944), 7, says they were "a qualified group with experience in politics, railroads, and regulatory commissions."

[16] This approach was consistent with the kind of classical legal thought that emphasized precedents and deductive reasoning. I am grateful to William W. Fisher III for the opportunity to read and learn from a draft of his chapter on "Legal Theory and Legal Education, 1920–2000," in Michael Grossberg and Christopher Tomlins, eds., *The Cambridge History of Law in America*, 3 (New York, 2008), 34–72. A critic such as Roscoe Pound called this "mechanical" reasoning.

[17] Stephen Skowronek, *Building a New American State*, 155.

[18] Marver H. Bernstein, *Regulating Business by Independent Commission* (Princeton, 1955) discusses this issue.

That's how this first stage of state building ended, but the matter wasn't settled. The learning process continued, this time in Congress, in the White House, and then eventually in the courts once again. By the time this process got reenergized, the progressive reform movement was in full swing in many of the states and public attitudes toward big business were extremely negative.[19] President Theodore Roosevelt was using the Sherman Anti-Trust Act to keep monopoly on the American political agenda, and it was in that setting that a new team of lawyers moved into play on the matter of railroad regulation.

Three were particularly important. Senator Stephen Benton Elkins was an attorney who had gone into business. He and his father-in-law had played a major role in the development of the railroad and coal mining industries of West Virginia.[20] Congressman William Peters Hepburn had practiced law in Iowa, and Congressman James Robert Mann, a lawyer from Chicago, had long been working to strengthen federal regulation in several important industries, including railroads. The laws these men sponsored between 1903 and 1910 gave the ICC the power it needed to control rates, services, and the thousands of businesses in the railroad industry.

By 1930, one could see both the accomplishments and problems of this newly rejuvenated system. The major accomplishment was to establish beyond serious challenge the federal government's role as a regulator of vital services in interstate commerce. The means to that end – the regulatory agency – was created as an organization of professional experts working relatively free from partisan political control. This was an anomaly in America's democratic society. But by 1930, the courts had backed off, except on matters of law and procedure, conceding substantial ground to the Commission's expertise.[21] Was twenty to thirty years too long for this substantial process of change to take? Despite the complaints of the participants in this extended state-building exercise, I don't

---

[19] Marc Schneiberg, "What's on the path? Path dependence, organizational diversity and the problem of institutional change in the US economy, 1900–1950," *Socio-Economic Review*, 5 (2007), 47–80, explores the role of contingency and alternative forms of institutional development from a somewhat different perspective.

[20] John Alexander Williams, *Davis and Elkins of West Virginia: Businessmen in Politics* (New Haven, Dissertation, 1967), especially 300–27. Williams provides an excellent treatment of Elkins' approach to the need for compromise in regulatory matters. Elkins' father-in-law was Henry Gassaway Davis, also a U.S. Senator from West Virginia.

[21] Ibid., 254–55. Stephen Skowronek, *Building a New American State*, cites 259 ICC v Illinois Central RR Co.

think that was too long to develop a major governmental innovation like the independent regulatory agency.[22]

Of more concern to me is the price paid for this major shift in political power. The ICC, as strengthened after 1910, served the interests of shippers and farmers by stabilizing rates, eliminating rebates, and preventing the worst aspects of discrimination in setting rates.[23] But the regulatory process adopted by the ICC was still unbelievably slow. And the system made it difficult for the railroads to fund improvements.[24] A lawyerly approach, case by case, favored stasis in a rapidly growing, changing economy.[25] This was a systemic problem that would arise in some (but not all) regulated industries.

Left carrying enormous debts, most of the nation's major railroad lines were either in bankruptcy or about to enter bankruptcy by the end of the 1920s. A dynamic industry that had spurred the nation's economy in the nineteenth century had become a sick industry, a problem instead of a source of entrepreneurial drive.[26] Nevertheless, the various organized interests that constituted the American public in 1930 clearly wanted to

[22] For the most effective presentation of a different position, see ibid., 123, 13. The author complains about "the early regulatory debacle in America" and says, "the most striking thing about this early regulatory effort remains the inability of the federal government to sustain concerted action in any interest at all." "A state that promoted pluralism promoted a formula for failure in regulation," the author concludes. But pluralism was, to my mind, one of the great strengths of the American system of government, as were experimentation and a slow evolutionary process.

[23] K. Austin Kerr, *American Railroad Politics, 1914–1920: Rates, Wages, and Efficiency* (Pittsburgh, 1968).

[24] Stephen Skowronek concludes that the ICC under Cooley established "a judicious case-by-case approach to administrative regulation" and then looked forward to extracting uniform rules from the separate cases *Building a New American State*, 153. But the uniform rules didn't emerge and the ICC was never able to overcome the burden of wading forever in a molasses-like sea of infinite details.

[25] Arthur Hadley, an economist, complained in 1898 that his profession was being ignored. Ibid., 161. Indeed it was. The lawyers were in the saddle and not about to yield authority to an upstart profession like economics. In a few decades, of course, that situation would change significantly and the economists would establish a beachhead in the upper reaches of American government. In an AEA presidential address, Henry Carter Adams wanted a Bureau of Railway Statistics where economists would gather accurate information "and with it pursue the scientific management of a national railway system." Ibid., 252–53.

[26] Stephen Skowronek sees it just the opposite way: "The Interstate Commerce Commission (ICC) emerged in 1920 as the signal triumph of the Progressive reconstitution." And later in the same paragraph: "The revival of the ICC was heralded as a vindication of the independent expert over the narrow interests of political managers and the usurpations of jealous judges. It became a symbol of a new democracy and a new political economy. It was all the promises of the new American state rolled into the expansion of national administrative capacities." *Building a New American State*, 248.

continue the experiment with regulation – that is, to improve the ICC and heal the sick industry. There was no well-organized movement to get rid of regulation. The doctor for this sick industry would apparently have to be the ICC itself.

Alternatives Explored

Fortunately, learning was taking place across a broad, not a narrow, front. The United States was developing alternative approaches to regulation while the ICC experiment was underway. That too reflects lawyerly input. Lawyers, unlike some other professionals, cannot practice effectively without changing to keep abreast of the most recent court cases and legislative innovations. Some try. But the courts are inclined to reward those attorneys who are quick and flexible rather than the laggards.

Flexibility paid off in the case of telecommunications, an industry that got a different style of regulation with dramatically different consequences for the businesses and the public. The government, guided throughout by lawyers, opted in this instance for a monopoly with state regulation of rates and service. Once the Bell System had reached an accommodation with the lawyers at the Department of Justice and begun to work closely with state regulators, the pressure to tighten the controls declined sharply. Economic logic pointed toward ICC-type national regulation in the telephone industry. But the Bell System managed to negotiate a better deal than the railroads did. At the state level, the regulatory agencies followed patterns similar to those of the ICC, but the problems were more manageable state-by-state, and the culture of the Bell System made for an easy accommodation with public authority.

The results of this experiment were important. By 1930, the United States had the best telecommunication system in the world and had received a lesson in how to construct a regulatory state that actually worked. There would continue to be tensions over the Bell System's monopoly power. Large monopolies are always unstable in a democratic society that privileges competition and loves the underdog. But as of 1930, the U.S. government and the phone company's customers seemed to be happy with America's style of telephone regulation and with the Bell System's technological and economic progress.

So forty years into this learning process, the United States had two relatively stable, working models of the right and wrong ways to go about regulation. In both, professional expertise was more important than democratic decision making. Most economic activities that generated a strong, organized movement calling for regulation were thus likely to end up under the control of either federal or state agencies, which by design were largely independent of party politics. The states were still the primary regulators of business activities, including corporate governance. In electrical power, for instance, state regulation and statewide organizations continued to be the norm for America long after the technology existed to create systems larger and more efficient than state boundaries allowed. In banking, the Federal Reserve System controlled the national banks with an ICC-type independent agency, but the Federal Reserve System left state banking to state control.

To the purist, the theoretician, regulation in America was an unsightly hodge-podge. To some ideologues, the most important feature of the Federal Reserve System was that it was designed and controlled by bankers. From that perspective, the most important feature of telephone regulation was the influence the Bell System had on the regulators and their decisions. Seen from a different, conservative perspective, the rise of the regulatory state in any form was threatening the sources of America's phenomenal economic expansion. But to the lawyers who molded the system, the essence of the matter was the outcome. This was just business as usual in coping with a world of myriad details, a world that was changing rapidly and needed the new government institutions and regulations the lawyers were crafting.

The emerging consensus about regulation persisted even though the United States had one experience with regulatory failure far worse than anything the ICC did. All of the experiments with regulation were more successful than America's most formidable venture into national social planning. Prohibition was the culmination of a multifaceted movement at the local, state, and federal levels. The policy had deep roots in America. Opposition to drinking alcohol had a long history in the United States, and the final triumph of the movement appeared to have been achieved with the ratification in 1919 of the Eighteenth Amendment to the Constitution. Guided by lawyers who should have known better, the United States prohibited the production, distribution, or even transportation of liquor.

By 1930, however, it was apparent to all but the most ardent teetotalers that national prohibition was a disaster. The unanticipated consequences – in crime and corruption – of this effort to change the habits of a nation long accustomed to drinking alcohol undercut the policy and redirected the movement back to local and state governments. In most of the nation's states and localities, however, prohibition simply slid off the political agenda and disappeared.

Far more popular in America was the style of sociopolitical *self-regulation* that was promoted as a viable alternative to governmental control. Many of the professions, including law and medicine, were able to achieve considerable control over their own economic activities in this way. So powerful was the appeal of self-regulation that Secretary of Commerce and then President Herbert Hoover attempted in the 1920s to build a shadow government alongside the federal government. Hoover's goal was an associative state that would bring to America the advantages of control without coercive political force. Hoover's program made some progress. But many of the new associative-state experiments of the 1920s quickly collapsed in the Great Depression. The appeal of self-regulation nevertheless persisted and was fostered by the professions that had acquired a direct role in controlling their institutions and practitioners.

All of these forms of regulation coexisted in America by 1930. The U.S. style of creating a regulatory state wasn't pretty and the outcomes certainly weren't logical. The new regulatory state was, however, flexible and innovative. In regulation as in higher education, the American system benefited greatly from that flexibility in dealing with a complex and rapidly changing economy. This form of government made it easier for the lawyers who dominated the intricacies of the political process to keep devising new compromises as situations changed. They could do so because the legitimacy of the regulatory state in its various forms was by that time firmly established in America.

The Welfare State

While there was little question as to whether America needed some form of a regulatory state, there was less consensus about welfare. This was, after all, an unusually wealthy and fast-growing society. By world standards and certainly by comparison with the European nations sending off millions of emigrants, wages were high in the United States for unskilled as well as skilled workers. There were comparatively few political, economic, or cultural barriers to mobility. There were even ample opportunities to become a professional by proclamation, as Lou Galambos and many others had discovered. The streets were not paved with gold. But there were many opportunities to better oneself in America. As a result, the organized labor movement was relatively weak and conservative by European standards. So too was the welfare movement.[27]

The United States lacked two ingredients that sparked the welfare movement in Germany and Britain. In Germany, Bismarck guided through the nation's pioneering laws in an effort to beat back the Marxist critics of the state. In Britain, a talented cadre of Fabian socialists provided effective leadership for a welfare movement that reached fruition with the creation of workmen's compensation (1906) and old-age pensions (1908).[28] Lacking either a vibrant Marxist movement or left-leaning Fabian elites, the United States was guided by middle- and upper-class professionals toward moderate measures designed to soften only the sharpest edges of industrial capitalism.

Looking over their shoulders at what was happening in Europe, a group of well-educated American professionals began to write about the need for social insurance to protect workers in an urban industrial society. Thanks to the research of Theda Skocpol, we can follow the intellectual trail of these academicians, ministers, doctors, and lawyers as they analyzed European innovations and the pressing needs of an American system in which workers were protected neither from injuries on the job nor unemployment. Retirement was an individual and family responsibility.[29] Like the first generation of regulators, the advocates of social insurance were also spokesmen for the new role of the expert in American government.[30] After all, they too were experts.

The gains were slow in coming, but some headway was made on two issues: safety and workmen's compensation. On broader issues like health insurance, the reform organizations and their leaders

---

[27] Edward Berkowitz and Kim McQuaid, *Creating the Welfare State: The Political Economy of Twentieth-Century Reform* (New York, 1988), provide a different explanation of the retardation of reform.

[28] Gaston V. Rimlinger, *Welfare Policy and Industrialization in Europe, America, and Russia* (New York, 1971).

[29] Theda Skocpol, *Protecting Soldiers and Mothers: The Political Origins of Social Policy in the United States* (Cambridge, 1992), especially 160–204. As the author makes clear, the federal government was deeply involved in this movement. The U.S. Department of Commerce and Labor sponsored the research on which one of the books was based and commissioned one of the others. Most such movements in modern American history involve similar mixtures of public, private, and nonprofit institutions. "Every one of these books surveyed recent European (and sometimes Australasian) approaches to workmen's compensation, sickness insurance, and old-age benefits; and several also examined measures to help the unemployed" (171). Brian Balogh, *A Government Out of Sight*, 352–78, sees these mixtures as the essence of progressive reform. I agree.

[30] Ibid., 187.

encountered formidable resistance, even from the American Federation of Labor, which was deeply suspicious of government controls.[31]

Meanwhile, state-level innovations helped generate the experience and expertise needed to promote additional reform policies. In many cases, businesses and business associations backed positive measures to deal with both safety and compensation for accidents. State-level changes led the way, with the legal profession developing alternative innovations when the courts were initially hostile to compulsory compensation measures like that of New York State. The lawyers for and against went head to head, but by 1917, the U.S. Supreme Court had given blanket approval to the plans for new laws. By 1920, almost all of the states had provided for workmen's compensation.[32]

The process in Pennsylvania, which was similar to that in several other states, was led by lawyers like William Henry Wilson of Philadelphia. Wilson was one of the new breed of lawyers. A graduate of the University of Pennsylvania Law School, Wilson was chairman of the House Committee on the Judiciary, which considered the proposals for workmen's compensation. He worked closely with lawyer William E. Crow of the Senate to prevent tension between the two houses.[33] The pressure to act had been mounting from 1911 on, partly as a result of the increases in litigation and in large settlements as a result of injuries.[34] Compromising on some issues, Wilson and Crow successfully gave Pennsylvania a new bureau to handle the claims and keep the applications from clogging the courts. The various states differed in these and other regards. But by 1920, only six states in the Deep South had failed to pass some kind of workmen's compensation law.

Safety regulation also remained for the most part in the hands of the states and in the particularly dangerous occupations – mining and railroading, for instance – little was done to prevent accidents and injuries.[35]

---

[31] Christopher L. Tomlins, *The State and the Unions: Labor Relations, Law, and the Organized Labor Movement in America, 1880–1960* (New York, 1985).

[32] Theda Skocpol, *Protecting Soldiers and* Mothers, 294–98.

[33] Crow, one of the old breed of lawyers, had acquired his expertise by reading law before passing the bar.

[34] As the 1912 Pennsylvania *Report of Industrial Accidents Commission* observed: "The compensation of injured workmen is a subject that has received exhaustive study in every civilized country; and within the past decade the current of public opinion in favor of such compensation has become so strong that no argument in its favor is necessary" (4–5). David A. Reed of Philadelphia was chair of the commission.

[35] The 1912 *Report* in Pennsylvania linked these two issues: "Every safety device that may be installed means a direct money saving to the employer" (9).

The first federal measure of note was the Safety Appliance Act of 1893, which mandated the use of air brakes and automatic car couplers on the interstate railroads. In mining, the federal government established a Bureau of Mines (1910), but its activities were informational rather than regulatory. Questions of safety were thus left in the hands of the courts and such agencies as existed in a few of the leading industrial states. Even without extensive regulation, accident rates were falling, as large firms sought to improve their safety measures, prevent injuries on the job, and avoid expensive, time-consuming lawsuits.[36]

These developments blended easily with the welfare-capitalism movement of the 1920s. As large corporations instituted their own programs for welfare, they successfully turned down the pressure for either federal or state-level innovations. Professionals like Owen D. Young (law) and Gerard Swope (engineering) guided General Electric into a series of experiments with pension and disability plans, as well as life insurance programs. Other firms, including AT&T, launched similar efforts to stabilize their workforces and forestall further efforts to extend the welfare state.

Corporate welfare and Hoover's associational state got their first real test after 1929, when the economy sank into the Great Depression.[37] Then it became apparent that neither experiment was up to the task of coping with the needs generated by a major economic collapse. Although both experiments left a residue of ideas and institutions that would continue to impact American policy for many decades, the associational state gave way to the administrative state in the 1930s.[38]

Broadening the Foundation of the Promotional State

The legal profession also helped shape America's elaboration of a promotional state – one that encouraged enterprise rather than regulating it. There was substantially less resistance to business welfare than to social welfare, and during the years between 1890 and 1930, the promotional state became deeper and broader at all levels of government. The nation

---

[36] See Edward Berkowitz and Kim McQuaid, *Creating the Welfare State*, 40–43 on the early efforts to establish minimum wages. The Supreme Court came down against the minimum wage for women in 1923.

[37] Sanford M. Jacoby, *Modern Manors: Welfare Capitalism Since the New Deal* (Princeton, 1997), 11–34.

[38] Jennifer Klein, *For All These Rights: Business, Labor, and the Shaping of America's Public-Private Welfare State* (Princeton, 2003).

had provided enormous subsidies to railroad companies in the nineteenth century and had a well-developed system of tariffs that had long given protection to American industries. Instituted to protect infant industries from the competition of British and Continental producers, the tariff walls remained high and imposing after the United States became the world's leading industrial power.

Although this form of protection came under fire during and after the election of 1912, it was extremely difficult in the American system to get rid of subsidies, even indirect ones. Alliances between capital and labor made the job painfully slow, and during the 1920s, tariff walls were once again raised. In 1930, Congress increased the protection, making it clear to the world that even though the depression might be international, the United States would deal with it on purely national terms.

Consistent with the spirit of the tariff were the new institutions congressional lawyers and company lawyers created to protect two specific industries: oil and air transportation. The arrangement for the oil industry was especially ingenious. It was designed to protect the industry from itself, that is, from competition and oversupply. This time the lawyers came up with a special blend of federal authority over interstate commerce and state authority exercised through the Texas Railroad Commission. So-called "hot oil" – that is, oil produced in violation of the Commission's rulings – could not cross state boundaries. What better way to protect the industry and stave off bankruptcies than to create a cartel reinforced with government authority?[39] Similar support was lavished on the country's tiny air transportation industry, one that, like oil, benefited from national security concerns.[40]

Far more important than the federal government, however, were the state and local governments that competed to bestow favors on their favorite industries. These subsidies were one of the means of drawing new industries away from older, East Coast regions to southern and western sites. Tax breaks were popular, as were provisions of police support and other favors that attracted industry to states where the unions were weak and labor relatively cheap.[41]

---

[39] William R. Childs, *The Texas Railroad Commission: Understanding Regulation in America to the Mid-Twentieth Century* (College Station, Texas, 2005).

[40] Richard H. K. Vietor, *Contrived Competition: Regulation and Deregulation in America* (Cambridge, 1994).

[41] Peter K. Eisinger, *The Rise of the Entrepreneurial State: State and Local Economic Development Policy in the United States* (Madison, 1988), focuses primarily on the post–World War II era but gives some historical background. The state and local tradition of

As we saw in the previous chapter, agriculture also received an ample share of benefits from the federal and state governments. This brand of welfare included a special bank for agriculture, a system that was created to ensure that farmers could borrow the money they needed on favorable terms. In 1922, Congress also gave agriculture freedom from prosecution under the antitrust laws if farm associations and cooperatives were able to "stabilize" prices. Of course, to farmers and business leaders alike, "stable" always meant "stable at a profitable level" – a target that few farmers could hit in the late 1920s and few businesses in the 1930s. The overproduction, low prices, and unprofitable operations persisted in agriculture, despite all of the efforts of these new institutions and of the extension service's farm-by-farm promotion of efficiency in agriculture.[42]

A Lawyer's Administrative State

So what kind of modern administrative state did the legal profession give us in the years between 1890 and 1930? Given that they were the leaders in creating the compromises that enabled the administrative state to get a firm foothold in the United States, we have every right to ask what sort of state they created and how well it worked.

Clearly the legal profession in America created a state in its own image. Its approach was case by case, with more attention to fact-specific detail than to any overall plan or theory of government. Precedents mattered. The resulting state was tailored to fit, rather than to change drastically, the existing power structure of the nation. Nonviolent adversarial processes tend to work that way. Where powerful interests demanded action, the

supporting economic enterprises, directly or indirectly, has deep roots that reach back into the origins of the nation. In the nineteenth century, transportation ventures received extensive support, as did other infrastructure projects. States competed to have lax corporate regulations and low taxes – an indirect form of corporate welfare. Many state and local governments were hostile to labor organizations, especially in the southern states.

[42] There are many excellent studies of the long struggle to stabilize agricultural prices and profits. You can start with Alan L. Olmstead and Paul W. Rhode, "The Transformation of Northern Agriculture, 1910–1990," in Stanley L. Engerman and Robert E. Gallman, eds., *The Cambridge Economic History of the United States*, III, *The Twentieth Century*, 693–742; and then read Murray R. Benedict, *Farm Policies of the United States, 1790–1950: A Study of Their Origins and Development* (New York, 1953); and David E. Hamilton, *From New Day to New Deal: American Farm Policy from Hoover to Roosevelt, 1928–33* (Chapel Hill, North Carolina, 1991). On the early development of the Department of Agriculture, see Daniel P. Carpenter, *The Forging of Bureaucratic Autonomy*, 179–254.

legal experts in government produced action of some sort, even though they could not be certain what the results would be. This was the case with the Interstate Commerce Commission in its early years. Every shift, every accretion of power, every change in procedure was looked at from every angle possible. That, of course, took time – expensive time. There were advantages to incrementalism, but there was also an opportunity cost buried in this political process: opportunities were missed while the new institutions slowly evolved.

The emerging administrative state took a decisive step away from democracy by shifting authority to professional expertise. That was one of the consequences of having agencies that were to a considerable degree "independent" of the nation's existing political institutions. This was a step that would be followed by others, after the leaders in the administrative state had consolidated their positions in government and begun the inevitable efforts to extend their power. Some of those efforts would succeed.

The new state began very quickly to influence its parent society. The administrative institutions pressured those who wanted to benefit from their services to organize. Whether they were in business, in the workforce, in the professions, or in government itself, organization was the key to representation, to achieving a voice that could be heard in America.[43] That pressure in turn created a growing need for expertise, for professionals, and, not incidentally, for the services of lawyers. The legal profession retooled in the twentieth century and was growing rapidly and strengthening its position in American society.

This new set of institutions quickly developed a great appetite for information.[44] This became especially evident during World War I, when the government tried to regulate the economy but found that it lacked the most elementary statistics on the activities it was trying to control. Unable to generate the information in a reasonable amount of time, the

---

[43] Hunter Heyck, "The Branching Tree: The Organizational Revolution and the Human Sciences (Manuscript courtesy of the author, 2007), explores a "new way of understanding science and nature," which he calls "the 'bureaucratic worldview' because those who shared this outlook understood all subjects of study as *complex, hierarchic systems* defined more by their *structures* and *processes* than by their components." This worldview meshed neatly with a legal outlook on the world of affairs. See also the same author's *Herbert A. Simon: The Bounds of Reason in Modern America* (Baltimore, 2005).

[44] Sarah E. Igo, *The Averaged American: Surveys, Citizens, and the Making of a Mass Public* (Cambridge, 2007).

War Industries Board simply gave up the task. But the drive to measure and record the characteristics of American society would continue.[45]

By 1930, some of the limitations of the new state were already becoming obvious. This new style of government provided Americans with substantially less equity than most reformers wanted. It provided less security than many Americans wanted, especially in 1930. The lawyer's administrative state, at both the federal level and in each of the forty-eight states, tended to give people and their organizations what a reasonable, white, middle-class professional thought they deserved. The central assumption was that the people being administered and judged had reached their current situation in life as a result of their own efforts. This embodied a commitment to equity, but it was a distinctly narrow form of equity.

There was already evidence of regulatory failure. When the regulatory state intruded on widespread social practices, like drinking alcohol, it generated disaster. When regulatory institutions moved too slowly for a fast-changing economy experiencing the second industrial revolution, they finessed disaster but cut off innovation. In effect, they traded a large measure of efficiency for a small measure of security. For those who were not organized effectively, the American administrative state favored neither security nor equity. For those Americans, both of these social goals were left to the forces of the market, just as they had been through the previous century. That looked like a stable position in the mid-1920s but not in the painful days of the 1930s depression.

The great strength of this highly variegated system was its flexibility. It was well adapted to a long-term evolutionary process that would gradually mold and remold the government. Each of the new institutions and their new leaders got a chance to prove their value in practice. True to the philosophical pragmatism expounded by John Dewey and others, American government would not move toward one overriding goal, some central idea that was above history. In the new American state, various theories of government and political ideologies would be deployed by those struggling for advantage. But theory would always yield to compromise in a setting designed and largely controlled by the legal profession.

---

[45] On the war experience and its aftermath, see Ellis W. Hawley, *The Great War and the Search for a Modern Order: A History of the American People and Their Institutions, 1917–1933* (New York, 1979); Robert Cuff, *The War Industries Board: Business-Government Relations during World War I* (Baltimore, 1973); and Marc Allen Eisner, *From Warfare State to Welfare State: World War I, Compensatory State Building, and the Limits of the Modern Order* (University Park, Pennsylvania, 2000).

Those compromises were central to the history of American government during the years prior to the Great Depression.

America's new institutions frequently left a large measure of authority and responsibility in the hands of the separate states, local governments, or some blend of state and federal control. This mixture was shaped in part by the Constitution and in part by the practical considerations involved in governing a large, heterogeneous country. What was solidly established was the authority of the federal and state governments to implement controls and to deploy professional expertise. That was a decisive governmental innovation and a credit to the lawyers who shaped it.

Those lawyerly results were not particularly important to Lazlo Galambos or his son Lou, the freshly minted "mining engineer." Lazlo had his own wine press, so prohibition created no hardship for him. He and his son Lou kept scrambling for work and both managed to avoid the welfare system. They weren't in any position to take direct advantage of the promotional state – although the bosses for whom they worked obviously did. Lou Galambos would later have a bitter encounter with the regulatory state, an encounter that would prompt many long dinner-table monologues. But that would follow some major developments that took place in the 1930s and 1940s. Through the end of the 1920s, Lou was, for the most part, oblivious to the fact that his society was tinkering with government, experimenting with new regulatory, welfare, and promotional systems.

5

Confronting the World

By the 1890s, the United States had consolidated its continental empire and was beginning to redefine its relations with the rest of the world. America was now a very large, unified nation. Its population had grown by more than 25 percent in the previous decade, and the great tide of immigrants was still flowing across the Atlantic. Having just become the world's leading industrial producer, the United States was tempted to flex its new economic muscles and maybe even assert its power abroad. Maybe even among the developed nations of Europe.[1]

It was not at all clear, however, what the United States would do or should do. It was unclear to most Americans that it was wise to intrude on the affairs of other powerful nations. George Washington's famous Farewell Address had established the central principle that had guided American foreign policy in the nineteenth century. Over two centuries later, it's still worth quoting.

"The great rule of conduct for us, in regard to foreign nations, is in extending our commercial relations, to have with them as little *political* connection as possible. So far as we have already formed engagements, let them be fulfilled with perfect good faith. – Here let us stop.

Europe has a set of primary interests, which to us have none, or a very remote relation. Hence she must be engaged in frequent controversies, the causes of which are essentially foreign to our concerns. Hence, therefore,

---

[1] In an effort to acquire more understanding of the significant changes in U.S. foreign policy during these years, you might turn to Walter LaFeber, *The American Search for Opportunity, 1865–1913* (Cambridge, 1993), and Thomas J. Knock, *To End All Wars: Woodrow Wilson and the Quest for a New World Order* (New York, 1992). LaFeber's synthesis is close to mine, whereas Knock's is very different.

it must be unwise in us to implicate ourselves, by artificial ties, in the ordinary vicissitudes of her politics, or the ordinary combinations and collisions of her friendships, or enmities."

There were plenty of Americans who thought that was still the right strategy for their country – when, that is, they gave any thought to foreign policy. If they lived away from the east or west coasts, foreign policy appears to have seldom been on their minds at all. People who lived in the vast center of the country certainly didn't feel threatened, didn't feel that the national security was at stake just because America had become a very wealthy nation with a powerhouse economy. If anything, we were manifestly more secure given our industrial strength and in that regard, they were, of course, correct.[2] So those Americans were content to carry on building their individual futures, their farms and businesses, while providing a better future for their children. For many, this meant adjusting to new jobs and to city life. During the 1890s, the people making those adjustments had plenty of problems to solve at home without overseas adventures. Their lack of concern about foreign power – whether that of Germany in Europe or Japan in the Pacific – is understandable.

The Professionals Disagree

There was another position on these matters, of course. Some of those who best understood military power had in mind a different strategy. One of these was a professional naval officer who was a prodigious writer and analyst of naval affairs. Alfred Thayer Mahan was no ordinary officer. A graduate of the Naval Academy and a teacher at the Naval War College, he published an entire bookshelf of histories that charted the abiding role of sea power in international relations.[3]

Surveying the rise and fall of nations, Mahan constructed a synthesis that appealed to many American leaders in the 1890s. Mahan envisioned a trinity, a triangular base that would ensure success in the endless struggle between nations. This was a struggle that he and others conceived in

---

[2] My guiding principle is that national security should be the primary goal of foreign policy and the only objective worth American lives. Other goals are worth money, but not American lives.

[3] Mahan's career reminds one of the career of Joseph A. Schumpeter. Although a failure in business, Schumpeter became the preeminent historian of capitalism. Mahan failed as a ship commander but became the world's leading historian of sea power. The Naval War College (established in 1884) accelerated the professionalization of U.S. naval officers. It was 1901 before the army established its counterpart, the U.S. Army War College.

Darwinian terms. One essential part of the base would be provided by a strong navy, a force capable of extending American influence around the world. The U.S. Navy had been created primarily to defend America from foreign intrusions. But the new battle fleets that professional naval officers, Congress, and the presidents set out to create were a force with the capability of striking abroad, beyond the shores of the Western Hemisphere, beyond the Caribbean where the United States already had important commercial and strategic interests. By the early 1900s, the U.S. Navy had the foundation for a seagoing force of the sort that Mahan had projected.[4]

The second part of the base was an extended commercial system that would turn away, at least in part, from the internal market that had occupied most of the attention of America's entrepreneurs through the entire nineteenth century. Foreign markets looked attractive to many American firms. The fabled China market proved elusive, but other markets beckoned. Large firms in automobiles, oil, and electrical machinery made sales abroad in a way that was appealing to the new apostles of sea power. America's success in the second industrial revolution was making itself felt.

The third side of the triangle for Mahan and the other champions of an imperial United States was a series of overseas bases. These stations would enable the Navy to refuel the fleet and keep an active American presence throughout the world. Coaling stations were needed to keep a steam-powered fleet in action, and that made some obscure islands important to the advocates of empire. Fortune shined upon America – or seemed to shine at first. A collapsing Spanish empire offered Americans opportunities to obtain new outposts in the Pacific and the Caribbean with relatively little effort or loss of life.

Cuba, under Spanish rule, was particularly attractive because of its existing commercial ties with the United States. In 1898, when the U.S. battleship *Maine* blew up in Havana's harbor, the Americans looking to

---

4 Dirk Bönker, "Militarizing the Western World: Navalism, Empire, and State-Building in Germany and the United States Before World War I (Doctoral Dissertation, Johns Hopkins University, 2002), especially 114–24. See also the author's insightful treatment "Of Experts, Science, and Militarism: Military Professionalism and the Sinews of Navalism," Part 4, 354–437. "In both countries, the makers of navalism forged a new body of professional thought and practices and cast themselves as . . . science-based groups of professional experts (355)." The institutional foundation for professionalism was provided by the U.S. Naval War College, the Office of Naval Intelligence (1899), and the General Board (1900).

expand the reach of U.S. power had an excuse for going to war. There were, of course, humanitarian reasons to unseat the Spanish. But there was little reason to believe that men like Assistant Secretary of the Navy Theodore Roosevelt were moved by sympathy. Instead, for Roosevelt, Mahan, and others, the Spanish-American war was an opportunity to flex the nation's muscles and nail down the third of Mahan's goals for a great nation.

The war was everything the advocates of an aggressive foreign policy could have wanted. It was quick, largely costless, and profitable. The Navy won glorious victories in the Philippines and Cuba. The U.S. Army, which was poorly equipped and poorly trained, nevertheless had more trouble with food poisoning and disease than it did with the dispirited, poorly armed Spanish forces. The war was over almost too soon to give the newspapers a full opportunity to exploit the conflict.

The spoils of this introduction to *realpolitik* were significant. Cuba was now in U.S. hands. As were the Philippines and Puerto Rico. Humanitarianism aside, the United States also ended up with Wake Island and Guam in the Pacific. It is doubtful that in 1898 many Americans knew where Wake Island and Guam were or cared about why one of the Ladrone Islands was important, but the nation's military professionals and the advocates of empire knew exactly where they were and why they mattered. These men knew that the new territories were important because they facilitated the thrust of American power into the Far East, where the British and German empires were solidly established and where Japanese power was growing. Shortly, the United States informed all of these nations what *their* commercial policies should be in China.

There is no evidence that the other powerful nations misunderstood what America was doing, but there was plenty of misunderstanding and disagreement in the United States. The Senate debate over the peace treaty with Spain brought to the surface serious doubts many had about exercising American power in this way and about acquiring foreign lands and peoples. In one form or another, this debate would echo and re-echo through American politics for more than a century. An echo or two has been heard recently in the bitter arguments over the U.S. military's presence in Iraq.

The questions raised about an American empire in 1899 were all important, but the two most significant questions of all were not really answered on Capitol Hill. First, would the extension of our empire beyond the continent enhance or diminish our long-term security? Second, could an empire be managed in a manner consistent with America's foundational values and democracy?[5] The experience in the Philippines, where the U.S. Army was forced to put down a bloody insurrection, suggested that the answer to the second question was likely to be "No."[6] The first question about American security would not be answered for several decades, and we'll look for a plausible answer to that question in the following chapters.

In part because of these political and ideological tensions, the American empire would be different than the empires established by other industrial powers. The United States would occupy very few foreign lands, acquiring only what it needed for its base system. The American empire would include those military bases and a number of client states that were protected by U.S. military power, that frequently received U.S. economic and military support, and that normally tolerated some degree of U.S. intrusion on their internal affairs and external relations. In the Caribbean, the U.S. intrusions would from time to time involve the exercise of military, economic, and political power.[7] Over the twentieth century, both the base system and the number of client states would grow much larger, especially during the Cold War. Even then, very few Americans wanted to call this a U.S. empire. But that's what it was and still is today, denial notwithstanding.[8]

Realpolitik Marches On

Despite the intense debates over the empire, the United States continued down the path marked out by the military and political leaders who had guided the nation into the war with Spain. The United States tightened its grip on the Caribbean. America acquired the Guantanamo Bay naval station in Cuba, seized the land it needed to build the Panama Canal,

---

[5] Elmer Plischke, *U.S. Department of State: A Reference History* (Westport, Connecticut, 1999). Robert D. Schulzinger, *The Making of the Diplomatic Mind: The Training, Outlook, and Style of the United States Foreign Service Officers, 1908–1931* (Middletown, Connecticut, 1975).

[6] Michael Kazin, *A Godly Hero: The Life of William Jennings Bryan* (New York, 2006), 46–62.

[7] Covert intrusions would also take place, especially during the Cold War.

[8] In 1915, President Wilson said that our approach to Latin America had "none of the spirit of empire in it. It is the embodiment, the effectual embodiment, of the spirit of law and independence and liberty and mutual service." *Papers Relating to the Foreign Relations of the United States, 1915*, p. xi. I am certain that the Mexicans who had been attacked (1914) at Vera Cruz by U.S. naval forces had a better understanding of the American empire than did President Wilson.

and intervened with military force in Nicaragua, Santo Domingo, Haiti, and Mexico. The new American empire was a bipartisan effort. In the Far East, U.S. power was far more limited, and America was forced to back away unhappily as Japan consolidated its empire in Korea and Manchuria. "Dollar Diplomacy" was no more successful in Asia than the Mahan triangular strategy was in bolstering America's overextended position in the Pacific. Unwilling to abandon that position or to focus all of its power directly against Japanese expansion, the United States left itself vulnerable to developments it could neither control nor avoid as Japan advanced.

Some of the problems the United States experienced during these years stemmed from the low level of professional expertise in the U.S. State Department.[9] A more talented and confident foreign service would have provided America's leaders with better information about the world they were confronting. A stronger State Department would have been a counterweight to the nation's military elite. The war with Spain had accelerated professionalization among America's naval and army officers, and both services had introduced new postgraduate training institutions in a determined effort to continue that process. The sentiment in favor of a General Staff á la Germany became very strong among America's military professionals, who now sought the sort of independence that the Prussian officer corps had. They were unable to achieve that goal. But even without guidance from a Prussian-style General Staff, the country appeared to be following very closely the strategies laid out by its most aggressive military officers.

The State Department was lagging behind the military in the process of professionalization. Steps had been taken in the 1890s to counter the effects of patronage on the State Department and to raise the level of talent in that organization. But State seemed always to be bringing up the rear, behind the military, behind the country's rapid economic expansion, and behind America's shifting position in the world. Conservative to a fault, the State Department lacked the influence to rein in U.S. policy. The presidents simply ignored the Department when it didn't give them

---

[9] When President McKinley asked lawyer Elihu Root to become Secretary of War, Root apparently responded that it was "quite absurd" because he knew "nothing about war" and "nothing about the army." But the President told Root he "was not looking for any one who knows anything about war or for any one who knows anything about the army." Quoted in James Brown Scott, "Elihu Root, Secretary of State, July 7, 1905, to January 27, 1909," in Samuel Flagg Bemis, ed., *The American Secretaries of State and Their Diplomacy* (New York, 1929), 193–94.

the policies they wanted. President Woodrow Wilson sitting alone at his typewriter in the White House composed messages dealing with the problems arising from the Mexican Revolution. Because he understood neither the language, nor the culture, nor the revolutionary process in Mexico, Wilson was unlikely to get it right. He didn't.

Where Europe was concerned, the United States was, of course, considerably less aggressive than it was with Latin America. But even with the European powers, America pressed forward with results that would lead slowly toward military intervention in 1917. President Theodore Roosevelt thrust the United States into the European politics of empire, and neither William Howard Taft nor Woodrow Wilson saw fit to pull back from that newly extended position. By the time war began in Europe in 1914, the United States had already abandoned George Washington's strategy. The nation had pushed its nose into the "vicissitudes," "combinations and collisions" of the European powers, nations that were consumed by the sort of "ambition, rivalship, [and] interest" that George Washington thought the United States did not and should not share.

The result in 1917 was one of the major blunders of American policy in the twentieth century. President Wilson was an accomplished political scientist and university leader, but his expertise was in domestic, not foreign, affairs. He needed strong guidance from the State Department, and he needed to listen carefully to what an experienced, talented Secretary of State could tell him.

Wilson ensured that wouldn't happen, however, by appointing William Jennings Bryan Secretary of State in 1913. A graduate of the Whipple Academy (Jacksonville, Illinois), Illinois College, and the Union College of Law in Chicago, Bryan had served in Congress and run unsuccessfully for the Senate and for the presidency as the Democratic candidate in 1896 and again in 1900. Bryan was a brilliant orator, most famous for the "Cross of Gold" speech that helped him win the party's nomination in 1896.[10] His ardent plea for an inflationary policy and his nonstop speaking tour in 1896 won Bryan almost six and a half million votes. But that wasn't enough to defeat Republican William McKinley, who won by a substantial margin in 1896 and an even larger margin in 1900.

In the latter campaign, Bryan emphasized his opposition to empire. He called on America to behave so well in international relations that the

---

[10] The cross of gold was the gold standard, which was the basis for America's currency. Bryan wanted to use silver as well, and since it was less scarce and valuable than gold, this would have promoted inflation.

nation would become "the supreme moral factor in the world's progress and the accepted arbiter of the world's disputes." Whereas a majority of the American voters opted for the Republican Party and its more aggressive stance on foreign policy, more than six million voted for Bryan. The election results suggested that there was still considerable ambivalence on the part of the American people about exercising the nation's power abroad. Two decades and some deadly experiences later, American ambivalence would evolve into forthright isolationism.

Rejected by a majority of America's voters, Bryan got one more chance to guide American foreign policy away from empire.[11] Because he helped Wilson win the nomination of the Democratic Party and the election in 1912, President-Elect Wilson felt obliged to appoint him to his Cabinet. Wilson met this political obligation by giving Bryan the most prestigious Cabinet position, Secretary of State. He did so knowing that Bryan lacked experience in administration and in the nuts-and-bolts of foreign relations.[12] Wilson handled that problem by simply ignoring both the Secretary of State and his Department.

As a result, the President was cut off from the advice he most needed after World War I began in 1914. Then, Wilson had to decide how the United States should position itself toward the European belligerents. Guided in large part by his long-standing, personal attachment to Great Britain, Wilson adopted policies that favored the British, the French, and their allies. This strategy nudged the United States toward more direct involvement.

Bryan, "the Great Commoner," was inexperienced in the formalities of diplomacy. Oddly enough, however, he turned out to be right about the central issue the nation was facing in 1914. His strength was his deep attachment to the ambivalences and doubts of all those Americans who knew less about Germany than they did about Missouri, who cared more about the crop reports than they did about the intricacies of French diplomacy. Bryan was an expert on that important aspect of the American mentality. Bear in mind that Bryan, the loser, had received more votes in 1900 than Wilson, the winner, received in the election of 1912. Bryan

---

[11] When Bryan ran in 1908, he did not make anti-imperialism a central issue in his campaign.

[12] Michael Kazin, one of Bryan's biographers, remarks that "On the eve of World War I, the State Department resembled a bustling campaign office more than a modern bureaucracy." *A Godly Hero*, 216. Kazin emphasizes more than I do the impact that the war in Europe had on the Wilson-Bryan relationship (215–38).

had reason to believe that on this issue, if no other, he had strong ideas that should command respect.

But Wilson wasn't listening to Bryan. The president was charting a different course and was working closely with his personal advisor, a Texas political insider "Colonel" Edward M. House, and the U.S. Ambassador to Great Britain, Walter Hines Page. Bryan and the State Department were left out in the cold.[13] Wilson guided the United States down a path that led inexorably toward a joint effort with the Allies and war with Germany. Bryan stubbornly pushed in a different direction. He wanted the United States to deal in an even-handed way with Germany and Britain. He argued for a truly neutral policy toward the belligerents and for a determined effort to bring about a negotiated peace. Bryan was surprisingly prescient for a politician as untutored as he was in diplomacy and national strategy. Victory by one side, he concluded, "will probably mean preparation for another war."

"It would seem better," Bryan advised Wilson, "to look for a more rational basis of peace." Although Bryan was willing to exercise American power in the Caribbean, he wanted the United States to seek peace by staying out of the war in Europe. More of a pacifist than Wilson or House, Bryan had guided the United States into a series of bilateral "Treaties for the Advancement of Peace." The treaties – now faded from our memory – provided for a cooling-off period when nations disagreed.[14] In 1914, however, the treaties were to no avail, and Wilson continued to squeeze Bryan out of his formal position as foreign policy advisor. Unable to countenance the president's drift toward the Allies, Bryan offered his resignation. Wilson promptly accepted it.[15]

---

[13] Charles E. Neu, "Woodrow Wilson and Colonel House: The Early Years, 1911–1915," in John Milton Cooper, Jr. and Charles E. Neu, eds., *The Wilson Era: Essays in Honor of Arthur S. Link* (Arlington Heights, Ill., 1991), 248–78. Neu captures House's stunning combination of ego, hubris, and naiveté about European affairs; House wrote (267) in 1915: "I thought if *our* plans carried true, the President would easily outrank any American that had yet lived; that the war was the greatest event in human history excepting the birth of Christ, therefore, if the President were able to play the part *I* hoped for, I was in favor of his retiring at the end of the present term." Emphasis added to catch a touch of House's inflated ego.

[14] "William Jennings Bryan: Secretary of State, March 5, 1913, to June 8, 1915." In Samuel Flagg Bemis, ed., *The American Secretaries of State and Their Diplomacy* (New York, 1929), 3–42. This essay is by an anonymous author and the quotation is not documented. It is in keeping, nevertheless, with Bryan's general position on the war and U.S. policy. For the details of the "cooling off" treaties see *Papers Relating to the Foreign Relations of the United States*, 1913, 8–12.

[15] Wilson was consistent. He also largely ignored Bryan's successor, Robert Lansing, who had a far more substantial background than Bryan in international relations.

Wilson rejected Bryan's recommendations and adopted policies that led to war against Germany and Austria-Hungary.[16] This was the case even though American national security was not threatened.[17] The United States insisted on unrealistic conditions for the freedom of the seas, conditions that the nation would itself ignore in that second great war that would arise from the ashes of the first (as Bryan seems to have predicted). The Wilson administration drummed up the same nationalist fervor that had accompanied the brief struggle with Spain and entered the war without imposing any conditions on the Allies. As Wilson announced grandly and naively, "The world must be made safe for democracy." If one assumes, as I do, that the goal of democratization was largely empty political rhetoric, then peaceful stabilization of Europe was the only significant American objective. It would not be achieved if one side won a clear victory.[18]

By the fall of 1918, the United States had enabled the Allies to break the German lines and force a surrender. The price of victory was not terribly high – unless you consider 116,000 American deaths and more than 200,000 American casualties an unreasonable sacrifice to the war aims of France, Great Britain, and Italy. The Galambos family had been either too old or too young to serve in the war, so Lazlo benefited from America's wartime prosperity without being forced to send his sons to fight in his former homeland. The European Allies had paid a much higher price than America: France lost more than 1.3 million killed; the British Empire more than 900,000; Italy 650,000. Those losses dictated who would control the peace terms, and the European leaders were determined to exact a heavy price from Germany and its allies. Little was done in the peace settlement to make the world "safe for democracy." Much was done to provoke further conflict and endanger democracy everywhere in the world.

---

[16] The United States did not declare war on Germany's other two allies, Turkey and Bulgaria.

[17] In his annual address to Congress in 1914, President Wilson said, "No one who speaks counsel based on fact or drawn from a just and candid interpretation of realities can say that there is reason to fear that from any quarter our independence or the integrity of our territory is threatened." *Papers Relating to the Foreign Relations of the United States, 1914* (Washington, 1922), xvii. Wilson was certainly right about that.

[18] Unlike historian/diplomat George Kennan, I do not object to Wilson's idealism – after entering the war. I object to his decision to enter the war and then to the manner in which he implemented that decision. The Kennan-Wilson issue is discussed in Thomas J. Knock, "Kennan Versus Wilson," in John Milton Cooper, Jr., and Charles E. Neu, eds., *The Wilson Era*, 302–26.

To its credit, the Wilson administration attempted to deploy professional expertise in its futile effort to achieve a Wilsonian peace. To serve that purpose, the administration pulled together a talented group of academics and other professionals, a group called the Inquiry, to provide the American peace commission with the information and ideas it would need for the negotiations in France. Ignoring the advice of his Secretary of State, now Robert Lansing, Wilson ventured forth personally to reform the world along lines set forth in his famous Fourteen Points. The Points, full of "should" and "must" like directions to school boys, were designated "the only possible program.... "

Ignoring reality didn't make it go away. France was not to be denied a punitive peace. Britain had its own objectives, as did Italy and the other twenty-four nations represented at the conference. While the Europeans understood America's contribution to the victory, they had overriding national concerns. They chopped up Wilson's fourteen points and buried most of them in hundreds of detailed settlements dictated by their national goals.

Few of these individual issues threatened America's need for international stability, but taken together, they ensured the instability of the postwar world. Britain and Japan stripped Germany of its colonies. France seized Alsace-Lorraine and the Saar Valley and took military control of the western bank of the Rhine. With Germany disarmed and weighed down with reparations payments, France seemed to have what it wanted, as did the new and reconstituted Eastern European states. But the settlement left the most powerful nation on the continent deeply troubled and damaged. Wilson and others hoped that the newly designed League of Nations would settle any disagreements arising from the Treaty of Versailles, but the League would shortly suffer a blow from which it would never recover.

To the east in Russia, the Bolshevik Revolution (1917) had created a powerful new challenge to a democratic, capitalist world order. The Russian Problem very quickly became a World Problem. After Russia left the war in 1918, the Bolsheviks were locked in a brutal civil war for control of the country. The United States responded to this phase of the Russian revolution with no more intelligent restraint than it had demonstrated during the Mexican Revolution.

America entered the civil war in Russia on the side of the counterrevolutionaries. American forces, along with those of Britain and France, joined in a muddled and unsuccessful struggle to unseat the Bolsheviks. The United States and its allies provided manpower at first and then supplies to the White army fighting the Reds, but that effort failed, as did their naval blockade. Although lacking the resources to launch attacks on the Allied and Associated Powers, the Third International (1919) raised the red banner of world revolution, a proclamation that prompted the Wilson administration to initiate a sweeping campaign to wipe out radicalism in the United States.

President Wilson's new world order thus started with a shaky base in Europe and soon encountered serious problems at home. By ignoring Congress and the Republican Party, Wilson had ensured opposition in the Senate to his strategy for a new American role in world affairs. After intense debate and bitter disagreement, the Senate rejected the peace treaty and the League of Nations. In the election of 1920, American voters confirmed that decision by rejecting the Democratic candidate for the presidency. Republican President Warren G. Harding had a wayward way with words as well as ideas, but his call for "normalcy" resonated with the voters. Americans were apparently ready to return to the Washingtonian principles of foreign policy, turning their backs on European intrigues.

The Isolationist Will-o'-the-Wisp

It turned out to be easier to get involved in the "combinations and collisions" in Europe than it was to get away from them. In the 1920s, three Republican administrations tried unsuccessfully to break away from the great powers of Europe and Asia. Their efforts to return to the American policies of 1913 – or maybe even 1890 – failed. Initially, the major problems were in Europe, where economic and political crises kept unsettling the stability the United States needed. Not too surprisingly, one of the first sticky problems to emerge involved money. The American economy came out of the war relatively unscathed by mobilization. Not so in Europe, where war debts and reparations payments soon began to strain the fragile postwar peace.

The Europeans couldn't possibly pay off the war debts, even if they had wanted to pay them. Britain had suffered a significant loss of foreign trade, a crucial element to an economy dependent for many years on exports and financial services to other countries. London was still the global economy's financial center. But the British economy emerged from the war badly weakened. Foreign markets that the British had controlled had been taken over by firms from other countries, including the United States.

France was in even worse shape in the 1920s. Severe wartime losses of men killed, wounded, or missing in action made it difficult for the French economy to recover. Enormous losses of capital and war debts magnified the problem, leaving the currency in a weakened state and industry struggling to get back to a prewar level of output and efficiency. Before the war, France had been attempting rather unsuccessfully to match the gains in Germany and the United States in the leading industries of the second industrial revolution. Now France was coming from farther behind in the electrical, chemical, and electrochemical industries, as well as those industries where the competition was in mass production of standardized products.[19]

French attempts to make Germany pay the price of French recovery and to lure the United States into bolstering the French position in Europe ran into trouble. Germany defaulted on the reparations payments and when its economy collapsed, hyperinflation made the paper currency useless. The United States stepped back into Europe in 1924 to provide American backing for the collapsing currencies and economies of Germany and France. Fiscal stability, however, was an elusive target. The problems in Germany couldn't be solved by American dollars, and the Kellogg-Briand Peace Pact (1928), with its "outlawry of war," couldn't ensure "peace in their time."[20]

From the vantage point of 1930, the United States had failed to achieve either one of its major objectives in Europe. It had not been able to swing back to the position it had held prior to the war. Nor had it been able to create a stable Europe that would enable the United States to get on with its impressive economic growth and its initial efforts to improve relations with Latin America. Searching for a better balance between American democratic ideology and power politics, the United States renounced some aspects of Teddy Roosevelt's brand of *realpolitik*.[21] But the economic collapse that started in late 1929 quickly refocused American policy. The Great Depression multiplied the problems in Britain and on the continent, paving the way in Germany for the rise of fascism, for the Holocaust, and for the deadliest war in history.

---

[19] David S. Landes, *The Unbound Prometheus: Technological Change and Industrial Development in Western Europe from 1750 to the Present* (Cambridge, 1969).

[20] Robert H. Ferrell, *Peace in Their Time: the origins of the Kellogg-Briand Pact* (New Haven, 1952).

[21] My reference here is to the State Department's Clark Memorandum of 1930.

In the Pacific, too, the United States found it impossible to create a stable order by slowing the rise of Japanese power. The U.S.-sponsored Washington Armament Conference (1921–1922) developed a formula for limiting naval expansion, but the Japanese cleverly demonstrated that they could expand their naval forces while observing the letter of the agreement. Japan extended its empire into Manchuria. Recognizing the weakness of the western powers and the unwillingness of the United States to use force to defend China, Japan pressed on, militarily and economically. Asian stability was hostage to Japan's desire for an empire appropriate for its growing economic power and population.

Failing to stabilize international relations either in Europe or Asia, the United States looked inward, hoping at least to control its own population. For some years there had been political pressure to choke down the flow of Central European and Asian immigrants. The country had excluded Chinese immigrants for many years and had long employed informal understandings, the so-called Gentlemen's Agreements, to cut back sharply on emigration from Japan.[22] But in 1921 and 1924, America for the first time in its history set formal quotas that sharply restricted the number and nature of the foreigners welcomed into the country. The new controls were directed especially at the Eastern and Southern European "huddled masses" who had poured into America by the millions before the war.

Fortunately for my future, Lazlo Galambos was already in the country before the clamp came down on Hungarian immigration. The new policy worked: instead of the more than 440,000 Hungarians who came in the previous ten years, fewer than 31,000 came in the 1920s. According to family lore, Lazlo had returned to Europe briefly in the years before World War I began. In the style characteristic of many working-class immigrants, he had made some money in America, established a family, and then returned to Hungary. Quickly, however, he turned around and came back to continue seeking his fortune in northern Ohio. There he could take advantage of the opportunities created by the rapid expansion of the automobile industry and be able to buy Hungarian delicacies in Toledo.[23] Thanks to the new immigration restrictions, he and his sons could get on

---

[22] The Gentlemen's Agreements were designed to achieve restrictions on emigration without embarrassing Japan.

[23] The delicacies included bacon that was boiled (not broiled), coated with paprika, and eaten cold.

with the job of slowly pushing their way toward the middle class without facing competition from a new wave of "Hunky" workers. From the narrow perspective of Lazlo and his family, this aspect of isolationism was wonderful.

Engagement Evaluated: 1930

In 1930, most Americans seem to have agreed with Lazlo that isolation was the best policy for America. There was no outcry against the decision that year to raise American tariffs and cut down on imports.[24] Even an imperfect policy of isolation seemed better than what had happened during the country's first round of heavy engagement with the world beyond the Western Hemisphere. The United States hadn't enhanced its national security in the four decades since 1890. The professionals in the armed services and in the State Department hadn't been very effective in providing the strategies and tactics America needed to chart a successful course in the world. The politicians who brokered America's strategy and the presidents who implemented it hadn't done very well either. Learning by doing wasn't going very well.

In the four decades following 1890, the nation had become a more aggressive, intrusive world power. It had begun, rather quickly, to acquire some pieces of an empire, a particularly American style of empire, but an empire nonetheless. Masking its aggression with humanitarian rhetoric, the United States ended up entangled in a messy and embarrassing struggle against revolutionary nationalists in the Philippines. The American position in that struggle was at least consistent. We were an opponent of revolutionary change, just as we were in Mexico and later in Russia. Of course each of these conflicts had its own unique characteristics. But in each case, the United States exercised its military power in opposition to a revolution. The country's citizens and leaders had lost touch with the history of the American Revolution. Now the United States was trying to achieve international stability by opposing change, and that required the country to do things that were deeply inconsistent with America's founding values. For good reasons, our Fourth of July rhetoric about freedom didn't resonate outside of our national frontiers.

The early experiences with empire exposed the difficulties the nation was experiencing in remaining faithful to its basic political values while

---

[24] The Hawley-Smoot Tariff of 1930 sharply increased the taxes on imports and prompted foreign countries to respond in kind.

sustaining a more aggressive policy toward the rest of the world. The debates in Congress and in the media revealed clear stress lines. In the Caribbean, the United States had used military force to impose on several struggling nations *our* solutions to *their* problems. The heritage of hatred that this meddling inspired bothered many Americans. It should have bothered them even more and still should today.

We had invested less in Asia, and had achieved results commensurate with our investment. Japanese power was on the rise. America's desire for stability was increasingly endangered. Our foothold in the East was not secure, and our attempts to restrain Japan had thus far failed.

The best measure of American policy, however, was in Europe. There we had prevented a stalemate in World War I and as a result instability and conflict would continue. Having little sense of what would enhance America's national security over the long term, President Wilson took it on himself to shape his administration's foreign policy. Ignoring his own State Department and its secretaries, he marched America into the war and upset the balance of power in Europe. Instead of making the world safe for democracy, the United States endangered its own security and that of the entire world.

It would have been far better if Wilson had allowed American policy to be debated, studied and restudied, "seasoned" for many months in the State Department. In 1916 and 1917, stasis was the optimal policy for a nation that had nothing to gain and much to lose from an Allied victory. That story would unfold in the 1930s, when the turn toward fascism in Germany would destroy the fragile Versailles settlement and thrust America back into full-scale involvement in European affairs. By that time, it was apparent that the effort to get back to an isolationist stance had been no more successful than our military venture in World War I.

Throughout these unfortunate episodes in America's history, the weakness of the country's professional diplomats made it difficult to adopt policies consistent with American values and more likely to enhance American security. In the aftermath of the war, Congress took up this problem and produced the 1924 Foreign Services Act.[25] For the first time, aspiring diplomats had to take examinations before they could be appointed to the Foreign Service. For the first time, promotion was to

---

[25] For the particulars of the reform and subsequent changes in the 1920s see Irvin Stewart, "American Government and Politics: Congress, the Foreign Service, and the Department of State," *The American Political Science Review*, 24, 2 (May 1930), 355–66.

be based on merit! Political patronage was not completely abandoned. Top-level ambassadorial appointments would still go (as they do today) to wealthy Americans who had supported the winning presidential candidate. In the rest of the Service, however, merit ruled and would over time raise the level of professionalism in America's diplomatic corps.

Unfortunately, the new policy couldn't keep the United States and its empire safe in the turbulent 1930s. The attempt to return to the Washingtonian principles of the Farewell Address had failed. The genie of international engagement was out of the bottle and couldn't be shoved back. Events in Europe and the Far East in the 1930s provided a bitter response to America's quasi-isolationism. Rather than achieving international stability, the United States was forced to fight in a second, deadlier world war.

6

Winners and Losers, 1890 to 1930

Despite America's difficulties overseas, there was much that was positive about the nation's experience and about its growing cadres of professional experts. The professional class was generating an impressive range of new ideas, helping American society continue growing and changing in decisive ways. The managerial and political brokers who were responsible for converting the ideas of experts into policies and organizations were successful in many of the institutions they served. In the cities, where much of the new growth was taking place, people were healthier than they had been in the previous century. They were likely to enjoy longer as well as healthier lives. This was true, in fact, for the entire population as a result of the advances in public health and medicine. Some of the worst aspects of the industrial economy were being brought under the control of the administrative state. Guided by the legal professionals who were defining and frequently running the agencies, government at the federal and state levels was gradually, sometimes hesitantly, developing new capabilities.[1]

At the heart of these positive developments was a massive educational system that worked to sift out winners and send them through the nation's growing number of professional schools. Easy access to public education provided an escape valve for the children of the millions of immigrants

[1] The student who might be inspired to read more about this era in U.S. history should turn to Mary P. Ryan, *Mysteries of Sex: Tracing Women & Men through American History* (Chapel Hill, 2006): Ellis W. Hawley, *The Great War and the Search for a Modern Order, a History of the American People and their Institutions, 1917–1933* (New York, 1997); and Ronald Takaki, *A Different Mirror: A History of Multicultural America* (Boston, 1993).

pouring into the United States. A few of the immigrants had enough talent and luck to get a foothold in one of the professions, as did the marvelously successful Michael Pupin. For most, however, it was the second and third generations that were able to climb the educational ladder into the professional middle class.

Fortunately, for the immigrants and for the rest of the society, the educational system of those years was extremely flexible – responsive to new demands and new opportunities. Urban reform improved schooling in the cities, as did the growing number of high schools in the urban centers and smaller communities like Fostoria, Ohio. Private schools at all levels continued to play a significant role in American education, but the most decisive changes came in the public sector. By 1930, the United States had the largest, most elaborate set of educational institutions in the world. Few of them were world-class institutions. Far from it. State universities that started out as glorified high schools were common throughout America. Pride of place, however, and a keen eye for economic opportunity persuaded state legislatures and executives to provide the funds these universities and colleges needed to improve. Competition within the system then pushed upward and outward onto the more established private schools and universities, some of which began, department by department, to creep toward European standards of excellence.

The gloomiest predictions of grumpy reactionaries and of those citizens who had been working for a socialist future had not proven to be true. The economy had recovered from the deep depression of the 1890s and spawned new businesses, many of which actually thrived in markets dominated by a few giant firms. The energy provided by the entrepreneurs of the second industrial revolution was driving America forward in the 1920s, generating new jobs, new products, new services. America's experts were alive to the opportunities as well as the problems this growth was generating. They were creatively organizing or transforming their professional institutions as the society evolved. That's how the history could be recorded if it was only viewed from the top, that is, from the perspective of the winners.

But there was a different America if you looked at the society from the bottom up during these same years. For those closer to the bottom of the social pyramid, the innovation and efficiency of America looked a great deal like instability and painful competition. The giant gap between the bottom and the top seemed to be unfair. That gap appeared to be growing. The newly created administrative state was providing those near the bottom and their families with neither equity nor security, and their concerns rapidly multiplied with every downturn in the economy.

Worst off were those who gave their lives as the United States was trying to learn how to become a major world power. As the nation started to acquire an empire overseas and to get entangled with the "ordinary vicissitudes" of the European nations, a price had to be paid. This transition turned out to be far more complicated and substantially more dangerous than the country's international experiences through most of the nineteenth century. America poked its nose into the Far East and then had to back off in the face of Japan's aggressive expansion. Learning by doing in the Far East and among the European powers was certainly not cheap. It proved to be costly in terms of both American values and American lives. By 1930, the toll was almost 120,000 killed and more than 205,000 wounded in the Caribbean, in the Philippines, and especially in Europe.

These would have been acceptable losses if the United States had been able to achieve its major strategic goal. But instead of a stable balance of power, U.S. policies fostered a tragic instability in Europe. The United States was certainly not alone in bringing about that unfortunate result. But the United States alone had the power in 1917 and 1918 to force the European combatants to arrange an armistice without victory. Or the United States could have just allowed the combatants to fight on until they had exhausted themselves. That policy might have failed. But it could hardly have had a more disastrous result for America and the rest of the world than the fragile postwar peace that broke down in the 1930s.

The working-class Americans who had sent their sons into combat in World War I suffered anew when the prosperity of the 1920s gave way to a deep and puzzling national depression. The professional experts didn't seem to understand the depression any better than the country's political leaders. From a working-class perspective, the experts were doing all right for themselves, but they didn't appear to be doing much for the people at the bottom, those who didn't have a secure position in this new society.[2]

---

[2] On the economic returns to professionals, see Thomas Goebel, "The Uneven Rewards of Professional Labor: Wealth and Income in the Chicago Professions, 1870–1920," *Journal of Social History*, 29 (Summer 1996), 749–77. Also see Milton Friedman and Simon Kuznets, *Income from Independent Professional Practice* (National Bureau of Economic Research, 1954).

African Americans and the Road to the Top

Professionalization had been providing a road to the top of society, or at least to the top of the middle, for millions of Americans. But that road was only open to a tiny percentage of African Americans. Professor William E. B. Du Bois found his way onto the path, and he recognized how important it could be for other African Americans.

Brought up in Great Barrington, Massachusetts, Du Bois was a "village prodigy" in a region where there were probably only about thirty blacks. The town favored public education and had a high school that played a crucial role in Du Bois' storied career. Great Barrington was not color-blind, but Du Bois' education continued even though he was the only black student to complete the high school program.

Encouraged to take the college preparatory course by his mentor, Du Bois was one of the star pupils in his small graduating class. After completing a second college prep course at Fisk University in Nashville, Tennessee (1888), Du Bois entered Harvard University, the school of his "youngest, wildest visions." Although he later said he was "in Harvard but not of it," he graduated cum laude in 1890, and his successful commencement address aroused favorable media attention. Graduate work in history and political economy followed, as did study in Germany, and in 1895, Du Bois received his Ph.D. in history from Harvard. He published his dissertation, *The Suppression of the African Slave Trade*, the following year.[3]

Many books and academic appointments followed, and Du Bois built from the pattern of his own career a theory and ideology of racial progress.[4] Rejecting Booker T. Washington's conservative, accommodating prescriptions for industrial education, Du Bois called for leadership by the Talented Tenth, an educated elite. It could, he said, provide a leadership cadre capable of uniting black Americans and altering the oppressive social, political, and economic restraints they were forced to endure in their own country.[5]

Looking back on those bitter struggles, we can see that Du Bois and his opponent were both right. In the short term, Booker T. Washington had much to offer the African-American people. The Tuskegee Institute

[3] David Levering Lewis, *W.E.B. Du Bois: Biography of a Race* (New York, 1993), 11–161.
[4] See ibid., 179–210, on the first few turns in his frustrating but ultimately successful professional career.
[5] Ibid., 73, 133, 165, 206, for the early development of Du Bois's ideas. See also Manning Marable, *W.E.B. Du Bois: Black Radical Democrat* (Boston, 1986), 51.

program of incremental gains and accommodation paid off in a setting hostile to any significant changes in race relations. In the long term, however, Tuskegee could not change the system that was oppressing African Americans. Du Bois's Talented Tenth could. Ultimately it did: first for those African Americans who were able to make it in business or squeeze into a profession; later, for many others. But changes were slow in coming, and Du Bois became understandably discouraged by the lack of progress in his own lifetime (1868–1963). America, he decided, needed a proletarian revolution of the sort that transformed Russia.

As Du Bois knew, the educational system was stacked so completely against blacks that they were unlikely to get the kind of representation they needed in the American professions. They could not get a voice in the institutions shaping the nation's private, public, and nonprofit sectors. In all, education and especially advanced education was the ticket for admission. But the Supreme Court had ruled in 1894 that educational institutions in America could remain divided by race. Blind to the reality of African-American education, the Court said the country could keep systems that were "separate but equal." The systems that existed were almost entirely separate but tragically unequal.

As a result, it became almost impossible to develop a black elite. In 1900, the largest number of black professionals consisted of clergymen.[6] They far outweighed the combined number in law, medicine, and dentistry. There were a large number of blacks in teaching, where the introduction of merit and educational standards was just beginning to reshape the occupation for white, urban Americans. But the impact of these reforms was not felt in African-American urban education, in large part because of segregation.

As the white professions improved their educational standards and raised their admission requirements, some opportunities for African Americans actually shrank. Elite professionals like those in law, dentistry, and teaching had every reason to believe that society would benefit from their reforms. But this was not true for all of society. Blacks who wanted access to the status and income that professional careers promised were denied chances to remake their lives and careers. Where immigrants were impacted by professional reform, they could fight back through their state

---

[6] As noted in Chapters 1 and 2, all of the statistics, unless otherwise cited, come from Cambridge University Press's *Historical Statistics of the United States*. In this case, for instance, I am using volume 2, *Work and Welfare*, 182–91, with figures for nonwhite males. Throughout the book, I am using my expanded version of the professions.

legislatures and state schools. They voted and made their votes count.[7] But in the South, most blacks were denied the vote and, increasingly, access to the professions.[8]

Blocked from the educational path that was being used by second-generation immigrants in America's cities, blacks were also suppressed by the threat of lynching, by exclusion from jobs, and by humiliating segregation in public facilities. Du Bois first encountered racial violence in Tennessee and later in horrible circumstances in Atlanta, Georgia. As he came to see, race relations were a blind spot for most American liberals. President Theodore Roosevelt, who became a leader of the Progressive Party, showed his true colors on race in the Brownsville Affair. The Republican President gave dishonorable discharges to an entire Army company of black troopers who would not provide evidence against those colleagues who may or may not have been involved in a shooting incident in Brownsville, Texas.[9] Democratic President Wilson kept the party score even by yielding to his party's southern wing and segregating official Washington and the U.S. Post Office system.[10]

It was a harsh world that Du Bois and other African Americans lived in, and it didn't get any better after African Americans gave their lives for their country in World War I. The military was of course completely segregated, with white officers commanding all of the black units. African Americans were widely used as orderlies for officers and were confined to low positions in the mess halls. The officer corps in the U.S. Army had for a long time been recruited heavily from the southern United States, where the worst forms of prejudice and racial subjugation took place. Even in death, blacks were not treated equally with white soldiers who were killed in combat.[11]

---

[7] Paul J. Miranti, Jr., *Accountancy Comes of Age: The Development of an American Profession, 1886–1940* (Chapel Hill, 1990).

[8] J. R. Oldfield, "A High and Honorable Calling: Black Lawyers in South Carolina, 1868–1915," *Journal of American Studies*, 23, 3 (1989), 395–406. Oldfield says that black lawyers in the state were never admitted to the South Carolina Bar Association. They were "consistently frustrated by impoverished clients, local prejudice and, except for a fortunate few, lack of business."

[9] Kathleen Dalton, *Theodore Roosevelt: A Strenuous Life* (New York, 2002).

[10] Lewis, *W.E.B. Du Bois*, 509–13.

[11] Blacks were not buried or honored in the same manner as white combatants. Du Bois wrote a famous editorial that proclaimed "We return. We return from fighting. We return fighting. Make way for Democracy! We saved it in France, and by the Great Jehovah, we will save it in the United States of America, or know the reason why." Lewis, *W.E.B. Du Bois*, 578.

After the war, African Americans made important contributions to the jazz, which many considered to be one of the hallmarks of the 1920s, but most blacks continued to be tightly locked into the lowest tier of America's economy and society. The black exodus from the South created new working-class opportunities but not openings into the middle class. Race riots – as we've seen – were part of what awaited blacks in northern cities, and the revival of the Ku Klux Klan in the Midwest suggested that more violence would be coming in the future. Seeing how few blacks could follow his educational path into the professions and into the American elite, DuBois began to look away from his native land. In the Soviet Union, he saw a vast experiment with an extreme form of social planning taking place. A two-month tour in 1926 helped push him toward the blending of Marxist and racial ideology that would be central to his thought for the rest of his life.[12] His radicalization may have been out of touch with the reality of life in the Soviet Union, but it was certainly not out of touch with the realities of African-American life in the United States.

Little Women

Knowing nothing about history, one might assume that during the four decades after 1890, white women faced fewer barriers to equality of opportunity than African-American men.[13] Although some white women had been indentured, none had been enslaved – at least none that I know of. Women had greater access to property, to education, and to social

---

[12] As a result of his trip to the Soviet Union, Du Bois began to elevate class analysis to a new position in his theory and history of modern society. He was especially impressed by the spirit of the people. Du Bois did not, of course, see what had happened to the people who had been forced off of their farms. As became apparent later, this was merely the first act in the development of a regime that would, under Stalin's leadership, kill millions of its own citizens. Stalin was just then beginning to consolidate his position in the Communist hierarchy. Other American visitors to the Soviet Union had similar experiences and came to similar conclusions about the promise of the Soviet style of planning. David Levering Lewis, *W.E.B. Du Bois: The Fight for Equality and the American Century, 1919–1963* (New York, 2000), 194–204. At about this time, Du Bois began work on his second novel. Jack B. Moore, *W.E.B. Du Bois* (Boston, 1981). His novels, like most, had autobiographical streaks and it was thus probably not an accident that in *Dark Princess* (1928), the hero of the novel was bent on a professional course. The hero was prevented by racism from getting his degree in obstetrics, perhaps reflecting Du Bois's disappointment at being blocked from receiving a much-coveted doctorate in Germany. On the degree see Lewis, *W.E.B. Du Bois*, 145.

[13] Throughout this section of the book, I am talking exclusively about white women. African-American women were doubly discriminated against on gendered as well as racial grounds.

mobility than did blacks. True, they trailed along, for the most part, behind their ascending or descending husbands. But on the way up or down, they could enjoy the advantages conferred by greater income and wealth and might as a result be able to make or influence decisions of considerable import to others and to society.

Normally, however, those decisions had to be filtered through a male power structure. Inside and outside the home, women were junior partners at best, commonly referred to with diminutives like "the little woman." In the age of iron and steel, of brawny men and imposing bosses, it was a solid put-down to be commonly referred to as "little." This insult was a good measure of the culture of gender in America.

Emma Goldman, lecturer, author, and revolutionary, was sensitive to that culture and the power structure it reflected. An immigrant (1886) from Russia, where her Jewish parents had been able to give her the advantages of a middle-class education, Goldman struggled to make a living in her new home. She found that the land of opportunity offered little to a poor seamstress. Already a revolutionary in mind and heart, Goldman's experiences in America deepened her radical bent. She was stunned by the Haymarket Riot in Chicago (1886) and its outcome.[14] Four of the anarchists charged with throwing a bomb at the police were hanged, as much for their radical challenge to authority as for their direct involvement in the bombing. Goldman didn't look to that kind of government for reform. Deeply dedicated to anarchism, she leaned hard against America's seemingly relentless drive toward organization, bureaucratization, and professionalization.

Goldman's ideology was difficult for most Americans to understand – then and now.[15] This was especially true when her radical vision spilled over onto issues of gender and the family. Goldman wanted to free the little women from a social system that was, in her view, as oppressive as the economic system of capitalism. "Nowhere," she wrote, "is woman treated according to the merit of her work, but rather as a sex. It is therefore almost inevitable that she should pay for her right to exist, to keep a position in whatever line, with sex favors. Thus it is merely a question

---

[14] The riot was prompted by police efforts to disperse a demonstration in support of striking workers. The facts were vague, and the court seemed more concerned about the political views of the anarchists than their involvement in the deaths of the policemen.

[15] Almost all of my university students have, for instance, always been baffled by anarchism. "How would things run?" they ask. Bent on getting things done and looking forward to professional careers, they find it impossible to believe that an intelligent person would find Goldman's ideology convincing.

of degree whether she sells herself to one man, in or out of marriage, or to many men."[16] "Marriage," she concluded, "is primarily an economic arrangement, an insurance pact. It differs from the ordinary life insurance agreement only in that it is more binding, more exacting.... The institution of marriage makes a parasite of woman, an absolute dependent. It incapacitates her for life's struggle, annihilates her social consciousness, paralyzes her imagination, and then imposes its gracious protection... [it is] a travesty on human character."[17] This was a heady dose of ideas for early-twentieth-century America, an ideology that prefigured some of the central ideas of the women's emancipation movement half a century later.

To a nation still imbued with Victorian ideas about the family and gender, Goldman's ideas were revolutionary. In politics, women were considered inherently inferior as late as World War I. Long after African-American males could vote in much of the country, women were denied equality at the ballot box.[18] Through their organizations they could influence politics.[19] But the political system in America, from the cities through the states and into the national government, was a hunting ground for opportunities restricted to men.

In the workforce too, women were placed in subordinate roles in 1900. There were plenty of women working in America: well over a million were employed in personal services in homes, almost 300,000 as teachers, and many more as sales clerks and laborers, on and off the farm. But there were only 1,500 in law. The census in 1900 discovered no female economists, no engineers, none in the agricultural and biological sciences – indeed, no women college professors. Power in higher education remained in the firm grip of the men whom a distinguished president of Harvard University had declared were the only Americans fit for the highest forms of higher education.[20] There were many women clerical

---

[16] Emma Goldman, "The Traffic in Women" in Richard Drinnon, ed., *Anarchism and Other Essays* (New York, 1969), 179.

[17] Emma Goldman, "Marriage and Love," in ibid., 228, 235.

[18] The exceptions in state elections were interesting, if only because of their geographical locations.

[19] Paula Baker, "The Domestication of Politics: Women and American Political Society, 1780–1920," *American Historical Review*, 89 (June 1984), 620–47.

[20] My reference is to Charles William Eliot, president of Harvard University from 1869 to 1909. He had decided early on that poor but talented men should attend Harvard, but "only after generations of civil freedom and social equality" would women be prepared for the rigorous demands of a first-rate university education. Lewis, *W.E.B. Du Bois*, 81.

workers, but few who were bosses, even in companies that sold services.[21] For many, paid work was an interlude before marriage, but for many others, staying at home was an unaffordable luxury.[22] They were locked into poorly paid jobs in a rapidly expanding urban, industrial economy that was run by and for men.

There were a few cracks in the dominant institutions and culture, even in the professions where the assumption that women were inferior seemed beyond question. One of those cracks is instructive and close to home for me. It was produced by a woman who had reaped all of the advantages of America's second industrial revolution and was perched near the top of society, in a position far removed from seamstresses like Emma Goldman. Mary Elizabeth Garrett got her opportunity to be an academic entrepreneur when Johns Hopkins University was trying to establish a school of medicine. When the University ran low on money, Garrett and three of her friends, all well-placed daughters of trustees, tried to help. They organized a Women's Medical Fund Committee (1889), which was able to raise $100,000 for the new school.

Almost half of the money came from the wealthy Miss Garrett. The daughter of the late president of the Baltimore and Ohio Railroad, Garrett had been educated at a school for girls. Privately tutored when she traveled in Europe, Garrett had the kind of advantages that only the wealthiest Americans could afford.[23] Although she didn't attend a university, Garrett was interested in education and particularly in education for women. She had helped the Bryn Mawr School in Baltimore get started and continued to take an active interest in its finances and administration. She wasn't anyone's "little woman."

Playing hardball, Garrett's Committee offered the money to Hopkins only if the medical school would admit women on equal terms with men. The distinguished president of the University, Daniel Coit Gilman, wasn't happy with the conditions of the offer and neither were the trustees. But they badly wanted a medical school. They needed more money than the trustees could provide. After Miss Garrett added over $300,000 more to her gift, Gilman and the trustees suddenly realized that this was a matter

---

[21] Telephone service is a good example, but there are many others.

[22] Mary P. Ryan, *Mysteries of Sex*, 201–8. As Ryan observes, "the law of supply and demand operated through dual labor markets, separate tracks for male and female workers" (204).

[23] Albert J. Beveridge III and Susan Radomsky, *The Chronicle of Catherine Eddy Beveridge: An American Girl Travels into the Twentieth Century* (New York, 2005), provides an excellent guide to what woman of this class could afford.

of principle. The University accepted the money and became one of the few leading medical programs to accept women.[24] Given the fact that only about 3,000 women worked as physicians or surgeons in America in 1900, and none worked as dentists, this was a significant breakthrough.

Other breakthroughs followed. Between 1900 and 1930, the number of Americans in public high schools increased eightfold and the number in private high schools threefold.[25] The number of women graduating from high school increased steadily and the number in colleges and universities jumped from 85,000 to slightly more than 481,000. Almost 50,000 of these women earned BA degrees in 1930 alone. Private universities, including the elite schools of the East, were changing slowly, but higher education to the West was more open, more obliging to women. The University of California at Berkeley had admitted women since its opening (1869), as was the case with other state universities in the West.[26] These coeducational admission policies at the state level were not just a hollow, public-relations formality. The policies were implemented, as well as proclaimed. Meanwhile women's colleges throughout the country were also increasing their enrollments.[27]

The second important change for women at the turn of the century involved employment and living conditions. In the growing service sector, employers were alerted to the fact that they could lower their labor costs by substituting women for men. This was not a unique revelation. Textile manufacturers and farmers had long ago discovered that women were cheaper to employ than men and that children came even cheaper than adult women. But now this knowledge began to spread. As a result, the

---

[24] Jane Eliot Sewell, *Medicine in Maryland: The Practice and Profession, 1799–1999* (Baltimore, 1999), 87–88.

[25] See volume 2, *Work and Welfare*, in Cambridge University Press's *Historical Statistics of the United States*.

[26] Alison Comish Thorne, *Visible and Invisible Women in Land-Grant Colleges, 1890–1940* (Logan, Utah, 1985). As Thorne notes, there were not many women in these schools at first, but those who were enrolled took the same courses as men. Later that changed, as a special curriculum for women was created. Thorne observes that "educators believed that too much intellectual effort would cause a woman's uterus to atrophy, an attitude which affected the curricula for women in most educational institutions across the country." The course that became most popular for women was "domestic arts," which evolved into "home economics."

[27] See Thomas Woody, *A History of Women's Education in the United States*, vol. 2 (New York, 1980), pp. 184–233, and especially 224–303, on coeducation. By 1900, 98% of the public high schools (reporting) were coeducational and they enrolled 93.6% of all the students enrolled in high schools. (p. 229). As the author notes, "the Western state universities were influential leaders in the movement" for coeducation (p. 239).

number of women in the paid workforce increased steadily. No longer living in maternal or paternal settings, many of the young women of these years began to break out of a protective family environment and confront urban life on their own terms. By 1920, women had also cracked one of the barriers to power in America by acquiring the right to vote. Psychologically, economically, and socially, a base was being laid in the 1920s for the astonishing transformation of gender relations that would take place in the next generation of American women.

As late as 1930, however, that decisive transformation was still in the future. Public policy in the early 1930s was still being framed and the administrative state defined by men. There were still many more women librarians than lawyers. This was true as well in most of the other important professions. Nursing was becoming a largely female profession, but – Johns Hopkins notwithstanding – the medical sciences and clinical medicine were not. In the universities and colleges of the entire nation, there were only 200 women teaching in the social sciences. There were almost 5,000 in fields like home economics, but the power structure in higher education continued to mirror the more traditional aspects of American society.

Materially better off than most African-American men, women by 1930 had still failed to break down the imposing gender barriers to most of the professions and leadership positions in the nation's important institutions.[28] In the high schools, universities, and colleges, women were acquiring the educations they would need to define new roles for themselves and a new concept of the nation's gender relations. Similar changes were taking place in the workforce. But these were just promissory notes that couldn't be cashed for many years. Meanwhile, the Great Depression would set women back for an entire decade.

Immigrant Building Blocks

For immigrants like Lazlo Galambos, there were also imposing barriers to getting ahead. Poorly educated and unfamiliar with American institutions, men like Lazlo struggled in factories and fields where twelve-hour days were the common rule. Split apart by languages and churches,

---

[28] Even at Cornell, where women comprised a quarter of the graduating class in agriculture (1923), Barbara McClintock was not allowed to do graduate work in genetics. To her credit, she worked around this barrier and ultimately won a Nobel Prize for her research on the genetics of maize. Alison Comish Thorne, *Visible and Invisible Women*, 6–7.

Hunkies and Wops and Polacks made good strike-breakers and bad union members. Understandably, many worked a few years and then returned to their homes in Europe. Lazlo, a Catholic, went back to Europe once, but he returned to stay, having apparently had enough of the Eastern European class system, political turmoil, and poor opportunities. For Jews, who faced a much more hostile environment in America, the option of returning to Europe was seldom available. Although they may have missed home, in the United States they did not have to fear pogroms. Here, their powerful tradition of intellectual achievement could play out in a system of public education that was open to all.

For Lazlo and other immigrants, the key to making it in America was education. What is rather astounding is how many of them perceived just how important education would be for their children. That doomed most of the first generation to jobs as low-skilled laborers, to craft jobs at best, maybe to politics for a few, to crime for some, and to an insecure future for most. Andrew Carnegie was a wonderful exception to the rule, an inspiration but not an appropriate model.[29] Great wealth was beyond the reach of most of America's millions of immigrants. If security loomed large in their thinking, they had every reason to be concerned about a nation with only the flimsiest of welfare networks to catch them if they failed, became ill, or were injured on the job. Their wives and young children had more to fear. Even in the states that adopted workmen's compensation, the payments were small and were no substitute for a working husband.

Fortunately for second- and third-generation immigrants, public education was available and the system was steadily improving. So Lazlo, undeterred by his own poor command of English or by Ohio's various brands of hostility toward immigrants, shoved ahead in the foundry while he and his wife pushed their three sons to get educations.[30] All three of the sons made it into high school, which was a tribute that can be evenly

[29] There are three good biographies of Carnegie. Harold C. Livesay, *Andrew Carnegie and the Rise of Big Business* (New York, 1999 edition), is short and insightful. See also David Nasaw, *Andrew Carnegie* (New York, 2006). Joseph Frazier Wall, *Andrew Carnegie* (Pittsburgh, 1989).

[30] As a child visiting Toledo, I was impressed by the fact that the African-American children living near Grandfather Lazlo's home referred to their Hungarian neighbors as "white trash." Lazlo didn't talk much except when he was upset about something; then, he would exclaim: "Son-a-ma-bisch," with the emphasis on the "Son." Like many first- and second-generation Eastern European immigrants, Lazlo and Hazel wanted their children and grandchildren to become completely Americanized as well as educated. So they didn't teach you any Hungarian. As a result, the only Hungarian I learned was

divided between Lazlo's determination and the changes taking place in American schools. From that point on, the educational accomplishments of his sons were varied, but all three learned enough to get at least one notch higher than their father in the workforce. Instead of being defeated by the trying American environment, the sons became aggressive competitors, would-be entrepreneurs, and in the case of Lou Galambos, an instant (although tenuous) professional by proclamation.

Education was also the path that Lou Galambos' wife, Ruth, had followed. She and her sister, Geraldine, had grown up in difficult circumstances in Fostoria, as we saw in Chapter 2. After their father abandoned the family, the mother, Carrie, was forced to return to her own family for help. For working-class women, perceptions of insecurity were well grounded in reality. The daughters and Carrie moved into a small house with her mother and two other members of the family. Support was scrambled together with resentment. But both Ruth and Geraldine were able to make it into high school – a considerable achievement for that time – and to graduate.[31] Geraldine, as we saw, excelled in music and school, wrote the high school's alma mater, and was able to move on to a teacher's college.[32] Ruth took the secretarial course that was more common for young women. After graduation, she found a local office job and began to provide some income for the family. Her older sister's success in school left Ruth with a permanent streak of resentment, but she had a trump card she could always play after she married Lou. Geraldine never married.

These family stories are the common stuff of American working-class life in the 1920s. The tales of hardship and of educational and economic progress are familiar to all of us. The stories reflect and refract the general experiences of many European immigrants and their families. But what those anecdotes and the Horatio Alger tales mask is the inequality of wealth and income, the inequality of educational opportunities, and the problems many immigrant families experienced in making their first steps into American society.[33]

Hazel's term of endearment ("Edge mega seved") which apparently means "You eat my heart out."

[31] As I mentioned before, the third daughter, Kathryn, died of appendicitis.

[32] Geraldine Himburg graduated in 1919 and her alma mater was sung at the Commencement in that year. Her younger sister, Ruth, graduated a few years later and received the only graduation gift her mother could afford – a cheap set of book ends.

[33] For a long-term perspective on inequality, see Thomas Ferguson and James K. Galbraith, "The American Wage Structure: 1920–1947," in James K. Galbraith and Maureen

Some of the markers for their troubles can be traced through the violent battles that took place between labor and capital in the depressed 1890s and the more prosperous years after 1900. In the aftermath of World War I, these struggles took place against an international background of communist revolution and American efforts to suppress a perceived threat from foreigners like Emma Goldman. Goldman's brand of anarchism and feminism was seen as a threat to the foundation stones of one of the most politically stable societies in world history. Having been imprisoned on three occasions, Goldman was finally sent back to Russia.[34] She and hundreds of others were deported for advocating and working for more change than America could tolerate. As the young J. Edgar Hoover explained to the Department of Justice, she was one of "the most dangerous anarchists in this country and if permitted to return to the community will result in undue harm."[35]

So What Was the Price?

Looked at from the bottom up, the price of the American brand of progress between 1890 and 1930 was high. High in terms of lives lost and destroyed, families ripped apart, and talent wasted. People and resources were blown away in the efforts to suppress revolutions and in a disastrous war in Europe, a war that ultimately came close to destroying the democracies it was supposed to save. The United States had by 1930 established patterns of national behavior that would persist and make it extremely difficult for the government to relate to the larger world in ways consistent with the nation's democratic values. Professional expertise would continue to be ignored almost as frequently as it was consulted.

At home, Americans of color were, with few exceptions, pressed down into the lower class, cut off from the educational opportunities that could have served America by making full use of their intelligence and imagination. Forced into ghettos in northern cities, African Americans were better off than they had been in the South. But not by much. Like the

---

Berner, eds., *Inequality and Industrial Change: A Global View* (Cambridge, 2001), 33–75; and Peter H. Lindert, "The Distribution of Income and Wealth," *Historical Statistics of the United States*, 2, 621–62.

[34] Time does not heal all wounds, but it does provide relief for some. In post–World War II America, the U.S. government provided money to support the editing of the papers of Emma Goldman, and in at least one course at Johns Hopkins University, the professor required the students to read a collection of Goldman's writings.

[35] Candace Falk, *Love, Anarchy, and Emma Goldman* (New York, 1984), 290–91.

hordes of Eastern European immigrants, urban blacks lived on the edge, confronting on a daily basis the insecurities and inequalities of American urban life.

White women were stymied by similar barriers to progress. Some were beginning to push through the economic, political, and cultural fences that kept them in subordinate roles. But it was not at all clear in 1930 that their progress would continue, and it was entirely clear that black women would not be allowed to follow them out of the lower reaches of urban America.

When white women and the children of immigrants made progress, it was generally through education. They were, in effect, building a base that might eventually enable them to climb into the middle class. Professional careers were the reward for success in education. The professions promised opportunity, greater security, and even access to the power to reshape American institutions.

Viewed from the comfortable reaches of middle- and upper-class America, the price paid for the country's progress seemed reasonable – even in 1930. From that point of view, the society's professional experts, political brokers, and business leaders still had the country headed in the right direction. Middle-class Americans could still muster hope that the depression that had begun in October 1929 would be short and the recovery decisive. After all, that was what had happened before. The young administrative state seemed to be arming itself to help those most damaged and politically effective, like farmers, bankers, and railroad leaders.[36]

There had been serious tremors of doubt in the immediate aftermath of the stock market crash in 1929. As the bodies of some financiers wiped out by the crash hit the ground in New York, the upper class briefly shuddered. The worries deepened as holding companies collapsed and corrupt business leaders were exposed in 1930 and 1931. But President Hoover, the Engineer in the White House, seemed determined to set things right without destroying the economic system that had elevated upper-class Americans to positions of great wealth and power. With Emma Goldman and her radical friends out of the country, America seemed safe from revolution, secure in its traditions.

---

[36] My reference is to the following three measures: the Reconstruction Finance Corporation, which was a miniature form of the measures being taken in 2008 and 2009 to pump money into the financial system; the Agricultural Marketing Act, a response to the farmers' distress in the late 1920s; and the Hawley-Smoot Tariff, which raised rates on agricultural as well as industrial products.

All too soon, however, that confidence withered like flowers in a hard freeze. In the 1930s, the fears and doubts of the working class began to spread into middle- and upper-class America, undermining the resistance to another round of state building and bringing forth new professional experts. Like most experts, they would assume there was always one best solution to any problem the nation faced. They would struggle to move a political system built on the central assumption that all solutions lend themselves to compromise, to the shaving and reshaping that always accompanies innovation in America's brand of democracy. The legal profession's central role in shaping those solutions would be diminished but not destroyed as the depression deepened.

7

New Deal Experiments

In the 1930s, there were a few winners, but most of the people were losers in small towns like Fostoria, Ohio, and Princeton, Indiana. It seemed the depression would never end.[1] Princeton, which was a slightly smaller version of Fostoria, was nestled in the southwest corner of Indiana, about 11 miles from the Wabash River to the west and 25 miles from the Ohio River to the south. Princeton's fortunes turned on agriculture, on coal, and on the railroad, its commercial lifeline. The Southern Railroad Company had a big repair shop on the edge of town, and the Deep Vein Coal Mine, just a few miles to the south, used the Southern to ship its soft coal. Out near the mine was the headquarters for a large commercial agribusiness that sprawled over 12,000 acres of rich farmland. The investors who owned the coal mine had amassed the land to control the mineral rights. A few years later, under the watchful eye of Orville "Reddie" Redenbacher, they built up a substantial operation in hybrid corn and then in popcorn. But that enterprise was just getting underway in the late 1930s, and meanwhile, the only other business of note was a Heinz plant. We didn't know much about it, but we were told they made catsup.[2]

Because Princeton was the seat of Gibson County's government, there was a red-brick courthouse in the middle of a square that was the center of the town's dwindling retail life. Like most other small towns in the heartland, it had a Penny's Store, a pool room that kept the men off

---

[1] Although it was published many decades ago, William E. Leuchtenburg's book, *Franklin D. Roosevelt and the New Deal, 1932–1940* (New York, 1963) is still the best single volume on the 1930s.

[2] On Redenbacher, who much later became a famous popcorn tycoon, see http://www .wyandotpopcornmus.com/interview.htm

the streets, and a candy and soda shop know universally as "Greeks" in "honor" of the family that ran the establishment. When teenage boys left the Palace Pool Parlor, they'd stroll over to Greeks to meet their girlfriends. All of these institutions played central roles in the lives of young people growing up in Princeton, Indiana, in the 1930s.[3]

More important to adults was Highway 41, which ran through the center of the town, past the courthouse. If you took that road south, you'd pass the coal mine and the Highway Machine Shop that serviced the mine. In the shop, mechanics turned out axles for the mine's coal cars, sharpened the teeth of the metal bits used to tear chunks of coal out of the ground, and repaired everything else that broke in the business of getting coal to the surface and into the railroad cars that carried it to market. The mechanics in the shop were defined in part by their toolboxes.[4] Although the shop owned the lathes and drill presses on which they worked, a mechanic owned his own micrometers, files, and wrenches. When an axle broke, he made a new one on the lath, one at a time. When a metal wheel or strap broke, one of the welders, who had a different skill and a different toolbox, would repair it on the shop floor and send it back to the mine. The Highway Machine Shop also took care of equipment from the big commercial farm because all three businesses – the farm, the mine, and the shop – had the same owners. This was a two-family enterprise.[5]

In the late 1930s, the machine shop needed a new boss, and Lou Galambos needed a new job. Despite the depression, neither he nor his father, Lazlo, had been out of work, but the depression finally caught Lou in 1937. He and his family were forced to leave Shawneetown, near Harrisburg, Illinois, by the Ohio River flood of that year. Everyone was evacuated from Shawneetown, which was completely underwater. Even Harrisburg, thirty miles from the river, was almost wiped out by the flood.[6] Lou took the car out on a raft made of wooden planks and oil

---

[3] At the five-and-ten store, you could buy an inexpensive musical instrument called a "Jew's Harp." If you don't know what it is, you should Google it. It never occurred to us that this name and the reference to "Greeks" might be derogatory.

[4] All of the mechanics, welders, and other workers were men, as symbolized by the fact that there was no restroom at the Highway Machine Shop for women.

[5] The families were the Hulmans and the Smiths, from Terre Haute, Indiana. Tony Hulman, Jr., (famous because of his presidency of the Indianapolis Motor Speedway) and Donald E. Smith (a prominent banker) were linked through their families, their love of sports, and their complex business interests in a manner familiar to all those who study family enterprises.

[6] The Ohio River flood that year covered 978 square miles and forced a mass evacuation. After the water receded, Shawneetown was moved to higher ground, leaving behind a

drums, and my mother and sister and I left in a canoe, courtesy of a rescue team. The coal mines around southern Illinois were flooded and weren't buying the machinery Lou had been trying to sell for the J. F. Joy Company, so he and the family headed back to Ohio to look for a new job.

This kind of odyssey wasn't unusual for our family. We'd lived in Kansas City and St. Louis for a time, following Lou's relentless search for work that was suited to a "mining engineer" with more experience than education. The depression had seemed to be lifting, but the economy had turned back down in 1937 and 1938. Then came the worst flood since 1927, followed by a drive across southern Illinois and into the western edge of Indiana.[7]

When we got to Princeton, Indiana we had to stop. I was ill, and Lou had to go in search of a doctor. While that was being taken care of, he had some good luck. I got well quickly and in the meantime, Lou landed a job running the Highway Machine Shop, a job that would keep the family in Princeton for the next fifteen years. After having followed the mining business from city to city, it was a relief to the family, and especially to Lou's wife Ruth, to settle down in Princeton. Although Lou had to scale back his goals and work for a salary rather than a commission, he now had the opportunity to build up a business that would make good use of his mechanical skills. That would keep this restless man fully occupied until the Midwestern oil fields beckoned.

The Depression

Lou Galambos was one of the millions of Americans who were on the move in the 1930s, getting away from a flood or a drought, looking for a new job or in some cases just a meal. In 1933, when Franklin D. Roosevelt was inaugurated as the thirty-second President of the United States, more than ten million American workers were unemployed. By

---

tiny community known as Old Shawneetown. This was the same flood on the Mississippi River that inspired Johnny Cash to write his song, "Five Feet High and Rising." See the account at http://www.island63.com/article.cfm?articleID=5. Despite the efforts of the U.S. Army Corps of Engineers, the floods continued and 75 percent of Old Shawneetown was under water in March 2008.

7 The 1927 flood was so disastrous that Congress passed the Flood Control Act of 1928 and set out to develop through the U.S. Army Corps of Engineers a plan for flood control on the Mississippi and its tributaries, including the Ohio River. The levees and floodways did not, however, protect Harrisburg in 1937. See the Corps of Engineers account at http://www.mvn.usace.army.mil/pao/bro/misstrib.htm.

1937, New Deal programs and business recovery had cut that figure in half, but in the following year, the economy sagged again, leaving 6.8 million out of work. So it was a good time to be a boss and a very bad time to be on the road with a family and no job.

The President had promised the nation "a new deal for the American people," and more than 28 million voters had given him their support while turning their backs on Herbert Hoover and the Republican Party.[8] By 1933, when he left office, Hoover could claim with justice that he had done more than any previous president to spur an economic recovery.[9] But the Hoover programs had failed, and President Roosevelt quickly demonstrated that he would be more flexible than his predecessor. He quickly abandoned an effort to balance the budget and set out to do more, much more, than Hoover had done to get the economy going again. He could do more in part because he had the support of a Congress in which the Democrats controlled both the Senate and the House of Representatives. The federal government was united under one party and ready as of March 4, 1933 to move forward to help "the forgotten man at the bottom of the economic pyramid."[10]

Political rhetoric aside, however, what Roosevelt still needed in 1933 was a plan that would work. He needed a specific program that was grounded in a new set of economic ideas – that is, the sort of theory that only professionals were likely to provide. The economic ideas that Hoover embraced were discredited. The country wanted and needed a new paradigm. In the election campaign, FDR had anticipated this need and had clearly acknowledged that he had to have professional expertise to generate the guiding ideas for a Roosevelt-led recovery. He had organized a "Brains Trust" with that in mind.[11] Turning to Columbia

---

[8] The quotation is from Franklin D. Roosevelt's address accepting the Democratic Party's presidential nomination. John T. Woolley and Gerhard Peters, *The American Presidency Project* [online]. Available at http://www.presidency.ucsb.edu/ws/?pid=75174.

[9] Joan Hoff-Wilson, *Herbert Hoover: Forgotten Progressive* (Boston, 1975). Richard Norton Smith, *An Uncommon Man: The Triumph of Herbert Hoover* (New York, 1984). David M. Hart, "Herbert Hoover's Last Laugh: The Enduring Significance of the 'Associative State' in the United States," *Journal of Policy History*, 10, 4 (1998), 419–44. David E. Hamilton, *From New Day to New Deal: American Farm Policy from Hoover to Roosevelt, 1928–1933* (Chapel Hill, North Carolina, 1991).

[10] The Twentieth Amendment to the Constitution (1933) changed the inauguration date from March 4 to January 20, which is the current date.

[11] According to Jean Edward Smith, *FDR* (New York, 2007), 262, Sam Rosenman said to FDR, "You have been having good experiences with college professors. If we can get a small group together willing to give us some time, they can prepare memoranda for you. You'll want to talk with them yourself, and maybe out of all the talk some concrete ideas

University in his home state, he picked Raymond Moley, a professor of public law, Adolf A. Berle, Jr., a professor of corporation law, and Rexford Guy Tugwell, a professor of economics, to formulate a program for the New Deal. Of the three professors, Berle was the most brilliant, Moley the most practical, and Tugwell the most ambitious about reshaping American political economy. All three men would continue to serve the Roosevelt administration following the election: Moley briefly; Berle and Tugwell for many years.

Professor Tugwell had already published some of his ideas for changing America. Although he had attended the University of Pennsylvania's Wharton School of Finance and Commerce (MA, 1916), he had emerged from his business-school interlude with a deep skepticism about capitalism. Completing his graduate work at Columbia (Ph.D., 1922), he remained at the school to teach economics and to research and write about the wastefulness of the American economy. Instead of looking to markets and competition as the central mechanisms of recovery, he looked to the public sector and to national planning. He was particularly enthusiastic about marshalling government power behind the ideas of Frederick W. Taylor, the guru of efficiency analysis in American industry. A more efficient system, Tugwell reasoned, would enable the nation to solve the problems of business and agriculture, problems he had identified in the 1920s.[12] The farm crisis of the late 1920s was, he said, symptomatic of the major problems of the capitalist system. With central planning, Tugwell believed, the government could bring supply and demand into proper balance and eliminate the fluctuations and hardship created by a market system.

In 1933, Tugwell tried to translate his academic inclinations into a coherent program that would help the lawyers in Washington, DC, devise policies that would provide relief for business as well as agriculture, for commerce as well as finance. Certain elements of the problem were obvious to anyone who could read a newspaper. The workforce needed more jobs and higher wages. The business system needed more consumer

---

will come." Roosevelt was worried they might leak too much information too early, but decided he would just have to take that risk.

[12] As a young welder, Lou Galambos had an unfortunate experience with corporate efficiency controls. He was welding large parts piled in the company yard under a piece-work system. He and the other welders laboriously took each piece down, welded it, and placed it back in another pile. Seeing an easy opportunity to increase his income, Lou threw a ladder over the fence and welded each part without taking it out of the pile. He was fired for using a ladder that didn't belong to the company.

demand and increased orders for capital goods. Farmers needed more money for their crops. The banking system needed to have collapsing institutions weeded out and the remaining banks supported and reorganized along new lines. Tugwell – an energetic, articulate champion of an active federal government – tried to help the Roosevelt Administration and Congress create the new agencies and new policies that would solve these problems and get the American economy growing again.

What was missing was a solution that could somehow cut across all of these problems and spur the entire economy ahead. That was Tugwell's dilemma. He was unable to come up with ideas that linked banking, industry, agriculture, and labor. When he did some serious thinking about this problem in the early 1930s, all he could offer was a program focusing on improved efficiency à la Taylor. By gathering all of the nation's coal mines under one umbrella organization, Tugwell said, the government could eliminate the marginal producers and restore the health of the mining industry. But where, in that case, would the laid-off workers go for their next jobs? Tugwell didn't know. And there is no indication in anything he subsequently wrote or did indicating that he had an answer to that question.[13]

In this regard, Tugwell was not alone. No one in either the executive or the legislative branch had an answer to that fundamental question. Lacking a coherent theory that cut across the entire economy, Tugwell, the lawyers in government, and the other professionals who were concerned with economic policy had to live with a series of separate solutions for each problem, for each sector of the economy, without worrying about whether they might have conflicting results.[14] Something had to be done. So for Tugwell, for Congress, and for President Roosevelt, it was perfectly acceptable to build a new branch of the regulatory state to control the output of agricultural commodities, to subsidize the property-owning farmers for cutting back production, and thus to raise farm prices and income. It was particularly acceptable if the new system received input

---

[13] Rexford G. Tugwell, *The Industrial Discipline and the Governmental Arts* (New York, 1933). Michael V. Namorato, *Rexford G. Tugwell: A Biography* (New York, 1988) offers a more charitable perspective on Tugwell's role as a "practical planner" (p. 4). So too does Jean Edward Smith, *FDR*, 262,

[14] The categories used were functional: they were sectoral (industry and agriculture, for instance) and within those broad sectoral groupings, the breakdowns were by product and service. This type of thinking is what carried the National Recovery Administration down into the mop industry, where they had to distinguish – as did the trade associations – between wet and dry mops. For teachers who touch on public policy, this is an excellent illustration of how ideas and the lack of ideas influence the exercise of power.

from dirt farmers, the organized ones, at the local level. That left out the sharecroppers, most of whom were African Americans in the South, but they were not organized so their voices were not heard.[15]

If this hurt urban consumers, well, they would have separate programs to deal with their part of this awesome national problem. The administration offered them banking legislation designed to protect them and to insure (under the Federal Deposit Insurance Corporation) any savings they might have left or might acquire as recovery got going.[16] The government entered the mortgage market for the first time, initially to prevent owners from losing their homes and later to encourage homeownership.[17] Relief payments, government employment programs, federal suburban home building, urban public housing, a new food stamp policy, and a minimum wage law all helped many urban Americans – some of those who still had jobs and many of those who were unemployed.[18]

For business, as for agriculture, the New Deal's central solution was another regulatory innovation: a government-authorized set of cartels, with trade associations offering guidance in "stabilizing" their respective industries.[19] The National Recovery Administration (NRA) was built on

[15] There is a substantial literature on the interest groups pressing for a new agricultural policy, on the agencies that implemented the policies, and on their impact on prices and production. If you have an interest in this subject, the best place to start is with David E. Hamilton's book cited in note 6 to this chapter, and with Theodore Saloutos, *The American Farmer and the New Deal* (Ames, 1982). As you will see, the historical literature on the New Deal programs adopted the same sectoral and functional categories that the policy planners and legislators and agencies employed.

[16] Geraldine Himberg, the schoolteacher who you last met in Chapter 6, lost money in one of the failed banks of the Great Depression. After that experience, she would only save $10,000 in any one bank because that was the amount covered by the Federal Deposit Insurance Corporation's original legislation. Once burned, twice shy – or in Geraldine's case, "always shy."

[17] Similar policies were adopted for farmers facing the loss of their farms.

[18] Peter Temin, "The Great Depression," in Stanley L. Engerman and Robert E. Gallman, eds., *The Cambridge Economic History of the United States, III, The Twentieth Century* (New York, 2000), 317–28, briefly reviews the legislative initiatives. In the same volume, see Eugene N. White, "Banking and Finance in the Twentieth Century," 757–73; Richard H. K. Vietor, "Government Regulation of Business," 975–88; and W. Elliot Brownlee, "The Public Sector," 1013–46.

[19] As numerous historians (including myself) have pointed out, the trade association programs of World War I and the 1920s had an impact on the NRA. But the Roosevelt program added a coercive element that was missing from the previous policies. For the strongest statement about the influence of World War I policy on the New Deal, see Marc Allen Eisner, *From Warfare State to Welfare State*. For my own work, see Louis Galambos, *Competition & Cooperation: The Emergence of a National Trade Association* (Baltimore, 1966).

the hope that recovery would quickly follow the stabilization of prices. But no one in the government could actually explain why that would happen.[20] Consumers were given a formal foothold in the NRA, but their representatives had a hard time formulating positions to take on the narrow and highly specific issues vital to the producers and to labor. Their problem was similar to Tugwell's quandary.[21]

This type of thinking played into the lawyerly bent of Congress, which hustled the New Deal measures through in a dramatic tribute to Roosevelt's political leadership and the intense interest voters all over the country had in escaping the deadly grip of the Great Depression. Neither the Administration nor the Congress could really be blamed if the cartel strategy of regulation failed – as it did – because there were no well-placed professional experts providing better ideas in this first, dynamic phase of New Deal state crafting. When the Supreme Court overturned the National Industrial Recovery Act in 1935, there were few who mourned the disappearance of the NRA.

Other additions to the regulatory state were less innovative than the NRA, but several of them proved to be more durable. Congress created a new agency, the Federal Communications Commission (FCC), to take over the job of regulating interstate communications, including radio, telegraph, and telephone. Where the telephone was concerned, the FCC sat atop an elaborate structure of state regulatory agencies that had enabled the Bell System to remain efficient and innovative while it worked toward the goal of universal service in the United States. By 1929, that target was in sight, and fortunately federal regulation in the 1930s did not supplant the state-oriented combination of public and private authority that had given the United States the best telephone system in the world.[22]

The contrast between a growing, technologically advanced telephone system and a collapsing railroad system should have caused deep concern in Congress. But the regulatory state and the cartel philosophy had such momentum in the 1930s, that the failures of the Interstate Commerce

[20] The idea that successful stabilization would restore "confidence" unfortunately hearkened back to Hoover's initial approach to the depression.

[21] B. Lizabeth Cohen, *A Consumers' Republic: The Politics of Mass Consumption in Postwar America* (New York, 2003), presents a different perspective on the consumer representatives.

[22] In 1929, 41.6 percent of America's households had telephones (more than 20 million were in service then). The percentage declined in the 1930s and did not pass the 1929 level until 1942. According to Professor Kenneth Lipartito, the only rival to the American system was the much smaller system in Sweden. See also *Bell System Statistical Manual 1920–1964*, p. 504.

Commission (ICC) were largely ignored. Indeed, Congress ensured that the agency would become more deeply mired down by extending its control to buses and trucks. The new technology of trucking was a threat to the railroads. But rather than allowing competition to play itself out in transportation, the government did just what a private cartel would have done: it reached out to bring the competitors under the umbrella of the existing controls. Neither the President, nor Congress, nor the experts wanted to give up on the traditional style of regulation. What was new about this phase of the New Deal was the great extent of government control rather than its basic structure or process.

Some of the other changes in the regulatory state did, however, represent significant innovations in American state crafting. To promote electrification in rural and small-town America, the government made a bold move toward state-owned enterprise by establishing the Tennessee Valley Authority (TVA) in 1933. The TVA's program, which combined public power with planning under a federal authority, covered a region that reached from western North Carolina to the Mississippi River and from southern Kentucky to the northern parts of Mississippi, Alabama, and Georgia. TVA's region included the cities of Nashville, Memphis, and Chattanooga and touched the lives of millions of Americans. Much was riding on the success of the TVA. To many New Dealers, successful regional planning was seen as the next step toward a form of national planning that would be more centralized and effective than the National Recovery Administration's cartel program.[23]

A different approach to the Great Depression and the expansion of the regulatory state was taken with the creation in 1934 of the Securities and Exchange Commission (SEC). The SEC blended elements of professional self-regulation with New Deal government control.[24] The SEC's mission was to bring under federal authority the New York Stock Exchange and other securities markets, as well as the stocks and bonds they traded. The key goal was "transparency." The SEC brought a new level of reliable

---

[23] Thomas K. McCraw, *TVA and the Power Fight, 1933–1939* (Philadelphia, 1971). Erwin C. Hargrove, *Prisoners of Myth: The Leadership of the Tennessee Valley Authority, 1933–1990* (Princeton, 1994).

[24] The role of the accounting profession in the SEC mirrored Hoover's concept of the associative state – a state in which organized interests worked together to promote the public interest. But, as with the National Recovery Administration, the SEC added a powerful element of government authority to the Hoover plan. Thomas K. McCraw, "With Consent of the Governed: SEC's Formative Years," *Journal of Policy Analysis and Management*, 1, 3 (1982), 346–70.

information to this important part of U.S. capitalism. Anyone opposed to transparency in public corporations and their securities should be required to read with care the business and financial history of the late 1920s, an era when small investors were routinely cheated by insiders and corporate reports were frequently designed to deceive rather than to inform stockholders.

In setting out to achieve transparency and make markets work better, the Commission astutely decided to extend its reach by using the accounting profession as part of its regulatory network. This distinctly American blend of public and private authority worked. It enabled the SEC to broaden its control of the nation's complex markets for securities and gave the accounting profession the authority it needed to resist pressures from its corporate clients. In this basic form, the SEC was a great success story for sixty years, an unusual run for any American institution, public or private. The accounting profession, which had already created a solid base in state educational institutions, was strengthened by having a power-sharing role in a crucial federal regulatory system.[25] By extending power and status to professional experts, New Deal state crafting actually decentralized authority.[26] This process would continue long after the 1930s reform drive had waned and would enhance the roles of other professions. Those chosen to be supported would vary, but all would be comfortable sharing with lawyers the advantages of being able to influence America's expanding administrative state.[27]

There was more to come in 1935. Having failed to protect union labor under the National Industrial Recovery Act, Congress and the Administration provided ample protection to the unions and their organized workers under the aegis of a new and potentially powerful National Labor Relations Board (NLRB). The Board and its regional operations were dominated by lawyers who grounded the organization and its procedures "firmly in professional legal practice."[28] Within a few years, the NLRB's presence was felt throughout America, in communities large and

---

[25] Paul J. Miranti, *Accountancy Comes of Age: The Development of an American Profession, 1886–1940* (Chapel Hill, North Carolina, 1990).

[26] This type of centrifugal change was taking place amid a political process that appeared to be entirely centripetal. It was in that regard typical of the American style of politics.

[27] On the political and legal dynamics of the administrative state see, especially, Daniel Ernst, "Morgan and the New Dealers," *Journal of Policy History*, 20, 4 (2008), 447–81.

[28] Christopher L. Tomlins, *The State and the Unions: Labor Relations, Law, and the Organized Labor Movement in America, 1880–1960* (New York, 1985), 154.

small. This included Princeton, Indiana, where the miners and shop workers were organized. Bosses accustomed to having their way on the shop floor discovered that some part of their authority was now held by the shop's union steward. There were bruising encounters over the unions. Bosses like Lou Galambos frequently ended up with more bruises than they thought they deserved.[29]

Once the New Deal had established political momentum and the economy slowly began to recover, a powerful blend of party concerns, interest-group politics, market failures, bureaucratic impulses, and ideas from home and abroad combined in ways that kept the administrative state – including the welfare state – growing through most of the 1930s. Able to follow the lead of the developed economies of Europe, the Roosevelt administration included social security – old-age insurance and a federal-state unemployment and welfare plan – in its second great wave of reforms.[30] The 1935 legislation was carefully crafted after extended expert debate, and this time, the lawyers in government shared influence with professionals trained in liberal, Wisconsin School economics.[31] This diffusion of professional influence would continue and accelerate in the following decade, when economists would acquire a special role in the federal government.

As designed in the 1930s, Social Security was a brilliant achievement in political economy. It was based on payments by both workers and their employers. Initially there were many more workers paying Social Security than were retired and drawing out benefits, so the program was in great shape economically. It also had the political appeal of providing funds that Congress could use for other purposes – including, some critics have said, reelection. Everyone was a winner.

From time to time, this emerging welfare state elided into the promotional state, as was the case with the increases in federal spending for construction. Attempting to increase employment, the administration launched several programs that provided opportunities for private contractors to help the nation solve its economic problems while helping their own firms get ahead. This was consistent with the ideology of the promotional state, which always claimed that all parties were winners in these situations. The New Deal's progress with this form of economic development was slow at first, especially with projects that had to pass

---

[29] Ibid., 103 ff.
[30] The welfare provisions covered needy dependent children and blind and needy citizens.
[31] Edward Berkowitz and Kim McQuaid, *Creating the Welfare State*, 106–46.

the scrutiny of Harold Ickes, the meticulous Secretary of the Interior. Determined to spend every dollar effectively, Ickes dribbled money into post office construction and other programs.

Fortunately for economic recovery, not all of the New Dealers were this parsimonious, so there were many opportunities for a well-connected entrepreneur like Henry Kaiser to build a thriving enterprise on the edges of a growing public sector. As the pace of spending picked up, so did the opportunities in Washington, DC, and around the country to profit from government expansion. Kaiser built a West Coast economic empire in construction, then in primary metals. A promotional-state entrepreneur, he became during the 1940s one of the best known and popular tycoons in America.[32] After the big floods on the Mississippi, Ohio, and Tennessee rivers, there was plenty of work to do for Midwestern contractors who, like Kaiser, benefited from the expansion of the promotional state. Whether it was flood control, the development of public power facilities in Tennessee, or dam construction in the western states, businessmen were able to take advantage of opportunities created by an administration whose rhetoric was increasingly anticapitalist but whose reality had a close fit with the American tradition of the promotional state.

The Keynesian Breakthrough

After four years of vigorous, multifaceted reform efforts, the United States government would never be the same. The federal share of the U.S. gross domestic product had more than tripled. Government at all levels was providing more services to Americans, employed and unemployed, than it ever had before 1933. The regulatory state had been extended and the welfare state at last given a solid national foundation. The promotional state had grown quietly, obscured behind the front-page news about reform.

As late as 1938, however, the economy had yet to recover the vigor it had displayed through most of the 1920s and the years prior to World War I. Even in 1937, when the official figures indicated that unemployment had been cut to about five million, an additional 2.7 million workers were in Federal emergency jobs such as those provided by the Civilian

---

[32] Stephen B. Adams, *Mr. Kaiser Goes to Washington: The Rise of a Government Entrepreneur* (Chapel Hill, North Carolina, 1997).

Conservation Corps and the Works Progress Administration. Then, during the recession that hit in 1938, the economy faltered again. More than three million workers lost their jobs. It would in fact be 1941 before the gross domestic product reached the pre-depression level of 1929 and the population in the meantime had increased by more than 12 million. Viewed from the vantage point of the late 1930s, the New Deal appeared to be a rousing political success but certainly not a breakthrough in economic planning.[33]

The distinguished British economist John Maynard Keynes had tried to help the Roosevelt Administration. Keynes had developed a new and exciting theory that seemed to some professional economists to provide the paradigm and integrated policy prescriptions that the New Deal needed to encourage a nationwide recovery. Keynes called for the government to make up for the gap in investment spending by pumping substantially more money into the economy than it earned from taxes and tariffs. With deficit financing, the government wouldn't draw out of the economy as much as it was distributing through its spending programs.

Keynes' theory, however, made slow progress in penetrating the American economics profession.[34] Academics are almost as conservative about their intellectual domains as they are about office space and parking. Reaching out to FDR, Keynes published an open letter to the President and in 1934 went to tea at the White House. To no avail. Roosevelt was still talking about balancing the budget.[35] Admittedly, Keynes' formulations were not easy to digest. They were especially difficult to digest by those formulating public policy. Neither the Congress not the Executive

---

[33] Michael A. Bernstein, *The Great Depression: Delayed Recovery and Economic Change in America, 1929–1939* (New York, 1987), 184–206.

[34] For a different opinion on this issue, see Mark Blaug, *John Maynard Keynes: Life, Ideas, Legacy* (London, 1990). But one of the interviews printed in the book is with Paul Samuelson, who said, "He shook us up. I have put in the records how much I resisted. No Jesuit fighting against disbelief ever worked harder than I did to keep my classical convictions. . . . I was at the University of Chicago, the inner temple of classical economics. . . . " After World War II, he continued, "in Britain, Keynes had become a revered part of the Establishment. But in America, there was still a long way to go before Keynesianism came to be accepted in academic circles" (56, 60).

[35] Arthur M. Schlesinger, Jr., *The Politics of Upheaval* (Cambridge, 1960), 236–37, 401–05, 408, 506, 656, describes the links between Keynes and the administration. The authoritative account is by Ellis W. Hawley, *The New Deal and the Problem of Monopoly: A Study in Economic Ambivalence* (Princeton, 1966). See also Robert Skidelsky, *John Maynard Keynes, 1883–1946* (London, 2003), 490, 506–10, 546.

Branch was well staffed with advisors open to the British economist's innovative ideas.[36]

This sort of thinking was alien to the lawyers who controlled Congressional budgets and to FDR, who had run for office on the promise of balancing the budget. Indeed, one of the early New Deal measures had been an effort to pay off on that promise. Events, however, had overwhelmed tradition, and the New Deal deficit had increased between 1933 and 1936.[37]

Keynes, however, was proposing a much larger deficit, purposefully created. Could a nation actually spend its way out of a depression? Many Americans were skeptical about that idea. Keynes' prescriptions had an uphill fight at a time when common sense told you that neither individuals nor the government could increase prosperity by going further into debt. Indeed, the government was just then creating new agencies and policies to help individuals who were already deeply in debt and in very serious trouble.

At that time, academic economists, along with businessmen, had been largely discredited by the economic collapse. There were exceptions like Tugwell and a few other New Dealers. But the profession's input during the early stages of the crisis had been dismal. Now Keynes was calling on the administration to do something that no American government had ever done. His ideas were explained in a book that hardly anyone in Washington could read and understand.[38] Little wonder that he couldn't convince FDR to change the administration's policies. Keynes's stunning new ideas about the relationships between consumption, investment expenditures, gross national product, and employment thus made slow headway in Washington, DC. It is thus not surprising that the administration allowed the first payments into Social Security (1937) to chop into consumer spending and help send the economy back into a sharp recession in 1938.

---

[36] Ibid.

[37] The increase was from $2.6 billion to $4.4 billion, which seems trivial today. In the 1930s, these numbers were impressive to Americans, but not, as noted, to Keynes.

[38] Keynes' *The General Theory of Employment, Interest and Money* was published in 1936, but the author had been setting forth his central ideas since the early 1930s. D. E. Moggridge, *Keynes* (Toronto, 1993), 84–121. A contemporary, R. F. Harrod, *The Life of John Maynard Keynes* (New York, 1963), 432–86, devotes more attention to Keynes' varied political and intellectual activities during the 1930s. In advancing his ideas on *Monetary Reform* (New York, 1924), 216, Keynes had noted wryly, "One cannot be quite certain that some Senator might not read and understand this book."

That experience, however, inspired some quick rethinking on the part of the Administration and Congress. Perhaps fiscal policy – the government's expenditures, taxes, and debts – could indeed have the impact on the national economy that Keynes's general theory indicated. Given the dismal experiences to date with economic planning, it was worth a chance. Inspired to change course, the Administration and Congress were able to promote a quick recovery from the 1937–1938 downturn. By 1939 and the beginning of new wars in Europe and Asia, unemployment was down to 16 percent and the economy was almost back to its 1929 level.[39] Soon, wartime purchasing and heavy deficit spending in America sparked a complete recovery that inspired a conversion experience among American economists. They quickly made Keynesian economics America's "conventional wisdom" for professionals.

So What Kind of Deal Did Americans Get?

The answer is, of course, that different Americans got different deals in the 1930s. For millions, the major positive effect was increased economic security. Those who were employed outside of agriculture now had the protection provided by Social Security, as did those who were retiring or unable to work. For many who couldn't find work, there were temporary government jobs. Opponents of the New Deal made bad jokes about those public jobs. The WPA (the Works Progress Agency), they said, actually stood for "We Poke Along." But given the fact that the rate of suicide and serious illness went up with the unemployment figures, this was not a laughing matter. Nor was the increased support for unions under the New Deal. The American Federation of Labor (AFL) and the Congress of Industrial Organizations (CIO) created an important element of job security for millions of workers, women as well as men. Even companies that were able to resist unionization were forced to adopt policies that favored their workers.[40] Farms, homes, and bank accounts were protected in new ways. Millions of farmers who owned their land now had a sturdy government floor under the prices for their crops. If they lived in the Tennessee Valley, they could enjoy the wonders of electricity at prices they could afford.

---

[39] The unemployment figure is for the civilian private nonfarm labor force.
[40] Sanford M. Jacoby, *Modern Manors: Welfare Capitalism since the New Deal* (Princeton, 1997), especially 35–56.

Similar effects were felt in the nation's industrial cities, where both the regulatory and the welfare states had decisive impacts. Middle- and upper-class Americans could now invest their savings with greater certainty. For white working-class Americans in the cities, the New Deal's minimum wages and regulation of hours were welcome, as were the opportunities to join a CIO or AFL union.[41] New Deal programs encouraged homeownership and inspired those city and state leaders who were working to substitute urban planning for the traditional style of growth attuned to market forces and business interests.

The New Deal did less to encourage innovation and efficiency, but here too there were some important and largely unanticipated payoffs. The biggest payoff came in agriculture, following the stabilization of commodity production and prices. Doing better in a public cartel plan that increased and stabilized their incomes, many farmers began to invest in labor-saving equipment and other innovations. They bought tractors and fertilizer. They began to pay more attention to the improvements they had long shunned as "book farming." In the late 1930s, America's massive, subsidized system for agricultural innovation began at last to yield significant positive results for farmers and the rest of the nation. As we saw in Chapter 3, this system included the research conducted by the Department of Agriculture, the A & M colleges and universities in states like South Dakota, the extension service, and the farm interest groups. Farm productivity began to creep upward as the United States edged into what would later be recognized as an agricultural revolution, a green revolution, the counterpart of the industrial revolutions that had already reshaped the American economy.[42]

There is a lesson in political economy hidden in this agrarian history: it took a half century of patient institution building to create the amalgam of state, federal, nonprofit, and for-profit interests that finally began to yield revolutionary advances in productivity in the late 1930s. Patience is not generally recognized as a common American virtue. Had farmers not been overrepresented in state and federal politics, had the myth of agrarian goodness been less widely revered, had the tragedy of the Great Depression not taken place, the United States might well have abandoned

---

[41] Compare B. Lizabeth Cohen, *Making a New Deal: Industrial Workers in Chicago, 1919–1939* (New York, 1992) with Christopher L. Tomlins, *The State and the Unions*.
[42] Sally H. Clarke, *Regulation and the Revolution in United States Farm Productivity* (New York, 1994).

the public components of this elaborate agrarian network in mid-course. As it was, America emerged from the depression with the most productive agricultural system in the world, a source of envy in communist nations, and a model for many nations seeking to emerge from poverty.

The United States was not a model, however, in race or gender relations. For most African Americans, the New Deal was a mixed blessing. Many were helped by the new welfare system and by minimum wages. Some could now join labor unions and have strong national organizations bargain for their wages, hours, and fringe benefits. But the agricultural programs controlled in the South by white landowners drove many black sharecroppers off the land. Alternative jobs were scarce in the South, and African Americans headed in growing numbers to northern and western cities. So too did many white farmers driven out of agrarian life by drought and depression.

Following the long trek to cities like Detroit and Chicago, blacks found life in the urban ghettos hard and opportunities for advancement few. For many, the most disappointing aspect of the urban politics of the 1930s was the failure of city governments to provide the educational resources their children needed to escape from the slums. The door to the middle class was through the schoolroom, as W. E. B. DuBois had discovered. But too few blacks were going through that door. Too few were making it onto the professional paths that would lead to roles that would make full use of their talents. The entire society thus paid a price for America's urban ghettos.

America also paid a price for the setbacks the women's movement for equality suffered during the depression. Married women benefited from the new welfare measures and from the protection now provided to farms and homes, but they had a rough time in the workforce during the 1930s. Married women were routinely fired in government and business so that jobs could be given to men. Women working in households as maids or cooks – so-called domestic services – were not protected by wages and hours legislation. Some women were able to organize effectively under the protection of the National Labor Relations Board, but few office workers or teachers were able to take advantage of the country's growing labor movement. These women were lucky if they kept their jobs. The number of women graduating from high schools, colleges, and universities continued to increase in the 1930s, but the percentage of women getting into professional jobs was actually lower at the end of the decade than it had been at the end of World War I. Having the vote didn't seem to matter in terms of opportunities for advancement. All in all, it was a dismal decade for the women's movement.

It was as well a difficult decade for immigrants and their families. To those with few skills and little education, the depression was a disaster. The New Deal relief and work programs helped, but the United States was no longer the land of great opportunities. They voted with their feet. From 1932 through 1935, more of them returned to their homelands than came to America.[43] Prejudice still closed off many jobs and educational opportunities to immigrants, especially if they were Jews. Anti-Semitism was a powerful force in American society in government, business, and universities – in cities, small towns, and the countryside. Universities were no different than other American institutions in this regard, and firms – in particular, those in industries such as chemicals and pharmaceuticals – almost never hired Jews in any capacity. Immigrants who had learned a craft and found good jobs in industry could benefit from unionization in either the AFL or the CIO, but political rhetoric aside, the New Deal had not done much to tip the balance of income and wealth in their direction. Those near the top of the heap, in the top 1 percent of the population, had lost some ground on income, but they had actually gained ground on wealth – hardly the stuff of an economic revolution.[44]

What was most revolutionary about the New Deal would not become apparent for many years to come. Looking back today, we can see that once recovery took place, the total mix of New Deal programs and policies – a more active administrative state – made it possible for the United States economy to continue growing without experiencing another great depression. Looking backward from 1929, we can see that just about every twenty years during the previous hundred years, America had slumped into a depression deeper than a normal, cyclical downturn. These were major, extended depressions – so damaging that Marxists thought they were an intrinsic aspect of capitalism and would eventually lead to its collapse. But in the decades since the 1930s, this has no longer happened, and a good deal of the credit for that has to be given to the New Deal innovations in state crafting.

[43] The number arriving exceeded the number going home from 1936 to 1939, but even the beginning of the war in Europe in 1939 only brought a net immigration of slightly more than 56,000.

[44] The share of income for the top 1 percent of Americans had declined from 12.14 to 11.80 percent between 1933 and 1939. Their share of household wealth had increased from 36.4 to 39.8 percent during the same years.

The View from Princeton, Indiana

Out in the heartland, in Indiana, people in the late 1930s were not concerned with historical turning points. Their concerns were more immediate and personal. Rocked by unemployment and bank failures, a state that had been solidly Republican in the 1920s had voted for FDR in 1932 and given the president and the New Deal an impressive victory in 1936. By 1940, however, Hoosiers had grown skeptical of the deal they were getting, and the state drifted back into the Republican fold.

That was pleasing to Lou Galambos, who had made a success of his job managing the Highway Machine Shop. The coal mine and the shop were humming with business as wartime orders began to mount at the end of the 1930s. Never having belonged to a union or been on relief, Lou identified with his employers and with the Americans one historian called the "Go-Getters."[45] Like most Americans of that ilk, he was instinctively suspicious of welfare, bitterly opposed to organized labor, and convinced that neither government agencies nor churches could save America's soul or its economy. His wife, Ruth, never disagreed with him (in public, at least), and she and his children knew that the dinner table was a place for monologues, not debates. Events in Lou's life and the nation's experiences in the next decade would deepen his conservatism and provide even better opportunities for him to exercise his entrepreneurial bent.

[45] Daniel Boorstin coined this expression in his magisterial history of the United States.

8

Fighting On God's Side

World War II changed America and the rest of the world in ways impossible to predict in the late 1930s.[1] The war transformed the country's international relations, drew three new professional elites into the top tiers of the nation's power structure, and opened the door to an "American Century" that was more frightening and more rewarding than anything the country had experienced since the Civil War.[2] None of these changes could be anticipated in 1939, when the war began in Europe. Then, the United States was turned inward, still struggling with the problems of the depression, still trying to find the government policies that would restore prosperity. Most Americans wanted nothing to do with another European war. It was better, they thought, to stay safe, isolated in Fortress America from the European struggles.

By September, 1941, however, in the big northeastern cities like Boston and New York, anxious eyes looked toward Europe where the powerful Nazi war machine had occupied Belgium, the Netherlands, and most of France. After invading Denmark and Norway, Hitler's forces had swept into the Soviet Union, conquering most of the Ukraine and threatening Moscow. Germany's new ally, Japan, was continuing its conquest of China and Indochina, a Far Eastern war that was starting to cause

---

[1] A brief guide to the war is provided by Michael J. Lyons, *World War II: A Short History* (Upper Saddle River, NJ, 2009).

[2] Donald W. White, *The American Century*, 8–12, carefully describes the origin of the expression. Henry Luce, who published *Life* magazine, popularized the expression in a 1941 editorial that characterized the twentieth century as one in which the United States was the dominant power (much as Britain had been the dominant power of the nineteenth century),

nervous tremors in the cities along America's Pacific coast. Even to the east of the Rocky Mountains and through Midwestern farm country, in little towns like Princeton and Fostoria, there was now some interest in wars that were threatening, although still distant. In Washington, DC, in the White House and the State Department, there was deep, growing concern about an international struggle that might any moment involve the United States.[3]

Unlike Woodrow Wilson, President Franklin D. Roosevelt sought professional advice as he charted America's course in these difficult times. FDR didn't always take the advice he solicited. But he listened. At the beginning of his first administration in 1933, he had rejected internationalism, embraced an exclusively domestic response to the Great Depression, and punched a hole in the efforts to achieve monetary stabilization at the London Economic Conference. This last decision was consistent with the administration's cartel policies, which would only work if America was relatively isolated, economically, from its former allies and other nations. By 1940, however, neither FDR nor his closest advisors in the State and War Departments thought that a policy of isolation would protect American security while war raged in Europe and Asia.

Secretary of State Cordell Hull – another lawyer in government – had labored through the 1930s to consolidate the U.S. position in the Western Hemisphere on new terms.[4] His diplomacy, which took him through a seemingly endless series of Pan-American conferences, was dedicated to giving substance to the country's new "Good Neighbor Policy."[5] This innovation suggested that up to that point, the United States had been a Bad Neighbor, and in many regards that was true. The long heritage of military interventions and dollar diplomacy could not be overcome with a proclamation. But the new policy was important because it brought America's commercial empire in the Western Hemisphere into closer alignment with the country's basic democratic values – as well as its need to cultivate more allies close to home in the late 1930s.[6] Hull

---

[3] For an early and detailed account, see W. L. Langer and S. E. Gleason, *The Challenge to Isolation, 1937–1940* (New York, 1952), and *The Undeclared War* (New York, 1953). For a more recent perspective on the same events, see Jean E. Smith, *FDR* (New York, 2007).

[4] Hull, who was from Tennessee, had received his law degree from Cumberland University in 1891.

[5] Harold B. Hinton, *Cordell Hull: A Biography* (Garden City, 1942), 240–348, provides a friendly description of Hull's role in the new policy.

[6] Frederick B. Pike, *FDR's Good Neighbor Policy: Sixty Years of Generally Gentle Chaos* (Austin, 1995).

counseled aggressive preparation for war against the Axis powers, as did Henry Stimson, who was Secretary of War as of 1940.[7]

Stimson, Hull, and Roosevelt all turned to General George Catlett Marshall for guidance in mobilization and in military strategy. Marshall was one of a new breed of professional military officers. A graduate of the Virginia Military Institute, Marshall was an expert in planning and directing military operations, a role he had played to perfection during World War I. He broadened his experience in the 1920s, taught for a time at the Army War College, and published an influential study of *Infantry in Battle*. Although Marshall had proven himself adept at directing an offensive in World War I, his great skill was as a strategist, top-level executive, and coordinator. His forte was the organizational rather than the heroic side of combat. He was especially skillful at working along the boundary between the nation's military and political leaders. He was the counterpart in military life of the president or chief operating officer of a modern multinational firm, an executive who advised on policy and guided operations. In 1939, FDR appointed him Army Chief of Staff.[8]

Reinforced in his determination to support the Allies and the Soviet Union, Roosevelt skillfully guided the country toward war.[9] Now there was no chance to create a stalemate in either Europe or Asia. Germany and Japan were too strong, too well positioned, and much too ambitious to consider a stalemate. Nevertheless, the President and his advisors had to move ahead slowly, with Machiavellian guile, because as late as 1941, many Americans still doubted that the nation's security was at stake. Roosevelt, Hull, Stimson, and Marshall knew the doubters were wrong.[10] With a superbly subtle touch, they led the country and its many reluctant citizens toward a war that would cost more American lives than all of its previous foreign wars combined. The Japanese surprise attack on Pearl Harbor on December 7, 1941, made consideration of the price of war

[7] Henry Lewis Stimson, also a lawyer, was an anomaly in the New Deal administration: a life-long, blue-blooded Republican, he had served as Secretary of War under President William Howard Taft, Governor-General of the Philippines under President Calvin Coolidge, and Secretary of State under President Herbert Hoover.

[8] Forrest C. Pogue, *George C. Marshall: Education of a General, 1880–1939* (New York, 1963); and *George C. Marshall: Ordeal and Hope, 1939–1942* (New York, 1966).

[9] The Administration and Congress collaborated in this ongoing effort, from the 1939 amendment of the neutrality laws, through the increased aid to Britain and the Soviet Union, to the Lend-Lease Act, and the Atlantic Charter in 1941.

[10] The Neutrality Acts of 1935 and 1937 reflected the attitudes of those voters and their representatives who thought the international situation in the mid-1930s was comparable to the situation that had existed in 1914–1917. Unfortunately, it was not.

superfluous. The drums of war quickly drowned out debate as America set out to fight for the first time on two oceans and several continents.

Mobilizing for the War

The contrast between mobilization for World War II and World War I could not have been more complete. The New Deal had expanded the administrative state, providing a more formidable bureaucratic and informational base for mobilization. By 1941, the nation could muster significantly greater levels of knowledge and expertise than had been the case in 1917.[11] The administration had started the process of bringing American advanced science and technology to bear in 1940 by appointing Dr. Vannevar Bush to chair the National Defense Research Committee (later the Office of Scientific Research and Development).[12] This was an abrupt change of course for the New Deal. During the depression, the only top member of the administration with any background in modern science was Secretary of Agriculture Henry Wallace, who had studied crop genetics in school.

By contrast, Bush, president of the Carnegie Institution of Washington and a former professor and dean at MIT, was an accomplished scientist and science administrator. He had worked in Washington during the 1917–1918 mobilization and fully understood what had to be done in the 1940s. Indeed, he had proposed the creation of the National Defense Research Committee and was ready to staff and organize the operation quickly. The level of expertise involved was in part a measure of Bush's vigorous leadership and also an indicator of the progress American science and engineering had made by the early 1940s. The huge public investments of the interwar period in American higher education and professional training now paid off richly. So too did the successful, ongoing efforts of American corporations to use internal resources in science and advanced engineering to sustain innovation.[13]

---

[11] Alfred D. Chandler, Jr., and Louis Galambos, "The Development of Large-Scale Economic Organizations in Modern America," *Journal of Economic History*, 30, 1 (March 1970), 201–17.

[12] Dr. Bush was not related to President George H. W. Bush.

[13] See, for instance, the trends charted in Arnold Thackray, Jeffrey L. Sturchio, P. Thomas Carroll, and Robert Bud, *Chemistry in America, 1876–1976: Historical Indicators* (Dordrecht, 1985). Daniel J. Kevles, *The Physicists: The History of a Scientific Community in Modern America* (New York, 1978).

Typical of the talented professionals Bush mustered was Dr. Frank B. Jewett, the distinguished physicist who had recently headed the Bell Telephone Laboratories.[14] In addition to Jewett, Bush turned for help to Dr. James B. Conant, one of the nation's leading chemists and president of Harvard University since 1933. Joining their effort was Ernest O. Lawrence, the one-time South Dakota student still in the afterglow of his 1939 Nobel Prize – the first to be awarded to a U.S. scientist at a state institution.[15] Lawrence and his scientific colleagues set out to use their knowledge of physics to develop weapons. They would succeed beyond anyone's expectations – and that too would change the course of history in a decisive way.

While Bush was priming his new organization, Walter S. Knudsen of General Motors was working on the mobilization of industry. In World War I, President Wilson had, after some floundering, turned over industry to a Wall Street investor, Bernard Baruch.[16] Now the administration wisely looked to the leader of the country's largest multinational production firm and paired him with a trusted union leader, Sidney Hillman. The hope was to convert industry to wartime output quickly, without precipitating fights between labor and management.

Mass-production of standardized goods was one of the crucial drivers of the American economy throughout the second industrial revolution, and General Motors was one of the leaders in developing the multidivisional (M-form) organization that played a crucial role in that process.[17] Like R&D, organizational innovation along these lines yielded competitive advantages. By breaking the corporation into divisions, the M-form business decentralized authority and helped large U.S. firms balance the need to remain flexible and innovative with the ability to achieve economies of scale in production and distribution. Knudsen provided the mobilizers with planning strategies and tactics that had been honed in the difficult years of the Great Depression. Central to the new approach

---

[14] When he was appointed, Jewett was serving as president of the National Academy of Sciences.

[15] Herbert Childs, *An American Genius*, 294–307.

[16] Baruch was a skillful negotiator. He served the country well in what was, in fact, a virtually untenable position in which he had neither the staff support nor the information needed to coordinate and speed up the mobilization process. Robert D. Cuff, *The War Industries Board: Business-Government Relations During World War I* (Baltimore, 1973).

[17] Alfred D. Chandler, Jr. was the pioneer in analyzing this development; see *Strategy and Structure: Chapters in the History of the Industrial Enterprise* (Cambridge, 1962).

were techniques developed at General Motors and DuPont to forecast needs and allocate resources. As of 1942, these tools were the primary means of controlling the nation's enormous industrial system.[18]

Even with effective leadership, great resources, and the pressure of a national emergency, it was 1943 before the full effects of U.S. economic mobilization were felt in the war. By then, Donald M. Nelson, an expert in mass-distribution, was leading this vital program.[19] Using price controls to prevent inflation and rationing to ensure that the resources went where they were most needed, the United States had a controlled economy under a bureaucratic hierarchy for the first time in its history. Although it took three years to complete this conversion, the governmental process was neither exceptionally wasteful nor inefficient. Given America's antibureaucratic culture and the size and complexity of the world's largest industrial economy, the transition was, I believe, creative and successful – a tribute to the experience and expertise the United States could now bring to bear.

By 1943, the surging industrial economy was pressing hard on the available supplies of labor. Strapped for skilled and unskilled workers when well over two million men were in uniform, companies began to lure mothers with young children into the workforce by offering childcare. This was a stunning innovation, and even more stunning was the fact that it worked so well. By 1944, large numbers of women with families were getting their first experience in factory production. Many of them looked forward to staying in the workforce after the war. African Americans and first- and second-generation immigrants also benefited from the sharply increased demand for labor. Wartime production helped blacks pull out of the agricultural South and get experience in manufacturing throughout the country, but especially along the eastern seaboard and in the Midwest.

These were triumphant years for Detroit, for Cleveland, Boston, Chicago, Baltimore, St. Louis, Los Angeles, and Toledo – production centers that benefited greatly from wartime contracts. There was plenty of work for anyone with metalworking skills, and Lazlo Galambos, as well as his sons, prospered. Then, in 1943, Lazlo was driving home after a

---

[18] Alfred D. Chandler, Jr., and Louis Galambos, "The Development of Large-Scale Economic Organizations in Modern America." See also R. Elberton Smith, *The Army and Economic Mobilization* (Washington, DC, 1959), especially 567–70.

[19] Nelson was a chemical engineer who had graduated from the University of Missouri. He spent thirty years working in Sears, Roebuck. An executive vice-president before going to Washington, DC, during the war, Nelson brought to the WPB his expertise in purchasing, allocating, and distributing goods.

busy day in the Toledo foundry when he died suddenly of a heart attack. While the family drew together for the wake, the sons all had to get back to their jobs quickly.

In the war effort, all cities and all regions were equal, of course, but some were more equal than others: the big gainers were the Northeast and Middle Atlantic regions.[20] With the government paying the way, about half of America's manufacturing facilities were government-owned but most were privately employed by companies that leased the facilities. This distinctly American style of public-private organization was a central aspect of World War II mobilization.

Mobilization reached all the way down from the Washington, DC, headquarters into southern Indiana, where parts for American tanks were subcontracted to small entrepreneurs. One of them was Lou Galambos, who set up a tiny production unit in the family garage. Using labor from the Highway Machine Shop in the evenings, he made shifter forks for American tanks. The American tanks were not as good as those of Germany, but so far as I know, this was not because they couldn't shift gears. Redesigned after their encounters with German forces in Africa, American tanks played important roles in the combat in Europe and Asia.

Americans at War

On both of those fronts, the American military's introduction to war didn't start smoothly. War puts unique pressures on a society's institutions and individuals. The pressure finds the weak spots, including the weak leaders. America was fortunate in 1942 and 1943 to have a large enough pool of professional military leaders to draw on as the process of sifting out began.

Early on, there were serious problems of coordination in the Pacific. There, the American military commanders included General Douglas MacArthur, a brilliant graduate of West Point with a thorny personality. MacArthur was paired with Admiral Chester W. Nimitz, a graduate of the Naval Academy who matched MacArthur in determination but not in style or eloquence. Not too surprisingly, these leaders came up with different strategies for blunting the Japanese advance. MacArthur's plan favored a campaign aimed at quickly putting the Army back in the Philippines. The Navy's proposal would focus American forces on a

---

[20] Carol E. Heim, "Structural Changes: Regional and Urban," Stanley L. Engerman and Robert E. Gallman, eds., *The Cambridge Economic History*, 3, 129.

naval and marine attack through the islands of the central Pacific.[21] The gap between these two plans had to be closed by General Marshall, who backed the Nimitz strategy and then had to struggle to keep the military's primary focus on Germany. The big decisions often came down to what appeared to be minor requests for the men, machines, munitions, and fuel that would keep the war machine moving. All were in tragically short supply in 1942 and 1943.

Marshall persisted, dribbling out resources to his outspoken commanders while maintaining America's emphasis on Europe. He could do nothing to resist British pressure to move first into North Africa. That decision was reached primarily as a result of Churchill's clever bullying. To this point in the war, the British Prime Minister had done nothing to upset the opinion that he was an inspiring leader and a miserable strategist.[22] He would reinforce that conclusion by insisting that the Allies attack Germany through the "soft underbelly of Europe," but fortunately he would lose that debate to FDR, Marshall, and his commanders.

While preparing for the African campaign, the Allies were suffering severe losses in the Pacific. At first, the Japanese forces proceeded with very little effective opposition. Having seized the Philippines, Japan pressed forward into Southeast Asia, weakened the British fleet, and occupied Singapore and Hong Kong. MacArthur's forces had fallen back and were attempting to consolidate their positions in New Guinea, Australia, and Hawaii. At sea, Nimitz's naval and air forces stymied the Japanese advance in the Battle of Midway (1942), Japan's first major defeat. By that time, however, Japan's empire already stretched from Burma to northern New Guinea, from the western Aleutian Islands to Korea and through southern China. The outlook in the Pacific was grim in 1942, as the Allies anticipated that only a slow, difficult island-by-island advance would defeat Japan.

In North Africa, American forces completed a successful landing but then suffered a stunning defeat. General Dwight D. Eisenhower, whom Marshall had pushed ahead of other senior officers, was in command, and his study of the defeat at Kassarine Pass produced some disturbing conclusions about the Army's leaders. Starting at the top, he replaced the

---

[21] On retreating from the Philippines in 1942, General MacArthur had left his mark on the press and military history by proclaiming as he splashed through the surf off Bataan Peninsula, "I shall return."

[22] Churchill's reputation in military planning was solidly grounded in the British experience during World War I in the disastrous Gallipoli campaign.

commander whose II Corps had been routed by the German attack.[23] Ike turned to an old friend, General George S. Patton. Patton, Ike knew, would provide the kind of decisive professional leadership the American forces needed to be successful against the German army. Improvements in American equipment, including the tanks, followed, and the Allied forces completed the conquest of North Africa in 1943.

Following the British strategy, the Allies initially attacked Europe through the Mediterranean. They moved into Sicily and then into a difficult and deadly Italian campaign fought over mountains and valleys that gave little advantage to their superior forces and mobility. As an introduction to terrain similar to what the British had said was the "soft underbelly of Europe," the Italian campaign reinforced Eisenhower's and Marshall's conviction that it was necessary to launch a cross-channel invasion of France as soon as possible.

By D-Day in 1944, America's military forces were hardened by combat and their leaders tested against a German army that was, man for man, the best in Europe. General Eisenhower, in command of an enormous Allied force of nearly three million men, guided this difficult operation to a successful conclusion, and his battle commanders, especially British General Bernard Montgomery and Americans George C. Patton and Omar N. Bradley, drove the German forces out of France by the fall of 1944. With the Soviet Union defeating the bulk of the German Army in the East, the Allies were able to complete their thrust into the Ruhr Valley and then to the Elbe River by April. Germany surrendered, unconditionally, on May 7, 1945.

In the Pacific, the Allies won a series of naval battles in 1943 and 1944 that left the Japanese forces isolated and fighting a holding action. Hold they did, at a great price in American and British lives. Admiral Nimitz's island-hopping strategy was successful, however, and in the fall of 1944, General MacArthur was at last able to make good on his promise to return to the Philippines. As the bombing campaign against Japan's homeland grew more intense, the Allies looked forward to a complete victory in the following year. Even this late in the war, however, the intensity of the resistance surprised the Allied commanders. Suicide bombing missions took a heavy toll on the U.S. Navy, and the battle for Okinawa was one of the deadliest in the Pacific War.

[23] Dwight David Eisenhower, *Crusade in Europe* (New York, 1948). Alfred D. Chandler, Jr. et al., *The Papers of Dwight David Eisenhower, The War Years* (Baltimore, 1970), II, 882, 955, 972–73, 981, 984–85, 990–93, 1020.

This was the situation in August of 1945, when the United States used a new weapon, an atomic bomb, against the cities of Hiroshima and Nagasaki. The bombs wiped out the entire centers of both urban areas, with a terrible loss of civilian and military lives. Japan's surrender followed in a matter of days. World War II was over, and the victory elevated the nation's military and scientific professionals to new and more important positions in American society and political life. Their leaders would play important roles in shaping America's position in the postwar world.

The Atomic Age

My perspective on these wartime events was filtered through the values of a small, Midwestern town. I was only ten years old when America entered the war, but I quickly became fascinated with the victories and defeats in Europe and the Pacific. My obsession was fed by the National Geographic Society, which provided the maps I hung on the bedroom wall. I used pins to mark the advances and retreats. At school, we all helped collect scrap metal and paper to support the troops.

Coming of age during the war, I had a well-nourished hatred of the Japanese and Nazi Germany. I don't believe I had ever met anyone from Japan, any real Japanese Americans, or any actual German people. I knew plenty of German Americans, but they were mostly my own aunts and I didn't relate them in any way to Hitler's Nazi Germany. During the war, my education in international affairs included reports of the Death March on Bataan, brutal Japanese attacks on Chinese cities like Nanjing, and the Nazi Holocaust. Newsreels, newspaper headlines, and comic books fed my new interests. By 1945, I was convinced that the Japanese and Germans were uniquely cruel and beastly. I was not alone in these feelings, and I can't remember a single word said against the use of atomic bombs to end the war. That doesn't justify what happened, but it needs to be part of the history of why it happened.

Also part of that history should be the immediate events prior to the use of the new atomic weapons. Given the importance of this subject, those events are worth a brief digression. To understand the decision to bomb the cities, you need to look to the island campaigns and the losses America suffered in those bitter battles. It was realistic to assume that the conquest of Japan would not have been any different. Victory in the Pacific was obtained at great cost to America and its allies, but those losses were also not questioned. No price seemed too great for a generation of

Americans longing for victory over Japan. From the perspective of 1945, neither morality nor national security would have been served by not using the atomic bomb and invading Japan.

Since then, heated debates have bubbled up from year to year about the development and first use of those weapons of mass destruction. The most telling critique is, I think, the charge that only one bomb had to be dropped and that it could have been demonstrated without destroying a city like Hiroshima.[24] This kind of counterfactual is appealing (and has been to me in the past), but the argument only carries the day if you strip out of the historical context the possibilities for error. After the fact, we know that the bomb was delivered correctly, that it worked, and that the Japanese were persuaded after the second attack to surrender. But none of this was known before the decisions were made and the bombs dropped. Given those imponderables, it is hard for me to imagine America's leaders making any other decisions.[25]

Most recently, these issues have been revisited in an even broader context, one in which the fundamental morality of the entire war against the Axis powers has been questioned. It is impossible to claim, this line of reasoning goes, that we were "on God's side." We were, in fact, on the side of the Soviet communists who were themselves responsible for the deaths of millions of their own people in their effort to perfect and stay in control of an authoritarian society. Nor were the Allies beyond reproach for their cruel behavior during the war. Hitler, it is said, was driven to make war by Winston Churchill's unwillingness to emulate Neville Chamberlain and yield to Nazi demands.[26]

This way of looking at the past involves an elaborate, although largely unexplored, counterfactual, as do all analyses that say "it could have been different." So perhaps we can explore the problem with a slightly different counterfactual. Let's discuss briefly what would have happened if Germany, instead of the United States, had developed atomic weapons. Would the world have been a better place? Germany had the scientific

---

[24] For an excellent study of the issues and the literature, see Michael J. Hogan, ed., *Hiroshima in History and Memory* (New York, 1996).

[25] For a good introduction to a recent controversy over the bomb, go to http://www.afa .org/media/enolagay/chrono.asp for information on the Smithsonian imbroglio of the 1990s.

[26] Munich became a symbol for the futility of attempting to compromise with Adolf Hitler and prevent further aggression through appeasement. British Prime Minister Neville Chamberlain flew to Munich in September 1938 to sign a peace pact that condoned Germany's annexation of the Sudeten region of Czechoslovakia.

resources to develop an atomic weapon and was leading the world in rocket science and engineering. Germany would quickly have turned London and other major British cities to radioactive cinders. No moral concerns there! The massed Soviet forces would have been destroyed and Moscow bombed out of the war. Imagine then a Europe completely controlled by Nazi Germany, with the Holocaust deepened and broadened as the Nazis found new populations to destroy. Meanwhile Germany would be developing intercontinental rockets that could reach the United States. Would this have been a better, more moral social order? I find it difficult to understand how anyone who has thought seriously about the twentieth century could answer "yes" to that question. What prevented that terrible outcome was the failure of German political and military leadership. Japan was no threat to develop atomic weapons. The country lacked the science and resource base needed to explore the ideas, freely available to all physicists, on which the new weapons were based. Germany had the scientists and resources to build an atomic bomb, but Hitler drove off a generation of brilliant Jewish scientists and misused the remaining scientists and advisors who might have countered his bad judgment. Paradoxically, they could have given him the power to win the war.

In the United States, a vigorous, productive, broad-based scientific community was able to work with the government and the military leadership to shape public policy and concentrate enormous resources on one history-making task – the Manhattan Project. The nation's leading research universities came into play, providing personnel and in some cases their organizational base for research, as did the University of California at Berkeley and Cal Tech. Science managers, science brokers, technicians, administrators, and staff contributed to that massive project.

Leading one wing of this unique research program was Ernest O. Lawrence, the inventor of the cyclotron.[27] In addition to Lawrence, Lyman Briggs, the one-time agricultural scientist, popped back into our history as head of the government's Uranium Committee.[28] Too slow-moving for the scientists, Briggs lost his control of the vital fuel for the atomic bomb, and Lawrence, Oppenheimer, and Teller became the scientific dynamos of the U.S. program.[29] There were many possibilities for mistakes, and some of the research efforts ran down blind alleys. But

---

[27] Lawrence signed on, verbally, for the next several years of his life. Gregg Herken, *Brotherhood of the Bomb*, 41

[28] On Briggs see Chapter 3 of this volume.

[29] Ibid., 32ff.

by 1945, the U.S. teams were able to test one of the weapons – success-fully – in the Arizona desert. The results were at the same time exciting and terrifying. There had never been a weapon that could destroy not just a small target, but everything surrounding it for several square miles. Now there was. The age of total war had suddenly acquired an entirely new dimension as a result of an entirely new scientific-military-political network.

The atom bomb was not the only contribution modern science made to Allied victory. Intricate links were developed between the military and scientists through the country's leading research universities. The Massachusetts Institute of Technology, which had already contributed Vannevar Bush to the war effort, organized a full-bore effort that led, among other things, to the development and improvement of radar. At Johns Hopkins, a new organization – the Applied Physics Lab – became a nonprofit wing of the military and produced the proximity fuse, an inno-vation that greatly increased the effectiveness of antiaircraft fire. Sonar, too, depended on the application of scientific knowledge, as did many other innovations that came out of California, particularly at Cal Tech. Atop this vast network of institutions and creative individuals was Bush's Office of Scientific Research and Development, a science and technology broker operating in the upper reaches of America's government. By the end of the war, the scientists had joined the military as leaders in what would later be called the "power elite."[30]

War's End in Washington, DC

As the war drew to a close, the American economy was pouring out goods and services at an almost unbelievable rate. To the man or woman on the street, to many executives in U.S. companies, and to the some of the nation's political leaders, the economic impact of the war on America didn't make much sense. As late as 1938, millions had been unemployed and the gross domestic product (GDP) was still very low, hovering around $86 billion.[31] Then, as war orders from overseas poured in, the economy started to recover. That made sense. But after the United States entered the war, the recovery continued. The government and U.S. industry produced thousands of planes, tanks, and ships. The country turned out billions of shells and drew millions of men and women into the armed services. As

---

[30] C. Wright Mills, *The Power Elite* (New York, 1959).
[31] Compare this figure with the $103.7 billion GDP of 1929.

the war progressed, many of America's new planes were shot down, the tanks were destroyed, and the ships sunk. But still, the national economy prospered. By 1945, the GDP was $223 billion and there was virtually no unemployment. It was almost as if the New Deal in the 1930s could have rearmed the nation, dumped all of the war material in the ocean, and America would have quickly been restored to prosperity. How could that be?

The answer of course was provided by Keynesian economic analysis, and by 1945, the most accelerated conversion experience in American academic life had made Keynes America's economic guru. His *General Theory* provided the model needed in the 1930s, but the lawyers in American government, like FDR, had been skeptical, as we have seen. Even most economists, who should have known better, were slow to abandon their version of neoclassical theory. Forced by the war to do what Keynes had suggested and his theory explained, the economy recovered and grew at a tremendous clip. By the end of the war, the "facts" that mattered – the statistics on output and income – were beyond question. It had worked.

Not all Americans were optimistic as the war ended, and that included some of the economists who had undergone forced conversion experiences. John Kenneth Galbraith wanted the United States to keep price controls on products and services after the war. By extending the wartime controls into the late 1940s, he reasoned, the United States could create a more stable, equitable form of capitalism, with the government firmly in control of the economy.[32] Economist Alvin Hansen at Harvard University worried that the country would quickly sag back into a depression. Instead of a glowing future, Hansen thought America had to face up to long-term stagnation. The government, he reasoned, had artificially pushed the American system to higher levels of output and employment. With the war's end, however, stagnation would follow simply because the great inventions and great investment opportunities that had sustained American capitalism would no longer drive the business and agricultural systems ahead.[33]

Pessimism frequently scores points in academic discourse, but in American politics, optimists usually win. That was true in Washington, DC,

[32] Hugh Rockoff, *Drastic Measures: A History of Wage and Price Controls in the United States* (New York, 1984).
[33] Alvin Hansen, *Full Recovery or Stagnation* (New York, 1938). Theodore Rosenof, *Economics in the Long Run: New Deal Theorists and their Legacies, 1933–1993* (Chapel Hill, North Carolina, 1997).

in 1945 and 1946. Most economists and most of the nation's political leaders were ready to place their bets on the style of modified capitalism that the United States had created by the end of the 1930s. The government quickly abandoned price controls. The factories, the pipelines, and many of the transport ships built during the war were sold off to astute investors at bargain prices as government surplus. Confident now that the Keynesian political economy would work, business leaders from some of the nation's largest firms were organized and prepared to work with the government to keep the economy growing. Riding this wave of optimism about the Keynesian conversion, Congress gave to the economists a special, statutory role as advisors to the federal government. The economists were the third professional elite – joining the military and the scientists – to emerge from World War II with a new and more important position in America's government.

A New World Order

During World War II, the realists appeared to have their way in shaping America's links to the rest of the world. But long before the war's successful conclusion, American tensions between realism and idealism emerged and were, in fact, institutionalized in a new world order. The United States initially played the lead role in building and funding that new international structure. Roosevelt and his advisors worked hard to avoid the problems created by the struggles and fatally flawed settlement that had followed World War I. The Atlantic Charter of 1941 set forth the basic principles that the United States and Great Britain hoped would guide the world to peace, and both China and the Soviet Union accepted those guidelines the following year. Of course some of that posturing was just posturing, and some of the concepts would become irrelevant. But those early efforts to make possible a lasting peace were not irrelevant. They helped provide an intellectual foundation for a series of new international organizations.

First to take form was the United Nations (UN). Important as these international institutions were and still are, they frequently give Americans a bad case of MEGO (My Eyes Glaze Over). So you might want to zip ahead to the Cold War, while I, a relentless teacher, briefly describe the new world order, starting with the UN. It grew in pieces during the war, first with a food and agricultural organization, then with a similar institution dedicated to relief and rehabilitation. Both of these were dependent on U.S. financial support. Finally in 1945, representatives of fifty nations met in San Francisco for the formal organization of the UN.

Although grounded in an idealistic search for lasting world peace, the UN's organization reflected certain realistic assumptions. Chief among these were the assumptions that shaped its bicameral organization: the General Assembly included all of the signatories, large and small, but the Security Council included the big five nations as permanent members with vetoes and six others on a rotating basis. The UN, which built on Woodrow Wilson's failed effort to create a new style of peaceful international relations, also included a high court of international justice at The Hague.

Peace and justice would both prove elusive, but the creation of a firm institutional base for a new world order was an impressive accomplishment. At Bretton Woods, New Hampshire, in July 1944, more than forty nations had worked together to create two more organizations designed to prevent a recurrence of the economic nationalism of the 1930s. The participants hoped in that way to help the UN prevent a third world war. The Bretton Woods institutions included the International Monetary Fund (IMF) and the International Bank for Reconstruction and Development (the World Bank). These two institutions and the UN would evolve in the years that followed the war, and all three would arouse substantial controversy in both the United States and abroad. Insofar as they were created to prevent a war that has not taken place, we should probably all give them the benefit of the doubt. Insofar as they blended a measure of realism about power with democratic values, Americans should be especially inclined to be tolerant of their problems and hopeful about their futures.[34]

The Realists and the Empire

Not everyone in America was getting ready for peace. During the last two years of the war, there were many in Washington and overseas who were anticipating a new political and military struggle with a greatly strengthened Soviet Union. The Atlantic Charter renounced territorial gain as a result of the war, but that principle was in direct conflict with Soviet

---

[34] Edward S. Mason and Robert E. Asher, *The World Bank Since Bretton Woods* (Washington, 1973). Devesh Kapur, John P. Lewis, and Richard Webb, *The World Bank: Its First Half Century* (Washington, 1997), I, *History*. J. Keith Horsefield, *The International Monetary Fund, 1945–1965* (Washington, 1969).

ideology calling for worldwide communist revolution. With German forces defeated and Soviet tanks and soldiers controlling Eastern Europe, there was little hope that Stalin would tolerate anything except communist regimes in the states closest to his own. These regimes would be closely aligned with their powerful Soviet neighbor.

The United States and its allies tried to prevent that outcome through negotiation at a series of conferences that have faded from the memory of all but the scholars who still parse them for historical meaning. For our purposes, it is sufficient to acknowledge that the Moscow Conference of Foreign ministers (1943), the Cairo Conference of Heads of State (1943), the Teheran Conference (1943), the second Moscow Conference (1944), and even the Yalta Conference (1945) did nothing to disperse the Soviet tanks and soldiers and thus the extension of the communist empire through Eastern Europe and into East Germany. Just as the realists expected. George Kennan, then an obscure *chargé d'affaires* in Moscow, suspected that the Soviets had overextended their empire. But his expertise wasn't being tapped by the leaders who were guiding U.S. policy at the war's end. Soon, however, Kennan's voice would be heard.

Those who, like Kennan, were deeply concerned about Soviet power and intentions were at work at several levels of the government, within the military and foreign policy establishments. When German rocket bases, knowledge, equipment, and personnel became available, they made certain these resources were quickly seized by American or British forces before the Soviets could get them. When plans had to be developed for a postwar base system, the planners looked forward to sites ringing the Soviet Union.[35] Although the Soviets finally entered the war against Japan in 1945, the Allies excluded the communists from the peace negotiations and military control of Japan. In brief, the realist position was well represented in a government that would shortly appoint its most distinguished military professional, George C. Marshall, as Secretary of State. Marshall was backed up by a substantial tier of professionals in the military and foreign services who were placing their bets on force rather than international organization as a means of controlling communism's expansion.

They looked for support to the networks that had produced the atomic bomb and other modern weapons. Enlisting Congressional support, military planners helped ensure that even our closest allies, let alone the

---

[35] See the outlines of the plans for a postwar base system around the world in Louis Galambos et al., *The Papers of Dwight David Eisenhower, 9, The Chief of Staff* (Baltimore, 1978), 2293, 2294–97.

Soviet Union, would not share our atomic secrets.[36] They also made certain that the Navy would not have to abandon the Applied Physics Laboratory and the Air Force could maintain its support for the Rand Corporation. In effect, a shadowy form of what Eisenhower would later call the military-industrial complex was already marshalling its strength for a new international struggle as World War II drew to an end. Idealism was in short supply where *realpolitik* was the central ideology. If the realists had their way, the United States would not abruptly shed its warfare state as it had after World War I. Like the internationalists, the military and foreign policy realists wanted a new order, but one solidly based on America's economic and military power.

War's End in a Small Town

There is nothing like peace and prosperity to make the American people hum with excitement, and they were certainly humming in 1945 and 1946. Out in Princeton, Indiana, we had been feeling the effects of prosperity long before we could celebrate peace. When the wartime economy recovered, the Galambos family had been able to move to a new and much larger house. We were still renting, but we were now living on the north side of town, away from the railroad shop, in a predominantly middle-class part of Princeton. That class element was far more important to my mother than the lawn or the beautiful pecan tree we now had in our yard. She remembered too much about railroad tracks and working-class poverty. She was very pleased to have some of the symbols of middle-class life, even if my Father still drove a Chevy truck to work and still swore eloquently in Hungarian from time to time.[37] When he wasn't angry, Lou was incurably optimistic, like any good salesman, and in 1945, he was looking forward to spending on a new car some of the money he had made producing tank parts in the garage.

My concerns were more immediate. I just wanted to celebrate the great victory marked in the maps on my bedroom wall. Because my father had been able to land those defense subcontracts for the Highway

---

[36] Gregg Herken, *Brotherhood of the Bomb*, 149–52, 153–56. The McMahon Act of 1946 made it impossible for the United States to exchange atomic information with the United Kingdom.

[37] He was from time to time reminded of his lower-class roots. On one memorable occasion, a local baker made pointed remarks to him about people who cook with garlic. This raised the intensity of Lou's monologue that evening to a level that made it stick in my mind – as it still does today.

Machine Shop as well as his own garage enterprise, I was well equipped for this occasion. I owned a chemistry set and had a little laboratory in the basement, next to our coal furnace. Working at a feverish pace, I filled a wooden cheesebox with homemade gunpowder. Looking for spectacular results, I added magnesium and aluminum shavings that I knew would flash and burn brightly when my bomb went off. I already knew where this celebration would take place. Half of the town, or so it seemed, was already on the square around the courthouse. Accompanied by my buddies, I put the cheesebox on one of the large concrete banisters at the courthouse – careful to leave the top open so it wouldn't kill anyone. It went off with a satisfying flash. Smoke filled the air as the shavings and the box blazed.

I had successfully marked the end of the war, and this marking would persist. My homemade firebomb burned a very large brown circle on the courthouse banister. It would stay there for years, reminding me of the end of a war that had already reshaped the world and would soon recast the American empire.

9

The New Aristocracy, 1946 to 1969

Victory in World War II and a prosperous economy gave the growing professional class a powerful position in American society. The images were compelling. The nation's scientists and engineers had helped win the greatest war in American history – a moral as well as a military victory. They had given the country more than just weapons to use overseas. At home, they were opening new frontiers in the medical sciences with remarkable innovations in the treatment of human and animal diseases. New drugs – the sulfa drugs and penicillin especially – had given doctors the ability to treat internal infections for the first time in the world's history. Physicists had made breakthroughs as well, expanding our understanding of the material world and, perhaps, the universe. Economists were no longer locked into a brand of classical and neoclassical analysis that left them and their governments with little room to maneuver when problems arose.[1]

Good news like this vibrated through America society, out of the research universities, out of the big cities and into the countryside and the small towns. In our small town of Princeton, Indiana, the professions were revered.[2] With the exception of Lou Galambos' early self-promotion as a

---

[1] For a short introduction see Olivier Zunz, *Why the American Century?* (Chicago, 1998).

[2] Asked which professions they trusted the most in 1949, the Americans polled gave doctors (32%) first place, followed by professors/teachers (26%) and bankers (18%). Lawyers lagged badly (3%). Gallup Poll #439T. See also #439K. The category "Engineer-Builder" received substantial support in this and subsequent polls. See #456, 1950; #516, 1953; and #748, 1967. This and all subsequent polls (unless otherwise indicated) are at http:// institution.gallup.com/documents/questionnaire.aspx?

"mining engineer," neither he nor my mother had been able to buck the odds and acquire a coveted place in the professions. But they knew how important the professions were and so did many people in Princeton. This knowledge was so deeply planted in the small-town culture that it seldom had to be discussed. I can't remember it ever being a subject talked about at home or in the schools. But our teachers all considered themselves to be professionals, as did the school administrators. They all pointed us toward a college or university as the next big step toward a professional career. There was a steady stream of "suggestions" about schoolwork and about what it took to make that next step, about the difference, say, between a "B" and an "A" in one of your courses. It started early and it never let up.

It seemed as if there was a professional perch in Indiana for all sorts and conditions of white mankind. If you couldn't become a surgeon or a general practitioner, you could become a veterinarian or a dentist. Maybe you didn't have the grades to become a research scientist, but you could certainly earn a good living as a pharmacist. You might not be able to be a president or chief financial officer of one of the state's leading firms, but you could develop a technical skill, take some courses in a master's program, and become a professional business manager or maybe an accountant. It was a bit harder to become a certified public accountant (CPA), but even that position was open to those who could pass the state exam. A judgeship might be out of reach, but you could develop a good local practice in one of the state's many small towns where you could have a decent income without bucking up against the big law firms. Unwilling to leave southern Indiana, you could go to nearby Evansville or Terre Haute, get a teaching degree, and come back to work in the local school system.

As long as you could get into one of these programs – some had difficult entrance requirements, but most were relatively easy to get into – you could bump your career ahead as soon as you received your degree and your certification as a professional. The concept of "professional" was very broad, the edges were ill-defined, and the number of professions and professionals was growing. The G.I. Bill encouraged ex-servicemen to jump onto the professional path, increasing the demand for new programs. Indiana and other states responded by quickly jacking up the supply of educational services. This was hard to do quickly, so most states expanded existing schools, used World War II buildings for living quarters and classes, and extended state aid to small institutions that could accommodate more students.

Stagnation Threatens

You could do all of this getting ahead so long as the economy didn't level off and dip back into a serious depression. To those who studied economics, it was apparent that there was no guarantee in Keynesian analysis that this would not happen. There was a guarantee that a sharp decline in federal spending would follow the end of the war. There was a guarantee that millions of service men and women would return to civilian life and start looking for jobs. Unless the economy could develop new markets, new products, or new technologies to sustain a high level of output, the United States was probably in for some tough years of adjustment after the war. At least that was what Professor Alvin Hansen and the other "stagnationists" concluded. They looked to federal spending, not private investment or consumption, to prevent a return to the Great Depression.

This was a perfectly reasonable conclusion. Every successful economy whose growth had been studied and quantified had followed a path that looked like a sloping S-curve. At first, growth had accelerated as industrialization got underway. Then at some point, the growth had leveled off, population increases had slowed, and the government had begun to play a larger role in the economy. During the postwar years, another tribe of American economists led by Professor Simon Kuznets was focusing its attention on developing good international statistics so that these economic patterns could be compared and analyzed in systematic ways. Population studies indicated very clearly that natural increase in America had been slowing for many decades. Without large-scale immigration, the U.S. population would have stabilized a long time ago. The logic of the S-curve seemed to define a new and less prosperous American future.

The stagnationists concluded that the powerful industries of the second industrial revolution were no longer likely to experience rapid growth. Their markets were saturated and their industries mature. Unable to see new "drivers," new industries developing, the stagnationists worried about the future of the economy. The agrarian frontier was gone. The great sources of cheap raw materials had been discovered and exploited. The great surges of economic growth that had brought the United States to the top of the global economy were, they thought, a thing of the past.

This outlook made sense to those who saw analogies between economic growth and human growth. As children, most of us grew larger and taller very fast. But then as adults, that pattern of growth slowed and then stopped. We could continue to grow out, to get fatter around the waist. But we didn't get any taller. In fact, in old age, we tended to shrink somewhat. It all made sense, common sense, to believe that the great days of rapid growth in the American economy were over. Perhaps, then, it was time to behave differently as a nation, just as we do as individuals in middle age – and after.

Stagnation Confounded

But as demobilization accelerated, as the massive war plants stopped turning out planes and tanks, as the government's elaborate system of controls shrank, the economy jerked once or twice and then took off in another growth spurt. There were many doubters, but the optimists won. A great deal of money had been saved during the war, and Americans set out in the postwar years to spend it. As one of the nation's leading car salesman explained, "All you had to do to sell a new car was smile."

The salesman, Lido Iacocca, was one of a new breed of businessmen. A second-generation American, he had grown up in Allentown in the Lehigh Valley of Pennsylvania and read the American roadmap to success.[3] His Italian father, Nicola, had only finished the fourth grade, but Lido worked hard in school and was "usually second" in his class, just behind the Jewish girl who was always first. As he later explained: "As an Italian, I was seen as a cut above the Jewish kids – but not by much." Both Jews and Italians were nevertheless in a different league than the local African Americans: "I never saw a black person in Allentown," Iacocca said, "until I was in high school."[4]

Doing well, this "diligent student" learned to write and demonstrated a flair for math. From Allentown, he went on to nearby Bethlehem, Pennsylvania, to Lehigh University, a private school with a strong engineering tradition. Majoring in industrial engineering and taking a number of courses in the business program, Iacocca graduated in 1945.[5] On the move – socially as well as academically – he accepted a scholarship from Princeton University and got a master's degree in one year. Ready now to make his mark in business, he took a job at the Ford Motor Company as a student engineer. Ford broke in these young engineers by having them tour, so they could learn something about each of the firm's operations.

[3] Yes, this is the same Allentown that was the subject of Bruce Springsteen's famous song.
[4] Lee Iacocca, with William Novak, *Iacocca: An Autobiography* (New York, 1984), 14.
[5] Like many colleges and universities, Lehigh suffered at first as men left to go to war. The school partially recovered by offering Army training and then expanded in higher education's postwar boom.

The orientation gave Iacocca a good introduction to the business but it also convinced him that his real interest and the "real action" at Ford were in marketing and sales. Successful during the postwar boom in sales, he moved ahead quickly. He was intense, focused, clever, and flexible: "Lido" had become "Lee," one of the sales stars in America's second biggest automobile firm.

While Iacocca was mastering sales, another college-trained professional was helping redesign the Ford organization. Iacocca and Robert S. McNamara were both on fast tracks at the company. McNamara, a graduate of the University of California at Berkeley, shared with Iacocca a bent toward mathematics. But McNamara gravitated toward economics and then accounting, not sales. His gift was for ordering and analyzing information and for understanding how people and modern organizations used information to develop new strategies and evaluate their operations. These skills earned him respect at the Harvard Business School, which in 1940 appointed him an assistant professor of accounting, only one year after he received his master's degree.

Instead of interrupting McNamara's astonishing ascent, World War II actually accelerated his progress. As a captain in the Army Air Force, he worked with Colonel Tex Thornton in the office of statistical control, evaluating the success of bombing campaigns and developing new approaches to the use of air power. Thornton and his team provided the top command with the same kinds of evidence and forecasting techniques that America's leading industrial corporations were using. The U.S. Army – like most American institutions – had long depended on the common sense and judgment of experienced officers to perform these functions. But that was changing as new, professional concepts of decision making and planning began to replace traditional patterns of behavior inside the military establishment. The heroic style gave ground grudgingly to the behavioral style of running military operations. But it did give ground, as McNamara and his colleagues built a new professional, information-based foundation for the military-industrial complex.

After the war, Henry Ford II brought Thornton and his team, nicknamed the "Whiz Kids," into the company in an effort to reorganize Ford along the lines pioneered by its chief rival, General Motors. Ford needed a revolution. In his declining years, Henry Ford, Sr., had allowed the organization to sag badly in the marketplace and to develop a negative, often vicious internal environment. The reorganization transformed that environment and revitalized the firm. It also rapidly carried McNamara to the top of the company. By the early 1950s, McNamara was heading the Ford Division. In 1960, he became president of the company. By that time, the firm had reacquired a strong position in the U.S. market and was doing very well overseas. By that time, too, McNamara started moving Lee Iacocca into the upper reaches of the firm, along with a large number of Harvard Business School graduates.

Better trained and better equipped to manage a multinational firm, these new executives and managers came to control the entrepreneurial process in Ford and in many other large postwar businesses in America. The new professionals were able to understand the technologies and the sciences essential to their businesses and were familiar with the multidivisional, decentralized organizations (the M-form) that became the norm in U.S. industry in those years. Their careers were focused on the tension between the ongoing need to compete with new products, services, and processes and the natural tendency of any massive bureaucratic organization – public or private – to settle into a routine and oppose change. Businesses like General Motors, American Telephone & Telegraph (AT&T), Ford, DuPont, Standard Oil, and General Electric were certainly massive. Economically, GM was larger now than most of the nations in the world. All were bureaucratic: AT&T, for instance, had seventeen layers of managers and executives, all of whom occupied positions carefully defined in the firm's organizational chart.

To be successful, professional managers had to be obsessive about both innovation and efficiency. McNamara, who once came up with a new set of car specifications while sitting in church, was relentless about improving the performance of every branch of Ford's business.[6] This was not unusual behavior for this generation of professional managers. Whether they were developing innovations internally or scooping them up by acquiring small, entrepreneurial firms, they helped the United States reinforce its position as the world's leading industrial economy. Increases in productivity and the development of new goods, services, and ways of organizing businesses made the United States a dynamo for the world economy while Europe and Asia were still struggling to recover from World War II.

The service industries made important contributions to the success of this new American business system. Firms like AT&T, which controlled the Bell System, were pushing the entrepreneurial frontiers forward in

---

[6] At Ford, the tension was apparent in the struggles between the "bean counters" and the "hot dogs." The "hot dogs" were the "car guys" who designed the two-seater Thunderbird; the "bean counters" were the executives who added two more seats.

their industries. We usually associate increases in efficiency with intense competition in mass-production industries, with the assembly line in automobiles, for instance. But the Bell System, a regulated monopoly, was achieving this same goal in services. Using innovations coming out of Bell Laboratories, the system was making the jump from electromechanical to a much more efficient form of digital switching. Electrical generation – a heavily regulated industry – was also compiling a surprisingly good record for increased efficiency. So too was retailing, where chain stores and firms like Sears were taking markets away from small grocery and appliance stores.[7]

In all of these businesses, professional managers played central roles, but in none of them did professionalization go as far as it did in medicine or law. Why? In business there were no licenses to practice, no central body of abstract thought, no controlling associations policing training or entry. But there was certainly expertise at a high level, and in many staff functions there was expertise that called for extensive education. In finance, in human resources, in public relations, and in many other staff as well as line positions, higher education became a prerequisite for appointment and promotion. Certification, the license to practice, was not. Why?

This is an engaging question, and the answer can probably be found in two places: in the organizations hiring them (the demand side) and in the people being hired (the supply side). On the demand side, the businesses had no desire to yield more power and money than they had already yielded to their employees. Professionals were hard to organize – remember the struggles with scientists in the early development of R&D. They were also more expensive. So the businesses encouraged the development of new capabilities but had no interest in further professionalization of their managers and executives. On the side of those being hired, the immediate benefits from further professionalization were outweighed by the costs. Their "mystery" – the ancient word for their central body of knowledge – stayed for the most part within the organizations that hired them. Their knowledge was firm- and industry-specific and was acquired

---

7 I had a good perspective on the destructive side of this episode of capitalism's creative destruction. I was working for a small grocery store that was trying to compete with the A&P chain store around the corner. One means of competing was to offer delivery services instead of low prices. One of my jobs was to deliver the groceries, riding a bicycle with a very large basket on the front. In the end, of course, A&P's low prices beat the bicycle boys.

on the job.[8] Technical training got people into the jobs, but employees had to demonstrate leadership ability and a knack for innovation to make the important jump into the upper levels of management. So educational standards went up sharply in business but leveled off at the MBA, the master's degree in business administration. That was all McNamara and Iacocca needed as the base for their meteoric careers.[9]

In agriculture, as well, the American system experienced dramatic changes during the postwar years. By the late 1940s, farmers were only a small percentage of America's very large workforce, but they were continuing to make an important contribution to the nation's economy. They were riding the wave of a stunning revolution in productivity. The long-term public investments in research, in professional training, in systems that encouraged dirt farmers to innovate – these at last paid off. Not just for America. But for the world as well. And, as we noted before, that payoff came when prices and production for farm commodities were stabilized under a public cartel and subsidy program. The manner in which the cartel and subsidy system encouraged innovation was unanticipated and counterintuitive. The New Deal planners had not been concerned with agrarian entrepreneurship. But their programs and the tremendous wartime boost in demand had created an astonishing burst of innovation in American farming. The new-era farmers provided abundant supplies of food and other products both for domestic use and for foreign markets. Techniques and crops were exported, and American farming quickly became a model for much of the developing world.[10]

The Wonders of Science

The sciences emerged from World War II with a new measure of political standing. Their leaders were soon able to translate standing and political access into very impressive amounts of public funding for research and professional training. Impressed by the accomplishments of science and advanced technology, Congress created a National Science Foundation (NSF) to ensure that big science would have the continuing financial support it needed. The NSF was, like the SEC, a network organization.

---

[8] I have benefited from Christopher McKenna's analysis of the limits of professionalization in management consulting: *The World's Newest Profession: Management Consulting in the Twentieth Century* (New York, 2006), especially 26–50, 192–215.

[9] This was also the situation in most nonprofit and public institutions during these years.

[10] Sally H. Clarke, *Regulation and the Revolution in United States Farm Productivity* (New York, 2002).

NSF depended on the evaluations contributed by thousands of scientists as well as a specialized staff. Training and research grants were funneled through an elaborate and rapidly expanding network of universities and research organizations, all of which received substantial sums through overhead payments. The leading research universities quickly became dependent on those grants to keep their programs going.

The development of atomic weapons helped make physics the leading player in this new science network, but the medical sciences quickly began to share in the funds provided by Congress. The enlarged National Institutes of Health (NIH) stood at the core of the public-nonprofit-private medical network, a nationwide network that would experience tremendous growth in the following decades. It is still growing today. The Institutes supported research around the country, as well as conducting studies at Bethesda, outside of Washington, DC. NIH, which performed clinical as well as research functions, became by the mid-1950s one of the world's most innovative institutions in "hot" fields such as enzymology, biochemistry, and molecular genetics. Sprinkled throughout this network were talented Jewish scientists who had sought sanctuary in North America after fleeing the Nazi regime. They helped accelerate the development of America's medical sciences. The big payoff for America came after the 1940s, when the United States crept ahead of Europe in the development of new knowledge, new drugs, and life-saving vaccines. By the end of the 1960s, the United States, not Europe, was the nation for first-class researchers to visit in order to stay "at the tip" in their fields. This was a dramatic shift in a matter of three decades.

The United States also made rapid advances in engineering education and research. In some fields, such as chemical engineering, America had created the new subdiscipline and maintained a substantial advantage over foreign rivals. In others, the United States was playing catch-up, but that process was going very fast as the money flowed in from federal and state governments. As the links between science and engineering became stronger, American universities and technical schools quickly adapted to the new conditions. The practical, shop-centered aspects of engineering gave way to science-based bodies of knowledge and innovation.[11] Mechanical engineering became material science. Electrical engineering

---

[11] I briefly attended Purdue University before this transformation took place and was instructed in welding (which I already had learned from my father) and surveying (in which I might have done better if they had invented the handheld calculator by then). Some years later, at Rice University, I was an observer as science supplanted the craft tradition in all but one branch of engineering (civil).

was transformed by solid-state physics. Competition between the nation's engineering schools accelerated these transformations.

The changes taking place in engineering and science created unusual opportunities for new programs and new universities to make especially rapid advances. This was the experience in California, where Stanford, Cal Tech, and the University of California experienced rapid progress in engineering and the sciences. Military research money helped in fields like aeronautics and electronics, propelled by Cold War spending. The older, more established eastern universities had to hustle to stay up with the California system and frequently, the elite schools fell behind in the 1960s. Midwestern state universities were not far behind in the race to achieve higher academic standing by developing new fields, subdisciplines, and interdisciplinary programs. The pace of expansion accelerated dramatically in the 1960s, as the New York state system took off. By the end of the decade, the local, state, and federal governments were pumping more than $11.5 billion a year into this large, complex system of higher education. Across the entire system, quality doubtless lagged size. But the flow of Nobel Prizes toward the United States suggested that in many fields, America had established a dominant position.[12]

Triumphant Years for the Administrative State

The promotional state was vibrant and expanding rapidly during the postwar years. For professionals, as we have seen, the enormous government outlays for education at all levels were important, as was government's direct support for research and development. The more than $4 billion the federal government spent on space research and technology in 1969 translated into jobs and income for scientists, engineers, and administrators. The more than $33 billion that local governments spent on their schools that year provided new opportunities for teachers and school administrators all over the country. The subsidies for those striving to get on a professional path were enormous. Tuition in the state universities was very low, and even the professional schools charged relatively little.

Some of those who graduated and received their degrees were given a ticket to practice in restricted markets and allowed to share the power

---

[12] These developments in professional education appear even more important when they are placed in an international context. During the 1960s and 1970s, for instance, the People's Republic of China was launching a cultural revolution that would be particularly destructive to the country's professional elite.

of professional self-government. They could turn to their professional organizations for help when there were sticky problems involving jurisdiction over particular jobs.[13] It was not, for instance, self-evident that psychiatrists should be able to perform some functions that were not open to psychologists. The struggles between nurses and doctors were always resolved in favor of the MDs who controlled the hospitals and had a good measure of political power in state capitals. The physicians continued to have skirmishes on the boundaries of their profession, but they normally won these battles in the postwar years.

Government promotion of the professions and business was a common feature of the postwar economy. Tax breaks and expenditures for transportation were given to new enterprises and to businesses looking for low-cost locations outside of the older industrial areas of the East Coast and the Midwest. The drift toward the Sunbelt was not some kind of natural phenomenon, beyond man's control.[14] Large sums of money were spent to affect location decisions, and on balance, the expenditures were successful in encouraging businesses to move. The promotional state doesn't explain the sudden rise of Silicon Valley, California. But if you add the educational systems to the formula and then combine federal, state, and local support for business and the professions, you will be getting close to understanding why so many new and established firms were locating in California and other Sunbelt states.

It was often hard to find a boundary between the promotional state and the warfare state. When the Cold War against communism got into full swing during the late 1940s, the United States had to remobilize for a long and expensive struggle. A great deal of the government's money was funneled back into American businesses that could provide the weapons and services the federal government needed. How much money are we talking about? In 1960, the federal government was spending more than $48 billion on defense. By the end of the decade, the figure had increased to more than $82 billion. Inspired by the adventurous spirit of the space race, very few Americans wondered where the liquid gases that fueled the rockets came from. But there were businesses in places like Allentown,

---

[13] Jurisdiction, and thus power, is the central theme of Andrew Abbott's brilliant study, *The System of Professions: An Essay on the Division of Expert Labor* (Chicago, 1988). Although I disagree with Abbott on some issues, I still consider this the best book written on the modern professions.

[14] The Sunbelt is usually considered to encompass the states of the South, the Southwest, and the southern part of the Far West.

Pennsylvania, that were supplying that market and were attentive to every twitch in America's defense spending.[15]

The welfare state as well as the warfare state was growing – slowly in the 1950s and then more rapidly in the 1960s. While continuing to think conservatively about government, Americans were behaving more and more liberally about the government services they were receiving and the new ones they demanded. Within agencies like the Social Security Administration, professionals who really understood the system used their knowledge to expand services. They worked closely with the small number of representatives and senators in Congress who also understood the technical aspects of funding and administering welfare. Even during relatively conservative presidencies, like those of Dwight Eisenhower (1953–1961), these administrative and informational networks were able to push forward with new funding and expanded programs. Freed from the control of a conservative president in the 1960s, the government introduced a wave of innovations that more than doubled welfare spending.

The regulatory state grew more slowly, but there was a steady, almost invisible expansion as regulators gradually extended the reach of their agencies. There was now an internal dynamic to the regulatory state. Three-sided alliances – the so-called Iron Triangles or Triocracies – between regulatory agency experts, legislative committees, and interest groups organized by those who would benefit from the regulations gradually extended these bureaucratic controls. The process can be seen at work in many regulated activities, including energy and transportation as well as communications. Expansion was dictated both by an interest in acquiring power and by a well-meaning effort to adjust regulations to America's changing economy and technology. The regulators seemed always to be reaching for but not quite grasping the control they needed.

From time to time, this political process had a tendency to create unanticipated problems, as it did in the energy field. Following World War II, the government had quickly sold the pipelines it had built to carry gas and oil from Texas and other Southwestern states to the East Coast. The pipelines became crucial suppliers to the Eastern and Midwestern markets they served. Because they were engaged in interstate commerce, the pipelines came under federal control. But the gas supplies themselves didn't. When the regulations on the pipelines became too onerous, the companies owning gas simply decided to stay within

[15] Andrew J. Butrica, *Out of Thin Air: A History of Air Products and Chemicals, Inc., 1940–1990* (New York, 1990).

their state boundaries. Unfortunately, that left Eastern and Midwestern cities without gas for heating, cooking, and electricity production. This condition became politically intolerable, so the government followed the customary cartel approach by extending control to the wells, the sources of the gas. That solution failed, however, to deal with the intolerable problem of shortages, and these made legislators squirm. By the end of the 1960s, Congress, the industry, and the professional energy experts were all seriously considering alternatives to this branch of the regulatory state. Experiences like these laid a foundation for the deregulation movement of the 1970s.

The Search for Equality

A far more successful experience with the regulatory state took place in the field of civil rights. Here new leaders emerged and set out to transform the lives of African Americans and the white society that denied most blacks access to the path into the professional class. The National Association for the Advancement of Colored People (NAACP) combined lawyers and academic experts in a legal attack against segregated schooling. In 1954, their campaign reached fruition in the Supreme Court's decision in *Brown* vs. *the Board of Education*, which struck down the "separate but equal" doctrine.

The other route to a new order of civil rights was trod by those religious leaders – the black clergy – who were no longer willing to tolerate America's conditions of disenfranchisement and segregation – especially but not exclusively throughout the South. They and their followers suffered humiliations, attacks, and sometimes murder as they challenged the power structures of Southern communities and their schools. This movement from within the black community forced the hand of the federal government and finally fostered growing white support for reform. Two steps toward a new order came in 1957 and 1958: the first when Congress passed the initial civil rights legislation of the modern era; the second in a historic meeting in Washington, DC.[16]

In the summer of 1958, a small group of black leaders met with the President of the United States in the White House. Dr. Martin Luther

---

[16] The Civil Rights Act of 1957 was the first such measure to be passed by Congress since the end of the Reconstruction Era following the Civil War. It fell short of the Administration's goals but provided federal protection for blacks seeking to register to vote.

King, A. Philip Randolph (Vice President of the AFL-CIO), Roy Wilkins (Executive Secretary of the NAACP), and Lester Granger (of the National Urban League) met with Eisenhower, Attorney-General William Rogers, and two other members of the White House staff. One of the staff members was Fred Morrow, the first African American to hold a professional job in the White House, and the other was a young Italian American who had recently taken on the administration's civil rights issues. Rocco Siciliano had worked with Sherman Adams to arrange the meeting. Siciliano had pushed ahead with the plans even after Ike got testy when he was asked not to use the words "patience" or "tolerance" when he talked to the black leaders.

The path that had taken Siciliano into this meeting was in many regards typical of the new aristocracy. A second-generation Italian American, he had excelled in school and then done equally well at the University of Utah in the early 1940s. Like many of the western universities, Utah's small campus had yet to grow out of the "'super' high school" phase. That was a good setting for a determined high achiever propelled by the slights and sarcasms that were the steady diet for "wops" and "dagos" in Middle America. Siciliano threw himself into campus politics, political science, and his first love affair.[17] The romance between a Mormon and a Catholic collapsed, but Siciliano succeeded in school and also as an infantry officer in the brutal Italian campaigns of World War II.

After the war, Siciliano got back on the professional path that would soon carry him to the White House. He graduated from the law school at Georgetown University and then served as an assistant with the National Labor Relations Board. Later, he became an assistant secretary of labor responsible for the Bracero Program for immigrant Mexican laborers. In 1957, he was appointed – at age thirty-five – as a special assistant for personnel management in the White House. A year later, his job was stretched to include minority affairs.

Siciliano's experiences in Washington, as well as his upbringing in Utah, shaped his approach to minority issues. His parents had both been born in southern Italy, in the poorest and least advanced part of the country. In Utah, they were part of a tiny minority. Catholic instead of Mormon, southern European instead of Scandinavian, a young boy with a name like Rocco Siciliano had to dig hard to find respect and a niche in

---

[17] The love affair was with a Mormon girl and, as Siciliano discovered, even love could not breach the Mormon/Catholic barrier at that time.

Utah. From a surprisingly early age, Rocco had decided that niche would be in the government. Later, he became equally certain that his public service would be in the nation's capital. Successful in school, in the army, and in his new profession, he built a network of friends and supporters who helped him advance his career in Washington. As he clambered up the political ladder, he didn't forget where he came from. He worked hard to help those who were still trying to get off the lower rungs in American society.

That included the African Americans whose leaders he helped bring into the White House. They had much in common with Siciliano. All four of the black leaders had attended or graduated from college. Granger from Dartmouth in 1918. Wilkins from the University of Minnesota in 1923. Randolph had taken classes at City College in New York, and King had a doctorate from Boston University. They were the latest version of Du Bois' talented tenth.

What did they get out of the meeting with Ike? Against the background of their legal victory in the Brown decision, the Administration's quasi-military victory in Little Rock, Arkansas, and their legislative victory in the passage of the Civil Rights Act of 1957, the meeting with Ike symbolized the fact that the leaders of the movement now had access to the upper reaches of power in America. That access and their influence would wax and wane. Indeed, the administration didn't embrace their specific demands. But by keeping the pressure on the white leadership, they would ensure that African Americans would not return to the conditions that had existed before the 1950s.

The climax to this transformational movement came after the assassination of President John F. Kennedy in 1963. Then President Lyndon Baines Johnson and his supporters in Congress broke the Southern logjam and pushed through two landmark laws in 1964 and 1965. They ensured that voting rights would not be denied to African Americans, who quickly demonstrated their interest in taking part in democratic government. The new laws also prohibited the common forms of segregation by race in public transportation, eating establishments, and other institutions. What the black lawyers and clergy sought was equality before the law, not merely a change in the American political system. Thurgood Marshall's 1967 appointment as the first black justice on the Supreme Court ensured that the demands for equality would continue to be heard. By the end of the 1960s, the African-American leaders had achieved substantial legislative and judicial success. Then their task became one of translating the new laws into the same kinds of progress Italian Americans and other immigrant groups had already achieved.

The Brothers Arrive

During these same postwar years, Jewish Americans began to break down many of the barriers that blocked their progress in America. To get into the professions, they needed access to higher education and professional schools. To ensure equality over the long term, they also needed the opportunity to teach in those schools, many of which were still profoundly anti-Semitic.

What accelerated this process in higher education was the tremendous expansion taking place throughout the states and local communities. In the 1960s in particular, the demand for excellent scholars greatly exceeded the supply as schools in California, New York, and other states grew at astonishing rates. Adding twenty or so faculty members in a single department within a year or two left a school with restricted choices. Anti-Semitism became too expensive at the same time that it was becoming less acceptable socially. In the aftermath of the Holocaust, professional Americans were less inclined to tolerate blatant anti-Semitism of the sort that had been routine before and immediately after World War II.

Jews and other immigrant groups quickly took advantage of these new opportunities to acquire strategic positions in this new, performance-oriented aristocracy. The old New England stock that had long dominated higher education was simply absorbed by the rush of new people into the professions and the academic settings where they were trained. Surveying the scene at an academic convention after this process was well underway, one prominent Jewish historian turned to a colleague and said: "The brothers have arrived." He didn't need to explain.

Pleasant as this conclusion might seem, it is important to recognize that anti-Semitism didn't just evaporate. Some of it did, but some of it went underground, staying unspoken but sticking around nonetheless. It could pop to the surface after a few extra drinks as it did with one of the deans at an eminent Southwestern university. Staggering down the hotel hallway at a national convention, he was confronted with the suggestion that the history department try to appoint an outstanding American historian who was Jewish. "We've got enough of THEM," he blurted and reeled off to bed. Anti-Semitism and racism lurked beneath the surface long after they had become impolite.

The Sisters Would have to Wait

Another wave of change was gathering force in these postwar years. Women were taking new positions in the American economy. Following the war, many women had returned to the home life celebrated in American television shows during the 1950s.[18] But many more stayed in the workforce and were joined each year by a growing number of women seeking work outside the home. By 1970, more than 40 percent of women in their early thirties were in the workforce, and they constituted a growing proportion of the white middle class.

Now the coeducational progress made in high schools, colleges, and universities prior to and during the war began to pay off, as more and more women pressed to enter the professions. The number of women on science faculties had increased during World War II from 2,412 to 7,746, and even though women accounted for less than 3 percent of the scientists and engineers in the entire nation during the immediate postwar years, they had established a beachhead in a male domain.[19] It was harder and harder for academic institutions to resist this pressure, in part because professional women were beginning to organize effectively to put pressure on the institutions. Federal manpower policy also emphasized the need for women with professional training.[20] Women had gone to war. They could vote. They had effective leadership and a well-educated group of followers. Like most African-American leaders, women in these years were demanding equality of opportunity, in work and in education. They were especially effective at reshaping the academic environments at schools to the west of the elite East Coast institutions.[21]

[18] There was public approval for a return to the pre–World War II situation. Asked in 1947 if women could do as good a job as male ministers, 46% of those questioned said "No" and 45% said "Yes." The balance was slightly more favorable to women (34% "Yes" vs. 33% "No") who might serve as governors, senators, doctors, and lawyers. Gallup Poll #396.

[19] Margaret W. Rossiter, *Women Scientists in America Before Affirmative Action, 1940–1972* (Baltimore, 1995), 11, 29. Rossiter's careful research uncovers the many ways in which women were, however, still blocked from receiving professional training in science and engineering in the postwar years (30–49).

[20] Ibid., 50–94. Between 1963 and 1973, almost 12% of the NSF's grants and 22.5% of the NDEA's grants went to women. Between 1956 and 1973, however, there was only one black women scientist who received a Ph.D. (Shirley Ann Jackson, Physics at MIT; she became president of Rensselaer Polytechnic Institute in 1999).

[21] Ibid., 86–87. The top ten schools in awarding science doctorates to women 1947–1948 to 1962–1963, were Columbia, California Berkeley and UCLA, Radcliffe/Harvard, NYU, Chicago, Wisconsin, Michigan, Cornell, Ohio State, and Illinois. Antinepotism rules still barred many women from academic appointments in schools where their spouses were employed. Between 1968 and 1972, Rossiter concludes, women scientists sharply increased the intensity of their protests against these and other conditions in public, private, and nonprofit institutions (360–82). The Equal Employment Opportunity Act and the Education Amendments Act of 1972 provide a bookend for Rossiter's study.

In the postwar corporate world, however, they still had an uphill fight. The stereotypes of the fast-track manager were all male and white, a jumble of sports analogies and corporate-speak. Women were pressing into corporate America by way of staff appointments, but the best line positions were still reserved for the men who had dominated these organizations since the previous century. Education and ability notwithstanding, this generation of women would have to wait before they could take positions along side stars like Iaccoca and McNamara.[22]

The Indiana Perspective on All This

From southern Indiana, where the Galambos family was happily settled, these developments all looked completely natural. The children, it was assumed, would go from the local public high school to the state public university. Tuition was low and a university education was affordable to most high school graduates in Indiana. Many didn't go. Many tried it and left school after a year or so. The high dropout rates increased the cost of the American system of higher education, but they accurately reflected the democratic urge to make opportunities for advancement widely available.

Those who persisted included Peg Galambos and her younger brother – that's me; known then as Skip, but now and henceforth in this history as Louis.[23] Both of us graduated from Indiana University in Bloomington. Peg's path was linear and quickly productive. After finishing at Indiana, she went to Richmond, Virginia, and following clinical training, she received an advanced degree in physical therapy.

My educational path was full of twists and a few dead ends. Fortunately, in America's enormous, expensive, decentralized educational system, you could fail and still get back into a school, find a new program and perhaps a new career. I first tried chemical engineering, but that was a disaster, and I left school on probation in my sophomore year. Next came a year and a half in a more disciplined setting: the U.S. Navy. Having time to read, reflect, and grow up, I came out of the Navy with an intense desire to write. I just didn't know what I wanted to write. Back in a university in Columbus, Ohio, I tried history because that, I reasoned, included everything.

[22] See Pamela Walker Laird, *Pull: Networking and Success since Benjamin Franklin* (Cambridge, 2006), especially pp. 124–77, 246–65.
[23] My grandfather, Lazlo in this history, my father, Lou, and I were all blessed with the same name. To prevent confusion, I have given us three different names: Lazlo, Lou, and Louis.

Transferring to Indiana University in Bloomington, I started to get some of the kinks out of my education for a professional career. I had finally learned how to study and began to understand why history was important. After acquiring a mentor and a BA, I managed to squeeze into the graduate program at Yale, where I started studying diplomatic history with one of the creators of the subdiscipline, Samuel Flagg Bemis. Uncertain about that field of history, I gave my education another twist and backed into the study of political economy in nineteenth- and twentieth-century America. After a year at Harvard University's Graduate School of Business Administration, I finally finished my dissertation, received a Ph.D. from Yale, and set out to teach modern American history. I didn't know it at the time, but I was going to spend the next half century trying to get a better understanding of that subject.

When I got a job, my father and mother were pleased but a bit baffled by what I was doing in Houston, Texas, teaching at Rice University. Lou and Ruth had understood that I was at Yale to get a degree, and they more or less understood why I went to the Harvard Business School. But the inner reaches of academic life were a mystery to them. I didn't seem to spend much time teaching, and I was interested in subjects that seemed to them about as useful as a Do-Do Bird. They were curious about my interests, but all that was really important for my parents was knowing that both of their children had become professionals.

We had all left Princeton, Indiana. Lou and Ruth had moved to Evansville, Indiana, when he ventured into the oil business with three partners. As my parents moved from Princeton, they bought the first house they had ever owned, situated not by accident in a thoroughly middle-class section of the city. In a sense, we had all arrived at a common American destination.

From the vantage point of my Houston corner of the middle class, I was trying through my teaching and research to get a better understanding of the changes taking place in America. Actually, I was starting this book without knowing it. I was gradually learning more about the particular nature of American creativity and beginning to get an inkling of the price that was paid for that style of progress. Deeply engaged in professionalization, however, I had yet to realize that the new aristocracy of professionals had some serious flaws. Some of the flaws would surface in the 1970s, some much later.

10

The Suburban Conquest of the 1960s

Houston, Texas, in the early 1960s was typical in many regards of the fast-growing southern and western cities of the United States.[1] It was growing out, with new minicores of banks and shopping centers spreading around a flat exterior. The Gulf Plain was low and marshy and inviting to the real estate investors who were guiding Houston's growth. The city was miles from Galveston and the Gulf of Mexico, but Houston's avid promoters had long ago developed a channel that brought oceangoing ships right up to the city. The oil, gas, and petrochemical industries were thriving, as were the banking, legal, and transportation businesses.[2] These provided services to the core industries and jobs for all those non-Texans pushing into the suburbs. They were moving into new apartments and ranch-style houses, sending their children to new suburban schools. Everything seemed new.

The suburban culture and economy were omnipresent in Houston, which had virtually no downtown, hardly any city center as late as the

[1] Matthew D. Lassiter, "Suburban Strategies: The Volatile Center in Postwar American Politics," in Meg Jacobs, William J. Novak, and Julian E. Zelizer, *The Democratic Experiment*, 327–49, provided a preview of his book, *The Silent Majority: Suburban Politics in the Sunbelt South* (Princeton, 2006). For other aspects of suburbanization, see Lizabeth Cohen, *A Consumers' Republic: The Politics of Mass Consumption in Postwar America* (New York, 2003), and for an outstanding analysis of the urban core, see Thomas J. Sugrue, *The Origins of the Urban Crisis: Race and Inequality in Postwar Detroit* (Princeton, 2005 edition).

[2] Joseph A. Pratt, "A Mixed Blessing: Energy, Economic Growth, and Houston's Environment," in Martin V. Melosi and Joseph A Pratt, eds., *Energy Metropolis: An Environmental History of Houston and the Gulf Coast* (Pittsburgh, 2007), 21–51. See also Pratt's *The Growth of a Refining Region* (Greenwich, Connecticut, 1980); and David G. McComb, *Houston: The Bayou City* (Austin, 1969).

1960s. The automobile was as important to everyday life in Houston as it was in Los Angeles. As the new houses went up, the city often didn't even bother to build sidewalks. Who would walk? Highways cut through the city, linking the suburbs, the shopping centers, and the public schools that were the essential base for the universities and the professions. The schools were growing in pace with the suburbs. The roads that were the city's lifelines also brought workers from the other side of the city – the African-American and Hispanic laborers, men and women who played as crucial a role in Houston life as air conditioning. Houston had the temperature and humidity of Calcutta, India, and on hot summer nights you could hear the steady dripping of water from the broad leaves of the tropical bushes.

Coming from an eastern, urban life to Gulf Coast Suburbia, I experienced a brief fit of culture shock. Everything seemed too new. Everyone seemed too cordial. Coming directly from Cambridge, Massachusetts, where apartments were a privilege, I was stunned to encounter landlords who were eager to rent you a place to live.[3] It was a hyper-version of the friendly Midwest, with football taking the place of basketball and supporters of the John Birch Society edging out the kind of conservative Indiana Republicans I knew.

Rice University: A Darwinian Paradise

Once the first wave of culture shock had passed, I discovered that Rice University was a paradise for anyone interested in teaching history. Established as a tuition-free school for the white residents of Houston and vicinity, it attracted a large share of the region's best academic talent.[4] If a high-performance high school senior didn't get into Harvard or one of the other Ivy universities, he or she came to Rice for a first-class, free education.

When those bright, eager students got there from Lubbock or Dallas or Texarkana, they quickly discovered that they had been lured into an institution dedicated to a thoroughly Darwinian approach to learning. The talented history and literature students were required to take a

---

[3] My stay in Cambridge, Massachusetts had been courtesy of the Harvard Business School (HBS), where I was a Business History Fellow for a year. I had a great deal of catching up to do, and HBS was an ideal environment in which to learn more about modern political economy and to start the networking that is an essential aspect of any professional career.

[4] On the early years of the university, see John B. Boles, *University Builder: Edgar Odell Lovett and the Founding of the Rice Institute* (Baton Rouge, 2007).

calculus course in competition with the science, engineering, and math majors. Worse still, the grades were placed on a curve in which the lowest 10 percent *automatically* failed! A program based on survival of the fittest weeded out plenty of those former valedictorians and sent them skittering to the University of Texas and other schools with less hostile requirements. In the Rice setting, even a beginning assistant professor with a sincere interest in his or her students' progress could be a smashing success as a teacher.

That success could be dangerous, though, because it sharpened your identification with The Other, the visitors from the new aristocracy who didn't understand the local community of scholars. The faculty was split between Texans – many of them graduates of Rice, who found the school's approach to education completely reasonable – and the imported scholars, The Others, who were astonished by the fact that the school had no psychiatric counseling to deal with the emotional problems produced by the Darwinian Struggle.[5] Gradually, and painfully for all, the imports began to control a number of the departments.

This was especially true a year or so after the Rice Board of Trustees indicated its desire to go big time by appointing Kenneth S. Pitzer as president of the university in 1961. A distinguished chemist who had been involved with Ernest O. Lawrence, Oppenheimer, and the other members of the "brotherhood of the bomb," Pitzer set out to make Rice a worthy, Southwestern counterpart to the nation's leading technically oriented universities like Cal Tech and MIT.[6] Along the way, Pitzer tried to build first-class graduate programs in the humanities and social sciences, a task actually more formidable than upgrading science and engineering. President Pitzer, the master Otherman, had a great deal to work with, because Rice was a well-endowed school.[7] He persuaded the courts to change the

[5] This is not the customary use of "the other." For the customary usage, see the conferences sponsored by the Common Bond Institute (http://www.cbiworld.org). The third international conference explored "the roots of fear based belief systems and stereotypes, prejudice, polarization, enemy images, and artificial barriers of misunderstanding and distrust that divide us." Given that all of these patterns of thought existed at Rice in the 1960s, I feel justified in expanding the coverage of "the other" to include the new people at that University.

[6] Pitzer's undergraduate degree was from Cal Tech and his doctorate was from the University of California at Berkeley. On his appointment and presidency, see John B. Boles, *A University So Conceived: A Brief History of Rice University* (Houston, 3rd edition 2006), 37–46.

[7] We were told that George and Herman Brown arranged for the University to acquire the Rincon Oil Field, a deal that apparently provided substantial income to the school and

will of Rice's founder and admit students without regard to geography or race. The university began, as well, to charge tuition. While all this was happening, the balance on the faculty between Jews and Gentiles quietly shifted, and Rice's anti-Semitism went underground.

After the first round of academic battles had been won by the Others, however, Pitzer discovered he needed more resources than even the Houston elite on the Board of Trustees could provide. Rice was known locally as "George Brown's little university," and Pitzer apparently needed more endowment than even the Brown brothers and their business colleagues were able to muster. After a quiet but intense battle, Pitzer left Rice to become university president at Stanford. He left behind a school more suited to its suburban Texas surroundings than to the national and international competition that existed among America's leading research institutions. Rice became a very good feeder school for the graduate programs of the top-flight universities. If you choose, you can see this outcome as support for a Darwinian social analysis of the evolution of American research institutions during these years: only the fittest survived.

The Sunbelt Suburbs

The suburbs that housed Rice and the University of Houston, part of the state system, were remarkably similar to those evolving across the entire Sunbelt. Atlanta, for instance, had a school somewhat similar to Rice (Emory University) and a similar pattern of residential development oriented to the car and the shopping mall. Atlanta started with more of a downtown than Houston and was less aggressive about annexing land to keep the city's tax base growing. But otherwise, the larger outlines of urban development were much the same.

The suburbs in Atlanta, Houston, and elsewhere in the Sunbelt provided middle-class, white Americans with the single-family residences, the green yards, the good schools, the convenient shopping, and the safety from city crime that they wanted.[8] The price included the long-and-getting-longer commute to work. The American answer to that problem was to improve the roads into and around the city. These were the

___

substantial tax relief to the previous owners. Junior faculty members identified with the Other were not, however, privy to these Texas-size operations.

[8] See Lizabeth Cohen, *A Consumers' Republic: The Politics of Mass Consumption in Postwar America*, especially 194–289; although the author's focus is more on the Northeast, and especially New Jersey, than the rest of America, her generalizations about suburbia ring true. In Houston, crime and residences were both segregated.

years when inner and outer loops were being built, all linked by a new interstate highway system launched by the Eisenhower administration, Congress, and the construction industry. The call for such a system had emerged from the highway engineers who were familiar with what had been accomplished on Germany's autobahn. The White House support had come from a retired five-star general who had once experienced a slow, painful cross-country trip in the 1930s. Anyone who had survived an uphill drive behind a mud-slinging, slow-creeping West Virginia coal truck could well understand the support that emerged for this innovation in the promotional state.

The interstate highways were crucial out west as well, to California and certainly to the development of Los Angeles. Here too the city had distinctive characteristics, including a very large Hispanic population and a postwar industrial base that included high-tech airplane production. The large businesses fostered nodes of city and suburban concentration, much as they had decades earlier in Chicago and other Midwestern and Eastern cities. But in Los Angeles, the distances between the suburbs and the city were much greater. Although there was good public transportation, the new, improved highway network was vital to suburban life. Favored by its climate, by its newness, and by a touch of romanticism associated with Hollywood, Los Angeles was one of the places Americans went when they dreamed of finding a new life as well as a new job and a new place to live.

Some of them probably succeeded, but the suburbs of Los Angeles were, alas, very similar to those of every other large city in the Sunbelt. In LA you might have the desert as a backdrop, instead of a south Texas marsh, but the homes, the cul-de-sacs, the schools, and the entertainment – increasingly supplied by the televisions that were bumping radio out of its home market – were much the same in all of these cities. So were the problems. With sprawl and the automobile came a new level of pollution and painfully slow commuting. The middle-class, suburban lifestyle was also accompanied by an oppressive set of gender roles for the white women who were expected to stay at home and use the ubiquitous crock-pots to prepare dinners for their children and husbands (if the traffic allowed the Dads to make it in time). The culture and gender relations were captured in TV programs like "Leave It To Beaver." That show had all the set pieces of the suburban family: two children, the youngest of whom was nicknamed Beaver, and the mother who kept the house running while the father toiled at his profession in the city. They all engaged in an endless array of harmless, humorous social games with happy endings. All the major pieces were white so there was no checkmate, at least until the last episode was finally shown in 1963.

That big slice of wholesome, imaginary Americana inspired emulation, but it also aroused some new and serious questions about the meaning of life, especially suburban life and "Momism." Suburbia was and still is anathema to many, if not most, intellectuals. The blandness, the sameness, the lack of serious intellectual expression nettles those who favor city centers and the past glory of the walking city.[9] The "Momism" of suburban life would shortly come under serious assault. The foundation stones for what would become a major women's reform movement had been in place for a number of years. The steady advances women had been making in the workplace and in education – first in high schools and then in the universities – were creating an audience for change. The rapidly expanding university systems of the postwar era were offering many new opportunities for women to advance in the professions. And they did. Between 1950 and 1970, the number of women completing law and medical degrees increased rapidly. Even in engineering there were more and more women graduates.

This new, ambitious, well-educated generation of women was not going to be satisfied being a foil for Beaver and a cook for Dad. Something had to change. Then Betty Friedan published *The Feminine Mystique*, a 1963 bestseller that dropped sparks in dry intellectual tinder all over the United States. The author had a well-honed, personal knowledge of the gender relations she analyzed with devastating insight. Capturing in her book the tensions millions of well-educated white women were experiencing, Friedan gave the elite leaders in the new women's movement an ideological position in opposition to America's suburban culture. Friedan and those who followed in the movement wanted to get all those university-educated women out of the kitchen and into society.[10]

This was, after all, the era of the "multiversity," an institution that was created in an effort to deal effectively with all of society's demands for well-trained professionals, regardless of gender or race. By the end of the 1960s, the California state system of higher education had more students than Germany and Great Britain combined. UCLA dwarfed the schools of other countries. Even then, the University of California could

[9] Jane Jacobs, *The Death and Life of Great American Cities* (first published in 1961, but now available in a new edition, New York, 1993). For a recent essay, see Lee Siegel, "Why Does Hollywood Hate the Suburbs?" *Wall Street Journal*, December 27–28, 2008.
[10] Mary P. Ryan, *Mysteries of Sex*, 238–42.

not fully satisfy the growing demand for a ticket into the professions and the "good life."

In California and other states, there was a perpetual race between the population, the suburbs, and the state educational institutions. This race was particularly fast in Los Angeles. Between 1940 and 1970, the population of Los Angeles and its suburbs grew by 300 percent. This growth bred incredible opportunities and equally incredible problems. Even the Bell System had trouble keeping up with the demand for telecommunications in a setting where the telephone was almost as essential as the automobile.

That was not the only tension in California in the 1960s. The multiversities also bred a new movement concerned about the entire drift of American society, including the drift toward suburban life. The emerging New Left was bitterly opposed to a culture excessively dedicated to consumption, to the extended foreign empire America had acquired in the postwar years, and to the bureaucratic order of hierarchy and discipline, including the order that surrounded them in universities like those in California and other states. The New Left was primarily a middle-class phenomenon. It was led by young people, many of whom were well educated, who had enjoyed the physical comforts of suburban life and had been helped onto the paths that led to the professions. In effect, they were now rebelling against themselves, against their past, their families, and the future laid out for them by people they now said they hated. For some, religion pointed the way to "authentic" communities free of the hypocrisy of suburban life. For others, organized religion was the enemy of their free-flowing life style.[11]

The New Left gathered force and targets from the civil rights movement as it honed an ideology in opposition to almost every aspect of white, middle-class, suburban life. Seeing the suburban life as fragmented, the movement sought community. Seeing the middle-class culture as pinched and excessively rational, the movement looked to emotion, to freedom of expression, to music, drugs, and sexual liberation as expressions of opposition. If America was controlled by interest-group politics and giant national parties that stifled minorities, they would be truly democratic, open to all ideas and all people. If Robert McNamara, now U.S. Secretary of Defense, was the high priest of a bureaucratic order, then they would

[11] Doug Rossinow, *The Politics of Authenticity: Liberalism, Christianity, and the New Left in America* (New York, 1999).

follow Ken Keysey and his merry pranksters into a life of deliberate disorder.

Keysey carried his message of liberation to Houston and to Rice University, where he visited his friend, the novelist Larry McMurtry. After parking their day-glow bus outside of McMurtry's house, the merry pranksters popped over to Rice University where they demonstrated how to build a human pyramid. Their effort to sit on the conveyer belt and go through the cafeteria's dishwasher was less successful. The water was very hot, and it couldn't be imagined away.

Perfection through Planning

Insofar as their target was a suburban way of life, the New Left was beating on a giant mattress that could absorb almost any blow without losing its shape or comfortable appeal to the middle class. Millions of Americans still aspired to be middle class and to live in a Beaver-style dream house. The suburbanites and wannabes continued through the 1960s to buy Americana real estate as fast as the developers could lay concrete slabs and plant ranch houses on them. The lawyers in Congress, the real-estate moguls, and the Federal Reserve System combined forces in the well-grounded tradition of the promotional state to keep them buying. Home mortgage interest payments and property taxes were (and still are) deductions on your income tax. The Federal Housing Administration kept downpayments low and mortgage rates reasonable to encourage homeownership. Housing was one of the markets most affected by the enlarged administrative state. Direct and indirect subsidies also came from the states and local governments that extended road and water systems and built the new schools that kept the suburbs growing around every American city. If ever Americans voted with their dollars and cars against a European style of urban life, it was during the American Century.

There were now significant experiments in perfecting that style of life through planning. Prior to World War II, most American cities had adopted the style of "fringe planning" that Chicago had employed. Fringe planning improved urban life by adding attractive fringes – a park here, an improved waterfront there, a beautiful sculpture or a concert hall – without attacking the major problems that plagued the inner cities. Now that changed, and no single person symbolized the planning efforts of those decades better than Robert Moses of New York. Immortalized in construction, New York's "power broker" spread parks and parkways, bridges, tunnels, playgrounds, public housing, and expressways through and out of America's financial center. His first great project involved opening up Long Island to New Yorkers who could afford a car or tickets on the bus or train. Before Robert Moses, Long Island was largely the private preserve of upper-class New Yorkers who built remarkable homes in which to summer and entertain. These elites fought to preserve their class turf. But the promotional state provided Moses with the federal and state funds he needed to make Long Island available to hoards of working- and middle-class Americans.

Intoxicated by his success and the adulation it inspired, Moses pressed on and on and on. An urban hero in the 1950s, he became an urban monster in the 1960s. No longer in touch with the people he was supposedly serving, Moses drove through projects that scarred the city and many of those New Yorkers least able to help themselves. Skilled in bureaucratic and fiscal manipulation, Moses became the fallen angel of urban planning, the man who did as much as any single planner to discredit all of the efforts in the 1960s to eliminate "the great social and economic evils obtaining in every city in the form of slum and blighted areas." Moses did a great deal of "urban renewal," but it was difficult to distinguish that process from his other ventures. Residents were displaced, buildings went up, and some portion of a slum looked better – even though that didn't prevent the inner city from declining.[12]

In the 1960s, however, other planners in different settings were developing more holistic goals both for inner cities and for suburbs. One of the suburban planned communities was Columbia, Maryland, a product of the fertile mind, great energy, and resources mustered by James Rouse.[13] Rouse, who came of age in the Great Depression, was slow to settle on a career. After the death of his parents and his family's bankruptcy, he struggled to find a calling. A mediocre student in high school, he left the

---

[12] Robert A. Caro, *The Power Broker: Robert Moses and the Fall of New York* (New York, 1975). Moses had an article in the *New York Times Magazine*, December 5, 1948, on "Practical or Long-Haired Planning." This prompted the president of the American Society of Planning Officials, Charles B. Bennett, Director of Planning, Los Angeles, CA, to defend his brand of planning. Bennett conceded that Moses "has the welfare of the great mass of less fortunate people at heart...." But Bennett favored a different approach to urban problems: "For the first time in our history legal and financial tools are available, permitting us to do a first job first, namely, the elimination of the great social and economic evils obtaining in every city in the form of slum and blighted areas." American Society of Planning Officials, *Planning 1949* (Chicago, 1949), 209, 212.

[13] There were, of course, "new towns" built long before Rouse's experiment in planning, and the government's "greenbelt" towns also preceded Columbia. What changed were the breadth of the planning movement and its new mixture of social and economic goals.

University of Virginia in 1933 and went to work in Baltimore, where he earned a law degree in night school. Then he began to master the urban real estate market, first in a government position and then in the mortgage business. By the 1950s, he was a very successful developer with experience in a variety of urban renewal projects. In the early 1960s, he decided to build a city that would not have to be renewed.

Rouse designed Columbia in opposition to the architectural sameness and vacuous lifestyle of suburbia. Columbia was laid out so that each sub-division would have a different character and style. It was built around a small downtown and an entertainment area. Because suburbs were largely segregated, Columbia was designed to be integrated. Because most sub-urbs used zoning and other restrictions to keep out minorities, Columbia used low-priced housing to attract them. Rouse was a practical planner as well as a reformer: Columbia offered easy access to recession-proof jobs in Washington, DC. In most regards, Columbia was an antisub-urb suburb and a successful innovation.[14] Soon, attempts to duplicate its success began to sprout up around other major cities. Most, however, soft-pedaled reform and concentrated on middle-class amenities.

Those amenities were so popular that the Rouse strategy was pirated by developers who had a wealthy clientele and an interest in social stability rather than reform. They began to build gated communities for the upper-middle-class and upper-class Americans who had no desire to mingle with minorities. Indeed, insofar as those minorities were associated in buyers' minds with crime and drugs and inner-city decay, these gate-guarded suburbanites deliberately used their fences and high-price properties to keep minorities out. In these cases, good fences made bad neighbors. The residents behind the gates didn't want Columbia's mix of entertainment, shopping opportunities, and social betterment. They didn't want schools. They wanted quiet and safety, including the safety of being surrounded by people exactly like themselves. Fortunately for them, they got the same tax breaks that the promotional state gave to every other U.S. homeowner. The gated communities affirmed the suburban lifestyle by refining its middle-class culture and adding the expensive touches appropriate to an affluent clientele.

---

[14] On James Rouse and Columbia, see Joshua Olsen, *Better Places, Better Lives: A Biography of James Rouse* (Washington, DC, 2003). Nicholas Dagen Bloom, *Merchant of Illusion: America's Salesman of the Businessman's Utopia* (Columbus, 2004), especially 126–49, is suspicious of Rouse's liberalism and critical of the halfway measures Rouse and other businessmen implemented.

Lyndon Johnson and the Planning Impulse

In the aftermath of the Kennedy assassination and the Civil Rights Acts, President Lyndon B. Johnson (1963–1969) launched a new program to eliminate poverty in America. We could, he proclaimed, afford both guns and butter. We could fight a war in Vietnam while using tax dollars to create a better society at home – the Great Society, he called it. Like Robert Moses, Johnson would leave his mark on America in the concrete and steel of new public buildings – the projects that were central to his effort to rid the United States of "slum and blighted areas."

To design and build this great society, Congress and the administration reached out to the professions and sought to ally them with the poor people the government was trying to help. This brought urban sociologists, anthropologists, and urban planners into the embrace and funding of the growing administrative state. The mission of these professional experts – who, with some exceptions, had been ignored by the federal government – was to feed ideas into the new grassroots political organizations that the Great Society was now sponsoring. Like the Tennessee Valley Authority, the Agricultural Adjustment Authority, and other New Deal programs of the 1930s, the Johnson planning institutions attempted to mix elite oil with grassroots water in a democratic way.

President Johnson had come of age politically during the Great Depression and he clearly thought of himself as a new version of FDR, a leader who could help America win two wars at the same time. One of these wars was far away, in Southeast Asia, on the outer fringes of the American empire. It seemed winnable, if only because North Vietnam was a small, weak country that, to quote Robert McNamara, "couldn't make ice cubes." The other war was here at home, in the slums of America's major cities. It was harder to set odds on winning the War On Poverty because it was such an innovative task.

Johnson's reform policies were innovative and bold – no doubt about that. The New Deal had not targeted the slums. Neither had the cities' fringe planners. There were grounds for hope because the president had the political brokers in Congress on short, tight leashes. No doubt about that either. Johnson understood Congress better than any of the U.S. presidents since FDR. Even Machiavelli would have appreciated the way he controlled his Democratic congressmen and pummeled the Republican opposition. His skills were evident when the White House, the administration's social security experts, and legislative leaders were able to push through Congress a breakthrough health insurance law.[15] The new order subsidized health care for all welfare recipients (Medicaid), but balanced this provision with an appealing package (Medicare) of hospital and physician insurance for those aged sixty-five and older who were covered by social security. This cleverly designed combination of benefits cut across class and party lines, defusing much of the opposition to government intervention in health care markets.

It was necessary to be Machiavellian because the War On Poverty offered very little to the suburbs. Other than Medicare, it seemed only to promise a vague goal of urban peace. Ideally, the suburbanites would be able to drive to work, park their cars, and even get out to lunch without worrying about the poor people in surrounding inner-city slums. The War On Poverty also fitted well in the ideology the late President Kennedy had eloquently stated: "Ask not what your country can do for you. Ask what you can do for your country." Johnson was giving the suburbs an opportunity to do something for America without getting their hands dirty.

But to do that, the federal, state, and local governments enlisted in this crusade had to learn how to mix oil and water, blending the well-educated social scientists with some of the country's poorest and poorly educated citizens. Let's go back to Chicago and look at how the program actually worked in that setting. As we've seen, Chicago had a long and frequently successful experience with the "fringe innovations" that had given the city a more attractive waterfront, a less congested downtown, and some outstanding cultural attractions. There were many reasons to be proud of what Chicago's planning efforts had accomplished. But now, for the first time, the improvement plan was reaching deep into the city's long-ignored slums. The first step, the planning and organizational phase, went smoothly. Chicago had plenty of political expertise and a host of ardent social scientists eager to take on this challenge. The University of Chicago was alive with planners who were enthused about the task and ready to go.

In the second phase of reform, however, out in the neighborhoods, the war bogged down very quickly. It turned out that the people most affected by the War On Poverty in the 1960s had very specific needs. They were happy to tell the experts what they wanted and they were able to

---

[15] The congressional compromises are analyzed with great care and insight in Julian E. Zelizer, *Taxing America: Wilbur D. Mills, Congress, and the State, 1945–1975* (New York, 1998), 212–54.

find their own homegrown leaders very quickly. As a result, the consensus the Johnson administration had envisioned never emerged. What did emerge were media-grabbing fights that rocked the administration and left the urban wing of the Great Society in shambles. There were important lessons buried in those experiences, lessons about the tensions that inevitably exist between democratic and professional authority. Neither Johnson nor his advisors, however, had the inclination to reflect on this defeat. They were moving on to solve other serious problems, trying to remain positive about reform and that other war, the one in Southeast Asia.

What came out of the reform experience was a more centralized, typically American program to deal with hunger by giving poor people food stamps and to deal with the need for better housing by building apartment buildings in the city centers. The food stamps provided relief in the worst cases of urban poverty, but they also created a secondary black market in food stamps sold by those who wanted to buy other things than bread. The buildings, the "projects," concentrated poverty. They proved vulnerable to crime and in particular to the drug dealers who were beginning to get a solid foothold in urban markets. The suburbs handled stress through psychiatry and psychology. In the slums, the people went for more direct relief through alcohol, marijuana, and increasingly by the end of the decade, heroin.

Seen from the perspective of the suburbanites, the Johnson programs were neither an unexpected nor an entirely unsatisfactory solution to the problems of inner-city poverty. The projects reinforced the segregation the suburbs were already imposing. Like the other pockets of poverty spotted throughout an affluent society, the projects provided the cleaning ladies, nannies, and day laborers the middle class employed. The lower ranks of the working class continued to be replenished by migrants from the South and the new immigrants who continued to be drawn to America in search of jobs. Fortunately for the suburbanites, the War On Poverty increased income taxes but not their property taxes. Nor did the increase in taxes really cut into the inequalities in income and wealth that were an essential aspect of middle-class life in America. While the Johnson program thus left the suburbs unchanged, the failed effort at reform seriously tarnished the reputations of the professional urban experts. They were not the only professionals under attack in the late 1960s, but they were the ones who were discredited the most completely and quickly by this great national experiment in urban social reform.

President Johnson was also discredited and ultimately disrespected for losing the War On Poverty. His experiment was indeed a failure – an expensive one. But the problem he attempted to solve was a real, major social crisis, and to his credit, he attempted to use the society's professional expertise to improve conditions in the inner cities. He wanted to apply that expertise without diluting democracy. He failed. But the Johnson administration certainly made a laudable effort to solve problems that are still with us today.

The War On Poverty ended in a messy but thoroughly democratic manner. By 1968, when Richard Nixon was elected president, the suburbs could claim a complete victory over their challengers in Washington, in the states, and in every big city in the country. Most Americans lived in the suburbs, enjoying the amenities of the grass, the schools, and the nearby shopping centers.[16] Never was a victory more complete in American politics. Never were vocal, well-organized, talented opponents more thoroughly crushed than Johnson's urban reformers. Suburbia's triumph left the legislative foundations of the nation's welfare state intact, but it quickly ended the Democratic Party's effort to reduce inequality by giving new support to those inner-city minorities who were locked in the slums.

A Maryland Perspective

When Nixon was inaugurated in 1969, I was temporarily at Johns Hopkins University in Baltimore, Maryland, on a research grant. I was, by dint of my postdoctoral status, "at Hopkins" but not "of Hopkins." From that vantage point I started to look back, look more closely, and look more critically at a society in which I had been completely immersed, professionally and personally. I could now see just how difficult it was to change America or any of its major institutions from the top down. Even with the most effective, articulate leadership, it was extremely hard to budge a society of more than 200 million people and a federated government that left substantial powers in the states and localities. In this

---

[16] According to Sarah E. Igo, *The Averaged American: Surveys, Citizens, and the Making of a Mass Public* (Cambridge, Massachusetts, 2007), 291, "The mass public of the Gallup polls and the Kinsey Reports was born of a specific conjunction of cultural preoccupations and social scientific innovations. The same is true of the differentiated America found in survey research today." I disagree. The mass public was, for the most part, the product of the prolific mass-production, mass-distribution economy, the cultural dominance of the suburbs, and the new technologies of communication.

regard, then, the accomplishments of the Civil Rights Movement were historically phenomenal, and the meager domestic accomplishments of the New Left were understandable. The New Left was working against the grain of a suburban, increasingly professional society with a politically effective middle class. The promotional state worked with the grain of the society, in tandem with a public sphere of professional experts and interest groups.

The professionals were constantly bumping up against democratic institutions, creating serious tensions, as they had most clearly in the War On Poverty. By the end of the decade, however, that tension had been resolved in a way that had to be reassuring to the millions living in the suburbs. That's where my family and I were: in Towson, in Baltimore County, Maryland, which was as suburban as a community could be. From the busy YMCA to the little shops scattered around the town center, complete with a county courthouse, Towson was just the sort of white, middle-class community that continued to attract white, middle-class Americans throughout the postwar years. A decisive moment in the triumph of the suburbs came when Towson sent Spiro Agnew to Washington as Richard Nixon's Vice President. What better spokesman for the suburbs could you have? A Greek American and a lawyer, Agnew had served as Baltimore County Executive and then governor of the state.[17] America, it appeared, was finally about to settle down after the turmoil of the 1960s.

---

[17] Agnew's immigrant father had changed his name from Anagnostopoulos when he came to the United States. Spiro Agnew attended Johns Hopkins but did not graduate. After serving in the Army in World War II, he graduated from the University of Baltimore School of Law in 1947.

II

Empire in the American Century

If we're going to understand America's post–World War II empire, we need to jump back in time, back to 1945. For most Americans, the war erased the boundary between realism and idealism in foreign policy, easing the nation toward a new style of vastly extended empire.[1] Having just won a great victory over immoral fascism, this generation of Americans had reason to believe their exercise of global power would always serve moral as well as military, economic, and political ends. There were doubters. The brilliant scientist Robert Oppenheimer publicly confessed that he and the others who had developed atomic weapons had "known sin." But his colleague, Earnest O. Lawrence, denied that his experiences in science and war had ever brought him into a new relationship with sin.[2] Most of his fellow scientists and citizens seem to have agreed.

With concerns about idealism tabled or left to the friends of the UN, the realists plowed ahead with their plans for the postwar world.[3] Shortly after Japan surrendered, military planners in the Air Force already had in hand a strategic plan that included fifteen cities in the Soviet Union, cities that could be the targets for atomic weapons like the ones used

---

[1] Desiring a deeper, more complex synthesis, the student would do well to explore John Lewis Gaddis, *Strategies of Containment: A Critical Appraisal of American National Security Policy during the Cold War* (New York, 2005 edition).

[2] Gregg Herken, *Brotherhood of the Bomb*, 149–51, 166–67. J. Robert Oppenheimer, "Physics in the Contemporary World," Arthur D. Little Memorial Lecture at M.I.T., November 25, 1947. He also apparently told President Truman, "I feel we have blood on our hands," Nuel Pharr Davis, *Lawrence and Oppenheimer* (New York, 1968), 258.

[3] Until the victory was certain, the desire to cooperate with the Soviets was an important factor shaping U.S. policies. John Lewis Gaddis, *The United States and the Origins of the Cold War, 1941–1947* (New York, 1972), 63–94.

against Hiroshima and Nagasaki. No moral quivers there! No doubts either about the next enemy. Other professional strategists had more specific plans for the empire and its nemesis, the Soviet Union.

These were the military and foreign policy professionals who had been content to see the Soviets excluded from the peace negotiations with Italy and had been eager to see American and British forces outrace the Soviets to the German rocket bases and personnel in the endgame of the war. Looking ahead, they mapped out the U.S. bases that would ring the USSR and extend the American empire into Europe, the Middle East, and Asia.[4] The empire, as they conceived it, would continue to be loosely jointed, linked by trade, foreign aid, and military cooperation. Its new controlling rationale would be anticommunist. Insofar as the nations of Western Europe were now dependent on the protection provided by American military power, they were client states, important parts of a greatly extended American empire. The empire's means would be primarily military and economic, and although the United States and its European allies would continue to use democratic rhetoric, they would happily work with any of the dictatorships that supported the central mission of this refurbished, anticommunist empire.

The spokesman for the new empire was a professional diplomat who understood the USSR and the communist movement better than any of Washington's political leaders. Certainly better than Henry Wallace, the former U.S. Vice President, who looked forward to "One World," a friendly world, in the aftermath of World War II. Wallace's One World would be something like the farm country in Iowa where the Wallace family had thrived and put down deep roots. He looked forward to a world in which differences would be settled amicably by legal authorities. International cooperation would simply absorb national goals.

The Arch-Duke of Realism

The Arch-Duke of the Cold War, George Kennan, knew there would be three worlds when the war ended: a communist world led by the USSR; a capitalist world led by the United States; and a third world of underdeveloped, less powerful nations swaying back and forth between the dominant nation states and their allies. Kennan was contemptuous of the

---

4 On the base system, see the maps in Louis Galambos et al., eds., *The Papers of Dwight David Eisenhower, The Chief of Staff*, 9 (Baltimore, 1978), 2292–97. On the rocket bases, see volume 6, for Eisenhower's cable to General Marshall (June 7, 1945), 143–45.

professionals who hoped the United Nations would bring all the world's governments together in peace. He was deeply distressed by the idealism of the One Worlders and by their lack of historical understanding. He knew that the communists also wanted "one world," but he could see that this would be a world controlled by authoritarian communist parties, not by the UN or the dreams of the Atlantic Charter.[5]

Well trained in the diplomatic corps to keep his mouth shut, follow orders, and implement with skill the policies that came down the State Department's chain of command, Kennan at first played by the rules.[6] He finally broke out of this cage in 1946 and published his conclusions in a journal whose audience included the professional experts and analysts who could, he hoped, squash dangerous American idealism. Guided by his style of realism, he hoped the readers of *Foreign Affairs* would implement policies attuned to the real world of communist power and aggression.[7]

Kennan was right about the Soviets. He was not the only American expert who was calling for policies attuned to the Soviet tanks and soldiers in Eastern Europe. But he was the most articulate of those experts. He was the one who broke ranks and explained what needed to be done by those professionals and political leaders who had not gotten around to reading *Darkness at Noon* or to mastering the communist vocabulary in which "communist dictatorship" became "people's democracy" and "crushing the peasants" became "agrarian reform." Kennan published his article anonymously, but as he understood, the cover of Mr. X would soon be blown.

It was. Then the American media world – the *New York Times* to the north, the *Washington Post* to the south, the *Louisville Courier Journal* in the Midwest, and the *Los Angeles Times* out west – wanted to know everything about the mysterious author. What they found out wasn't very surprising. It was only newsworthy because of the Soviet presence

---

[5] John Lewis Gaddis, *Strategies of Containment*, 24–52.

[6] For Kennan's account, see George F. Kennan, *Memoirs, 1925–1950* (Boston, 1967), 294–97, with excerpts (547–59) from his long telegram of February 22, 1946: "In summary, we have here a political force committed fanatically to the belief that with US there can be no permanent modus vivendi, that it is desirable and necessary that the internal harmony of our society be disrupted, our traditional way of life be destroyed, the international authority of our state be broke, if Soviet power is to be secure (557)."

[7] Ibid., 354–67. Kennan later said, "Feeling like one who has inadvertently loosened a large boulder from the top of a cliff and now helplessly witnesses its path of destruction in the valley below, shuddering and wincing at each successive glimpse of disaster, I absorbed the bombardment of press comment that now set in (356)."

on the front pages of their papers. Kennan had been a career diplomat since the 1920s and an expert on Russia and the Soviet world since the 1930s. He had just completed a term as deputy head of the U.S. mission in Moscow, and he based his article on a long telegram he had sent to the Secretary of State calling for a new policy of containing Soviet power. Back in Washington, Kennan was now heading the State Department's policy-planning staff.

Kennan's plan for the U.S. empire was bounded and carefully tailored to fit the Soviet threat.[8] He understood that empires could become too large and indeed he thought the USSR had already tried to swallow too many nations, too many ethnic groups. The United States needed to strengthen its defenses and block further Soviet expansion through "a long-term, patient but firm and vigilant containment of Russian expansive tendencies. . . . " Time would be on the side of the anticommunists, Kennan reasoned. He held out the possibility that the USSR would eventually mellow or might even fall apart – a conclusion that was too bold for most American experts to contemplate at that time. His hard-line approach to American policy provoked an intense, public debate over containment.

The Realists and the Empire

The realists reacted quickly and positively to Kennan's call for action. They didn't have at their command all the tanks the Soviets had. But they had the tanks trumped by the atomic bomb, the apparently ultimate weapon when it was combined with the air power to deliver it. The United States had both.[9] The Soviets had neither the bomb nor the means to deliver it in the first years of tense peace. They did, however, have their own skilled physicists and an espionage system that helped give them their first atomic bomb by 1949. To the realists, the spying of Klaus

---

[8] Upon returning to the United States shortly after the presidential election in 1952, Kennan gave a talk in which he explained what one of the limits on the exercise of power should be. He advised Americans to "be extremely careful of doing anything at the governmental level that purports to affect directly the governmental system in another country, no matter what the provocation may seem. . . . To the extent it may be successful, it would involve us in heavy responsibilities." George F. Kennan, *Memoirs, 1950–1963* (Boston, 1972), 172–73. Some subsequent administrations would have been wise to heed this warning.

[9] The process of professionalization in the military continued at an accelerated pace in the Cold War setting. In 1959, for instance, the new Air Force Academy graduated its first class.

Fuchs and others was no surprise.[10] Their outlook was grounded upon a Kennan-like suspicion about communist intentions. The spies and the Soviet success with an atomic bomb illustrated all too well why it had been wise to move ahead quickly in developing what the realists considered the truly ultimate weapon, the hydrogen (or thermonuclear) bomb.

The United States had the scientific and engineering expertise and the resources needed to develop this new and deadly weapon. The original "brotherhood of the bomb" had produced some doubters, some defectors, and a raft of spies and "might-be" spies, but the core group that included Lawrence and Teller pushed ahead.[11] Within three years, America was once more on top in this accelerating arms race. The successful test in the South Pacific (Eniwetok) pushed the United States over a unique threshold, into an age more dangerous than the nation had experienced since the early years of the nineteenth century. This was especially true after the Soviets tested their own hydrogen bomb in 1955.

Long before that event, the realists, led by Secretary of State Dean Acheson, General Marshall, and the Joint Chiefs of Staff, had guided the United States into acceptance of the global responsibilities entailed in the containment policy.[12] One of the first products of that policy was the Marshall Plan, created to encourage the economic recovery of Western Europe and provide a bulwark against the Soviets. President Truman was an enthusiastic supporter of Marshall Plan aid, most of which was actually spent in the United States to buy the goods Europeans needed. Even though Europeans didn't rush to accept the entire Marshall Plan package of an American-style political economy, the program helped pump up the economies of nations vital to U.S. security.[13]

---

[10] The extent of the spying and the guilt of particular spies, including especially Alger Hiss, have been and continue to be much discussed. See, for instance, the debate over Allen Weinstein's book, *The Haunted Wood: Soviet Espionage in America – the Stalin Era* (with Alexander Vassiliev): David Lowenthal, "Did Allen Weinstein Get the Alger Hiss Story Wrong?" http://hnn.us/articles/11579.html. By vastly exaggerating the extent of the spying and using it as the basis for corrupt and misleading attacks on American individuals and institutions, Senator Joseph McCarthy cast an evil shadow over America between 1950 and 1954.

[11] Allen Weinstein and Alexander Vassiliev, *The Haunted Wood: Soviet Espionage in America – the Stalin Era* (New York, 1999), 172–222, 311–37, is, I believe, a remarkable account, in part because it uses both western and Soviet sources. The Soviet code name for the bomb was "Enormoz."

[12] Walter Isaacson and Evan Thomas, *The Wise Men: Six Friends and the World They Made: Acheson, Bohlen, Harriman, Kennan, Lovett, McCloy* (New York, 1986).

[13] Michael J. Hogan, *The Marshall Plan: America, Britain, and the reconstruction of Western Europe, 1947–1952* (New York, 1987).

The second phase of the realist program involved military alliances. The centerpiece was the North Atlantic Treaty Organization (NATO), which initially included the United States, France, Great Britain, Italy, the Netherlands, and Belgium.

Unlike previous U.S. agreements, which had made provision for military cooperation, NATO carried the alliance a giant step forward by creating a formal, international command structure for NATO forces. In the Mediterranean, the United States had already brought Greece and Turkey into its military ambit, and in the years that immediately followed, American treaties were also completed with Southeast Asian nations and with Australia and New Zealand. By 1952, the U.S. military presence was being felt throughout the world. When former enemies Germany and Japan were brought into the fold, the strategic objectives of Kennan's 1947 proposal were met.

The central accomplishment of postwar America's professional realists was the containment of Soviet power and expansion in Europe. Soviet pressures constantly tested the NATO allies, and the inevitable disagreements within the alliance called for many rounds of tinkering at all military and diplomatic levels to keep the system operational. The French were, as always, a problem to keep inside the NATO structure. Proud of their history and resentful of American power and intrusive leadership, the French government found it difficult to provide the support NATO wanted. Still, NATO persisted and gradually built up a force that made it a formidable counterbalance to the Soviet military power in Europe. Standing behind NATO were America's nuclear weapons and its Strategic Air Command.

The greatest challenges to the realists came from the national socialist revolutions that rocked the world during the American Century. China's communist revolution was distressing. U.S. realists were aligned with the Nationalist regime of C.K. Sheik, our ally. Corrupt? Yes. Weak? Yes. But he appeared to be the only alternative to the communists. So once again, American military aid and forces were deployed in a futile effort to beat back a revolution. Once again the United States failed. Too little power was used to keep the Chinese Nationalists going. Too much was employed to convince today's historian that the United States had learned how to conduct its empire without squandering its power.

In dealing with the Chinese revolution, there was a serious disconnect between those experts who best understood China and its political development and those who were now guiding the nation's military policies. The United States was already suffering from the overweening pride that would create problems for the realists for the next half century. Hubris fed denial. Denial was the antithesis of the professional expertise the United States badly needed in formulating a new China policy.

The Idealists and the Empire

The realists and the idealists didn't agree on many things, but they did agree on efforts to unify Europe. Rather than worry about the challenge a unified Europe might eventually pose to American leadership, the realists looked to European unity as the best possible means of containing Soviet power. Many European leaders looked to unity as the best possible means of containing German power. To the idealists, European unity promised to remake Europe along the lines of the United States, ensuring a peaceful and prosperous future of democratic capitalism.

On other important issues, the idealists and realists disagreed. To the idealists, it was natural, acceptable, and even desirable to see colonies in the twentieth century throwing off the empires of the European powers just as the United States had in the late eighteenth century. If those new nations opted for centralizing socialist regimes, well, that was their choice to make. Hadn't Woodrow Wilson, now a patron saint of the idealists, included self-determination in his Fourteen Points? That was one of the pillars of the Atlantic Charter ideology and of the United Nations. The United States should learn how to get along with the new regimes peacefully and as soon as possible. If trade had to be conducted on their socialist or even communist terms, that too was OK if only because the United States was the wealthiest nation in the world. America could afford to be magnanimous with both trade and foreign aid.

Most idealists were not One Worlders, but they supported the United Nations as the best hope that mankind had of avoiding a third world war. After the hydrogen bomb was developed, the UN became even more important to the idealists's plans. Now it was mutual destruction and perhaps the annihilation of all life on earth that had to be prevented. Whereas the realists turned to the Rand Corporation and the Joint Chiefs of Staff for plans and leadership to cope with these problems, the idealists looked to the UN. The efforts to bring atomic and nuclear weapons under international control failed, however. National interests ruled. Even the closest of allies – the United States and United Kingdom, for instance – were unable to share nuclear knowledge and weaponry. Fear and suspicion of the UN made it impossible for the nations in the small nuclear club to turn over control of those awesome weapons to any international agency. That hope went down the drain.

In other areas, the United Nations was able to build up its standing and establish new capabilities. In relief work, the UN played a vital role in what for many in the underdeveloped world was a life-threatening struggle. The UN's World Health Organization (WHO) provided assistance with public health in some of the poorest regions of the world. There were areas of Africa, Latin America, and Asia that had virtually no experience with the modern life-saving medicines and vaccines that Americans and Europeans were now using. Before World War II, the developed nations had reached out to the weak, undeveloped nations to colonize and exploit them. WHO reached out to those people in new ways, seeking to prevent or treat diseases like smallpox and measles.[14] This was an earth-shaking historical change that encouraged idealists to look forward eagerly to further accomplishments by WHO and the United Nations.

The UN continued to evolve, as did the International Monetary Fund (IMF) and the World Bank – the Bretton Woods institutions. Some of the greatest problems of the immediate postwar period involved the fiscal difficulties of both the developed and the developing countries. During the war, debts had piled up. Trade relations had been shattered. Confidence in currencies other than the dollar had been fractured.[15] The system developed at Bretton Woods in 1946 tried to deal with these problems by stabilizing international currencies. They were linked to the world's strongest currency, the dollar. When the economies of countries like Britain sagged under their debt load and stood on the brink of fiscal collapse, the IMF and the U.S. Treasury were able to work together to avert financial disaster. At first, recovery was slow, and the IMF had plenty of time to work on improving and extending its program of fiscal stabilization. Neither the IMF nor its member nations were perfect in this regard, but the contrast between the post–World War I and the post–World War II records of international monetary policy left no doubt as

---

[14] For a positive interpretation, see Ruth Levin et al., *Millions Saved: Proven Successes in Global Health* (Sudbury, Massachusetts, 2004); and Ruth Levine et al., *Millions Saved: Case Studies in Global Health* (Sudbury, Massachusetts, 2007). For the negative side, see William Easterly, *The White Man's Burden: Why the West's Efforts to Aid the Rest Have Done So Much Ill and so Little Good* (New York, 2006); and Laurie Garrett, "The Challenge of Global Health," *Foreign Affairs*, 86, 1 (2007), 14–38.

[15] Harold James, *International Monetary Cooperation since Bretton Woods* (Washington, 1996).

to which approach was best. Between 1946 and 1969, Bretton Woods performed a crucial role in fostering recovery.[16]

The World Bank started its postwar career as an agency of reconstruction, but the Marshall Plan soon took over that particular role.[17] Instead of shutting its doors, the Bank took on a new role astride the great gulf that existed between the industrial countries and those that had yet to feel the direct effects of the second industrial revolution. Many Americans were and still are automatically bored when they see an article on the World Bank; however, they should try harder to understand the activities of an institution that loaned large sums of money to the governments of underdeveloped countries. Dominated initially by engineers, the Bank staff primarily promoted bricks-and-mortar projects: dams to provide electrical power, flood control, and irrigation; roads and bridges to improve access to a country's natural resources and markets.[18]

The Bank's development model was based loosely on the economic histories of western nations and regions that had passed through various "stages" of growth. One of the world's leading economic historians, Walt Whitman Rostow, charted the path in his articles and his book *The Stages of Economic Growth*. According to Rostow and many other economists, the Bank's goal was to help underdeveloped countries like India, Kenya, and Brazil achieve a "take off into sustained growth." Rostow's model – and the Bank's – was a "one size fits all" theory that emphasized heavy investments in infrastructure as a first step toward accelerating economic growth.[19] The Bank, armed with low-interest loans, sought to close the entrepreneurial gap that plagued the underdeveloped economies. When it became clear early on that professional expertise in those countries was also underdeveloped, the Bank began to train the experts the counties needed.[20]

---

[16] J. Keith Horsefield, *The International Monetary Fund, 1945–1965: Twenty Years of International Monetary Cooperation* (Washington, 1969).

[17] Michael J. Hogan, *The Marshall Plan.*

[18] Edward S. Mason and Robert E. Asher, *The World Bank Since Bretton Woods: The Origins, Policies, Operations, and Impact of The International Bank for Reconstruction and Development and the Other Members of the World Bank Group: The International Finance Corporation, the International Development Association, The International Centre for Settlement of Investment Disputes* (Washington, 1973).

[19] The desired path was seen as a great slopping S curve, with growth accelerating, then staying on a long positive slope, and finally leveling off at very high levels of gross domestic product (GDP) and GDP per capita. Walt Whitman Rostow, *The Stages of Economic Growth: A Non-Communist Manifesto* (Cambridge, 1960).

[20] Devesh Kapur, John P. Lewis, and Richard Webb, *The World Bank: Its First Half Century, I, History* (Washington, 1997).

What did this trio of new institutions – the Bank, the IMF, and the UN – accomplish in the early years of the American Century? They both reflected and reinforced a new approach to the relations between strong and weak countries. Instead of the traditional colonial exploitation model that had characterized centuries of empire building, the postwar international organizations were working to implement a new ideology. It called on the strong nations to help themselves in the long run by helping the weak countries improve their lot in the short term. Running against the grain of centuries of exploitation was not an easy undertaking, and all three of these organizations had trouble with nations that were slow to abandon their customary international relations. The organizations also had trouble with the personal failings of their own leaders and followers, the kind of failings that pop up with regularity in all institutions and provide solid evidence that even the grandest intentions can founder in sin as well as error.

These institutions nevertheless helped promote a new wave of globalization that would eventually transform the United States and its links to the rest of the world. A number of the world's most economically advanced countries, led by Britain and the United States, attempted to break down the national barriers to global trade. This strategy for avoiding World War III was introduced with the Bretton Woods settlement and embodied in the International Trade Organization (ITO). You've probably never heard of that organization because the U.S. Congress rejected it.[21] The ITO proposal for sudden and sharp reductions in trade barriers hit too many of the Congressional lawyers and their colleagues where they were most vulnerable: on the issue of reelection. That set off more rounds of negotiation, which produced the General Agreement on Tariffs and Trade (GATT), which was less intrusive and less dangerous to the careers of congressional incumbents.

This framework of international organizations and programs would evolve through the following decades, but it is still, in one form or another, with us today. We deal, for instance, with the World Trade Organization (WTO) rather than GATT. And the World Bank has become the World Bank Group. But all still exist – a testament to the need for international governance in a global system.

The greatest failure of the idealists was their inability to bring the communist bloc into the new international organizations, with the exception

---

[21] Scott Newton, *The Global Economy, 1944–2000: The Limits of Ideology* (London, 2004), especially 28ff.

of the UN, where the Soviets had veto power. Bretton Woods was dedicated to free trade, but the Soviet bloc was dedicated to communist control of trade. The Bank was dedicated to helping underdeveloped nations achieve economic progress, whereas the communists were dedicated to world revolution against democratic capitalism. For the realities of Soviet and Chinese power, the idealists had no answer except to respect national sovereignty more than did either of these communist regimes.

Balancing Idealism and Realism

When Dwight "Ike" Eisenhower – a professional military leader – became President of the United States in 1953, he inherited a world split between communist and capitalist nations, with the current of national policies and international relations running strongly against America.[22] Ominous developments were taking place both inside and outside of the U.S. empire. Inside, Ike was concerned that the nationalization of industries and the implementation of extensive central controls would leave the United States with too few allies dedicated to American-style capitalism.[23] Outside of the empire, many of the "nonaligned" nations appeared actually to be aligning themselves with the communist or socialist left. They too were opting for central controls on their economies. Meanwhile, the two nations at the core of the communist movement, the USSR and China, were rapidly gaining economic and military strength. It was difficult to be an optimist about the future of democratic capitalism.

Even though Ike had roots planted deeply in the small-town agricultural Midwest, he didn't line up with Henry Wallace's one-world brand of idealism. Ike was a fervent believer in democracy. He understood the American values that made the struggle against totalitarian systems necessary, and he was unwilling to sacrifice those ideals in a futile effort to achieve perfect national security. But he blended those ideals with a well-grounded realism developed in World War II and perfected when he was the first supreme military commander of NATO forces (1951–1952). As president, Eisenhower and his military and diplomatic professionals formulated a Cold War strategy that would carry the United

---

[22] The reader should be aware that I served as editor or coeditor of volumes 6 through 21 of *The Papers of Dwight David Eisenhower*. The eight volumes on Eisenhower's presidency are available free and fully searchable at http://www.eisenhowermemorial.org/presidential-papers/index.htm

[23] *The Papers of Dwight David Eisenhower, The Presidency: The Middle Way*, vol. 14, 33–38, 88, 200–02, 552–53.

States through the dangerous 1950s and would still be guiding U.S. relations with the USSR when the Soviet empire began to experience a major internal crisis.[24]

Eisenhower and his strategists had no difficulty dealing with the threat of direct military attack. The president was certain the United States and its allies could withstand any attack and destroy the enemies' forces and homelands. He would use nuclear weapons in that case, and the threat of a nuclear holocaust would, he thought, prevent overt aggression by the communists. He made this strategy clear to America's enemies and allies alike.[25] Meanwhile, he patiently explored potential areas of agreement that promised to reduce the probabilities of a nuclear world war. He and his Secretary of State, John Foster Dulles, tried to do this without encouraging Americans to develop unrealistic expectations for détente.[26] The goal of Eisenhower's policies was to defend the United States and its client states without injuring either the democracy or the capitalist economy that were, over the long haul, America's greatest sources of strength.

Like all of the other postwar U.S. presidents, secretaries of state, and military planners, Eisenhower had trouble figuring out what to do about the forces of national socialist revolutions, including those in the Western Hemisphere.[27] In Latin America, forces on the left were powerful. When America tried to strengthen the economies and political systems of the weakest nations along democratic-capitalistic lines, leftists were able to disrupt the U.S. efforts. In the Middle East, Eisenhower was confronted by revolution, this time with an Islamic thrust. In France and Italy, where communist parties made large political gains, Ike was forced to consider what the United States would do if communist parties were freely elected to take control of two countries essential to NATO defenses.

In Latin America and the Middle East, Ike attempted to preserve the façade of American ideals while secretly using the Central Intelligence Agency to implement starkly realistic policies. In the short term, those

---

[24] On the Soviet's crisis, see Chapter 16 in this volume.

[25] For an outstanding history and analysis of the Eisenhower strategy (framed with events in the Soviet Union), see Melvyn P. Leffler, *For the Soul of Mankind: The United States, the Soviet Union, and the Cold War* (New York, 2007), 84–150.

[26] The exception to this rule was the indication in the political campaign of 1952 that the United States would attempt to "roll back communism" in East Europe. These statements came back to haunt the administration during the Hungarian revolt in 1956. See *The Papers of Dwight David Eisenhower, The Presidency: The Middle Way*, vol. 17, 2334–35, 2345, 2361–63.

[27] John Lewis Gaddis, *Strategies of Containment*, 174–81.

policies were successful in Peru and Guatemala, as well as Iran. But in the long term, this approach failed to satisfy the goals of either idealism or realism. In Latin America, the U.S.'s greatest accomplishments in the entire postwar era came from the patient exploration of mutual long-term economic interests – not from assassinations or manipulations by undercover agents. The United States has never been particularly good at that, and Allen Dulles' CIA was just about par for the course.[28]

These clandestine efforts notwithstanding, the Eisenhower administrations in the 1950s worked hard and did a reasonable job of balancing the country's democratic values with its need for national security.[29] Keeping the American empire's alliance system intact was a major accomplishment, as was the U.S.-led resistance in Europe and Asia to outright military aggression. This was the Eisenhower administration's policy even when the aggression was by its closest allies, as was the case in the Suez War (1956). Eisenhower stamped on that joint British, French, and Israeli assault, an attack that challenged Ike's basic strategy and was a throwback to the gunboat diplomacy of the pre–World War II years. Ike was not wedded to the Bretton Woods institutions, but he and his strategists were not going to preside over a return to the sort of nationalism that underpinned the old-style European empires. Eisenhower thought that one of his most significant accomplishments was to lead the loosely organized American empire without the loss of a single member of the American armed forces in combat overseas.[30] As he noted with a zing, "That didn't just happen!" Those words would come back to mock the United States in the 1960s, when a different brand of realism would be implemented.

A new breed of military experts would help plan that transition. Eisenhower had been too mindful of the idealist position to satisfy some of the country's leading military professionals in the late 1950s. Maxwell Taylor, for example, thought that the Eisenhower strategy was flawed

---

[28] Stephen E. Ambrose, *Eisenhower, 2, The President, 1952–1969* (New York, 1984), 189; Dennis E. Showalter, ed., *Forging the Shield: Eisenhower and National Security for the 21st Century* (Chicago, 2005). Israel seems to be the gold standard for these policies.

[29] See David Cannadine's nuanced exploration of *Ornamentalism: How the British Saw Their Empire* (London, 2001) for a discussion of the links between culture and empire. As Cannadine shows, the British had less tension between their values and their vast empire than the United States: "Only the United States of America," he says (xiii), "remains as the last authentic western imperial power, deploying its unchallenged financial might and unrivalled military strength around the globe, even as it still prides itself on its exemplary hostility to empire...."

[30] His statement was accurate for the years following the armistice in Korea.

and that the military could be revamped to fight effectively against the kinds of revolutionary outbreaks that had distressed the United States for so many years.[31] After John F. Kennedy took office in 1961, he bought into the Taylor strategy and began under his new Secretary of Defense Robert S. McNamara to recast the U.S. military so it could fight effectively against the world's revolutionary forces.[32]

Just that kind of war was waiting in Southeast Asia. From 1945 to 1954, France had fought a losing, increasingly expensive war aimed at preserving its Vietnamese colony. The United States helped support the French forces with extensive military supplies.[33] But in 1954, President Eisenhower had decided not to send ground or air units to Dien Bien Phu, where the communist Viet Minh had trapped a large part of the French army. Defeated, the French abandoned their colony and left Vietnam split between a communist north and a capitalist south aligned with the United States and its allies. America solidified its support for this new client state by creating SEATO, the Southeast Asia Treaty Organization.[34]

The Kennedy administration crept into the war, one carefully limited move at a time. The expansion of the U.S. effort began with a relatively small detachment of military advisors, but renewed attacks by Ho Chi Minh's Viet Cong kept forcing the U.S. president to reconsider and finally to bolster the South Vietnamese position. Within the administration, Secretary of Defense McNamara and the Joint Chiefs of Staff pressed demands to deploy U.S. combat troops. By 1962, U.S. military advice had become military assistance. There were now U.S. planes, ships, and about 16,000 troops dedicated to defeating a Viet Cong enemy that appeared

---

[31] There were others, including Bernard Brodie, who were interested in developing the capacity to fight limited wars. The split that took place among the military professionals was similar and had similar results to the one that developed among the experts in atomic energy. Brian Balogh, *Chain Reaction*.

[32] McNamara provides an interesting description of the meeting between Eisenhower and President-elect Kennedy and their respective associates on January 19, 1961. Indochina was the major subject, and Ike was apparently most concerned about Laos: "'President Eisenhower advised against unilateral action by the United States in connection with Laos," McNamara wrote in his memorandum of record.

[33] Melvyn P. Leffler, *The Specter of Communism: The United States and the Origins of the Cold War, 1917–1953* (New York, 1994), places these developments in the broad context of U.S. foreign policy. Leffler notes, "Although American fears were exaggerated, they were nonetheless understandable" (129).

[34] The peace settlement that split the country was negotiated at the Geneva Conference of 1954. In addition to representatives of the Viet Minh and South Vietnam, the Conference included representatives of Cambodia, Laos, France, Britain, China, the Soviet Union, and the United States.

to be ready to suffer any level of casualties to ensure an ultimate victory. That should have been clear from a careful study of the Viet Minh campaigns against the French. But America's political and military leaders were convinced that new policies would enable the client government in Saigon to defend itself. The problem was that the South Vietnamese military was poorly led, corrupt, and certainly less inspired than the communists. Our ally's political leadership – both before and after the coup we supported – was no better than it was in China during that country's revolution. With the same consequences.

After Kennedy's assassination, President Lyndon Johnson brought all of the force of America's revamped military and high technology to bear against the communist forces. To do so, he needed congressional support. To win that support and keep the money and troops flowing into Vietnam, the Johnson administration was forced to deceive Congress and the American people about a relatively minor naval incident in the Gulf of Tonkin during 1964. The Gulf, off North Vietnam's coastline, was being patrolled by Navy ships, including the destroyer USS *Maddox*. Under attack, briefly, by North Vietnamese torpedo boats, the *Maddox* returned fire and then went back out to sea. Two days later, the *Maddox* and a companion ship reported another attack when the ships were in international waters. This time, as subsequent studies showed, no attack had taken place.[35] Nevertheless, Johnson used the false information to persuade Congress to pass a resolution authorizing the president to use America's military power as he saw fit against the Vietnamese communists. Other deceptions would follow, as did the rapid buildup of American combat forces, a policy that many military and political experts had been recommending for several years.

The United States was no longer short of professional experts. Every discipline and subdiscipline, every corner of the society was full of them. Walt Whitman Rostow, National Security Advisor to President Johnson, was one of the leading experts. Rostow wasn't the sort of person who could win an election. But he could win a seat at the table where decisions were made, where power was deployed. Like most of the other gurus of the 1960s, Rostow was optimistic. His history had a happy ending in which the Cold War protagonists would gradually converge, via economic growth, on a common destination. This would, without another great war, leave the world in peace and prosperity. Americans and their

---

[35] Edward J. Marolda (Senior Historian, Naval Historical Center), "Summary of the Tonkin Gulf Crisis of August 1964," http://www.history.navy.mil/faqs/faq120-1.htm

allies would have to display true grit, would have to exercise their power realistically to get to that goal. But it could be done.[36]

In a public sphere dominated by experts like Rostow, one of the central problems of leadership in America became the choice and control of professional advisors. It was never completely obvious how to do this, and it would not always be done successfully. It certainly wasn't very successful in Washington, DC, in the 1960s or in Southeast Asia.

The military disaster that followed Johnson's decision to ramp up the war should have been an important turning point in America's experiment with empire. Vietnam should have taught Americans to show more respect for the revolutionary aims of other people and to have less confidence in the U.S. ability to thwart those aims with military force. But those were hard lessons for Americans to absorb. It should have been evident very early that America's allies in South Vietnam were corrupt and ineffective against the dedicated revolutionaries of the Viet Cong and their North Vietnamese allies. That failure gradually shifted the brunt of the war to the American forces, which adopted a variety of policies and programs to pacify the countryside and defeat the revolutionaries. The United States had, at best, isolated successes.

As the war dragged on and American losses mounted, the pressure at home to end the war became intense. The New Left movement began increasingly to focus on the war as the central issue in American politics. The wonders of technology – smart bombs, for instance – were paraded in front of the American public as our answer to the Vietnamese revolution. But most Americans were more concerned about the body bags coming home than the bombs destined for Vietnam's villages and jungles. There is a limit to what public relations can do in the public as well as the private sector. The resistance to the war finally drove Lyndon Johnson out of the White House, but his successor, Richard M. Nixon, refused to accept Ho Chi Min's wise analysis: "When you are gone, we will still be here." Nixon set out to reduce U.S. ground forces while expanding the war to North Vietnam and increasing the air power rained down on the revolutionary forces that were America's enemy. The domestic rhetoric was pianissimo and idealistic. The policies were those of brutal realism, fortissimo and completely insensitive to democratic values.

---

[36] Walt Whitman Rostow, *The Stages of Economic Growth: A Non-Communist Manifesto* (Cambridge, 1960). Rostow had published articles that set forth his stage analysis; see, for instance, "The Stages of Economic Growth," *The Economic History Review*, 12, 1 (1959), 1–16.

An Overview of the Empire in the Late 1960s

As the end of the decade approached, the U.S. empire in Europe was – in spite of the French disaffection – still very much intact. This was true even though the governments of the U.S. client states and their people were increasingly hostile to the United States and the war in Vietnam. Their hostility was exceeded only by their fear of the Soviet Union, a fear that held NATO together. In the Middle East, the U.S. position was stable, but the truce was fragile at best. In Southeast Asia, the limits of U.S. power had been exposed and the empire weakened as a result. Only Japan was still a determined ally. China had found it unwise to attempt to intervene more forcefully in Vietnam, as it had in Korea, perhaps because the U.S. was already losing to Ho Chi Minh.

Whether I was in Houston teaching at Rice or visiting Johns Hopkins as a postdoc, I was struggling to get a better understanding of the U.S. problems in dealing with the world. I knew there were serious problems. But I wasn't loaded with solutions. When I left my undergraduate school, I still knew more about Rome's empire than America's. In the years that followed, I had learned a great deal about American foreign relations. But the center of gravity in my knowledge was the middle of the nineteenth century, not the twentieth. I had begun to read and understand more about the Russian Revolution and Marxism.[37] But I still looked on the communist world as a big red blob, with no national borders or significant ethnic groups.[38]

Like many other Americans, I was just beginning to see the limits of military power in dealing with revolution, but I was not yet concerned about the tension between professional expertise and democracy. After all, I was a young professional surrounded by other professionals and would-be professionals. Soon I would have an opportunity to reflect more seriously on that tension and on the opposition to the war. I would have both America's New Left and Richard M. Nixon to thank for that next step in my education.

---

[37] I was being tutored during these years by Professor Leonard M. Marsak, an intellectual historian with an interest in the philosophy of history and a remarkable understanding of Hegel and Marx.

[38] Professor A. J. Matusow, a historian at Rice University, was trying hard to improve my grasp of this situation.

12

The Tattered Empire of the 1970s

After Nixon and Agnew took office in 1969, the victory of the American suburbs and the suburban mentality seemed complete. But the long-standing struggle between the realists and the idealists over the nation's empire had yet to be resolved.[1] The resolution for many in this generation of Americans would be achieved amid a great internal struggle that would array youth against age, professional expertise against common sense, and the powerful advocates of empire against those who were deeply concerned about the erosion of American democratic values. By the end of the 1970s, many who treasured memories of fighting on God's side in World War II would realize that they – like the scientist Robert Oppenheimer – had "known sin."[2]

By that time, the American Century was collapsing like a tire with a slow leak.[3] The leak should have been obvious to many Americans, to most of their leaders, and to all of the experts who now played decisive roles in framing the country's foreign policies and military interventions. It should have been clear to Walt Whitman Rostow, President Johnson's

---

[1] Questing for more knowledge about this dismal decade, the aspiring young scholar should turn first to David Halberstam's account of *The Best and the Brightest* (New York, 1992 edition), and then read Melvyn P. Leffler, *For the Soul of Mankind: The United States, the Soviet Union, and the Cold War* (New York, 2007).

[2] The popular version of this thought came from the comic strip Pogo: "We have met the enemy, and he is us."

[3] I am using the expression "the American Century" just to apply to the era following World War II. Other authors identify the American Century as the entire twentieth century. See, for instance, Donald W. White, *The American Century*. And Olivier Zunz, *Why the American Century?* (Chicago, 2000).

advisor on national security issues, that the U.S. position in the world had been sagging since the mid-1960s. But the smoke screen of over-weening pride made it difficult for the well-educated, talented experts to see what was happening. After all, the pundits of the new American aristocracy – the corporate and military leaders, the economists and other academics, the policy experts like Rostow, and the organizational wizards like McNamara – had reason to believe they had fought off or bought off their critics in the Civil Rights and New Left movements. Their optimism was not entirely irrational. But they were wrong.

The *realpolitik* of that era – like many elements of its idealistic counter-part – was based on the new aristocracy's sophisticated analyses. The new public sphere in America was a thoroughly professional sphere, radically transformed since the early decades of the twentieth century.[4] That's why a university professor like Walt Whitman Rostow could end up in the White House, close to the sources of power in the most power-ful nation in the world. That's also why his place would be taken in Nixon's White House by another expert, a man who was an immigrant, a Jew, and a remarkable example of just how far the professional path could take a determined, always brilliant, frequently ruthless political scientist.

Henry Kissinger was an exception to most of the rules, an outlier in the history of immigrant progress in America. It didn't take two or three generations for a Kissinger to make it into the upper reaches of U.S. professional and political life. Early on, it was not obvious that Henry, a bookish, introverted fifteen-year-old, was going to be particularly suc-cessful in his new home in New York City. He and his parents had landed there in 1938, when America was still struggling to get out of the Great Depression. The family had managed to escape Germany and Nazi per-secution, but it was not easy to get resettled in New York. His father, forced to abandon his career as a teacher, worked as a bookkeeper at a factory. Short of money, Henry (born Heinz) went to work at a shaving-brush company the following year and attended night school. He was an excellent student at George Washington High School, but after graduat-ing, he still couldn't think of anything more imaginative than following

---

[4] I have expropriated and twisted into a new shape Jürgen Habermas' concept of the public sphere. Jürgen Habermas, *The Structural Transformation of the Public Sphere: An Inquiry into a Category of Bourgeois Society* (Cambridge, Massachusetts, 1989 English translation of the 1962 German publication).

his father's occupation. He enrolled at City College of New York to get a degree in accounting.[5]

In 1943, the draft board interrupted his formal education and sent him into the U.S. Army. In that improbable setting, he acquired his first mentor and experienced the kind of epiphany that frequently bumps professional careers onto a new course. A well-educated Army colleague, Fritz Gustav Anton Kraemer, was the mentor who pushed young Henry toward history and philosophy and encouraged him to find a career commensurate with his intellect. With his ambition unleashed, Kissinger returned to the United States in 1947 and jump-started a new career at Harvard University.[6] Focused and unbelievably intense, he graduated *summa cum laude* in 1950 and only four years later completed his doctoral studies in government. By this time, he was already on his way to becoming something of an academic legend at Harvard.[7] Three years and two books later, he was back at Harvard as a lecturer and associate director of the Center for International Affairs.

One of Kissinger's books hit the *New York Times* best-seller list and made the author an instant national expert on *Nuclear Weapons and Foreign Policy*.[8] The dominant strategic paradigm of the 1950s involved massive nuclear retaliation if the Soviets threatened Western Europe. Seeking – as did Maxwell Taylor and others – greater flexibility, Kissinger proposed the use of tactical nuclear weapons to offset communist strength in troops and tanks. He said the new weapons could be employed without throwing the world into a nuclear holocaust.

Kissinger's other book was more modest, but it provided an interesting perspective on his approach to international relations. *A World Restored: Metternich, Castlereagh and the Problems of Peace, 1812–22* was, like most published dissertations, written for a tiny audience of experts, most of whom the author either knew or could identify by name, school, and

---

[5] Unless otherwise indicated, I have followed Walter Isaacson's impressive study, *Kissinger: A Biography* (New York, 1992). Isaacson acknowledges his subject's strengths while carefully cataloging Kissinger's flaws.

[6] As Isaacson explains, Kissinger's experiences in the Army's intelligence service and occupation in Germany involved the sort of responsibilities that in his case helped make him an unusually mature twenty-four-year-old student. *Kissinger*, 39–58.

[7] Kissinger had, for instance, organized and funded a special summer speaker's program – the Harvard International Seminar – at a point in his graduate studies when most students are nervously struggling to get through the reading lists provided by their professors.

[8] *Nuclear Weapons and Foreign Policy* (New York, 1957).

leading publications. The hero of Kissinger's history was Prince Metternich, the conservative Austrian diplomat who at the Congress of Vienna (1814–1815) led the effort to create a stable European order in the wake of the Napoleonic Wars. A skillful master of the balance of power, Metternich of course didn't have to contend with public opinion or democratic impulses.[9] He would, in these and other regards, provide a model for Kissinger, who would throughout his own career show no respect for American public opinion or democratic governance. Indeed, he would do as much as he could to keep them from interfering with his exercise of power.

Kissinger was an instinctive conservative who had already become a Republican when he was in high school. As his career unfolded, however, it became apparent that he was far more concerned with power and status than he was with any ideology. Thus, he could work as easily with the liberal Democratic administration of Lyndon Johnson as he could with the conservative administrations of Richard Nixon and Gerald Ford. He was a political chameleon who could adapt his language and many of his ideas to the leader he served. The only fixed points were his desire to have as much power as possible and to be able to implement his particular brand of *realpolitik*. When he joined the Nixon administration in 1969, Kissinger was supremely optimistic that he could restructure the balance of power and create a more stable order in the Cold War.

The optimism of Americans less historically sophisticated than Henry Kissinger was grounded in a much shorter sense of the past. The public's sense of history hinged on certain central events of the previous three decades: the victory in World War II, the economic recovery from the Great Depression, and the global triumphs of the postwar American Century. There appeared to be no limits to what a determined United States could accomplish. Keynesian economic policy was a magic wand that gave the federal government the power to guide the largest economy in the world through any difficulties. That's one of the reasons that the world's currencies were pegged to the dollar.[10] Science and modern engineering were giving Americans a new measure of understanding and control over their physical environment. The memory of the good war

---

[9] (Boston, 1957). Metternich, Kissinger observed (p. 19), "became the architect of peace, who would repair by cunning, patience, and manipulation what had been lost by total commitment."

[10] Robert Gilpin (with Jean Millis Gilpin), *The Challenge of Global Capitalism: The World Economy in the 21st Century* (Princeton, 2000), explores the issue, as does Harold James, *International Monetary Cooperation since Bretton Woods*.

with its spectacular atomic ending validated American optimism, as did the country's progress since 1945.[11] Facing down communist expansion, the United States would certainly win another glorious victory. Hadn't that always been the American story?

The Vietnamese Quagmire

But of course the analogies were false and the history flawed.[12] Instead of World War II, the United States was entangled once again in a foreign revolution. The country had always had trouble understanding and responding to these sorts of conflicts. Whether dealing with Latin America, Russia, or Asia, American policies in countering revolutions had been clumsy and unsuccessful. For the most part, the policies had been framed with an exaggerated sense of how much any country could reshape the internal politics and culture of another society – particularly another society in the midst of revolutionary turmoil. Instead of restraint, the United States had repeatedly inched forward, exercising its power timidly at first while trying to avoid the appearance (but not the reality) of interfering in another country's internal politics. In each case, controlling the empire made it necessary to ignore the approach to national self-determination that Woodrow Wilson had endorsed.

The American strategy for coping with the Vietnamese Revolution was a design for disaster. Those with the most knowledge of Southeast Asia had the least power in American government. Once again, those with the most power to act had the least knowledge. When Lyndon Johnson handed over the presidency to Richard Nixon in January 1969, the United States was already deeply involved in support of a weak, indecisive South Vietnamese government, as well as the governments of Cambodia, Laos, and Thailand. Each policy failure had been met with the only real answer the military professionals had to offer: the application of more force, perhaps in a different style. The cycle was repeated over and over again. There had been 50,000 American troops in South Vietnam in

---

[11] In addition to the data in volume 3 of the *Historical Statistics of the United States, Economic Structure and Performance*, see Christina D. Romer, "A Rehabilitation of Monetary Policy in the 1950s," *NBER Working Paper No. 8800* (February 2002), and Harold G. Vatter, *The U.S. Economy in the 1950s: An Economic History* (Chicago, 1985).

[12] On the use and misuse of historical analogies, see Ernest R. May and Richard E. Neustadt, *Thinking in Time: The Uses of History for Decision Makers* (New York, 1986).

the summer of 1965. Two years later, there were over 460,000. As the struggle continued to intensify, the U.S. commitment exceeded 540,000.[13]

In effect, the White House and the Pentagon had drawn a defensive line at the outer edge of the American empire. Then the line they had drawn became a central aspect of the problem. If the line gave way, the reasoning went, confidence in American military power would suffer. Therefore, the line had to be defended, and indeed, the military planners and security experts developed a program well suited to the defense of a frontier against an external threat. This was consistent with those global maps that showed communist governments as a great red blob, with no gradations for different countries, cultures, languages, or regimes. Consistent too was the domino strategy that posited an almost inevitable sequence of revolutions once Laos or Vietnam had fallen to the communists.[14] In this strategic plan, any differences between the Chinese and Vietnamese were insignificant because both countries were communist.

The Nixon Administration tried to tailor its military strategy to fit an increasingly volatile domestic political scene. Since the communist Tet Offensive of 1968, American voters, the media, and Congress had all been voicing more and more general concerns about the conduct of the war and very specific concerns about the mounting American casualties. While the Tet Offensive was costly to the Viet Cong and its North Vietnamese ally, the attacks demonstrated with clarity that the communist forces were capable of mounting coordinated campaigns against South Vietnam, including the major cities. Thousands of troops and tons of military supplies had been moved into place before the attacks, which began on the Vietnamese New Year (hence Tet). The assaults in Saigon, the capital, were especially troubling, even though they were not accompanied by the general uprising against the government that the communists had anticipated. The predictable military response was to request more troops and to look forward to broadening the war into Laos and Cambodia.

At first, Nixon decided to chart a different course. He tried to substitute "Vietnamization" for "Americanization" of the war. Thwarted in the ground war, the United States began to withdraw its troops, leaving the ground campaigns in the hands of South Vietnam's army. This was a distinction without a very impressive difference from the perspective of

---

[13] Robert S. McNamara, *In Retrospect: The Tragedy and Lessons of Vietnam* (New York, 1995), 283–321.

[14] The Eisenhower administration applied the domino concept to Southeast Asia and other parts of the world.

the Viet Cong. But many Americans were pleased to see their husbands and sons returning to the United States alive. Nixon's National Security Advisor, Henry Kissinger, was opposed to a unilateral withdrawal of ground forces. He believed his negotiations with the North Vietnamese could only be successful if they were backed by force. But he had to yield to Nixon on this policy.

Despite the withdrawal, there were ample opportunities to continue using force. The United States began to bomb Cambodia and the border areas of Laos in an unsuccessful effort to destroy the communist sanctuaries in those ostensibly neutral countries. Concerned not to foment more public demonstrations, Nixon and Kissinger kept the bombings secret, even from the U.S. Congress. In an effort to force North Vietnam to approve a truce, the United States finally started bombing Hanoi again in the spring of 1972. The United States secretly began mining North Vietnam's Haiphong harbor to prevent military supplies from arriving.[15]

To a realist like Henry Kissinger, it was far more important to extend the military campaign than it was to support American democratic values or institutions.[16] This late phase of the war involved an untenable extension of executive and professional military authority. Soon the new policies became public and came under intense attack from the media and the administration's political opponents within the United States and abroad. That pressure mounted after American and South Vietnamese ground forces moved into Cambodia and Laos to attack communist positions.

At home, the clash between American values and American policy on the frontiers of the empire had become widespread and intense. At Kent State University in Ohio, National Guardsmen actually fired on unarmed students demonstrating against the war. Four were killed. In 1971, Americans also watched the trial of a U.S. Army officer accused of massacring civilians in the tiny Vietnam village of My Lai. To the Army's credit, Lieutenant William Calley was convicted, but the vision of a massacre was

---

[15] George C. Herring, *America's Longest War: The United States and Vietnam, 1950–1975* (Philadelphia, 1979).

[16] Jeremi Suri, *Henry Kissinger and the American Century* (Cambridge, 2007) focuses on the "why" not the "what" of Kissinger's policies. He was, Suri claims, "a conceptual synthesizer. He combined a cosmopolitan vision of Western civilization (embodied by the transatlantic elites) with a deep commitment to the calibration of power for foreign-policy needs (the work of the strategic wizards)" (p. 142). As Suri notes, Kissinger "sought to mix force and diplomacy, increasing the military pressure on the ground and in the air, while also offering accommodation and compromise" (p. 189).

not erased. Television coverage of the war became important, especially when Americans had to look at a naked girl, burned by napalm, fleeing the bombers.[17] In 1973, Congress at last ordered a stop to the bombing of Cambodia, but the damage to public support for the war had already been done. Ignoring the serious collateral damage to American democracy, President Nixon appointed Henry Kissinger Secretary of State that same year.

Vietnamization, supported by U.S. bombing, was ultimately no more successful than Americanization had been – with or without widespread bombing. The poorly led and undisciplined South Vietnamese forces were no match for their opponents. The Paris Peace Accords that had won Kissinger a Nobel Peace Prize quickly collapsed as it became evident that the South Vietnamese had little reason to fight for a corrupt government dominated by a foreign power.[18] It was a bitter message for many Americans, but it was now evident that Ho Chi Min, who died in 1969, had been right. Eventually the American forces would leave and the Vietnamese would rule their land. That happened in 1975, when Saigon fell to the communists, erasing the frontier America's leaders had staked out for this wing of the empire.

The Wages of Defeat

The sight of American helicopters racing to evacuate U.S. citizens and allies as the communists approached was a bitter climax to a war that should not have been fought and could not be won.[19] The secret bombing of Cambodia had completed my personal conversion from a moderate

---

[17] The picture of Phan Thi Kim Phúc was taken on June 8, 1972 as she and other children fled the village of Trang Bang in South Vietnam. http://en.wikipedia.org/wiki/Kim_Phuc_Phan_Thi.

[18] Jeremi Suri, *Henry Kissinger and the American Century*, 192–96. Suri points out three mistakes Kissinger made: he wanted to put the revolutionary process in a state-centered context; he wanted the international system controlled by a grand master; and he wanted a rational world. On Kissinger's strategy, including nuclear posturing, see especially 215–22. For a distinctly more favorable view of U.S. policy, you can turn to Henry Kissinger, *White House Years* (Boston, 1979); *Years of Upheaval* (Boston, 1982); *Years of Renewal* (New York, 1999); and *Crisis: The Anatomy of Two Major Foreign Policy Crises* (New York, 2003).

[19] As John Lewis Gaddis, *Strategies of Containment*, 236, notes, George Kennan had carefully distinguished between those areas of the world that were vital to American interests and those that were peripheral. Kennedy, Johnson, and then Nixon and Kissinger had lost sight of that important distinction.

realist to a middle-class, coat-and-tie demonstrator against the war.[20] I was left pondering how one drew the line between expertise and democracy. How could you know when the nation actually needed less expertise and more everyday intelligence? I was still not certain. But I was beginning to appreciate the importance of leaders who knew how to use expertise without losing their common sense. Nixon, Kissinger, and the country's military leaders had turned the White House and the foreign policy bureaucracy into a nightmare of intrigues. Spying, wire-tapping, lying, and irrational outbursts had become the norm in an administration unable to win the war and unable to let go of an insignificant outpost of the empire.[21]

The defeat had a devastating impact on the nation's military morale and leadership.[22] General Colin Powell, who served with honor in Vietnam, would later reflect on that experience: "We accepted that we had been sent to pursue a policy that had become bankrupt. Our political leaders had led us into a war for the one-size-fits-all rationale of anticommunism, which was only a partial fit in Vietnam, where the war had its own historical roots in nationalism, anticolonialism, and civil strife.... As a corporate entity, the military failed to talk straight to its political superiors or to itself."[23] It would be years before the effect of the defeat would begin to fade in the top ranks of the U.S. services.[24] So too with the Central Intelligence Agency, which had suffered a severe blow to its prestige and authority.

The defeat took down the reputations of "the best and the brightest," the new professional experts who had moved into the upper reaches of government in the 1960s.[25] Left licking their wounds, they returned to various academic or foundation appointments where they could compose

---

[20] I had participated in a talk show in Houston, speaking in favor of the war and in opposition to my good friend and colleague at Rice University, Allen J. Matusow.

[21] Gabriel Kolko attempted to prove that there were natural resources in Southeast Asia that were vital to American business, but his analysis was flawed and his evidence unconvincing. *The Roots of American Foreign Policy: An Analysis of Power and Purpose* (Boston, 1969); and *Anatomy of a War: Vietnam, the United States, and the Modern Historical Experience* (New York, 1985).

[22] George C. Herring, "Preparing *Not* to Refight the Last War: The Impact of the Vietnam War on the U.S. Military," in Charles E. Neu, ed., *After Vietnam: Legacies of a Lost War* (Baltimore, 2000), 56–84.

[23] Colin L. Powell (with Joseph E. Persico), *My American Journey* (New York, 1995), 149.

[24] See also Colonel Harry G. Summers, Jr., "The Army after Vietnam," in Kenneth J. Hagan and William R. Roberts, eds., *Against All Enemies*, 361–73, for a less pessimistic evaluation.

[25] David Halberstam, *The Best and the Brightest*.

their own versions of the American failure in Vietnam. In fact, studying and restudying the war became a cottage industry in the next few decades. Blame had to be allocated. "What if" was explored and reexplored as American professionals mulled over the nation's defeat.[26]

The lost war weakened the support for the alliance system that was the skeleton of the U.S. empire. In Europe, the members of NATO still had to fear Soviet power, so they could do little else than criticize American policy. This is what they had done when Eisenhower used American force in the 1950s to defend the tiny islands of Quemoy and Matsu, off the coast of China. But Ike had won that standoff while Nixon, Secretary of State Henry Kissinger, and the Joint Chiefs of Staff lost their struggle to stabilize the empire's Southeast Asian frontier. American military power and advanced technology – including our first-generation "smart bombs" – had failed to contain the forces of revolution. Yet again.

In the aftermath of the defeat in Vietnam, the domino theory was at first confirmed by events in Southeast Asia. The dominoes didn't fall the way the Americans assumed they would, but some of them fell. The Khmer Rouge conquered Cambodia, and indigenous communist forces defeated the government in Laos in 1975.

But what followed had not been anticipated by the U.S. strategists. In Cambodia, the communist conquerors led by Pol Pot launched one of the world's most brutal genocides. They killed as many as three million Cambodians and soon became engaged in a war with their communist neighbor Vietnam. A failed economy in Cambodia and deep-set problems in Laos left both nations unable to feed their populations and dependent for decades upon foreign aid. The World Bank kept Laos going. Instead of advertisements for a global communist movement, these two nations became evidence of the brutality and incompetence that this revolution from the left had produced. More would be revealed about other communist regimes in the years to come.

All the dominoes in Asia didn't fall. Thailand successfully resisted the communist advance. Although handicapped by a government that swayed back and forth between military authority, constitutional monarchy, and democracy, Thailand managed to avoid the brutal excesses of Cambodia and the economic problems of Laos. By default, Thailand became the new boundary of U.S. power in Southeast Asia.

[26] Charles E. Neu, "The Vietnam War and the Transformation of America," in Charles E. Neu, ed., *After Vietnam*, 1–23, discusses this ongoing debate.

In the aftermath of America's defeat, the United States had a good test case of just how much "confidence" was worth. The fears of the realists who had emphasized the importance of international confidence proved to be exaggerated. This was true even though the country's stature in Asia was substantially reduced, and the Ford administration (1973–1977) did nothing to restore that prestige.[27] President Carter (1977–1981) attempted to rebuild American prestige by swinging sharply away from the realist camp of the military and national security experts. He tried to create a new balance between democratic values and the exercise of power, in part by cutting back on military expenditures. The resistance to cutbacks was fierce, however, and Carter had to settle for a virtual standoff.[28] Unfortunately, Carter's strategy – coming as it did right after the demoralizing defeat in Vietnam – further weakened the nation's military establishment. The humiliating failure of the United States to deal effectively with a hostage crisis in Iran (1979–1981) suggested that it might be some time before U.S. military leaders recovered the respect they had earned in World War II.[29]

Dollarless Diplomacy in the 1970s

America was floundering toward a new mix of idealism and realism, and the country's European allies in NATO had reason to wonder when the United States would get it right. Europe wanted to be defended by a stable ally. Reflect for a moment on the previous flip-flops in America's links to Europe. Start with the Versailles Peace Treaties, and then consider 1933 and the U.S. decision to abandon the London Economic Conference. Then there was the Suez Crisis of 1956. The U.S.-Soviet cooperation had restored what passed for peace in the Middle East, but it left America's

---

[27] During his twenty-nine months in office, President Ford was preoccupied with the poor state of the American economy, but the administration nevertheless provided covert aid to an anti-Marxist force in Angola and was forced to deal with the aftermath of the 1973 Arab-Israeli war in the Middle East. As Secretary of State under Ford, Kissinger continued his effort to squeeze all of the sentiment and moral issues out of American foreign policy while stressing the overriding goal of big-power détente.

[28] In constant dollars, total defense expenditures were $244.4 billion in 1977, $244.2 billion the following year, $244.1 billion in 1979, and $247.8 billion in 1980. So much for the so-called peace dividend.

[29] The American perspective on the hostages taken from the U.S. embassy is presented in Paul H. Kreisberg, ed., *American Hostages in Iran: The Conduct of a Crisis* (New Haven, 1985).

allies nervous about the protection they were receiving from their NATO ally.

In the 1970s, once again, the United States went its own way. President Johnson had proclaimed to the world that the United States had such a powerful economy that it could afford both guns and butter, but his boast now looked hollow.[30] President Nixon decided in 1970 that combined expenditures for the welfare and the warfare states were bringing the American economy to its knees. Nixon decided that the United States could no longer afford one of the central policies of the Bretton Woods settlement. Since the establishment of the International Monetary Fund and the World Bank, the United States had been providing gold backing for the members' currencies, all of which were pegged to the dollar. This system was important because it reduced fluctuations in the value of the different currencies and, to that extent, stabilized the global financial system. This was not the sort of policy that concerned many Americans. If they understood what President Nixon was doing, they probably still didn't care very much. But the importance of Nixon's decision was well understood outside of the United States.

When Nixon pulled out the gold peg, he explained that the United States could no longer afford to stabilize the international economy. Inflation was a problem for the United States, as was increasing global competition. The German recovery and the rapid expansion of Japan's industrial economy were putting pressure on the United States, driving some very large firms out of business and cutting into the markets of others. Europe was catching up to American productivity.[31] The bill for the war in Vietnam reduced the country's fiscal flexibility, leaving the United States more vulnerable to foreign competition. Quotas provided protection for some firms, but they were only a temporary shelter from those foreign competitors, especially in Japan and Germany, who were more efficient and innovative than many of their American counterparts. In automobile and steel production, the United States was falling behind.

---

[30] President Johnson said in his State of the Union message to Congress on January 12, 1966, that, "I believe that we can continue the Great Society while we fight in Vietnam." The newspapers picked this up and transformed it into the "guns and butter" imagery. http://www.lbjlib.utexas.edu/Johnson/archives.hom/speeches.hom/660112.asp.

[31] Robert J. Gordon, "Why Was Europe Left at the Station When America's Productivity Locomotive Departed?" NBER Working Paper 10661 (August 2004). See also Gordon's "Two Centuries of Economic Growth: Europe Chasing the American Frontier," NBER Working Paper No. 10662 (August 2004). Gianni Toniolo, "A Tale of Two Globalizations: Europe vs. America, 1860–2000," reports on a discussion held at Duke University (November 16, 2004).

Inflation was so serious by 1971–1972 that Nixon's economic advisors persuaded the administration to abandon Keynes and introduce price controls. The World War II conversion of the economics profession to Keynesian analysis and policy prescriptions had swollen the confidence of the economics profession. Convinced that control of the nation's fiscal and monetary levers would ease downturns and control inflation, the economists had largely neglected the negative side of Keynesian policies. This downside was created by the political dynamics of fiscal policy. It was easy for Congress to increase spending, to generate a deficit and thus to accelerate the economy. That had been clearly demonstrated in the 1960s. But when the economy started to race too fast and to create inflationary pressure, it was politically painful to apply fiscal brakes, to increase taxes or cut spending, or both. Pet projects would have to be abandoned. Constituents would be angered. Unemployment would increase.

Not all of America's professionals were oblivious to what was happening. There were heretics like the economist Milton Friedman at the University of Chicago who didn't run with the herd. He and others were warning the profession and the government about the downside of the Keynesian fiscal policies.[32] Friedman and the Chicago School of economics later became so popular that it is hard now to accept the fact that they were the unpopular outsiders in the early years of the great inflation. But they were. Concerned about fiscal policy, Friedman looked to monetary policy as the best balance wheel and the Federal Reserve Board as the most effective guide for the economy. Having little confidence in the lawyers on Capitol Hill, he looked to the Fed for leadership and his Chicago school for ideas.[33] But Friedman was an unpopular prophet in the early 1970s. Nixon's Council of Economic Advisors supported the sort of price controls on goods and services that were anathema to the leading Chicago School economists.

The controls were also anathema to the right wing of the Republican Party. Given that Richard Nixon had become the Republican candidate with strong support from that side of his party, the extension of federal

---

[32] As we saw in previous chapters, the experiences with wartime spending and the tax cut of 1964 had convinced many professionals and policy experts that the federal government's spending and tax policies were the appropriate mechanism for controlling the economy. The Chicago School emphasized the dangers of that approach and looked to monetary policies (interest rates and the supply of money/credit) as a much safer alternative.

[33] Johan Van Overtveldt, *The Chicago School: How the University of Chicago Assembled the Thinkers Who Revolutionized Economics and Business* (Chicago, 2007).

power through price controls was a startling swing to the left. At the same time, the administration was attempting to dampen international competition by using a self-governing quota system for important imports such as automobiles.[34] While these restrictions were more acceptable to the conservatives than price controls, the quotas backed the administration away from the free-trade position Republicans had been advancing since the 1950s. Free trade was and would continue to be hostage to the performance of the American economy. Free trade constrained nationalism, but it didn't take much of a spike in the unemployment rate to pump energy back into the nationalist cause.

Problems Galore

Although price controls were soon abandoned, America continued to pile up problems through the rest of the 1970s. Dependent for many years on Middle Eastern oil, America was paralyzed in 1973 when OPEC responded to Israeli belligerence with an oil embargo. Suddenly and decisively, the gasoline that had long been abundant, cheap, and absolutely essential to the American way of life was no longer available at the filling station around the corner. Alternate days were set up for those who wanted to wait in the long lines to buy gas. Unaccustomed to peacetime rationing, Americans looked for scapegoats and found them in the giant oil companies. But neither Exxon, nor Shell, nor Texaco was responsible for the gasoline shortage. Nor did the companies or the government have an answer to this crisis.[35]

The OPEC embargo had an even more devastating impact in Europe. Europeans had fewer alternatives than Americans to obtain energy supplies. As a result, industries were forced to cut back on production. Unemployment increased. All of America's NATO allies suffered directly from the decisions of the OPEC oil cartel and indirectly from the policies of America's Middle Eastern ally, Israel. The economic and political ties between the NATO countries and the United States were loosened by the embargo as each country turned inward to solve its energy problems. Instead of the coordinated policies that had characterized Bretton Woods, every nation now looked to its own devices.

---

[34] The system depended upon the exporting countries to restrain the volume of goods sent to the United States.

[35] Richard H. K. Vietor, *Energy Policy in America since 1945: A Study in Business-Government Relations* (New York, 1984).

That also included the underdeveloped nations, most of which were hit very hard by the shortage of oil and resulting market declines. The IMF and the World Bank rushed to help, making what were euphemistically called "structural adjustment loans." The premise underlying the loans was that the situation was temporary and that a quick recovery would enable borrowers to repay the loans. All too often, however, the recovery wasn't on schedule. Resentment of the burdens of the loans was focused on these two international organizations and their primary supporter, the United States. The gratitude borrowers felt when they received the money was brief. The hatred they experienced when forced to pay back the money was deep, long-lasting, and overwhelming. *Pax Americana* was producing a wave of global discontent.

The second oil shock of 1979 increased the hostility rife within and without the American empire. The U.S. economy suffered again. By the end of the decade, interest rates had reached paralyzing heights, unemployment was up, and productivity increases dipped toward zero. Europe was again hit hard by the oil shock and by the resulting declines in U.S. orders. In parts of the developing world, especially in Africa and Latin America, the first wave of structural adjustment loans had yet to be paid back when a second wave was needed. The IMF and the World Bank acted promptly to deal with the crisis, but their loans once again increased the animosity expressed toward these institutions. The loans that were meant to help were widely perceived as a new form of colonialism.[36]

Little wonder that these developments were seen by some observers as the final throes of a damaged capitalism, a system that seemed to be on the path that Marx and Lenin had charted – a path leading to a final collapse. Little wonder that most European countries were unwilling to abandon the postwar social networks and the state-owned enterprises (SOEs) they had created to provide stability and security to their populations. In the short term, the SOEs were slow to respond to the downturns that were experienced and responded to quickly in the United States. Unemployment was thus less of an immediate political problem in Europe than it was in America. With the U.S. model of political economy losing favor everywhere, socialism and communism appeared to be in triumphant control of the future.

---

[36] David Vines and Christopher L. Gilbert, eds., *The IMF and Its Critics: Reform of Global Financial Architecture* (Cambridge, 2004). Richard Peet, ed., *Unholy Trinity: The IMF, World Bank and WTO* (London, 2003).

In Europe, where NATO was central to the American empire's defense against communist expansion, America's allies appeared to be edging to the left again. France, always a reluctant participant in the empire's alliance system, withdrew from complete membership in NATO. The growing strength of the socialists and communists in France made it appear a matter of time before an elected regime would either betray NATO or withdraw completely. Similar changes in Italy were of great concern to America's military leaders. How would the United States cope with a freely elected communist government privy to all of NATO's strategic plans and its base system? This potential crisis brought into sharp focus the gulf between America's democratic values and the demands of the American empire.

There Was Still Some Water in the Glass

Not all of the news in the 1970s was bad. Nixon and Henry Kissinger had startled the far-right Republicans with an opening toward the People's Republic of China. After a series of secret negotiations handled largely by Kissinger, the United States suddenly and surprisingly recognized and established full diplomatic relations with China. Only twenty-three years after Nixon had built the first part of his career by attacking those in the United States government who, like General Marshall, were supposed to have "lost China" to the communists, the President did an abrupt about-face.[37]

Nowhere in the postwar history of the United States was there stronger evidence of the rise of the new aristocracy of professional experts. This incredible policy shift, which was guided through by Kissinger, left many Americans baffled. That is to say, the new policy was an outstanding innovation that should have prompted intense thought about America's relationships with the revolutionary process in Asia and the rest of the world. It didn't. Nevertheless, it was the high point of an administration that would shortly have a sad, damaged ending.

Optimists could also point to the spread of democracy. This was a countertrend in a world in which left-wing centralized authority had been growing for many decades. In Greece and Portugal, homegrown democratic movements brought an end to authoritarian, military regimes. There is a crucial moral here that many contemporaries and some scholars today have ignored. In neither Greece nor Portugal was the United

---

[37] Jeremi Suri, *Henry Kissinger and the American Century*, 234–36.

States a direct participant in the movements that led to democratization. Indeed, other than the immediate postwar conversions to democracy in Germany and Japan, the United States has never been able to transplant its form of government to another nation. Instead, democratic movements have arisen from the grassroots, from indigenous organizations that found authoritarian governments inflexible, ultimately unresponsive to their society's basic material needs, and unwilling to satisfy the demands for political participation and freedom of expression. Authoritarian governments have often been able to spur economic development in the short term, but the price in the long term has always been very high.

Grassroots democratization also took place in Spain, where local leaders and their organizations created a democratic movement that was able to change the nation's government. The United States was a useful symbol for Spanish reformers – but that was all. Symbolism, not intervention, was the proper role. The United States was most successful in spreading democracy when it provided moral, not military, support. Given the important role Spain had played in the Fascist movement of the 1930s, this was an encouraging transition in a nation that became a significant participant in the American alliance system and the European Union.

Above all, the United States managed to keep the containment policy intact and to absorb the losses in Southeast Asia without really losing the balance of power with the Soviet Union. This was a major achievement for a nation that, following World War I, had abandoned its international responsibilities. Seen in the context of the longer and more decisive containment policy, the détente strategy emphasized by Kissinger and Nixon was a relatively minor but welcome adjustment in the program originally conceived by George Kennan in the postwar years.

Despite its problems at home and abroad, the United States continued in the 1970s to support the United Nations, continued to work through the IMF and the World Bank, and continued to provide a military shield against overt Soviet expansion. The peripatetic Lou Galambos was involved with the shield, involved for the second time with America's national security. He was no longer making shifter forks in the garage as he had in World War II.[38] Now he was helping build missile bases in Montana and other parts of America. He had left the oil industry after acquiring a good understanding of drilling equipment and techniques. He was able to parlay that knowledge and experience into a position with

---

[38] See Chapter 8 for the shifter forks business during World War II.

Chicago Pneumatic Tool, which had government defense contracts at the new missile bases being constructed in Montana and other western states. The job involved traveling a great deal, and Lou had to remain on the site until the drilling was completed. The work was rough. The weather was often bad. But Lou was happy to be working with machinery, supervising a crew, and building something important for the country's defense.

The American military shield helped the European Union get on its feet without spending excessively on its own regional security. The EU made important steps forward, always with U.S. support. In this case – as was the case with democratization – the impulse for further European consolidation came from the bottom up, from the nations directly involved in the EU. In each nation, the political dynamics were different, but the end result was a Europe prepared to take the next important steps toward political and economic federation. Japan, which was also defended by the United States, was making even greater progress in the world economy.

A Sense of Impotence

Unfortunately, these accomplishments didn't get much attention near the end of the 1970s. Most Americans were distressed about their leaders, disappointed with the experts of the new aristocracy, and discouraged by an empire that seemed to be too expensive in lives and dollars for Americans to afford. The victory songs of the late 1940s had given way to a mournful national dirge. The media exaggerated America's decline, as did many politicians who reflected and refracted the negative ideas coming from their constituents and the evening news.

Painful questions surfaced about America's past and future. How could America, which had long led the world in technological progress, be falling behind its competitors in Europe and Asia? The helicopters that failed in the abortive attempt to rescue American hostages in Iran became a metaphor for a deeper social and economic malaise. The U.S. policies that had contributed to the Iranian situation came into question: Hadn't the United States under Eisenhower actually laid the basis for the Iranian Revolution and the anti-American response that followed?[39] Were we once again on the wrong side in a revolution? There were more questions

[39] Warren Christopher, who was Deputy Secretary of State during the crisis, later noted in the language characteristic of diplomacy that "the official American presence in that country had been drastically reduced after the Iranian revolution...." Stated more bluntly, our puppet government, under the Shah, was overthrown. "Introduction," in Paul H. Kreisberg, ed., *American Hostages in Iran*, 2.

than answers in the late 1970s, but it was already apparent that many Americans were anxious for a regime change in Washington, DC. Their empire hadn't collapsed, but it was certainly tattered by that time.

I was teaching and writing during these years, and I was weaving the professional experts into the history courses I taught on modern America. I was caught in a typical academic bind. On the one hand, I recognized the significant, positive contributions professionals had made and were continuing to make to American society. Looking around the world, I could see that the new aristocracy of professional experts gave the United States and its allies an important edge in the Cold War. While the USSR's government was dominating its professionals and sending many to the gulag archipelago, and while China was destroying an entire generation of professionals in the Cultural Revolution, the United States was continuing to support an enormous educational and research system that was providing the training grounds for its professionals and many from overseas.[40] I was certain the impact of that system would continue to be felt long after the defeats of the 1970s were forgotten.

But on the other hand – like most academics, I always have another hand ready – I began to see how the social process of professionalization tended to breed particular forms of hubris. Using a combination of well-trained minds and social skills, the leaders in the professions pushed their way to the top of society. Having mastered a well-defined body of ideas and perhaps added something special to those ideas – as Henry Kissinger had – they were likely to be full of themselves and contemptuous of the mass of people who made up the electorate. Successful in their professional domain, they were likely as well to be contemptuous of many of the values of the larger society.

That, I could now see, was why the country needed effective leaders to use and control the professionals and their expertise. Leadership without expertise could be clueless. Expertise without strong leadership could be dangerous, very dangerous. The United States didn't need better science or better economic or political theory. It needed better leadership, better judgment, and, in foreign policy, a better balance – a distinctly American balance – between realism and idealism.

[40] Aleksandr Solzhenitsyn made the string of brutal Soviet prison mining camps, the gulags, famous with his account of the murder and torture that accompanied imprisonment by the Soviet authorities (mostly under Stalin).

13

The Cracked Core

If this chapter reads like the front page of a newspaper – full of bad news – well, I hope you won't be too depressed. The fact is that the 1970s were a miserable decade for the United States, for most of its citizens, and especially for its professionals. For personal reasons, the Galambos family shared in this misery. The high points (and there were only three) made the rest of the decade look especially bleak by comparison. It was an unpleasant time for those who lived through it and it's still a difficult era for an optimistic historian to discuss.[1]

I began the decade teaching at Livingston College, in Rutgers University. I had finished my postdoc at Johns Hopkins, and I left Rice and Houston to be on the East Coast, where much of my research was focused. Livingston College provided an open window on the turmoil of the 1970s. The College was designed to be a revolutionary institution, perhaps the only state-subsidized revolutionary movement in modern American history. The College was initially shaped by the demands that higher education be responsive to the civil rights movement, to the New Left's antibureaucratic creed, and to the need to throw open admission to young people whose education had suffered under America's class system.

The result was some creativity and a great deal of chaos. Lacking good middle management – a bureaucratic phenomenon – it was hard for students to get the books they needed. Being open to demands for change, your classroom might be preempted by the Women's Defense

---

[1] Even if you have seen the movie, you should read Carl Bernstein and Bob Woodward, *All the President's Men* (New York, 1974). Then you can turn to Julian E. Zelizer, *Jimmy Carter: The 39th President, 1977–1981* (New York, 2010).

League or another reform organization. Opening admissions brought you some remarkable people like a multiracial former security guard who became a de facto middleman between the Hispanic and African-American students. But it also brought you students for whom error-free plagiarism represented commendable progress. To teach, you had to blend these struggling students with the brilliant transfer student from the University of Chicago who came hoping to find a truly diverse and united institution.

Higher education in those circumstances was a bracing experience. Near the end of the year, in the spring of 1971, the College was shaken by a growing awareness that the New Left movement was "going into its own head." Leaders and followers were apparently trading social concerns for introspection. In an effort to get back the spirit of the revolution as a social movement, some of those still dedicated to changing America called a Maoist-type student-faculty meeting at a local motel to discuss new strategies. One proposal was for the faculty and students to "live together." Another was for the faculty and students to "dress alike," to get rid of neckties and suits. One of my friends suggested that this latter goal could be achieved if the students wore neckties. But no one laughed, and that tiny corner of the New Left revolution continued to simmer down into psychology. Unable to imagine how I would move my wife, two daughters, and a dog into a commune, I didn't learn much from the meeting. But the New Left's suspicion of American leadership did prepare me for what happened during the next few years in Washington, DC.

Corruption

Lawyers and social scientists disagree about the precise meaning of corruption, but actually it's something we all understand. Most of us have gained some experience with minor or major examples of corrupt behavior during our lifetimes. Raised as I was in a small town in Southern Indiana, I understood petty corruption. I got my job on the county highway during the summer because Lou Galambos voted right, as did his wife, Ruth. Working on the highway, I understood why we graded some of the roads and mowed the long grass on the corners of some houses while we ignored the roads and weeds at other homes. There were a few Democrats in that part of heavily Republican Indiana. I also understood why the robbery at the poker game on the second floor of the Palace Pool Parlor didn't arouse any public concern. The illegal gambling was ignored, probably for a small price, so the robbery had to be ignored too.

Larger, more lucrative forms of corruption were beyond our experience, but in the 1970s, they became common knowledge. The country was rocked by a series of scandals. This was certainly not the most corrupt decade in American history. I don't believe it even came close to the records set on my "historical sin-dex" by Boss Tweed, Jay Gould, and other scoundrels of the Gilded Age.[2] But the corruption of the 1970s had some unique characteristics that made it particularly memorable. And shocking.

For one thing, the corrupt practices of that decade followed the ascendancy of the professional elite, the new aristocracy, that great cadre of experts who were supposed to have high standards as well as intelligence and technical ability.[3] That was why we bestowed such great respect on the professions during the immediate postwar years.[4] That's why we didn't laugh when the experts in Washington, DC, were called the "best and the brightest" in the early 1960s. Society granted many of the most prominent professions the authority to be largely self-governing, as were doctors and lawyers. Those privileges were called into question by the increasing evidence in the 1970s that the "brightest" often weren't the "best."[5]

The lawyers took a beating.[6] The Thirty-Ninth Vice President of the United States, a graduate of the School of Law at the University of Baltimore, was forced out of office for taking bribes. Spiro Agnew – the hero of the conservative suburbs – was caught receiving his bribes in a white paper envelope while he was sitting in the White House. The payments were from contractors who had bribed Agnew to get state business. Instead of contemplating a run for the presidency in 1976, Agnew was forced to resign in 1973 and plead no contest to the criminal charges.

---

[2] See Edward L. Glaeser and Claudia Goldin, "Corruption and Reform: An Introduction," NBER Working Paper 10775 (September 2004).

[3] See especially Brian Balogh, *Chain Reaction: Expert Debate and Public Participation in American Commercial Nuclear Power, 1945–1975* (New York, 1991).

[4] The impact of the new aristocracy is discussed in Samuel P. Hays, *Beauty, Health, and Permanence: Environmental Politics in the United States, 1955–1985* (New York, 1989).

[5] There is a tendency, I note, for people to forget that since the publication of David Halberstam's stunning account of *The Best and the Brightest* in 1972, the expression always carries a heavy negative evaluation.

[6] As Daniel R. Ernst notes in "Law and the State, 1920–2000: Institutional Growth and Structural Change," in Michael Grossberg and Christopher Tomlins, eds., *The Cambridge History of Law in America, III, The Twentieth Century and After (1920–)* (New York, 2008), 1–33, the position of lawyers in the state was challenged by the rise of other professions, most prominently the economists. Of equal importance, I believe, was the series of scandals that rocked the legal profession in the 1970s.

Disbarred and disgraced, he disappeared from American politics, leaving behind a diminished administration and a public wondering what to expect next from the many lawyers who were writing and enforcing the nation's laws.[7]

The answer came rolling out in the Watergate scandal that forced President Nixon to follow Agnew out of office. Nixon, a graduate of Duke University's School of Law, and his closest supporters, many of them also lawyers, became frightened that the Republicans might not win the 1972 election. Their efforts to prevent defeat slid across the line into reprehensible political activity and then kept sliding into stunningly illegal behavior. Whether they were collecting illegal cash payments for a political slush fund or breaking and entering to steal information at Democratic headquarters in the Watergate, the administration was violating the laws the president was sworn to defend. Relentless investigative reporting broke the case.[8] Then, behaving more like a petty criminal than an officer of the court, the president struggled frantically to beat back the charges the House Judiciary Committee considered in the summer of 1974. As the cover-up collapsed, the president faced certain impeachment. He resigned from office on August 9, 1974.[9]

Watergate took down a long list of other professionals, including the nation's top law-enforcement officer, Attorney General John N. Mitchell (Fordham's School of Law). He went to prison, as did John Ehrlichman, a graduate of Stanford's Law School. Ehrlichman's successor as White House counsel, John Dean (J.D., Georgetown University) turned state's evidence but he too did time and was disbarred. The president's personal attorney, Herbert Kalmbach (University of Southern California Law School) went to prison, along with Nixon's favorite hatchet man, Charles Colson (George Washington University School of Law). In addition to the lawyers, an engineer (Edwin Reinecke) and several former business executives (including H. R. Haldeman and Jeb Magruder) were all found guilty in the worst scandal to hit the presidency and America's professional elite in the twentieth century.

For the legal profession this was a major crisis, and the American Bar Association (ABA) responded to the growing criticism of its practitioners, practices, and culture. The ABA started in 1977 to develop new rules

[7] *New York Times*, obituary by Francis X Clines, September 19, 1996; also William Safire, in the same issue. Also http://www.senate.gov/artandhistory/history/common/generic/VP-Spiro_Agnew.htm.

[8] Carl Bernstein and Bob Woodward, *All the President's Men*.

[9] Stephen Ambrose, *Nixon* (New York, 1991).

of conduct for the profession. Six years later, after much debate, the association produced a set of "Model Rules of Professional Conduct." All of the states except California, Maine, and New York adopted rules based on the ABA's model. Among many other things, the new Rules required all students in ABA-approved programs to take a course in professional responsibility.[10] Some of the association's rules were designed to deal specifically with those patterns of professional misconduct that had been uncovered in the Watergate investigations: engaging, for instance, "in conduct involving dishonesty, fraud, deceit or misrepresentation," or "in conduct that is prejudicial to the administration of justice."[11]

Lawyers and other professionals found it necessary to display an aroused interest in ethics because there was so much evidence that many of them were unethical. Did the new rules and ethics courses matter? Yes, they helped some young lawyers understand what they could and couldn't do in specific situations.[12] It seems unlikely, however, that an ethics course would have changed the behavior of either President Nixon or his closest supporters. They considered themselves above the law and any kind of ethical code. The attitudes they displayed contributed to the growing suspicion that professional self-regulation was inherently flawed.

Indeed, while the ABA was developing its rules, two new scandals surfaced. One involved South Korean lobbyists who had been spreading money around Washington, providing thousands of dollars to prominent legislators. Tongsun Park, a South Korean businessman who described himself as "an American success story," had been handing out bundles of cash in an effort to influence U.S. policy. That was a cause for concern, as was the widespread suspicion that the intelligence services of South Korea had been able to manipulate Congress. As always, it was hard to find direct evidence of votes that were bought. The *New York Times* claimed that as many as 115 Congressmen were touched by the scandal. But the House Ethics Committee could only link ten members directly to the illicit lobbying campaign, and only one went to jail.[13]

---

[10] The ABA's Model Rules of Professional Conduct (1983) replaced its Model Code of Professional Responsibility (1969).

[11] http://www.abanet.org/epr/mrpe/rule_8.4.html.

[12] My evidence is anecdotal, and I would cite a reliable source if I knew one existed.

[13] Richard Thomas Hanna (Democrat, California) admitted to taking $200,000 from Park. Hanna, who was a graduate of the Law School at the University of California at Los Angeles, plea-bargained, and got six to thirty months in prison.

Americans had good cause to conclude that congressional self-policing wasn't working any better than the legal profession's self-governing associations.[14]

The confidence in Congress and the legal profession at large dipped even lower at the end of the decade when the ABSCAM sting became front-page news. The FBI set up the sting, using a phony organization, Abdul Enterprises, Ltd. (hence AB-SCAM), in 1978. The trap caught Senator Harrison A. Williams as well as Representatives John Jenrette, Richard Kelly, Raymond Lederer, Michael Myers, and Frank Thompson. The trail of corruption, of purchased favoritism, was long and complex. It led into the Immigration and Naturalization Service and from Washington into Philadelphia and Camden, New Jersey. Particularly stunning were the videotaped pictures of bribery, including one of Representative Richard Kelly stuffing $25,000 into his suit pockets. As the FBI's trap closed on four lawyers – two of them former judges – the public standing of the profession as well as Congress went into a freefall.

In the midst of all this turmoil, our family lost the guiding hand of Lou Galambos. He died in 1974, the same year that Watergate drove President Nixon from office. Lou, who had smoked all of his adult life, died of lung cancer. Like so many sons of immigrants, he had pushed his way up from the shop floor into what passed for the middle class in Southern Indiana. What were the symbols of middle-class status? Membership in the Elks Club counted, as did driving an Oldsmobile and owning a home in an indisputably middle-class neighborhood. Hardworking and frugal, he was able to leave his wife, Ruth, with a home and a comfortable income.[15] Generous, he had helped both of his children get through their educations, into the first houses they owned, and well into their professional careers. Tender about his own lack of education, he never wavered in his confidence that the professional path was the one his children should follow. This was true even when many Americans were having second thoughts about the kind of leadership they were getting from the nation's well-educated elite.

---

[14] According to a 1981 Gallup Poll (#178G), the honesty and ethical standards of medical doctors was still high (50% of the respondents rated the standards very high or high) compared to those of lawyers (24%) and Congressmen (15%). Senators did better (20%) and businessmen were not far behind (19%), unless they were in advertising (10%). Labor union leaders (14%) lagged behind businessmen, and only doctors were ahead of college teachers (45%).

[15] Ruth Galambos, who lived to be ninety, died in the spring of 1995.

Self-Governance and Self-Interest in Medicine

Lawyers were not the only American professionals to be challenged in this dreary decade. In the modern professional public sphere, academic criticism could have long-term negative effects on status and political standing, and much of the scholarship on the medical profession now became intensely negative.[16] Heroic biographies gave way to criticism of the high incomes of physicians, the licensing laws that controlled entry, and the degree of specialization in medicine. Few doctors wanted to be general practitioners, that is, the physicians portrayed in those sweet Norman Rockwell prints. Even fewer wanted to practice in the rural areas and small-towns that Rockwell loved.

As the critics pointed out, the United States was spending a great deal, in comparative terms, on health care, but most Americans were not receiving the best care possible. Too many people were slipping through the cracks in the system. Too many were forced to use emergency wards because they didn't have primary-care physicians. Too much was being spent on people in the last few months of their lives and too little on preventive medicine. Doctors were the visible symbol of medicine for most Americans. So it was the physicians who in the 1970s and 1980s were held responsible for the system's problems.[17]

Most doctors disagreed with this critique. Most were pleased with American health care, and they were well organized and politically effective. The American Medical Association (AMA) was a powerful lobbying organization, with its state and county groups, led by respected members of every community. One of their strongest arguments against change was to point to the accomplishments of medical science in America. The first phase of the therapeutic revolution – from the 1930s through the

---

[16] In regard to the legal profession, see, for instance, Jerold S. Auerbach, *Unequal Justice: Lawyers and Social Change in Modern America* (London, 1976) and Stephen Botein, "Professional History Reconsidered," *American Journal of Legal History*, 21 (January 1977), 60–79. On medicine, see James Gordon Burrow, *Organized Medicine in the Progressive Era: The Move Toward Monopoly* (Baltimore, 1977) and E. Richard Brown, *Rockefeller Medicine Men: Medicine and Capitalism in America* (Berkeley, California, 1977).

[17] Eliot Freidson, *The Profession of Medicine: A Study of the Sociology of Applied Knowledge* (New York, 1970) and his book on *Professional Powers: A Study of the Institutionalization of Formal Knowledge* (Chicago, 1986); Paul Starr, *The Social Transformation of American Medicine: The Rise of a Sovereign Profession and the Making of a Vast Industry* (New York, 1982); Rosemary A. Stevens, "Themes in the History of Medical Professionalism," *The Mount Sinai Journal of Medicine*, 69, 6 (November 2002), 357–62.

1960s – had produced a great wave of important discoveries: the sulfa drugs, penicillin, streptomycin (the first cure for tuberculosis), the polio and pediatric vaccines. The accomplishments of modern medicine provided a solid defense against any significant change.

The critics were, of course, not turned away by lists of miracle drugs and vaccines.[18] They were more likely to emphasize the crises over drug safety and efficacy that had brought about new regulations in the early 1960s. They saw a deeply flawed health care system with strong class and racial biases, a criticism that was supported by the statistics on life expectancy.[19] For those who couldn't afford hospitals or health insurance in the difficult years of the 1970s, most of the new wonder drugs were irrelevant.[20] A decade that should have been one of triumph for the medical professions became instead the first phase of an extended critique and a series of fundamental changes in American health care.

Big Science and Democracy

The concern about the medical sciences spilled over into all of the sciences, and especially the system of big science, of large government grants, of massive equipment and large research teams. These were all characteristic of American science in the postwar era. The critics began to ask where, exactly, big science had taken us? Were we really better off as a result of the astonishing developments of the 1940s, 1950s, and 1960s? The nuclear age was threatening to Americans – with good cause. A nation long accustomed to a high degree of national security could no longer feel secure.

There were serious questions about nuclear energy. The professional experts who proposed building a nuclear plant near Manhattan seemed

---

[18] As Albert O. Hirschman explained, we have three options for dealing with problems in businesses, other private organizations, and states: exit, loyalty, and voice. The critics were exercising their right to express their voices and were also loyal insofar as they assumed the problems could be corrected. In this sense, the Americans who brought lawsuits against their doctors were long on voice and short on loyalty. *Exit, Voice, and Loyalty: Responses to Decline in Firms, Organizations, and States* (Cambridge, 1970).

[19] In 1940, white Americans could expect, on average, to live about sixty-four years; African Americans could look forward to slightly more than fifty-three years. The infant mortality rate for blacks was almost 73 per 1,000; for whites, it was 43. By 1980, the differences were considerable smaller, but they hadn't disappeared entirely; the same figures were 74.4 years (white) and 68.1 (black), 22.2 (black) and 10.9 (white).

[20] The exceptions were the new pediatric vaccines that were required for school attendance and were available free in clinics for those who could not afford to pay for them.

to have no idea of the risks they would create for those living in the nation's largest city. Issues like this suggested that the best professionals and their bosses needed more common sense, not more expertise. Similar questions were raised when the experts built a plant over a fault line in California. Meanwhile, a political struggle developed over the problems of disposing of nuclear waste. There were many more questions than convincing answers about nuclear power in the 1970s, and while the experts debated, the nuclear power movement lost its political support and skidded to a halt.[21]

Other questions were raised about big science and the direction it was taking America. For some, the questions involved the cost of science. For others, it involved the dangers that were being created without adequate social controls. The new knowledge of molecular genetics was apparently creating wonderful opportunities in new drug development. Men in white lab coats, the new biomedical wizards, popped up on the covers of popular magazines. But there were widespread fears and controversies about the dangerous creations that might escape from laboratories or come out of the fields where genetically altered crops were growing.[22]

Of course they couldn't put this genetic genie back in the bottle. We were in the biomedical and nuclear age and had to learn how to live with it and with these new experts. What Americans could do was express their fears and doubts about new-era science. The media could question what science was creating, and the country's politicians could launch inquiries into whether or not the scientific experts were leading America into dangerous territory. And expensive territory at that. Were the expenses of big science really worth what America was getting out of these ventures? In the 1970s, the nation was trying to answer some of the questions that business leaders had been forced to answer at the beginning of the century when they began trying to harness science within their firms. They had to decide how to organize industrial labs and how to account for them. They weren't going to write blank checks for R&D, so they needed to decide where to draw a line and stop paying. In many cases, they had to plan large enterprises that took years, even decades, to come to fruition. Big science, like big business and big government, needed to be controlled. But who, other than scientists, could do that?

[21] Brian Balogh, *Chain Reaction*.
[22] Jeffrey Sturchio and I have discussed the literature and this subject in "Pharmaceutical Firms and the Transition to Biotechnology: A Study in Strategic Innovation," *Business History Review*, 72 (Summer 1998), 250–78.

Hubris and the New Age of Business Professionals

America's big businesses in the 1970s were bureaucratic marvels, larger economic organizations than most of the nations of the world. Great national and multinational enterprises, they employed large numbers of professionals and were run by professional managers, some of them trained at the nation's thriving business schools and others trained within their corporations. The largest of these massive organizations was the American Telephone & Telegraph Company, which had three million stockholders, more than a million employees, and an internal education system – the Corporation Education Center – that trained 4,500 Bell System workers each year. AT&T had also largely internalized its research in Bell Laboratories, which was widely recognized as the most outstanding industrial research organization in the world.

Bell executives, the so-called Bell Heads, had every reason to be proud of what their System had accomplished since the early 1900s. None were prouder than AT&T's new CEO in 1972, John Dulany deButts. A graduate of the Virginia Military Academy with a Bachelor of Science degree in electrical engineering, deButts started as a trainee in one of the Bell operating companies. He worked his way up the ladder to the central organization, AT&T, by excelling in a managerial system that was miserable for wives and children and wonderful for high-energy leaders like deButts. AT&T moved these fast-track managers every few years to give them experience in every facet of the business. He and his family bounced from Virginia to New York to Washington, DC, and then back to New York before a stint in Illinois, where he became the youngest president in the entire System. A dynamic, hands-on, intense problem solver, deButts had plenty of problems to solve in the 1970s.[23]

The AT&T monopoly was under attack. Aspiring competitors were trying to chip out some of Bell's business. The government was rethinking the need for a regulated monopoly, even one that was as efficient and innovative as the Bell System. These assaults had weakened morale in the System. Performance – the System's ace in the hole – was sagging. This sent the new CEO on a whirlwind tour. An inspiring leader, "deButts revved up the entire Bell operation and gave the Bell Heads a renewed sense of mission. He boldly assured them that the firm's traditional strategy was

---

[23] Yanek Mieczkowski, "John Dulany deButts," *American National Biography* (New York, 1999), vol. 6, 318–20. John Brooks, *Telephone: The First Hundred Years* (New York, 1975).

best for America as well as Bell. In effect, he tossed down gauntlets to the United States government and the firm's would-be competitors. They quickly picked them up."[24]

What this proud and forceful leader had forgotten was the essential lesson embodied in the Bell System's early history: a monopoly of a vital service in a democracy could not persist without compromising. In that spirit, the early Bell System had accepted state and federal regulation and endeavored to provide its customers with the best possible service at reasonable rates. This had sufficed to keep the monopoly intact until the 1970s. Then, however, a changing political and economic environment was creating the need for a new set of compromises. CEO deButts said, "No!" and the result was an antitrust suit that brought down the monopoly in 1982. The firm that had invented the transistor, launched the third industrial revolution, and given America the best telephone service in the world was done in by leaders like deButts who looked inward rather than outward to a changing world.[25]

Evidence of overweening pride could be seen sprinkled throughout American business leadership in the 1970s. The results of this hubris were devastating for workers, investors, and the national economy. Certain of their firms' technical capabilities and their own market savvy, the professional managers of too many U.S. firms lectured customers instead of listening to them. When foreign competitors developed superior products, like the radial tire, American executives tried to explain away the competition rather than meeting it.

The tire industry of the 1970s is a good one to look at if you want to understand the managerial culture of that decade. The United States, the world's most car-oriented society, had long supported a tire industry dominated by four very large producers: Firestone, Goodyear, Goodrich, and Uniroyal. They competed in two markets: one for the tires provided to new car manufacturers; and the other for replacement tires. Even though the Big Three car manufacturers (GM, Ford, and Chrysler) kept them on their competitive toes where costs were concerned, this was in reality a rather comfortable industry in which the companies all tried hard and successfully to avoid cutthroat competition. Labor was unionized and bargaining was industry-wide, which prevented any firm from getting an

[24] Alvin von Auw, *Heritage & Destiny: Reflections on the Bell System in Transition* (New York, 1983). Gerald W. Brock, *The Telecommunications Industry: The Dynamics of Market Structure* (Cambridge, 1981).

[25] Peter Temin with Louis Galambos, *The Fall of the Bell System: A Study in Prices and Politics* (New York, 1987).

advantage in labor costs over its American competitors. Innovation took place slowly in the tire industry.[26]

But then along came a new French product, the radial tire. It was made differently than American tires and performed differently. The large tire companies responded initially by turning up their noses at the new French tire. It was OK for little French cars, they said. But it wouldn't do for the big muscle cars Americans preferred. Instead of responding creatively to competition, the executives in this industry hunkered down and refused at first to change what they were doing.

In not too many years, there was only one American-owned company in the tire business, and today all of us have radial tires on our cars. The cars come that way from the factory. Ford was first to make the change, followed by General Motors and then Chrysler. A wave of foreign acquisitions left only Goodyear, which had adopted radials more quickly than its U.S. competitors, under American ownership. The foreign firms that now dominated the U.S. tire industry consolidated their positions by pumping more money into improved operations.[27]

This was not the only Darwinian struggle going on in American business – struggles that were raising questions about the nation's business leadership and its business schools. In the postwar era, the Masters of Business Administration had become steadily more important to American firms recruiting new managers. The MBAs and their close colleagues, the management consultants, had brought a new level of professionalism to American business. But the problems of the 1970s prompted a critical look at what these businessmen had learned in their professional schools.

Many of them had learned that a talented, well-trained manager could run anything effectively. Employing quantitative data, drawing on up-to-date theories of strategy and operations, and working within decentralized bureaucracies, they could run companies efficiently even though the firms spanned several continents, sold a broad range of products and services, and had employees of many different nationalities. By diversifying, firms had ostensibly lowered their risks. No longer was a steel firm limited to producing for one market. No longer was a great chemical firm limited by the markets for its specific chemical products. Ignoring

---

[26] Mansel G. Blackford and K. Austin Kerr, *BF Goodrich: Tradition and Transformation, 1870–1995* (Columbus, 1996).

[27] Raghuram Rajan, Paolo Volpin, and Luigi Zingales, "The Eclipse of the U.S. Tire Industry," http://gsblgz.uchicago.edu; Donald N. Sull, Richard S. Tedlow, and Richard S. Rosenbloom, "Managerial Commitments and Technological Change in the US Tire Industry," *Industrial and Corporate Change*, 6 (1997), 461–500.

the histories of the very businesses they were trying to run, many of the professional managers of this era believed there were no real limits to the range of products and services, to the size, or to the geographical spread of their organizations. There was, they thought, no point at which their firms would become dysfunctional.

They were wrong. But during the American Century, conditions had been so favorable for American business that the managers of that day had become unusually certain about what they were able to do. The multidivisional (M-form) firm, with presidents for each division, had encouraged this type of thinking, as had the managerial consultants who assisted with restructuring. R&D and strategic acquisitions, they said, would provide an endless array of new goods and processes – as they had for many years. This kind of confidence obscured risks and uncertainties and made it difficult to keep track of the competition.

Let's look at what the Ford Motor Co. did when the competition hit. As we saw in Chapter 9, Robert McNamara and his professional colleagues had begun the job of transforming the managerial ranks at Ford. Using the new structure, the company experienced very rapid expansion. Faced off against General Motors, Ford was able to increase its market share with hot new models like the Mustang and the Mercury Mark III. But then, like the tire manufacturers, Ford and GM both began to slip behind the new competition from overseas. Competitors in Japan and Germany were more innovative. They introduced disk brakes and front-wheel drive. Their quality control was better, as were their prices for similar products. By 1978, when I bought my first Honda, I personally estimated that dollar for dollar, the Japanese car was about 25 percent better. I've never owned anything but a Honda since that time.

What had happened? It didn't happen to every American industry, but many lagged behind the international competition, convinced that they would be able to make minor adjustments and hold their market shares. They couldn't. Too many of their professional managers seem to have been locked in on books lauding the American multinational corporation. They still imagined they were living in the prosperous 1950s when the American Century had been in full bloom. Motivation is a tricky problem for the historian to solve. It's hard enough to get a good fix on our own minds, let alone the minds of others. All we can do is make what we hope are intelligent guesses, and in this case, my educated guess is that a generation of professional managers had been convinced by twenty-five years of success to believe that they couldn't possibly be bested by foreign competition.

Ten years of intense competition, however, left America's professional business managers reeling. The competition had made deep inroads into automobiles, tires, into machine tools and consumer electronics – among others. With American productivity gains sagging toward zero, with inflation and interest rates unbelievably high, with bankruptcies and fire sales taking place in the corporate marketplace, Americans had every reason to believe the business core of their society was indeed cracked. Just like the political core in Washington, DC. And the military core of the American empire.

The master analyst of American malaise at this time was Christopher Lasch, who published a popular jeremiad in the late 1970s. *The Culture of Narcissism: American Life in an Age of Diminishing Expectations* didn't spare the rod.[28] The author lashed out at the schools, the universities, the businesses, the professions – all of which had combined to dumb down the population and undercut the good old American virtues. In governing, liberals had done no better than conservatives. The professionals so important to my account of American history were merely "a branch of modern management," in Lasch's perspective. He hoped for restoration but left his readers more impressed with America's "dying culture" than its "will to build a better society."[29]

Not so Fast!

Even in the 1970s, however, America had strengths that weren't apparent in Lasch's account or the nation's grim headlines. There were important parts of the core that weren't cracked. These boded well for America and its people, even though many Americans weren't paying much attention to them.

For one thing, the new women's movement made some astonishing gains in the 1970s. Betty Friedan's influence continued to be felt. Building on the solid educational and professional foundations rounded out in the postwar years, important changes continued to take place in the workforce and in America's educational institutions. For white women with a decent education, the 1970s was a decade of positive transitions. Admissions to professional schools were on the rise. At the beginning

---

[28] (New York, 1978).

[29] Christopher Lasch, *The Culture of Narcissism*, 234–36. Jack Nicholson was the movie counterpart of Lasch. As I pointed out in an earlier study of the 1970s, Nicholson was the symbol of "sardonic impotence," that is, of American failure. *America at Middle Age* (New York, 1983).

of the decade, less than 9 percent of the students in ABA-approved law programs were women. By 1980, that figure had more than tripled. This was an astonishing change for any decade, and it was just the first phase of a long-run trend.[30]

Women were a growing presence in the professional schools of educational institutions that had long been male preserves. This was important because it provided teachers and role models for the next generation of women. It also opened administrative positions to talented women in an era when more and more power and money were shifting to higher-education's bureaucracies. In all of the professions, women were making gains that would place them on the threshold of the top leadership in American institutions. For the most part, they could still only admire those positions, and the corner offices they provided, but now they could at least see them from up close. In politics, the progress was slow but significant. In medicine, it was much faster, in part because of the performance-centered nature of the admissions process and also because a high degree of specialization was creating positions that were especially attractive to women.[31]

In large corporations, women still tended to be bunched in staff, not line, positions, especially in legal departments and human resources. But that too was beginning to change. Increased enrollment by women in MBA programs like the one at the Harvard Business School pointed toward a new future for American enterprises, one in which women would soon be competing for the top executive positions.

The civil rights movement was by this time institutionalized, and the fracturing of the political side of the movement fortunately didn't stop the progress. Martin Luther King's assassination in 1968 was an American tragedy, but the movement for which he gave his life already had a great deal of social and political momentum. Some affirmative action programs ran into trouble, but they continued to make progress – even if it was less publicized than the problems. Academic institutions now experimented with minors and majors focused on African-American history, literature, politics, and culture. Each of these programs provided appointments for black scholars, and the best were in such demand that their salaries and statuses increased sharply. Like women in academic life, African

---

[30] http://www.encyclopedia.com/doc1G2-3468302724.html, August 10, 2008.
[31] In pediatrics, for instance, women were perceived as having important advantages, as they did in gynecology.

Americans were now being offered administrative positions that had long been reserved for white males. Outside the academy, black Americans were building a new power base in local, state, and national politics. In the 1950s, it had been a major breakthrough for President Eisenhower to meet with Martin Luther King in the White House.[32] By the end of the 1970s, white politicians were courting black support from the county courthouses to the U.S. Congress.

Carter's Two-Edged Sword

Certainly President Jimmy Carter's promotion of federal deregulation deserves a place in the accomplishments of the 1970s. Professional pressure against the style of regulation developed by the Interstate Commerce Commission had been building for many years.[33] Initially, the economic studies that created a base for the movement were written for, read by, and understood largely by other professional economists. Professors like Alfred E. Kahn and Herbert M. Kaufman were certain about their theories and their data, but you wouldn't expect a broad-based political movement to arise out of academic publications.

Or could you? This wasn't the way democracy was supposed to work, but it was the way the new public sphere of professionals was working.[34] Over a period of years, the academic publications began to influence people of power in institutions that mattered. Courses in leading universities used these materials. Their graduates weren't likely to become powerful senators or congressmen or even state legislators. They weren't likely to become state-level or federal executives either. But they could become members of – and in one important case (Alfred E. Kahn), the chairman of – a regulatory agency (the Civil Aeronautics Board). They could as well become staff members to people in positions of power, and one of the most important functions of the staff was to provide well-grounded ideas to those they served. This was the first major political movement in post-World War II America to have this kind of history, a new twist, a professional twist on the democratic model of political change.

---

[32] This was in Chapter 9.

[33] Regulations focused on the rate of return of the regulated companies were one of the chief targets of the deregulation scholars.

[34] As noted before, the original theory and history of the public sphere was provided by Jürgen Habermas, who located it in the eighteenth and early nineteenth centuries. For a different evaluation of the modern public sphere, see Lizabeth Cohen, *A Consumers' Republic*, especially 289.

Also unusual was the political support some of the new ideas enjoyed. To liberals, the message was clear. The regulatory state wasn't working properly because of the influence of big business. Businesses like AT&T had co-opted the regulatory process and controlled the rate and service structure to their own advantage. This reasoning was supported when the businesses opposed changes in a regulatory state that was working, they said, very well. To conservatives, the message was different but equally clear: America was suffering from regulatory failure. The regulatory state had failed to do what markets do to keep down costs and promote innovation as well as efficiency. In the short run, regulation worked. In the long run, conservatives claimed, it yielded results that were unfortunate for the public, for the companies, and for their employees.

With support from a broad range of political leaders and their staffs, the new deregulation policies were not likely to encounter any serious roadblocks in Congress. First to go was the elaborate regulatory system for the airlines. President Jimmy Carter strongly supported deregulation and backed up his words by appointing economist Alfred Kahn to head the airlines regulatory agency.[35] Congress resisted the pressure from the unions and airlines and approved the Airline Deregulation Act (1978). Later, Carter and Congress dismantled the regulations on interstate trucking, energy, and finance. Two of the agencies actually went out of business![36]

The mighty sword of deregulation cut two ways. One blade was directed at the regulatory state and the other sliced deeply into the concept of expert control. Based on a century of experience, Carter and his liberal/conservative coalition concluded that the experts weren't getting it right. The experts were too slow to change and were frequently more interested in consolidating and stabilizing the regulatory state than in promoting growth and technological change. The strongest arguments against the regulators were provided by the state of the economy in the late 1970s. A nation once all-powerful had lost its leadership position in the world economy. High inflation, paralyzing interest rates, and painful levels of unemployment were accompanied at the end of the 1970s by low

---

[35] Julian E. Zelizer, *Jimmy Carter*, 84, 86, gives a different picture of the deregulation legislation of the 1970s.

[36] Richard H. K. Vietor, "Government Regulation of Business," in Stanley L. Engerman and Robert E. Gallman, eds., *The Cambridge Economic History of the United States*, III, 995–1012. The Civil Aeronautics Board and the Interstate Commerce Commission both closed their doors, thus answering Herbert Kaufman's famous question: *Are Government Organizations Immortal?* (Washington, DC, 1976).

productivity increases, discouraging rates of job creation, and static economic growth. Little wonder that many Americans were ready for change. Some were actually looking overseas for models of political economy that might give the United States better results.[37]

I knew I wasn't the only American learning from the devastating negative experiences of the 1970s. What we were learning, I believe, was that America now had an impressive array of first-class universities, professional training programs, and experts. That hadn't been the case earlier in the century. But Americans had paid the taxes and tuitions needed to build up the universities and professional schools. Men and women had flocked to these programs, and by the 1970s, professional graduates of these programs populated all of society's most important institutions – in every part of the United States. Their expertise had accomplished a great deal for society. But now we could see the limits to what they could accomplish for America at home and abroad.

We could see, I believe, that America needed leaders who could manage the experts and do so in ways that served our national interests and were still consistent with American democratic values. Otherwise, we would be unable to make good use of America's great power and wealth. We would squander it, as we had in Southeast Asia and in the effort to pay for both guns and butter. We would squander it by encasing our entrepreneurs in regulatory spiderwebs like those woven by the Interstate Commerce Commission. The disastrous 1970s had provided a warning against corruption, overweening pride, and incompetent regulation – a harsh reminder that America still needed to learn how to balance professional expertise with effective democratic leadership.

---

[37] See, for example M. J. Piore and C. F. Sable, *The Second Industrial Divide: Possibilities for Prosperity* (New York, 1984). Otis Graham, *Toward a Planned Society: From Roosevelt to Nixon* (New York, 1976).

14

The American Solution, 1981 to 2001

Apparently down and out by the end of the 1970s, the United States made a remarkable comeback. Nations don't always come back, don't always make it through these transitions successfully.[1] In the early nineteenth century, the British had tremendous advantages on the basis of their success as the "first-movers" in the first industrial revolution. But the British steadily lost out to newcomers in the second industrial revolution.[2] So America's ability to change course, to transform many of its basic institutions and policies, and to recover its leading position in the world economy deserves some serious attention. This recovery is all the more important because it took place against the background of total collapse in the Soviet empire.

As became apparent during these decades, one of the great weaknesses of totalizing, authoritarian polities like the Soviet Union and the People's Republic of China was their tension with professional elites. Fascist regimes have normally had the same problem. The Gulag, the

[1] While the history of this transformation is as yet unwritten, the interested student might want to read Andrew Grove, *Only the Paranoid Survive* (New York, 1996) to get a feel for what was happening. Still desiring more information, he or she should turn to Manuel Castells, *The Rise of the Network Society* (Malden, MA, 2000 edition), to get a global perspective on the transition.

[2] We began this account (see Chapter 3) when American firms were well into the second industrial revolution, a technological and organizational transformation that began in the late nineteenth century and extended into the post–World War II years. Then, some of the leading industries were those in electrical products, chemicals, electrochemicals, and automobiles. These were the years when mass-production and mass-distribution combined to transform the American economy.

Cultural Revolution, the Nazi assaults on the universities – these experiences stunted the development of professional expertise. Professionals and professional institutions need to be nurtured in loosely controlled environments that foster debate. Authoritarian governments curdle professional discourse by encouraging intellectual and ideological conformity and compliance. The United States had vibrant professional cultures and organizations, and they played an important role in America's recovery from the serious stagflation of the 1970s. Professional elites also helped the European democracies catch up gradually with America's ability to generate productivity increases and economic growth.[3] The professionals on both sides of the Atlantic didn't always get it right, but they gave their societies the kind of public and private expertise essential to economic recovery.

The U.S. approach to this transformation was labeled "the American solution" by Europeans who claimed that Americans were too brutal about curbing welfare, too determined to change very quickly, too eager to embrace new approaches to public and private policies.[4] This evaluation was grounded in Europe's stronger dedication to economic security and equity and in a critique of what Europeans saw as America's coldhearted obsession with innovation and efficiency *at all costs.*[5]

In most regards, the European critics were right. The American transformation was fast, frequently brutal, and focused intensely on efficiency and innovation – at *almost* all costs. It was as well a class-specific transformation that cut deeply among blue- and white-collar Americans, hurting those without technical skills, without a good education, without a position protected from the forces of change. Most teachers and university professors were protected by tenure rules, but few outside of education were able to hide from the forces of change that swept through America in the last two decades of the twentieth century. Millions who felt the impact of global competition and the third industrial revolution learned

[3] Fredrik Bergström and Robert Gidehag, *EU Versus USA* (Stockholm, 2004). Robert J. Gordon, "Why Was Europe Left at the Station When America's Productivity Locomotive Departed?" NBER Working Paper 10661 (August 2004).

[4] See, for instance, two articles in *The Economist*: "French Railways," November 25, 1978; and "A Time to Dismantle the World Economy," November 9, 1985.

[5] There was probably an element of fear lurking behind this critique; fear that the American Colossus would get back on its feet and create new problems for European businesses. As it turned out, those fears were realistic.

all too well what the Social Darwinists of the late nineteenth century meant when they said "root hog or die." [6]

Globalization and information-age technology forced businesses all over the world to change. The United States and the other leading industrial nations aggressively promoted the lowering of barriers to trade as a means of fostering economic growth. Their efforts, many of which were channeled after 1995 through the World Trade Organization, were surprisingly successful. As a result, world trade between the developed and the developing nations increased dramatically after 1980.[7] So did competition at a time when the new technologies of the information age were also fostering rapid change in business. Very few, if any, American business firms were not touched in some way by the changes in information technology (IT). Retailing was transformed, as was design and manufacturing, by changes taking place quickly and across a very broad front.[8] Computer controls in manufacturing and design, bar codes in the checkout line, fiber-optic cables in communications, the personal computer on your desk – these and other innovations transformed business. These changes provided marvelous opportunities for some individuals and organizations and deadly threats to the wealth and income of those unable to adapt to this new environment.

Social Destruction Revisited

The resulting transformation was a painful case study in what Joseph Schumpeter called "creative destruction." As we saw in the Preface to this book, Schumpeter's idea was that capitalist entrepreneurship would produce new ways of doing things and new products and services. That was capitalism's creative side. But the entrepreneurs and their organizations would inevitably drive out of business the individuals and firms that didn't innovate. That was the destructive side of capitalism. This process was hurtful to many, Schumpeter acknowledged, but he maintained that entrepreneurship was the essence of capitalist progress.

---

[6] The expression, which roughly means "work or don't eat," was used by William Graham Sumner (1840–1910), the Yale University sociologist who was opposed to government intervention in the economy.

[7] Barry Eichengreen, "Global Imbalances and the Lessons of Bretton Woods," NBER Working Paper No. 10497 (May 2004).

[8] Robert J. Gordon, "Why Was Europe Left at the Station When America's Productivity Locomotive Departed?"

When journalists use Schumpeter's idea, they're usually more interested in destruction than creation. Newspapers don't report on airplanes that land successfully. In the case of the late-twentieth-century transformation of the American economy, the newspapers had plenty of bad news to report. It began with a Fed-led squeeze on the economy (1981–1983) that pushed the unemployment rate up above 10 percent of the nation's workforce. The policy worked. It brought an end to the great inflation that had been twisting the U.S. economy out of shape since the late 1960s. But the price was high for blue-collar Americans. Older workers suffered the worst effects, as did older regions of the country, especially the East Coast Rust Belt.[9] The broken windows and rusting hulks of factories were stark symbols of capitalism's destructive force.

As firms struggled to cut costs and improve operations, they also cut deeply into their white-collar ranks. Some managers were eased out with early retirements. Others were just eased out. This was the first time since World War II that major tremors of insecurity were felt among white-collar employees in large corporations. The bourgeoisie seldom evokes pity, but this time the shock was strong enough to bring expressions of social concern to the *New York Times* and other major publications. Corporate mergers were almost always accompanied by cuts in "redundant" employees as companies "right-sized" the workforce.[10] Deregulation had the same impact. When AT&T began to face competition across the entire range of its services, one of the company's responses was to dig deeply into the vast managerial force that ran the firm. Entire levels were wiped out as the company tried quickly to become an agile, low-cost competitor.

Less apparent and less publicized was the white-collar "stretch-out."[11] Managers and other administrators were given a greater range of responsibilities and a few more "direct reports" after cost cutting took out some of their colleagues. Increased workloads cut into what was left of family

---

[9] Adrian W. Throop, "Anatomy of the 1981–83 Disinflation," *Federal Reserve Bank of San Francisco*, March 23, 1984. William Robbins, "Data on Jobs Show Variety of Ills in U.S.," *New York Times*, January 11, 1982; William Serrin, "Recession and Spreading Layoffs Hitting the White-Collar Worker," *New York Times*, January 12, 1982.

[10] At first it was called downsizing, which is what it was; but the public-relations folks didn't like that because it sounded so harsh. There were other euphemisms, but right-sizing was probably the best of the lot.

[11] I first encountered this term when I was studying the intensely competitive cotton-textile industry. To cut labor costs, the manufacturers started running the machines before the workers arrived and ran them through the lunch period. They were increasing productivity by stretching out the labor, squeezing more work out of the lint-heads who tended the machines.

time. Those who were unwilling to make these sacrifices left for other jobs or early retirement. The laptop computer, the cell phone, and then the Blackberry brought the workplace into the home and the car. You could – and sometimes had to – do business when you were standing in line at Disney World or shopping for a birthday present. As the American Solution got fully underway, many white-collar employees could no longer plan on having both a successful corporate career and a well-rounded life. I was doing research in various companies during this long transition, so I was able to get a close view of this process and the price employees and their families paid for the powerful drive to improve efficiency.

The Turnaround Specialist

So pervasive was the transformation that it brought forth a new social creature, the turnaround specialist. These were executives who moved from one enterprise to another, reorganizing and revamping the businesses so they could compete effectively. Usually that involved unpleasant activities like getting rid of large numbers of employees, replacing fellow executives, and maybe even selling off part of the firm. Or maybe all of it. There had always been executives and bankers who performed some or all of these functions, but they usually did this within a single business or industry, often their own. Now the turnaround specialists were bouncing into new companies and entirely new industries. There were so many of them that they caught the eye of the business press.

None of this new business breed caught more eyes than Al "Chain Saw" Dunlap, who left no question as to whether he deserved his nickname. The son of a shipyard worker in Hoboken, New Jersey, Dunlap was the first person in his family to go to college. Getting an appointment to West Point, he quickly discovered that he "hated engineering," an important discipline at the Military Academy. He didn't like to lose, however, so he ground his way through the program using somewhat the same style he had as a West Point boxer: aggressive, tenacious, and hard to hit. After graduating in 1960, he spent three years in the army and then left to venture into business, where he thought his competitive nature would be an asset.[12]

---

[12] Albert J. Dunlap, with Bob Andelman, *Mean Business: How I Save Bad Companies and Make Good Companies Great* (New York, 1997 edition). See Roger Lowenstein's review in the *Wall Street Journal*, when the book was first published. Lowenstein fills in some of the big holes Dunlap left in his autobiography.

He was right. Dunlap started his civilian career in the paper business with Kimberly-Clark. This was a low-margin, mass-production industry in which firms carefully tended their costs. He was soon on the move, advancing to a supervisor's position in manufacturing and then going to a new company, Sterling Pulp & Paper, in Wisconsin. Four moves later, all of them advances, he got his first major turnaround job with Scott Paper, one of the giants in the industry. As Chairman and Chief Executive Officer, Dunlap was quick to use his chain saw at a 115-year-old organization that some thought was headed into bankruptcy. He had honed his techniques in his previous jobs, so he landed at Scott ready to go. He gave himself twelve months to finish the biggest part of the transformation. He launched his mission by selling off assets that were underperforming, getting rid of most of the upper-management team, and firing 11,200 employees – 35 percent of the workforce.[13] His focus was on the shareholders, not the stakeholders – who included the employees: "Stakeholders are total rubbish," he said. "It's the shareholders who own the company." After fifteen months on the job, he sold the company.[14]

True to his new specialty, he quickly headed into another turnaround job – this one with Sunbeam, a producer of appliances like blenders.[15] Now he targeted 12,000 employees for layoffs, got rid of almost 90 percent of the firm's products, and sold off 18 factories in the first year. The chain saw was just as sharp as it had been at Scott. The stock price turned up when Dunlap became Sunbeam's CEO and Chairman, but this time the fix didn't work. The company didn't recover, and Chain Saw was fired two years later. This was indeed a "mean business," and after he paid $15 million to settle a shareholder fraud case, the SEC banned Dunlap permanently from serving as an official of a public company.[16] The saw, like a sword, could cut both ways.

Chain Saw Dunlap was an extreme form of the American Solution, but he was close enough to the average for the *Wall Street Journal* to suggest that he might be needed at General Motors.[17] GM, Chrysler, and many of America's other large firms were struggling to survive in an intensely competitive global economy. At Chrysler, Lee Iacocca was brought in to

---

[13] He got rid of the managers who, he said, were "covering their butts."

[14] Kimberly-Clark bought Scott Paper.

[15] Like Scott Paper, Sunbeam was a well-established firm, almost a hundred years old.

[16] *New York Times*, June 16, 18, 21; July 10, 15; August 5, 7, 25, 1998. *Bloomberg News*, September 4, 2002. John A. Byrne, "How Al Dunlap Self-Destructed," *BusinessWeek*, July 6, 1998.

[17] This suggestion preceded the SEC ban.

"clean house" at the country's tenth largest corporation. He fired thirty-three of his thirty-five vice presidents. He copied the Japanese "just in time" inventory system, improved communications within the firm, and still had to lay off thousands of white-collar and shop-floor employees. In 1980, Chrysler fired 13,500 salaried workers.[18]

Even though the automobile producers received some temporary protection from the government, the long-term future was dismal for their businesses and any others that couldn't quickly cut costs, improve their ability to innovate, and meet the standards being set by foreign competitors.[19] Managers of troubled firms fought hard to compete, launching media campaigns and titanic court battles.[20] As these efforts to "turn around" U.S. companies in automobiles and other industries became pervasive, the specialists organized the Turnaround Management Association in 1988. Their march toward professionalization produced a journal in 1991 and awards to the leading turnaround professionals.[21] As "corporate renewal" matured, the leaders guided the association and its practitioners "beyond [the] simplistic things of getting rid of overhead, working strictly on the left-hand [cost] side of the balance sheet to shrink the company.... " As the association's chair explained, you had to have a new strategy for troubled companies. They had "to perform in a more efficient and productive manner" or go out of business.[22] The alternatives were stark – as they are today.

One good indicator of what was happening was the continued decline of organized labor in the private sector. As companies moved production overseas and imports swept into U.S. markets, labor union membership dwindled and "givebacks" became a common aspect of labor agreements. Because the foreign producers and branches of U.S. firms were outside the reach of American labor regulations, the New Deal settlement between labor, management, and the government broke down. Organized labor

---

[18] Lee Iacocca (with William Novak), *Iacocca: An Autobiography* (Toronto, 1984), especially 151–91. "With hindsight it's clear," Iacocca commented, "that Chrysler had been top-heavy, far beyond what was good for us" (191).

[19] Chrysler also got a controversial government loan, which it repaid early.

[20] Mark J. Roe, *Strong Managers, Weak Owners: The Political Roots of American Corporate Finance* (Princeton, 1994), 226–30, identifies this period of change as "An American Crossroads," and he is surely correct.

[21] There is abundant information at http://www.turnaround.org. The association has a built-in countercyclical aspect; as the economy sags, the turnaround business picks up. See, especially, *The Journal of Corporate Renewal*, 21, 10 (October 2008), which celebrated the twenty-year anniversary of the association.

[22] Interview with Gilbert C. Osnos, CTP, the association's chair in 1990–1991. For this and other materials on the association, I am grateful to Cecilia Green.

went into a long decline in membership and power in the private sector. By the end of the 1990s, only about 12 percent of America's nonfarm workers were union members. The only unions that were growing were those in the public sector where they were sheltered from the forces of global competition.

Gurus of the Transition

A social transformation on this scale – taking place in the largest economy in the world – was likely to produce a new set of intellectual leaders, and indeed the United States found a new crop of gurus in the business press. Leading the pack in 1982 were two talented managerial consultants, Thomas J. Peters and Robert H. Waterman, Jr., who wrote *In Search of Excellence: Lessons from America's Best-Run Companies*. Both authors came up through the professional education system of the new aristocracy. Peters had a degree in civil engineering (Cornell) and an MBA and PhD from Stanford. Waterman also had an MBA from Stanford and an undergraduate degree in geophysics. Early in their careers, both men wandered a bit, looking for the right niche. They found it when *In Search of Excellence* became the must-read book for America's professional managers.

Taking the solidly positive approach that appeals to U.S. executives and managers, Peters and Waterman walked their readers through the experiences of some of the country's leading corporations. There they discovered the "lessons" they had learned consulting for McKinsey & Company, where they became partners. They packaged their conclusions in the bullet heads normally used in business presentations. To be excellent, a company had to:

- Have a Bias for Action
- Be Close to the Customer
- Encourage Autonomy and Entrepreneurship
- Achieve Productivity through People
- Emphasize Hands-On, Value-Driven Activity
- Stick to the Knitting
- Use a Simple Form, Lean Staff
- Have Simultaneous Loose-Tight Properties.[23]

---

[23] Here I'm using the titles of Chapters 5 through 12 of Thomas J. Peters and Robert H. Waterman, Jr., *In Search of Excellence: Lessons from America's Best-Run Companies* (New York, 1982).

Fortunately, these guidelines to a winning corporate culture could be presented even more succinctly using the McKinsey patented 7-S Framework:[24]

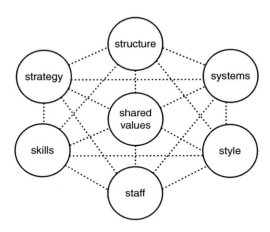

Don't scoff at this figure, the chapter titles, or the book. More than seven million copies of the book were sold, McKinsey & Company became the world's leading management consulting firm, and corporate culture became a central idea in the transformation of U.S. businesses in the 1980s and 1990s.

Let's look into one of this wildly successful book's chapter titles, the bullet urging firms to stick to their knitting. Using the multidivisional (M-form) structure we discussed before, many of the country's leading firms had diversified into an array of increasingly distinct activities.[25] Gradually, diversification had morphed into conglomeration, with companies making and trying to sell totally unrelated products and services. Some organizations could do it, especially during the American Century when the United States was dominating the world economy. Most couldn't do it profitably in an intensely competitive setting.[26] As they finally realized what was happening, their executives began to spin off unrelated divisions and departments so they could concentrate on their core functions. In the abstract, that sounds wonderful. It frequently was for the company bottom line. But if you were an employee or a manager

---

[24] For a succinct guide to the Framework and its origins see http://university-essays.tripod.com/mckinsey_7s_framework.html.

[25] See Chapter 9.

[26] During these years, one of the exceptions that proved the rule was General Electric.

in one of those divisions or departments, you had a good chance of suddenly discovering you were "redundant." If you were lucky, you might retire early; if not, you would probably be looking at a pink slip and searching for another job.

This process was closely linked to three financial practices that were widespread during this era of transition. One was the managerial buyout, which allowed the executives closest to one of the firm's divisions or departments to take over and run a subsidiary as a separate firm. Frequently, the managers didn't have the capital they needed to purchase the subsidiary, so they used large amounts of debt – the second practice – in what was called a leveraged buyout.[27] If the business could then grow into the debt, the new managers scored some big capital gains, as many of them did. The need for capital was frequently met by using "junk bonds," a third innovation. Junk bonds, which were originally developed by Michael Milken, a high-flying bond trader at Drexel Burnham and Company, had little or no backing.[28] This was a security well suited to economy-wide restructuring in a society that was still not frightened by risk.

Peters and Waterman were out in front, leading the way into this post-1980 transformation of U.S. business. You can imagine how many copies of *In Search* were sold the day the CEO of the nation's largest corporation was seen carrying the book into corporate headquarters.[29] As the authors accumulated royalties, they also accumulated competitors. This was a rich vein of business experience that attracted numerous academic and journalistic imitators.[30] Each of the corporate how-to books had a

---

[27] In this case, leverage simply means that a high percentage of their financing was done through bonds, not stock. Having a high ratio of debt (on which interest has to be paid to stay out of bankruptcy) makes a firm more vulnerable to downturns in the economy.

[28] Milken was brought to earth by the SEC and U.S. Attorney Rudy Guiliani. Milken pleaded guilty to six charges in 1990, paid a large fine, and served time in prison. He and Ivan Boesky were the only two financiers of this era to go to prison for practices that became widespread in the 1980s and 1990s. Drexel Burnham and Company failed as a result of the scandal.

[29] The CEO was Charlie Brown of AT&T.

[30] If you have a taste for this subject, see: M. Hammer and J. Champy, *Reengineering the Corporation: A Manifesto for Business Revolution* (New York, 1993); J. C. Collins and J. I. Porras, *Built to Last: Successful Habits of Visionary Companies* (New York, 1994). C. M. Christensen, *The Innovator's Dilemma: When New Technologies Cause Great Firms to Fail* (Boston, 1997), ran against the grain and became popular by frightening those executives who thought their firms were now in a strong position. To restore their faith, the executives could and did turn to N. M. Tichy and E. Cohen, *The Leadership Engine: How Winning Companies Build Leaders at Every Level* (New York, 1997).

slightly different formula for reengineering and restructuring and refitting the corporation. But all of them offered the same major lesson: you had to change, and change in dramatic ways, to be successful in this new economy. Because those changes will never be complete, the field of business books is still hot today, more than twenty-five years after the search for excellence began.

That search reached deeply into America's enormous corporate economy, and not all of the discoveries were as laudable as "sticking to your knitting." In an effort to cut costs, firms eliminated benefits by hiring temporary workers, by subcontracting to individuals and organizations, and in some cases by leasing employees. More and more work was sent "offshore" to Mexico, to Asia, to wherever labor and other costs were lower. Through the 1980s and 1990s, the service industries in America continued to grow, but manufacturing was in decline, caught up in fierce global price competition. For many Americans, the trade-offs between equity and efficiency, between security and innovation were painful indeed.

Creativity under Stress

When a local business was going under and your town or city was being stripped of jobs, it was hard to remember that the United States had tremendous strengths. In the 1980s and 1990s, however, America had three important assets that were often ignored because they weren't making headlines or short stories on the evening news. One was an abundant supply of capital accumulated during the country's successful experience in the second industrial revolution. By the 1980s, a strong venture-capital industry existed to help fund start-ups as well as mergers, acquisitions, and restructuring programs to revive companies in trouble. The financial sector in America was well developed, flexible, and innovative.

America's second ace in the hole was its labor force. There was much media and academic discussion of the American worker, who was often portrayed as poorly educated, unwilling to work hard, and unable to provide innovations from the shop floor. But in the 1980s and 1990s, in the midst of this great transition, it began to become clear that when American workers were given the right support, they matched or even exceeded the performances of foreign labor.[31] The media moaning was

---

[31] Richard Florida, *The Rise of the Creative Class*, 145. "Led by the Creative Class, the United States surged ahead of even Japan, long thought to be a nation of workaholics, in average hours worked."

excessive. U.S. labor proved itself capable of rising to the task of meeting global competition. If it hadn't, the transformation might not have taken place.

The third big advantage the United States had was the broad and deep array of academic institutions we've already discussed. They were continuing to churn out the professional experts and new knowledge the nation's enterprises needed. The schools were also training the brokers who could help translate the ideas and the activities of the experts into meaningful innovations. This gave the United States and its leading businesses an advantage that is hard to exaggerate and almost impossible to measure.[32] The educational system's rate of growth had slowed, but it was continuing to expand and change during the difficult 1970s.

That continued growth took place while the nation's universities were under attack on several fronts. California Governor Ronald Reagan, incensed by the New Left, had threatened to clean up "the mess at Berkeley." The Free Speech Movement and the riots and sit-ins challenged the authority of the university's administration and local government. Reagan's assault was followed by a taxpayers' revolt that struck a serious blow to the entire financial base of a very large and important set of institutions, local and state, from primary schools through to California's outstanding universities. As we saw earlier, the University of California at Berkeley had been able to attract brilliant scientists like Ernest O. Lawrence. Berkeley's physics department was one of the best in the world. The tax revolt threatened Berkeley and the rest of the Golden State's universities, and similar movements were underway in other states.[33]

Fortunately for California and America, the universities and their professional schools survived the struggles with cost cutting and with the New Left and were able in the 1980s and 1990s to provide American businesses with the professionals they needed to cope with global competition and the information age. As a result, U.S. firms took a leading role

---

[32] For an interesting exercise in comparative measurement and analysis for one industry, see L. Orsenigo, F. Pammolli, and M. Riccaboni, "Technological change and network dynamics: lessons from the pharmaceutical industry," *Research Policy*, 30 (2001), 485–508. See also Moses Abramovitz and Paul A. David, "American Macroeconomic Growth in the Era of Knowledge-Based Progress: The Long-Run Perspective," in Stanley L. Engerman and Robert E. Gallman, eds., *The Cambridge Economic History of the United States*, III, *The Twentieth Century*, 1–92.

[33] James Ring Adams, *Secrets of the Tax Revolt* (New York, 1984), 124–78; Robert M. Collins, *Transforming America: Politics and Culture in the Reagan Years* (New York, 2007), 39. By punishing the universities, Reagan apparently hoped to encourage their administrators and local authorities to bring the unruly students under control.

in the first stages of the information revolution. Taking advantage of the transistor, the integrated circuit, the large-frame and personal computers, and the Internet, American businesses like Microsoft, Intel, IBM, Google, and Hewlett-Packard acquired and then maintained strong global positions in the world's rapidly expanding IT industries.

Other large American businesses, like RCA and Netscape, have fallen to the kind of competition that persuaded Andy Grove of Intel to claim that *Only the Paranoid Survive*.[34] The IT-era competition favored "pure-play companies" that concentrated on a single function. These businesses were not vertically integrated like the M-form corporations of the second industrial revolution. They bought their inputs from other specialized firms. They worked through alliances in foreign and domestic markets, using partners to enhance their political and economic capabilities. In many cases, they became managers of other research and production businesses scattered around the world. This is a new business universe – one in which America is still in first place.

The IT revolution put tremendous pressure on American businesses, but it also created unusual opportunities for talented professionals, men and women, foreign and domestic, to get ahead. One of those who made it to the top was Carly Fiorina, who became CEO of Hewlett-Packard in 1999. This was a stunning event on a global scale. At that time, there was no country in the world other than the United States in which a woman could be the top executive of a leading, Fortune 50, high-tech company. Was this another American advantage? Of course it was! By breaking the glass ceiling, the United States would, over the long run, be able to make better use of about half of its population. Only a small number of women would get to the top, but they would provide models and mentors for those women who excelled in higher education, acquired professional capabilities, and learned how to manage in large, modern U.S. corporations.

Let's trace Fiorina's path to the top of HP because it will help us understand how and to what effect America was changing at the end of the twentieth century. She came to HP from Lucent Technologies, the firm that was once Western Electric in the old Bell System and was spun off by AT&T in 1996. A native Texan, Fiorina graduated from Stanford with a degree in history, made a one-year stab at law school, worked for a few years, and then finally found her profession in an MBA program.

[34] (New York, 1996).

Hired by AT&T in 1980, she had a front seat on the breakup of the Bell System and put the final touches on her business education at MIT's Sloan School. Picking up technical knowledge on the job, she demonstrated a talent that was in short supply at AT&T: salesmanship. High energy, imagination, and hard work carried her quickly up the phone company's hierarchy.[35] Already a vice president by 1995, she joined the team that took Lucent public. The spin-off was successful and so was Fiorina. She became president of a $20 billion division handling global service and headed *Fortune*'s 1998 list of the fifty most powerful women executives in America.[36]

While Fiorina was thriving at Lucent, Hewlett-Packard was in the market for a new leader. As the founders gradually retired, HP tried two inside appointments that didn't work. Then the company began to look outside for an energetic leader who could break the hold of a deeply planted culture and organization that was impeding change. HP's salesmanship was sagging and that made Fiorina an attractive candidate for the top job.[37] As soon as she took over at HP, she set out to restore luster to the HP brand, to tighten the organization's central controls, and to develop a strategy for dealing with the Internet. Then she made a truly bold move. To pump up HP's computer operations, she decided to make a bid for Compaq Computer Corporation.

While HP wanted a dynamic leader, her move to acquire Compaq appeared to some of the firm's powerful stockholders to be a mistake. The $20 billion bid for Compaq split the Board and prompted a bitter internal struggle that spilled over into the business press and the courts. Fiorina won that battle but then she had to focus on the slow grinding required for HP to digest its massive acquisition and become the next IBM. Unfortunately for Fiorina, this had to be done in the midst of a major recession. The dot-com bubble had burst and the entire IT sector was in distress. Fiorina had already laid off thousands of employees in an effort to cut costs. But in an intensely competitive market that was experiencing only moderate growth, HP was in trouble. The anticipated

[35] In 1983, when Cyndi Lauper brought out her hit song "Girls Just Wanna Have Fun," Carly Fiorina was launching her successful, hard-driving career at AT&T. That year, more than 490,000 women received bachelor's degrees and more than 140,000 received master's degrees. They apparently did not just "wanna have fun."

[36] George Anders, *Perfect Enough: Carly Fiorina and the Reinvention of Hewlett-Packard* (New York, 2003) carries the story through the HP acquisition of Compaq.

[37] *New York Times*, August 22, 1999; *Business Week*, August 2, 1999.

"synergies" from the merger were slow in coming. Earnings and the stock price were lagging. Rumblings came from the Board.[38] Then, five and a half years after she became CEO, Fiorina was suddenly ousted by HP.[39]

Carly Fiorina was gone from the big business stage, but she shouldn't be forgotten. For one thing, her successors at Hewlett-Packard have made a success of the merger that was the central accomplishment of Fiorina's leadership. HP has thrived.[40]

And the crack that Fiorina made in the glass ceiling has widened. More and more women are moving into top positions in American corporations. The list is long today. Mustering just below the top positions are those ranks of well-educated women who have moved along the professional path, through college, through graduate programs, and onto the corporate fast track. At the Harvard Business School in 1965, only 2 percent of the entering students were women. By 1975, the figure was 11 percent and by 1985, women made up a quarter of the entering class. By the early twenty-first century, the figure was 38 percent.[41]

Alongside this elite cadre of businesswomen are many first- and second-generation immigrant Americans who have also been able to take advantage of the new opportunities of the information age. India was sending America young people like Arun Sarin, a graduate of the Institute of Technology in Kharagpur. He continued his education at the University of California at Berkeley, where he received both an MS in engineering and an MBA (1978). At PacTel and then at Air Touch, a wireless spin-off, he quickly moved into upper management. He was not alone in making a quick step to the top. By the end of the 1990s, it was estimated that somewhere between 10 percent and 15 percent of Silicon Valley companies were being run by immigrants from India. For Sarin, the top of the

---

[38] *Wall Street Journal*, January 24, and February 8, 2005; Carol J. Loomis, "Why Carly's Big Bet Is Failing," *Fortune*, February 7, 2005.

[39] George Anders, "H-P's Board Ousts Fiorina as CEO," *Wall Street Journal*, February 10, 2005. Fiorina has been significantly less successful in politics than she was in business, but this does not change my conclusion about the significance of her corporate career.

[40] See, for instance, *Wall Street Journal*, May 17, 2006, and August 20, 2008. HP has been front-page business news recently as the firm was rocked by a series of scandals at the top; as yet, however, the company's problems have not unglued the merger that Fiorina consummated.

[41] For the entire nation, women make up about 30 percent of the enrollment in MBA programs, compared to 49 percent in medical and 47 percent in law schools. Sue Shellenbarger, "The Mommy M.B.A.: Schools Try to Attract More Women," *Wall Street Journal*, August 20, 2008.

business world was very high indeed. He later became the chief executive of the British firm Vodafone, the world's largest wireless company.[42]

Equally entrepreneurial was the new biotech industry in which the United States was an early leader. America's scientific strength in molecular genetics and recombinant DNA technology provided half of the leadership for the industry's new firms. It came from university scientists like biochemist Herbert Boyer, a codiscoverer of the rDNA technique.[43] Like most of the scientist-entrepreneurs, Boyer partnered with a venture capitalist who knew how to run a business and above all how to tap the financial markets for capital. Together, Boyer and Robert Swanson organized Genentech in 1976–1977 and took the company public in 1980. Two years later, the FDA approved the firm's genetically produced synthetic insulin. Alliances between biotech firms and large pharmaceutical companies followed, and the industry's rapid expansion continued into the twenty-first century. Genentech's total revenue by 2007 was more than $11.7 billion. By that time, the total capitalization of the biotech industry actually exceeded that of the pharmaceutical sector, one of America's most successful growth industries in the years since World War II.[44]

Global Challenges

Genentech gives us a window on a global economy in which national boundaries have become less imposing. A product of homegrown science and finance, Genentech is now owned by the Swiss pharmaceutical firm Roche Holding.[45] This has happened in industry after industry, with foreign companies acquiring U.S. operations and American firms pushing into foreign markets, frequently by buying into or establishing alliances with existing firms. National identity is still a powerful force. But in the business world, globalization has developed very fast and gone very far.

---

[42] Eric John Abrahamson and I tracked Sarin's career in *Anytime, Anywhere: Entrepreneurship and the Creation of a Wireless World* (New York, 2002). At the Harvard Business School in the early twenty-first century, one-third of the entering class was from outside the United States.

[43] The rDNA technology alters the DNA of living cells (yeast for instance) to produce drugs, vaccines, and other substances.

[44] Jeffrey L. Sturchio and I traced these developments through 1998 in "Pharmaceutical Firms and the Transition to Biotechnology: A Study in Strategic Innovation," *Business History Review*, 72 (Summer 1998), 250–78.

[45] Roche, which paid $2.1 billion for a 60% stake in Genentech in 1990, offered $43.7 billion for the remainder of the biotech's shares. http://www.iht.com/binprintfriendly .php?id=14650607. The acquisition was completed in 2009.

Since 1981, economic policy in America and then in Europe has encouraged combination into global-sized companies. In industries like aluminum, oil, steel, and cement, mergers and acquisitions have created a new generation of highly concentrated global oligopolies. The United States was, for instance, one of the initial innovators in the aluminum industry and its position is still important today. Alcoa, the Aluminum Company of America, was for many years an outstanding American monopoly – it was actually a smart monopoly! It achieved this status by doing what economists said monopolies don't do: innovating, holding prices close to a competitive level, and increasing its market share in primary materials. Even a smart monopolist could get crosswise with the antitrust policy, however, and that happened to Alcoa in 1945. But that setback was temporary, and today Alcoa is one of the leading aluminum producers in the world.

How did it do that? In part by cutting costs to meet foreign competition. The firm actually vacated the Alcoa Building in downtown Pittsburgh and moved to cheaper headquarters in which there were no corner offices for executives. It sold its fine-art collection, worked hard to improve labor relations, and reorganized its R&D. Then it got down to the merger business, acquiring two of its leading competitors, Alumax and Reynolds, as well as a French producer, an Italian firm, and a major share in a Korean company. Alcoa now operates in forty nations and is one of the largest aluminum producers in the world (along with UC Rusal and the Canadian firm, Alcan).

In the age of megamergers, even a global company like Alcoa could be bought. The market for corporate control – that is, the market for a controlling share of a company – is almost wide open in the United States, Britain, and a number of other countries. National feelings can be aroused by foreign takeovers. They were aroused recently in the United States when Dubai Ports World tried to purchase the firms managing six U.S. ports. But multinational megamergers involving billions of dollars nevertheless continued; they averaged twenty a year in the early 1990s and there were more than 200 of them in 2000 alone. When Exxon can absorb Mobil, and there are only two major competitors left producing commercial airplanes, we are clearly in the early stages of a new economy of global oligopolies.

Wide-open markets can produce profitable, efficient producers – as they have in aluminum – but they can also produce global-sized problems. Enron comes to mind, as does the recent financial crisis created by the market for mortgages. In the Enron case, a Houston company that mastered a perfectly legal and profitable energy-trading business attempted to expand into new fields where its techniques were less applicable and its risk higher. The smoke screen produced by its early success, high stock price, and sloppy accounting left investors and more than 20,000 employees unaware that Enron had quietly, illegally slid into bankruptcy. National and state regulators were as lax as the company's certified public accountants, and the result was a stunning, painful multibillion-dollar collapse. Night came in 2001 to Enron's "empire of the sun."

The Balance Sheet

Enron notwithstanding, the successful turnaround of the American economy since 1980 is a tribute in large part to the continuing flexibility of the country's economic institutions. This is a two-sided coin, as you can see by considering what happened to Enron, the other corporate criminals, and the millions of workers, managers, and executives who were "right-sized" out of their jobs and onto the street. That was an important part of the price Americans paid for the economic recovery, and there was even more to the downside. The same flexible financial and regulatory systems that eased capitalism through the recovery also gave us the dot-com bubble and its subsequent collapse. The price of the American Solution, which was high, was a warning of what might happen in the next few years. But following the recovery, no one was worrying about that.

In that regard and others, the transformation was well grounded in America's history. What mattered to the millions who were not on the street was the success in getting the United States back to the top of the global economy. What mattered to them – and they were certainly in the majority – was the stunning turnaround for the largest and most complex political economy in the world.[46] I was close to these events, studying the changes from inside and from outside of American business. As a professional historian, historical consultant, and editor, I was reading corporate documents, interviewing executives and public officials,

---

[46] As should be apparent, I am more optimistic than Donald W. White, *The American Century*, who says (426) that: "The era of American preeminence concluded not with the end of history and the fulfillment of national manifestations of abundance, aid, cultural exchange, and self-determination, nor with the end of military power. It concluded with the breakup of consensus and with the nation expending its resources, skilled labor, and wealth in unproductive ways and alienating parts of the world by the use of military force."

learning what modern firms could and couldn't do. In an era of corporate transformation, I was frequently within the corporation looking out. As a teacher, I was outside of business looking in and trying to fit the modern American corporation into the broader context of American society and American history.

One of the things I learned to appreciate during this transition was the importance of leaders who could guide and frequently even inspire their white- and blue-collar workers, their scientists and engineers, their marketing specialists, their managers and managerial gurus as their organizations tried to adapt to new conditions at home and abroad. Leadership was impossible to quantify, hard to evaluate. But in business, as in government and the nonprofit sector, it took a combination of good leaders and professional expertise to keep an organization efficient as well as innovative. They had to be both to survive, and many didn't survive during this era of brutal global competition.

15

Conservatism: Rhetoric and Realities, 1981 to 2001

Most historians struggle with the difference between what people say and what they actually do. This has become even more of a problem since the development in the early twentieth century of public relations, an organizational profession dedicated to providing us with the words and pictures we want to hear and see. Euphemisms abound. Advertising is so omnipresent that even our children soon learn to be cynical about the spoken and written word. As we look at the most recent cycle of conservatism in American politics, we need to be careful about separating words from actions, rhetoric from reality. As fascinating as developments were in the nation's capitol, we also need to use a wide-angle lens and try to bring some of the politics outside of the Beltway around Washington, DC, into this account of recent U.S. history.[1]

When we do that and let our gaze sweep back as far as the 1950s, we can see that a particular brand of conservatism was already beginning to acquire a base in a number of states.[2] This was originally a style of compromising, moderate conservatism that Ike referred to as the "middle way." It was from time to time accompanied by fierce rhetoric in foreign affairs. But the policies were, in reality, moderate and cautious in the

---

[1] For an insightful review of the outpouring of historical literature on conservatism, the reader can turn to Julian E. Zelizer, "Rethinking the History of American Conservatism," in *Reviews in American History*, 38, 2 (June 2010), 367–92.

[2] I disagree fundamentally with George Packer, "The Fall of Conservatism," *The New Yorker*, May 26, 2008, 47–55, who dates the beginning of the conservative era in American politics in 1966, when Patrick Buchanan went to work for Richard M. Nixon.

exercise of power abroad and at home. That kind of moderation was very popular when it provided Americans with peace and prosperity.[3]

Out in western states like Wyoming, Ike's leadership and ideology had enormous appeal. The voters appear to have quickly developed a taste for conservative values and for the policies of the Eisenhower administrations. This experience entrenched conservatism in a state that would later send Richard B. Cheney to Washington to occupy its only seat in the U.S. House of Representatives.[4] After casting its three electoral votes for Eisenhower in 1952 and 1956, Wyoming veered away from the Republican Party only once (1964) in the rest of the century. In 1980, Ronald Reagan carried the state by an overwhelming majority and then actually increased his lead in 1984. George W. Bush, with Cheney as his vice-presidential candidate, swept the state in both 2000 and 2004. Wyoming's stunning mountain ranges might seem unusual to many Americans, but the state's political configuration is similar to that great block of red states – that is, Republican and conservative states – in the American West and Midwest.

Alabama's conversion to Republican conservatism began differently than Wyoming's but ended up much the same. Solidly Democratic since

[3] In November 1954, President Eisenhower was irritated with his brother Edgar, who was "harping on the Constitution" and recommending that Ike swing his administration hard to the right. Eisenhower carefully explained his position: "Now it is true that I believe this country is following a dangerous trend when it permits too great a degree of centralization of governmental functions. I oppose this–in some instances the fight is a rather desperate one. But to attain any success it is quite clear that the Federal government cannot avoid or escape responsibilities which the mass of the people firmly *believe* should be undertaken by it. The political processes of our country are such that if a *rule of reason* is not applied in this effort, we will lose everything–even to a possible and drastic change in the Constitution. This is what I mean by my constant insistence upon "moderation" in government. Should any political party attempt to abolish social security, unemployment insurance, and eliminate labor laws and farm programs, you would not hear of that party again in our political history." Document #1147, November 8, 1954, in http://www.eisenhowermemorial.org/presidential-papers/first-term/documents/1147.cfm.

[4] Cheney would be elected in 1979 and would hold that seat for a decade. Connected through his father to America's unique agricultural outreach system (see Chapter 3), Cheney was one of those many Americans who got a second chance in our many-layered educational system (see Chapter 2). Failing to make it at Yale University, he returned to Wyoming and received his B.A. and M.A. degrees in political science from the state university. His first job in government was as an intern for Congressman William A. Steiger (1969), and during the next decade, he held a number of positions in Washington and in private industry. After his decade of service in the House of Representatives, he became Secretary of Defense in March 1989. Leaving that office in 1993, he joined the American Enterprise Institute – a sister conservative organization of the Heritage Foundation – and then became Chairman of the Board and CEO of the Haliburton Corporation (1995–2000). Elected Vice-President in 2000, with President George W. Bush, he and Bush were reelected in 2004.

the end of Reconstruction (1876), Alabama didn't break ranks until the passage of the 1960s Civil Rights legislation. Even before that happened, however, in 1952, Eisenhower received more votes in Alabama than any Republican candidate for president in the twentieth century. In Alabama and other southern and western states, religious conservatives gave the Republican Party a base on which to build its support.[5] Ike did even better in Alabama in 1956, and between 1964 and 2000, Democratic presidential candidates only carried the state when Jimmy Carter, a southern peanut farmer, was running for president (1976). Alabama continued to anchor the southern side of the red block through 2004.

In the Midwest, Ohio had a less decisive conversion experience. The home state of Senator Robert Taft, Ike's leading opponent for the presidential nomination in 1952, Ohio was staunchly Republican from Eisenhower's first election to Ronald Reagan's second. The only exception was 1964 when, like Wyoming, the state supported Lyndon Johnson and the memory of the late John Fitzgerald Kennedy. Ohio suffered badly from the decline of U.S. manufacturing and the difficult transformations we looked at in the last chapter, and this, as much as anything, appears to have kept the presidential votes very close. Overall, however, Ohio was a Republican state for ten of the fourteen presidential elections between Ike's first victory and 2004.

In these and other Midwestern, Southern, and Western states, there was a long, slow swing away from the liberal policies of the Democratic Party. That trend influenced Democrats as well as Republicans, all of whom were trying to control the middle of the political bell curve in American politics. Even a Democrat like President Carter could appeal to moderate conservatives by running against the government and then leading the charge for deregulation. It was thus no paradox that Carter's administration did more than any in the century to remove regulations from American companies.[6] Nor was it difficult to understand why President Clinton had to swing his administration sharply and visibly to the right to win the 1996 election.[7]

---

[5] For a recent exploration of southern conservative religion, see Bethany Moreton, *To Serve God and Wal-Mart: The Making of Christian Free Enterprise* (Cambridge, 2009).

[6] Martha Derthick and Paul J. Quirk, *The Politics of Deregulation* (Washington, 1985). Richard H. K. Vietor, *Contrived Competition: Regulation and Deregulation in America* (Cambridge, Massachusetts, 1994).

[7] See, for instance, Clinton's speech when he accepted the Democratic Party's nomination, August 29, 1996, http://www.pbs.org/newshour/convention96/floor_speeches/clinton_8-29.html. Opposed to "piling up another mountain of debt," Clinton lauded

Building a New Base

Behind the voting statistics were important institutional changes that helped sustain the move to the right. When Barry Goldwater, champion of the Republican Party's hard right wing, went down in a crushing defeat in the presidential election of 1964, many of his most ardent and well-heeled supporters were shocked into introspection. They realized that conservatives needed a new institutional base if they were going to acquire the power they needed to influence national and state public policies. The libertarian wing of the conservative movement was working through the Mont Pelerin Society that Friedrich Hayek had helped found in 1947.[8] In the 1940s and 1950s, American libertarianism had been energized by William Buckley's *National Review* and by the best-selling novels of Ayn Rand. Rand published *The Fountainhead* in 1943 and her most important book, *Atlas Shrugged*, in 1957. Encouraging as this was to some American conservatives, others were looking for a broader and more practical institutional base after Goldwater's overwhelming defeat. They were focused on immediate, practical goals – not on an intellectual transformation. They recognized that they needed more effective organizations in Washington, DC, and in those state capitals that had been leaning right before Lyndon Johnson reversed that trend and launched his crusade for the Great Society.

In effect, this group of conservatives was trying to bring the conservative movement into alignment with the new professional public sphere in America. They did this by getting right-thinking professionals and their ideas into communication with the nation's political brokers. The architects of conservative reform successfully developed an organization capable of bringing expert analyses and supporting data, especially quantitative data, to bear in national policy debates. After some experimentation and a few stumbles, the Heritage Foundation began to

the welfare reform measure that required "able-bodied parents to work for the income." His bridge to the next century included a plank calling for free trade. See also the president's second inaugural address, January 20, 1997, which looked forward to "a nation that balances its budget, but never loses the balance of its values." http://www.bartleby.com/124/pres65.html.

[8] On the Mont Pelerin Society, see Angus Burgin, "The Radical Conservatism of Frank H. Knight," *Modern Intellectual History*, 6, 3 (November 2009), 513–38; see also Burgin's "The Return of Laissez-Faire" (PhD dissertation, Harvard University, 2009). On Hayek, see his most famous and accessible work, *The Road to Serfdom* (Chicago, 1944). Thirty years later, Hayek received a Nobel Prize in Economics.

blaze a conservative trail in the legislative process in Washington, DC. Eventually, Heritage's success would encourage emulation by liberal Democrats seeking to reorient their party.[9]

A different kind of movement with somewhat similar results began among conservative lawyers. Worried that their liberal colleagues were controlling the activities of the profession and the appointment of judges, they mobilized foundations and academic leaders in an effort to change their profession's role in the public sphere. In the 1970s and 1980s, their leaders discovered, to their surprise, that conservative businesses didn't provide an effective base for political action. What was needed, they decided, was a movement focused on achieving intellectual and cultural standing in the profession – a movement that would be entirely different than Heritage. That came with such new institutions as the Federalist Society, which arose in 1982 out of the less formal law student organizations already active at Yale, Chicago, Harvard, and Stanford. The University of Chicago law program also promoted the law and economics wing of this conservative movement, an effort that resulted in a new publication, *The Journal of Law and Economics*, edited by economist Ronald Coase.[10] The impact of the new ideas about public policy spread into political science as rational-choice theory and into various law programs by way of the Economics Institute for Law Professors (Rochester University) and the Law and Economics Center (University of Miami and then Emory University). By the end of the 1980s, there was a dense network of conservative institutions in and around law programs throughout the United States.[11]

One of the founding fathers of Chicago's law and economics school was the learned and unbelievably productive Richard A. Posner. A 1962 graduate of the Harvard Law School, Posner has published an amazing array of books and articles. He became a founding editor of the *Journal of Legal Studies* only ten years after leaving law school and published his first major book, a blend of economic and legal analysis, the following

---

[9] Albert Beveridge has kindly allowed me to draw on his insightful manuscript, "Heritage Foundation: The New Think Tank – An Historical Perspective." See two articles by Matt Bai, "Notion Building," and "Wiring the Vast Left-Wing Conspiracy," *New York Times Magazine*, October 12, 2003 and July 25, 2004.

[10] Coase would receive a Nobel Prize in economics in 1991.

[11] My discussion of this subject is entirely dependent on the outstanding research and analysis of my colleague Steven M. Teles, *The Rise of the Conservative Legal Movement: The Battle for Control of the Law* (Princeton, 2008).

year.[12] At that time, he was also teaching in the University of Chicago law program and he drew on and extended Ronald Coase's ideas about the legal process. Posner, a tough-minded analyst, insisted that wealth maximization should guide almost every aspect of legal reasoning.

Posner's *The Economics of Justice* was a bold attempt to establish a new philosophical basis for the law.[13] His objective was to reconcile concepts that had normally been understood as competing principles: utility, for instance, and liberty. Even equality, he said, could be reconciled with his approach to wealth maximization, a claim that could hardly be better designed to infuriate the legal realists who looked to liberal political reform to achieve equity and security. Like his friend and coauthor Gary Becker, Posner applied his economic tools of analysis to all sorts of non-market behavior, including love and marriage, as well as crime. As an author, teacher, and jurist, Posner became a major force in reorienting American legal theory.[14]

The Center of Intellectual Gravity

As these and other publications poured out, the center of intellectual gravity in America was slowly sliding away from New York City and toward Chicago. Understandably, few New Yorkers seem to have been aware of or concerned about what was happening in the 1980s and 1990s. For most of the previous century, the intellectual leadership in American politics had been provided by liberal academics and intellectuals, most of them in the large urban centers on the East Coast. They drew on ideas that had long been dominant in a broad-based, left-oriented European intellectual world. Even American history was basically structured along liberal lines by the early progressive historians – most notably Charles A. Beard. He was followed by a long and distinguished line of talented progressive historians and political scientists.[15]

---

[12] *Economic Analysis of Law* (Boston, 1973). As of 2007, the book had gone through seven editions. Prior to 1973, Posner had already published eighteen articles and ten reviews.

[13] (Cambridge, 1981).

[14] William W. Fisher III, "Legal Theory and Legal Education, 1920–2000," in Christopher Tomlins and Michael Grossberg, eds., *The Cambridge History of Law in America, 3, The Twentieth Century and After (1920–)* (New York, 2008), 34–72.

[15] Richard Hofstadter, *The Progressive Historians: Turner, Beard, Parrington* (New York, 1968). John Higham, with Leonard Krieger and Felix Gilbert, *History: The Development of Historical Studies in the United States* (Englewood Cliffs, New Jersey, 1965).

As I made my first tentative steps toward a career as a professional historian, I was told by one of my professors that although I might be voting for Dwight Eisenhower in the 1950s, I would become a liberal historian after I had studied FDR's New Deal more deeply. The professor was right on target. When I began teaching some years later, I taught a course structured along lines that would have pleased Beard and his followers. But the times have changed, as did my perspective on America and indeed the world. Now when I teach global history, I'm certain that the all-seeing ghost of Professor Beard shudders at the role conservatism, innovation, the professional experts, the brokers, and the universities play in my courses – and in this book.

I was not the only academician who had developed a new appreciation for the central role of universities in American society. Professor Alan Bloom, a political philosopher at the University of Chicago, published his account of *The Closing of the American Mind* in 1987. This was a watershed book, a best seller that delved into Plato and Aristotle, into Hobbes, Locke, and Rousseau, and brought the Western Civilization Classics to bear on the problems of U.S. higher education in the 1960s and 1970s. Bloom could turn a memorable phrase: "nihilism with a happy ending," was the American way, he said, to digest "Continental despair." A scholar who could not be ignored by other academics, Bloom mounted a sophisticated professional assault on the New Left, the universities that tolerated violence in the 1960s and 1970s, and, above all, the cultural relativism that seemed to be making all values equal – or perhaps equally valueless.[16]

It was also difficult to ignore Thomas Sowell, an African-American economist and self-proclaimed libertarian. Trained at Harvard, Columbia, and the University of Chicago, Sowell also had solid academic credentials. He successfully blended economic theory with popular journalism and became the mirror image of W. E. B. DuBois. Instead of calling for a communist transformation of the capitalist democracies, Sowell dispassionately dealt with Marx's *Capital* as a study in the history of economic thought. He credited Marx for his advances in the economic

---

[16] The book's aim was to explain "how higher education has failed democracy and impoverished the souls of today's students." (New York, 1987). Along the way, Bloom gave us his particular concept of "creativity": "The artist is the most interesting of all phenomena, for he represents creativity, the definition of man" (p. 306). Scientists, he said, polluted the language by claiming that their professions were creative. If I didn't disagree, I wouldn't be writing this book.

analysis of prices and business cycles but concluded that "[i]n some ways, it was the last salvo of classical economics."[17]

Sowell was not, however, going to leave the country or rush to the ramparts. He had other battles to fight. He was, of course, very concerned about the civil rights issue, and his eleventh book was on *Civil Rights: Rhetoric or Reality?*[18] The reality was important: May 17, 1954, he said, "was a momentous day in the history of the United States.... A great nation voluntarily acknowledged and repudiated its own oppression of part of its own people." He also acknowledged that the Civil Rights Act of 1964 was a decisive watershed. Two decades later, however, Sowell said, the movement had "degenerated into the hustling rhetoric of [George Orwell's] Newspeak. 'Equal opportunity' now means preferential treatment. 'Voting rights' now include preferential chances to win. School desegregation no longer means the right to attend any public school, regardless of race, but being forced to attend where you are told, according to race. 'Equal justice for all' now means compensatory benefits for some – usually the more fortunate of those who share the political label 'disadvantaged.'"[19] Sowell was, in these and other regards, a true son of the Chicago School of economics.

Chicago economic thought was important because it provided an intellectual foundation for deregulation and privatization, a foundation grounded in respect for the power and efficiency of markets. The Chicago school blasted the empirical base of the nation's traditional antitrust policy and mounted a strong attack on the Keynesian fiscal paradigm in theory and practice. Chicago economists collected a string of Nobel Prizes, but the School's most enduring impact was on U.S. public policy. It was no longer possible for a third-rate theoretician like Rexford Tugwell (see Chapter 7) to play a large role in the Washington policy world. Milton Friedman and his colleagues were now the masters of that world, and their analyses and ideologies were of overwhelming importance within the Washington Beltway.

For the first time in the twentieth century, conservative authors were setting the intellectual table for many Americans. The ideas on offer frequently aroused painful screams of protest from writers and college professors long accustomed to liberal domination of the nation's intellect

---

[17] Thomas Sowell, "Marx's Capital after One Hundred Years," *The Canadian Journal of Economics and Political Science*, 33, 1 (February 1967), 72–74.
[18] (New York: William Morrow and Company, Inc., 1984), 13.
[19] Ibid., 13, 37, 110.

and central ideology. In the so-called culture wars within the colleges and universities, liberal and radical professors won the long struggle over what exactly should be taught.[20] Outside the academy, however, it was clear by the end of the 1980s that conservatives were winning most of the battles. Contempt had been replaced by angry resistance as the left dug in and tried to turn away the conservative advance. But the pressure points of public policy and ideology – welfare, for instance – were increasingly being defined by conservatives.

Their ideas were being broadcast outside the professional public sphere to the broader public by TV personalities and talk-show hosts. Rush Limbaugh has had an enormous following for years, but Bill O'Reilly on Fox TV is probably the most famous of these conservative spokesmen. He and his colleagues are brokers, translating conservative ideas into a popular form that appeals to those who might have heard about Alan Bloom or Richard Posner but aren't about to read their books. O'Reilly is an ideal middleman. After receiving an undergraduate degree from Marist College, he returned to school twice for more professional training. At Boston University, he finished a Master's program in broadcast journalism and some years later graduated from Harvard's Kennedy School of Government with an M.A. in public administration. Smart enough to digest the new professional literature but personable enough to carry those ideas to a broad audience, O'Reilly became a point man for the conservative campaigns to transform America.

Realities of Conservative Power

With the intellectual, ideological, and political winds blowing strongly from the right, the United States elected President Ronald Reagan (1980) to lead the charge against big government and big taxes. Reagan left no doubt about his position on the growth of the administrative state and on the professional experts who had been guiding that growth. In his inaugural address he focused on the nation's economic woes and the role the government should play in solving those problems. "In this present crisis," he said, "government is not the solution to our problem; government is the problem. From time to time we've been tempted to believe that society has become too complex to be managed by self-rule, that government by an elite group is superior to government for, by and

---

[20] See the twenty-year retrospective by Rachel Donadio, "Revisiting the Canon Wars," *New York Times Book Review*, September 16, 2007, 16–17.

of the people. Well, if no one among us is capable of governing himself, then who among us has the capacity to govern someone else?" "It is my intention," he said, "to curb the size and influence of the federal establishment.... It is no coincidence that our present troubles parallel and are proportionate to the intervention and intrusion in our lives that result from unnecessary and excessive growth of government.... So, with all the creative energy at our command, let us begin an era of national renewal."[21]

One set of policies up for "renewal" were those of the welfare state and the entitlements it bestowed on Americans. Reagan had long before proclaimed his opposition to a system of benefits that he thought was creating permanent, multigenerational welfare citizens. His rhetoric was harsh and memorable: He told Californians that he wanted to get the "welfare bums" back in real jobs. He wanted to "make able-bodied welfare recipients work at useful community jobs in return for welfare grants."[22] He wanted to find out who was "cheating."[23] One of the cheats was apparently the "welfare queen," the Chicago woman who was receiving welfare checks under multiple names at multiple addresses.[24]

Although many Democrats agreed that welfare should change, they were often at odds with the popular president about what, specifically, could be done. The lawyers and their liberal colleagues in Congress put a brake on the Reagan policy of cutting and changing welfare. Fiscal policy came to play a central role in this struggle over welfare. The conservative era began with a loud call to junk the Keynesian policies of the 1960s and 1970s. With Chicago economics firmly in control, the Reagan administration (1981–1989) pushed through Congress a dramatic tax cut that was apparently designed to achieve two objectives. One goal, which was achieved, was to reward those upper-income groups that were playing an important role in conservative political success. The other, less obvious objective, was to force Congress to make substantial cuts in entitlements. But even a very popular president couldn't convince a majority in Congress to rein in the subsidies that many of their constituents had received for a long time and on which they were dependent. That left the government mired in the sort of deficit financing conservatives had

[21] The speech is available at http://www.reaganlibrary.com/reagan/speeches/first.asp.
[22] Letter of November 4, 1981, in Kiron K. Skinner, ed., *Regan: A Life in Letters* (New York, 2004), 301.
[23] Letter of February 11, 1982, ibid., 310.
[24] Kiron K. Skinner, et al., eds., *Reagan's Path to Victory: The Shaping of Ronald Reagan's Vision: Selected Writings* (New York, 2004), 75–76.

long deplored. Conservative governance remained Keynesian by default, and the entitlements remained largely intact. What the White House was able to do was to toughen eligibility requirements and remove as many as 442,000 families from the welfare rolls. Job training was promoted as a means of moving families away from dependence on welfare. Soon, however, the number on welfare started creeping back up again, even when the economy had recovered after the mid-1980s. Well-established policies supported by dedicated professionals inside and outside of government are not impossible to change, but they can resist it – sometimes for many years.

The Reagan initiatives were just the first step in what would be an extended policy process in Washington and in the states. The conclusion to that process would come in the following decade. The second step came in 1993, when Congress and the administration of Democratic President William Clinton set out to encourage work over welfare by expanding the "earned income tax credit."[25] The third step followed after the states began to experiment with more aggressive programs to help those on welfare find employment. The experiments, twenty-seven of them by 1996, gradually yielded a substantial base of information and new ideas about what could be achieved through reform. Crucial to the debate was the entitlement concept: Should any person who was qualified automatically receive support?[26] Without limits? The consensus that emerged by the mid-1990s was that an entitlement without a limit encouraged families to remain on welfare, often through several generations.

A discourse launched under conservative leadership finally came to fruition in 1996 with strong support from both President Clinton and Republican leaders in Congress. The entitlement was eliminated. The states now received block grants that could be used in various ways. Authority was divided between the federal and state governments in a remarkable demonstration of federalism at work. States were urged to move recipients to work programs, eligibility was tightened, and

[25] See the excellent article by Rebecca M. Blank, "What Did the 1990s Welfare Reform Accomplish?" available at http://urbanpolicy.berkeley.edu/pdf/Ch2Blank0404.pdf, July 4, 2008. EITC either reduces taxes or pays subsidies to the working poor in low-income families.

[26] The cash-payment entitlement was written into the law under AFDC, Aid to Families with Dependent Children. Steven M. Teles, *Whose Welfare? AFDC and Elite Politics* (Lawrence, Kansas, 1998 edition). As Teles notes (182), "Ideas are not a side story in understanding political events and are not simply the reflection of more 'fundamental' things.... The essence of politics is the interaction of ideas, interests, conditions, and institutions."

specific time limits were established for government assistance. The results included a dramatic drop in welfare cases in the late 1990s and a significant increase in employment among single mothers. Many who left welfare did so to take jobs and to achieve higher incomes. The available studies fall short of providing a full evaluation of the policy changes in the 1990s, but most of what we now know is favorable to this effort to break the welfare culture and improve the system.[27]

So what didn't change? The answer is most of the most important parts of the social net created and elaborated since the 1930s. The innovations of the 1980s and 1990s didn't alter welfare's central policies: Social Security; Medicare, and Medicaid all survived. Periodic social security crises took place during these years, but nothing was done to change the program in any decisive way. Older people vote regularly, are well organized, and are very sensitive to changes in one of their primary sources of income. Legislators are also very sensitive to changes in the extra income the government receives from annual social security payments by individuals and their employers. These political realities don't make significant changes impossible. They just make it more likely that conservatives as well as liberals will either ignore or expand the system rather than contract it.[28]

The Regulatory State

Conservative rhetoric in the 1980s was also fiercely opposed to the regulatory state. Reagan came into office determined, he said, to get the government off the backs of American business through deregulation and privatization. He was initially successful in cutting the staffs in a number of federal agencies and in transforming the traditional antitrust policy. Reagan also took a shot at organized labor in 1981. But the White House and Congress were most concerned about macroeconomic issues – inflation, economic growth, and, for a time, unemployment. The regulatory state got lost in the government shuffle and stayed lost through the administrations of George H. W. Bush (1989–1993) and Bill Clinton (1993–2001). Conservatives settled for a truce rather than the political victory the rhetoric had promised. The truce was acceptable because market forces were reshaping the economy, undercutting significant parts of the country's regulatory systems.

---

[27] Rebecca M. Blank, "What Did the 1990s Welfare Reform Accomplish?" Part of the downside was the tendency for women who leave welfare to obtain less education.

[28] Federal social welfare expenditures per person grew from $500 to $623 between 1980 and 1990. Ballard C. Campbell, *The Growth of American Government: Governance from the Cleveland Era to the Present* (Bloomington, 1995), 34.

An uneasy truce emerged in environmental regulation after a flurry of proclamations and attacks on the elaborate structure of environmental controls that Congress, the White House, and the states had erected since the 1960s. As we saw in Chapter 9, Congress passed clean air measures in 1963 and 1967.[29] Interestingly, the high point of environmental advances came under conservative president Richard Nixon. As much as anything, this was a tribute to the increasing public interest in environmental issues and the steady expansion of green organizations. Sierra Club membership was 136 million by the early 1970s. Support for environmental programs came from a host of new institutions that could marshal the kind of political force Nixon and Congress had to respect. The new organizations had high levels of professional expertise that supported their efforts both in legislatures and in the courts. The result was a wave of new measures and the Environmental Protection Agency, arguably the most powerful regulatory institution in American history.[30]

Conservative efforts to revise the nation's environmental laws ran directly into this powerful network of public and nonprofit organizations, dedicated individuals, and professional experts. To every conservative action, there was an equal and opposite reaction. When conservatives pushed even harder to cut environmental programs, the membership of the green organizations shot up.[31] Economic arguments for growth-oriented policies fell on deaf ears. The institutional base of the environmental movement was so strong and the culture so firmly planted that conservatives couldn't compromise away any of the regulations: They simply gave up the battle. The walls of the green fortress were never breached, and the environmental movement picked up its pace again in the early years of the Clinton administration.[32]

When conservative administrations had discretionary power, as they did in antitrust policy, they were able to engineer more significant policy changes. In the early 1980s, the federal government in effect abandoned half of the traditional policy on antitrust. The Department of Justice

---

[29] Samuel P. Hays, *Beauty, Health, and Permanence: Environmental Politics in the United States, 1955–1985* (New York, 1987).

[30] Robert M. Collins, *More: The Politics of Economic Growth in Postwar America* (New York, 2000), 99, 137; and the same author's *Transforming America: Politics and Culture in the Reagan Years* (New York, 2007), 82. Michael E. Kraft, "U.S. Environmental Policy and Politics: From the 1960s to the 1990s," *Journal of Policy History*, 12, 1 (2000), 17–42.

[31] Samuel P. Hays *Beauty, Health, and Permanence*, 491–92, notes that "in being forced to recognize that environmental affairs were not momentary, limited, superficial, the administration, in fact, more firmly rooted their legitimacy on American politics."

[32] Michael E. Kraft, "U.S. Environmental Policy and Politics," 28–30.

and the Federal Trade Commission continued to enforce the prohibitions against price fixing and similar schemes, but they no longer attacked big business for achieving substantial power in American markets.[33] This threw the door open for acquisitions and mergers that enabled American firms to get up to global scale and compete with powerful foreign firms. A wave of combinations followed. These included the aluminum mergers that we mentioned in the last chapter and the combination of two of the world's largest energy companies, Exxon and Mobil. Steel mergers and numerous acquisitions in banking and finance resulted in dramatic changes in the American business system.[34]

The new policy of condoning oligopoly and near-monopoly stuck through the administrations of George H. W. Bush and William Clinton. The only exception was the suit against Microsoft, the world's leading software company. Even in that case, however, the suit was finally settled in a manner that left Microsoft with its market position basically intact. By the end of the twentieth century, antimonopoly policy appeared to be a relic of a U.S.-centric era – a change that conservatives had been the first to understand.[35]

Initially it appeared that Reagan was also going to send conservatives on the warpath against the nation's labor policies. After the Professional Air Traffic Controllers called a strike that violated their contract, the President abruptly fired more than 11,000 employees who didn't return to work. But very little happened after that explosive episode. In dealing with labor, the administrations of Reagan and Bush used their discretionary powers of appointment but didn't push hard for new legislation that would shift the balance of power from organized labor to management. In effect, both administrations left the fate of organized labor largely

---

[33] The only exception was the country's largest monopoly, the Bell System, which used government power to prevent entry into telecommunications.

[34] William E. Kovacic, "Failed Expectations: The Troubled Past and Uncertain Future of the Sherman Act as a Tool for Deconcentration," *Iowa Law Review*, 74, 5 (1989), 1105–50. See also Louis Galambos, "The Monopoly Enigma, the Reagan Administration's Antitrust Experiment, and the Global Economy," in Kenneth Lipartito and David B. Sicilia, eds., *Constructing Corporate America: History, Politics, Culture* (New York, 2004), 149–67. As Richard H. K. Vietor, *Contrived Competition*, 234–309, observes, technological and market forces were transforming banking and finance faster than the national and state efforts in the 1980s to deregulate the industry.

[35] The Supreme Court put a solid stamp on the new policy environment by refusing to consider damage to competitors in antitrust suits. The Court's position was and still is that the only damage to be considered is to consumers.

to be determined by the global market forces that had been weakening American unions since the 1960s.[36]

The Clinton administration was more supportive of the labor movement rhetorically, but the decision to promote the North American Free Trade Area (NAFTA, which we consider more fully in the next chapter) indicates just how fragile and perfunctory that support was. NAFTA sent factory jobs to Mexico, just as the unions had warned. Then, when Clinton began to look forward to his reelection campaign, he shifted even further to the right. As a result, the "enforcement mood" of his administration's labor program abruptly changed. The Department of Labor ducked down into the trenches. Violations of equal employment opportunities for women and minorities were ignored. Instead of aggressively enforcing and thus steadily increasing the specification of the law, the Labor Department foundered.

I had a family window on those developments. One of my daughters, Denise Galambos, was a lawyer in the Department of Labor at this time (1990–1995). She was happily enforcing the laws requiring equal opportunity and treatment for women and minorities. But now, suddenly, she was left sitting for months with nothing to do. The Department of Labor looked the same. The jobs were the same. The people were the same. The violations of the law were the same. But the administration's swing to the right took all the energy out of enforcement. Up to that point, she had made good progress in arranging settlements with various companies, including those in the construction industry, which were some of the worst offenders. But then, the investigations, the negotiations, and the litigation all stopped. Bored and no longer willing to sit in an office without working, she left the government and took a job in the private sector with one of the country's leading law firms specializing in employment matters.

The Promotional State

While the welfare state was under siege and the regulatory state adrift, America's promotional state was vibrant and growing. Leaving aside

---

[36] It is still difficult to understand why PATCO played into Reagan's hand in 1981 by challenging the newly inaugurated president. The controllers both violated their agreements by going on strike and endangered the public. PATCO's decision brings into serious question the quality of the organization's legal and political expertise.

spending for national security, which we'll take up in the next chapter, conservative leaders continued to promote economic activities at all levels of society. The growth orientation of their ideology seemed to justify these expenditures – as did America's efforts to compete in global markets in high-tech, science-based industries as well as commodities. Government expenditures for education more than doubled between 1981 and 1992, as did federal support for space research and technological development. Government spending on health research also increased.

Most telling of all were the realities of the farm subsidies. As we have seen, over the course of the twentieth century, the United States had developed a complex network of federal, state, local, and nonprofit institutions to foster innovation and efficiency in agriculture while keeping commodity prices (and hence farm income) relatively stable. From the late 1930s on, this intricate system had paid off for America with impressive increases in efficiency and total output. But over the years, more and more of the subsidies had gone to the very large corporate farms that produced almost all of our farm commodities. There was every economic reason to cut back sharply on the subsidies for this network in the 1980s and 1990s. But there was every political reason to continue them, while gathering for conservative candidates the votes of agricultural states. This was a powerful motive, and the administrations of presidents Reagan and Bush did just what you would expect. They ignored their conservative ideals and pumped enormous increases in subsidies into the farm pipeline. Federal expenditures for agriculture more than tripled between 1981 and 1990. Initially, the Clinton administration cut back sharply on the subsidies, but when agricultural prices sagged and another election loomed, the payments shot up again to very high levels.[37]

Manufacturing and the services were also dining at the national, state, and local subsidy troughs. States and localities continued their aggressive promotional activities, including their support for professional training programs. Despite conservative concerns about the liberals and radicals in American colleges and universities, funding for higher education continued to grow during the 1980s and 1990s. With the nation competing in a global economy and the states and localities competing against each other, all levels of government sought advantages by encouraging

[37] See Alan L. Olmstead and Paul W. Rhode, "The Transformation of Northern Agriculture, 1910–1990," in Stanley L. Engerman and Robert E. Gallman, *The Cambridge Economic History of the United States*, III, *The Twentieth Century*, 735–42, for developments in the 1990s.

research and professional development. Subsidies for businesses looking to relocate continued to be an important element in many state and
city development plans, with the South and West the big gainers in this
competition.

The Balance Sheet

The realities of conservative government in the last two decades of the
twentieth century were more akin to the middle way that Eisenhower
preached than they were to Reagan's campaign rhetoric. American government is designed to foster compromise and soften the edges of ideology. Its strength in this regard may someday be its weakness. But that
was not the case in the 1980s and 1990s.

Most revealing was the manner in which America responded to intense
global competition. Hard-pressed by efficient, innovative foreign competitors, many in America looked to the government for protectionist policies
of the sort that had fractured the global economy in the 1930s. But the
American choice was – and still is – to compete and encourage American
businesses to match foreign firms or go out of business. In this regard,
the harsh spirit of the American Solution carried over from the business system into government. On this crucial issue, a powerful American
consensus emerged. It was not universal. There was strong labor union
support for protection. But the unions were weak and getting weaker.
They were not in the mainstream of American political economy in these
two decades.

The best indication of how much had changed in America was the decision by Democratic President Clinton and Congress to support NAFTA.
This was the single boldest decision of a Clinton administration that had
powerful political reasons to follow the guidance of union leaders instead
of professional economists. Bringing Canada and Mexico into a single,
tariff-free market changed the American economy in a significant way. It
would never be the same, and down the road is the Free Trade Area of
the Americas (FTAA), the logical counterpoint to the European Union's
greatly expanded free-trade area. NAFTA and FTAA are the political
versions of the American Solution, harsh to many but promising for a
society firmly committed to globalization. As this indicates, most Americans seem still to be willing to sacrifice security and equity to achieve the
efficiency and innovation needed to remain the world's most competitive
society. There would, however, be new opportunities to reflect on that
balance after 2001.

16

The Hegemony Trap

There was serious work to do in January 1981 if the United States was to protect its empire.[1] The country's reputation had plummeted following the defeat in Vietnam. There were hairline cracks in the U.S. alliance structure after the nation's most important allies turned decisively against America's exercise of military power in Southeast Asia. There was no longer much confidence at home or abroad in a demoralized American military establishment.

It didn't help to have President Carter's bold 1980 rescue mission in Iran come to a humiliating conclusion. The Iranian revolution had overthrown the Shah of Iran, America's puppet ruler, and the Ayatollah Khomeini was transforming the nation's government into a theocracy bitterly opposed to the influence of the United States, the "Great Satan." Rumors that America was once again going to intervene in Iran prompted a small group of revolutionary students to take over the American embassy and seize American hostages.[2] After negotiations failed, Carter sent a small force on a secret mission to rescue the hostages. But the operation, Eagle Claw, was a disaster.[3] When the helicopters crashed,

---

[1] John Lewis Gaddis, *Strategies of Containment*, will help you through the last stages of the Cold War, and David Halberstam, *War in a Time of Peace: Bush, Clinton, and the Generals* (New York, 2001) carries the narrative through the 1990s.

[2] For the Iranian perspective, see Shaul Bakhash, *The Reign of the Ayatollahs: Iran and the Islamic Revolution* (New York, 1984), especially 114–19; see 16–17 for U.S. relations with the Shah during the crisis. The Iranian revolution, like most such upheavals, was particularly destructive to the professional class, including those in the military; see, especially 4, 136, and 242–49.

[3] Paul H. Kreisberg, ed., *American Hostages in Iran.*

they seemed to symbolize the nation's failure as the military, political, and economic leader of the world's capitalist democracies.[4]

The contrast between capitalism and communism was decisive, for all the world to see. America's Cold War opponents appeared to be thriving. George Kennan's predictions about the internal weaknesses of the Soviet empire seemed now to be wide of the mark, as was Walt Whitman Rostow's prophecy that the communist and capitalist nations would converge on a common destiny.[5] Instead, the protagonists were pulling further apart. The USSR was extending its military operations in Afghanistan and its diplomatic offensive in Africa. Its Polish client state was aggressively beating back internal opposition to communist authority, and in Asia, Vietnam was threatening to seize control of a substantial part of Cambodia.

While Ronald Reagan explained in January of 1981 that he intended "to curb the size and influence of the federal establishment...," the newly elected president also looked forward to "having greater strength throughout the world." The meaning was clear. The government was going to chop welfare and regulation and pump those billions into the military. He warned the nation's opponents. "Our reluctance for conflict should not be misjudged as a failure of will. When action is required to preserve our national security, we will act." Then, in a statement that didn't receive the attention it deserved, Reagan added, "We will maintain sufficient strength to prevail if need be, knowing that if we do so we have the best chance of never having to use that strength."[6] Congress, the American people, and the Soviet Union shortly found out exactly what that meant.[7]

When Reagan needed advice on foreign policy, he frequently turned to Jeane Kirkpatrick, a political scientist who was teaching at Georgetown University in Washington, DC. Kirkpatrick had come to Reagan's

---

[4] Secretary of State Cyrus Vance resigned over the decision to attempt to rescue the hostages. See also Richard Burt, "Many Questions, Few Answers on Iran Missions," *New York Times*, May 11, 1980. Maj. Gianni Koskinas, "Desert One and Air Force Special Operations Command," *Air & Space Power Journal* (Spring 2005), available at http://www.airpower.au.af.mil/airchronicles/apj/apjo5/spro5/vignette4.html. Maj. Joseph T. Benson, "Weather and the Wreckage at Desert-One," http://www.airpower.maxwell.af.mil/airchronicles/cc/benson.html.

[5] On Kennan and Rostow see Chapters 11 and 12 in this volume.

[6] Reagan's inaugural address is available at http://www.reaganfoundation.org/reagan/speeches/first.asp.

[7] The best treatment of Reagan's foreign policy is John Lewis Gaddis, *Strategies of Containment*, 342–79.

attention through her article, "Dictatorships & Double Standards," which launched a fierce realist attack on the foreign policy of the Carter Administration. "In the thirty-odd months since the inauguration of Jimmy Carter as President," she said, "there has occurred a dramatic Soviet military buildup, matched by the stagnation of American armed forces, and a dramatic extension of Soviet influence in the Horn of Africa, Afghanistan, Southern Africa, and the Caribbean, matched by a declining American position in all these areas."[8]

Kirkpatrick had not always been an East Coast hawk. Raised in Oklahoma and small-town Illinois near the Big Muddy River, she had climbed onto the professional path after making a big leap from Stephens College in Missouri to Barnard College in New York City. Barnard's intense coursework (BA 1948) prepped her for advanced study in political science at its affiliated university, Columbia (PhD 1968). She landed a teaching position at Georgetown University before she had completed her second great leap from a left-wing ideology to Reagan-style conservatism. Long active in the Democratic Party, she finally gave up on the left during the 1970s when the American empire seemed to be tottering. Her attack on the "architects of contemporary American foreign policy" catalogued the policy mistakes she said could be traced to a "lack of realism."[9]

Reagan's brand of realism began with a massive military buildup. The administration was in a hurry. It would take months and maybe years of grinding interservice struggle to formulate a new Cold War strategy.[10] So Congress and the White House made the money available and, in effect, asked the armed services to bid for the funding. The rush was awesome. The increases in spending were astounding: more than 38 percent by 1982, and more than 88 percent by 1985.[11] This was a great deal of money. By 1989, the United States was spending $303 billion on defense. One of the new weapon systems – Star Wars, for antimissile defense – would cost the country $27 billion.[12] Empires are never

---

[8] Commentary, November 1979.

[9] Ibid.

[10] For a good sense of how contentious and difficult this process can be, you should trace General Eisenhower's attempts to finalize a Cold War strategy when he was Chief of Staff in the U.S. Army. Louis Galambos, et al., eds., *The Papers of Dwight David Eisenhower*, volumes 7–9, *The Chief of Staff*. It is instructive to compare this with the similar problem of developing a common NATO strategy, as discussed in volumes 12 and 13, *NATO and the Campaign of 1952* (Baltimore, 1978 and 1989).

[11] These figures are for current dollars. Changing them to constant dollars reduces the first figure to slightly more than 18% and the second to more than 44%.

[12] Ballard C. Campbell, *The Growth of American Government*, 230. This figure is for the period 1983–1991. The official name was Strategic Defense Initiative.

cheap, and rebuilding a world-class military force cost the United States dearly.

With realists like Kirkpatrick and Secretary of Defense Casper Weinberger guiding the way, the United States became more aggressive about defending the frontiers of the U.S. empire.[13] Attempting to "roll back" communism, the United States began to pump money and military supplies into Afghanistan, Angola, and Nicaragua. The Heritage Foundation helped by targeting various nations for U.S. interventions under the Reagan Doctrine. The new strategy of "rollback" was in effect a hypercontainment policy that closely resembled a Republican campaign slogan of the 1950s. Nothing had come of the 1950s rhetoric about rolling back communism in East Europe – Ike understood war too well for that to happen. And history repeated itself in the 1980s. Little was accomplished by the realist efforts to provide support for freedom fighters on the edges of the U.S. empire.[14]

Taking a tough line on foreign policy, the Reagan realists were skeptical about the United Nations and the Bretton Woods organizations, including the World Bank and the IMF. Kirkpatrick, who served as U.S. ambassador to the United Nations from 1981 to 1985, ridiculed the UN's Universal Declaration of Human Rights as "a letter to Santa Claus." These sorts of "utopian expectations concerning the human condition are compounded," she said, " . . . by a vague sense that Utopia is one's due. . . . "[15] The UN, she argued, was built on the false premise that there would be a consensus about peace, the rights of people, and the sovereignty of nations. It had "not, even remotely, fulfilled the expectations of its founding fathers." The UN mattered, however, because it shaped "attitudes in cumulative ways. . . . The United Nations shapes agendas and focuses world attention and assumptions about what is and is not possible in what is euphemistically called the community of nations."[16] Kirkpatrick was the essence of Reagan realism.

---

[13] For Casper W. Weinberger's background, see the official Department of Defense biography at http://www.defenselink.mil/specials/secdef_histories/bios/weinberger.htm. That biography touches very lightly on his indictment and conviction for perjury over the Iran-Contra Affair.

[14] Steven Coll, *Ghost Wars*. George Shultz, *Turmoil and Trumph*. John Lewis Gaddis, *Strategies of Containment*, 370–73, on the Reagan Doctrine.

[15] Jeane J. Kirkpatrick, "Establishing a Viable Human Rights Policy," for Kenyon College's Human Rights Conference, April 4, 1981.

[16] Jeane J. Kirkpatrick, "The United Nations as a Political System: A Practicing Political Scientist's Insights into U.N. Politics," address at Georgetown University, June 14, 1983. See also her "Peaceful Dispute Resolution through the United Nations," *The Arbitration Journal*, 37, 3 (Sept. 1982), 3–9.

While they were trying to reshape the nation's foreign policy, the realists got a harsh reminder of American values in 1986 when the Iran-Contra scandal broke. What started as a simple deal to get back U.S. hostages with Iranian help morphed into a complicated three-way deal to sell weapons to Iran and send support to the anticommunists, the Contras, in Nicaragua. The catch was that Congress, exhibiting commendable concern for American ideals, had made it illegal to sell arms for this purpose or to intervene in Nicaragua. Lieutenant Colonel Oliver North of the National Security Council and seven other administration officials were indicted for their actions. Those who were convicted were later pardoned, but Iran-Contra was, like an echo of Watergate, a warning that the law and the values it reflected still mattered to many Americans.[17]

Hegemony Realized

A nation distracted by the Iran-Contra scandal and nervous about the quality of Republican leadership in foreign affairs was jolted in 1989 when the communist empire began to collapse. As Soviet authority in East Europe evaporated, the wall that divided East and West Berlin became a focal point for widespread demonstrations. In November 1989, the wall came down, followed by the East German communist government. The Soviet tanks didn't roll into East Germany, and less than a year later, East and West Germany were reunified.

Within the Soviet Union, Mikhail Gorbachev, the General Secretary of the Communist Party, had attempted for several years to spark economic growth by developing a sort of halfway house, *perestroika*, between communist centralization and capitalist market-oriented decentralization. He and his supporters were trying to close the entrepreneurial gap, just as many U.S. businesses were since the end of the American Century. That was what the American Solution was all about. In the Soviet case, however, the authoritarian bureaucracy was a powerful force resistant to change. The culture of control was deeply planted. The system was enormous, and the "apparatchiks," the party officials whose positions were threatened by change, had too many opportunities to block reform. Confusion and conflict followed Gorbachev's introduction of private property

---

[17] *Report of the Congressional Committees Investigating the Iran-Contra Affair* (Washington, 1995).

in a giant system built since the 1920s on the premise of state ownership of the means of production.[18]

All of this confusion was multiplied when Gorbachev set out to democratize the polity (*glasnost*) by making the communist party merely one of many parties. The atrocities of Stalin's labor camps hung around the necks of the communists – a dead albatross for the party and any in America and elsewhere who had hoped for an ultimate communist victory.[19] Now the threat to those Soviet party members who wielded authority was severe and immediate. A free election followed, and the political disintegration of the Soviet empire accelerated. With the government no longer ready to impose authority on East Europe, mass political resistance to communism quickly transformed the East European states into a variety of independent entities. The climax came in December 1991, when the Soviet Union formally disintegrated. The Cold War that had dominated world politics since the last years of World War II was over.[20]

Given the sizes, weaponry, and national incomes of the adversaries, this was, hands down, the single greatest diplomatic triumph in world history. Without a missile being launched or even a shot being fired, the alliance of capitalist democracies had won a complete victory. After the end of the Cold War, the alliance didn't even have to occupy enemy territory.

What role did the conservative policies of Ronald Reagan and George H. W. Bush play in the downfall of the Soviet Union? We will probably never have a satisfactory answer to that question, but we can start by recognizing that the conservative U.S. policies of the 1980s were just variants on the basic containment policy set forth under President Truman in the late 1940s, sharpened considerably in the 1950s under President Eisenhower, and carried forward by all of the subsequent administrations. Lashing out with attacks on the "evil empire" didn't change the policy in any fundamental way. Nor did the rollback efforts.

---

[18] Mark Kramer, "The Collapse of the Soviet Union (Part 2)"; Walter D. Connor, "Soviet Society, Public Attitudes, and the Perils of Gorbachev's Reforms," *Journal of Cold War Studies*, 5, 4 (Fall 2003), 3–80; and Amy Knight, "The KGB, Perestroika, and the Collapse of the Soviet Union," ibid, 5, 1 (Winter 2003), 67–93.

[19] Alexander Solzhenitsyn, *One Day in the Life of Ivan Denisovich* (New York: Praeger edition, 1963).

[20] See George Bush and Brent Scowcroft, *A World Transformed* (New York, 1998), for the manner in which President Bush and his National Security Advisor, Scowcroft, perceived and responded to these changes in the USSR.

To sketch some aspects of a conclusion, we need first to acknowledge that the primary causes for communism's collapse rested within the Soviet system, starting with its economy. It was no accident that perestroika was the first formal, public acknowledgment of the depth of those problems. What changed while the problems were emerging were the American military buildup and the heavy investments in Star Wars. These probably accelerated the Soviet collapse. The U.S. initiatives put pressure on their economy when it was already having trouble keeping up.

At that time, the transition to information-age technology was well underway in the United States. That too exerted competitive pressure on a Soviet system that was more effective in mass production using well-understood technologies than it was in generating breakthrough innovations.[21] The Soviets had, for instance, a good health care system, but they produced hardly any pharmaceutical or biotech innovations.[22] Lacking the private/public/university networks that conducted new drug development in the United States and Europe, the Soviets were dependent on western innovations. The Soviet centralized system had trouble coping with the high-tech industries characteristic of the third industrial revolution. Under pressure to change, the Soviets went to the bargaining table, but eventually their leaders recognized that they could no longer hold their empire together.[23]

Hegemony Exercised, 1990–2001

As the Soviet empire began to fall apart, the United States had its first experiences with hegemony. Like all other hegemonic powers, the United States would be repeatedly tempted to try to do too much, to overextend its power, to exhaust its resources and resolve. That was the trap. George

---

[21] As Robert W. Campbell, *Soviet Economic Power: Its Organization, Growth, and Challenge* (Cambridge, Massachusetts), pointed out in 1960, the Soviet railroads were extremely efficient. The problems arose – in chemicals, for instance – where the technology was changing rapidly.

[22] The Soviets conducted a very effective mass campaign to vaccinate against polio. But the vaccine was developed in the United States and initially provided to the Soviets. M. P. Chumakov, et al., "Some Results of the Work on Mass Immunization in the Soviet Union with Live Poliovirus prepared from Sabin Strains," *Bulletin of the World Health Organization*, 25 (1961), 79–91.

[23] Celeste A. Wallander, "Western Policy and the Demise of the Soviet Union," 5, 4 (Fall 2003), *Journal of Cold War Studies*, 137–77. Wallander also suggests that American criticism of Soviet human rights policies had an indirect impact on the breakup of their empire.

Kennan – who didn't use this expression – had long before explained how the Soviets had fallen into this trap at the end of World War II. They had simply acquired more nationalities and ethnic groups than they could eventually absorb and control.

Avoiding the trap, President George H. W. Bush and his advisors moved quickly but carefully as they developed a strategy for dealing with their first serious challenge: Iraq's dictator, Saddam Hussein. Hussein had designs on the oil produced by neighboring Kuwait, and he exploited a border disagreement to launch an unprovoked attack on that country in August 1990. His forces quickly crushed Kuwait's defenses, but Iraq's dictator had seriously miscalculated the diplomatic and military force that would be deployed against his invasion. The United States was officially neutral but unofficially determined not to allow Iraq to control Kuwait and threaten Saudi Arabia. President Bush, his Secretary of State James Baker, and his National Security Advisor Brent Scowcroft responded immediately to Iraq's incursion. All three men – professionals with extensive experience in government and law – knew exactly what to do to counter this threat to the world's oil supply and to an important U.S. ally.[24]

Bush, as Commander-in-Chief, turned for strategic guidance to General Colin L. Powell, then Chairman of the Joint Chiefs of Staff. Powell was an unusual officer with an unusual background and an unusually successful career. Like General Marshall, Powell was not a graduate of West Point. He entered the Reserve Officers Training Corp at City College of New York and received his commission in the Army when he graduated in 1958. Like General Eisenhower, one of the officers on whom he modeled his career, Powell was an average undergraduate student who continued his education during his Army career.[25] Successful during the 1970s, when many of the tattered empire's service leaders were dispirited, he became National Security Advisor to President Reagan (1987–1989)

---

[24] For the Secretary of State's account, see James A. Baker, III, with Thomas M. Defrank, *The Politics of Diplomacy: Revolution, War and Peace, 1989–1992* (New York, 1995), 276–77.

[25] Powell entered the MBA program at George Washington University and graduated in 1971. Colin L. Powell (with Joseph E. Persico), *My American Journey* (New York, 1995), 140–41, 149, 151–55. As Powell explained, "I have always felt a special affinity for Dwight Eisenhower, a war hero who did not have to bark or rattle sabers to gain respect and exercise command, a President who did not stampede his nation into every world trouble spot, a man who understood both the use of power and the value of restraint and who had the secure character to exercise whichever was appropriate" (312).

in the throes of the military buildup. In 1989, he became the first African American to head the Joint Chiefs of Staff.

As Powell and Bush prepared a military response to Iraq's invasion of Kuwait, Secretary of State Baker marshaled international support for the American forces. A Washington insider and Reagan's White House Chief of Staff, Baker had prepped for his role in the Gulf War as a member of the National Security Council. Now he turned to the United Nations in search of international approval for U.S. action. The response was overwhelmingly positive. Reacting quickly to the U.S. and Kuwaiti requests, the UN Security Council met and condemned Iraq's invasion. The UN called for Iraq to withdraw and a few days later imposed economic sanctions on Saddam Hussein's regime. In November, the UN authorized the use of force, and Baker's full-bore diplomatic offense provided the United States with thirty-three allies in Operation Desert Storm.[26]

With strong support at home and abroad, the American and allied forces quickly demonstrated the difference between the military power of the world's major nations and the best that Iraq could muster. The conflict that Saddam Hussein called "the mother of all battles" was actually a demonstration for the world of what hegemony was all about. Victory was achieved in six weeks without using the nuclear weapons that could have destroyed most of Iraq. The Iraqi air force was so overmatched that it attempted to flee into Iran, and the coalition air and missile campaigns quickly knocked out most of Iraq's electrical and water infrastructures. Coalition planes devastated the Iraqi forces as they retreated from Kuwait along the "highway of death."[27]

As the military action reached a decisive conclusion, Bush, Baker, and Powell made a crucial decision to declare a cease-fire.[28] Rather than pushing further into Iraq and toppling Saddam Hussein's government, they settled for the limited objective, freeing Kuwait, which had brought the coalition together.[29] The losses to the coalition were light and the

---

[26] James A. Baker, III, with Thomas M. Defrank, *The Politics of Diplomacy*, 277–408. The correct name is Desert Shield, but Desert Storm was used to name the air/ground operations and has become the common usage. I will use it throughout to avoid confusion.

[27] Jeffrey T. Richardson, ed., *Operation Desert Storm: Ten Years After* (2001), with documents including United States Central Command, *Operation Desert Shield/Desert Storm* (1991). Available at http://www.gwu.edu/~/hsarchiv/NSAEBB/NSAEBB39.

[28] President Bush also consulted with Scowcroft, Cheney, and General Schwarzkopf, who had led the campaign against Iraq. George Bush and Brent Scowcroft, *A World Transformed*, 485–87.

[29] Rick Atkinson, *Crusade: The Untold Story of the Persian Gulf War* (New York, 1993), 469–87, describes the decision and the final days of the war.

victory complete. One might have expected U.S. military leaders to insist that the coalition push on to Baghdad and depose Hussein. But General Powell, later nicknamed "the reluctant warrior," was solidly behind the decision to settle for a cautious, limited victory.[30]

Desert Storm set a high mark for America's relations with the rest of the world during the era of U.S. hegemony. Eschewing military force until a vast coalition was organized, Bush, Baker, and Powell ensured that the United States would not weaken its alliance structure as it had during the Vietnam War. They broke with Reagan's approach by turning to and strengthening the hand of the United Nations. The American position in the Middle East was improved – if only marginally – by the constrained manner in which the United States used its power.

There were important lessons to be learned from the first Gulf War and from the style of leadership that President Bush and his professional cohort displayed. They accommodated smoothly to the fact that America's NATO allies were no longer client states. The relationships had to be different now because Western Europe wasn't dependent on the American military shield to provide protection against the USSR's military might. NATO's central reason to exist had evaporated. Military planning had to give way to diplomacy between equals, a transition that was uncomfortable for some Americans and still makes them uncomfortable today.

For even a wary leader like Bush, however, the hegemony trap was hard to avoid completely. There was a powerful temptation to deploy U.S. military force unilaterally, to dip into collapsing states, revolutionary movements, and ethnic struggles. The world was filled with crises in which there was little threat to America's national security and hardly any likelihood of a favorable conclusion. Bush gave into the temptation in Somalia, an African nation wracked by civil war against a failed government. He left that problem, unsolved, in the hands of his successor, President Clinton, who tried the familiar American approach of increasing our military involvement. Unsuccessful, the United States withdrew, leaving behind a state in crisis, as it had been before U.S. intervention.[31]

Throughout his two administrations, Clinton was constantly tempted to use America's overwhelming power and abandon Bush's cautious

---

[30] Colin L. Powell (with Joseph E. Persico), *My American Journey*, 519–28.
[31] Kenneth Allard, *Somalia Operations. Lessons Learned* (1995). Mark Bowden, *Black Hawk Down: A Story of Modern War* (New York, 1999), gives you a remarkable sense of the chaos of combat. As Daniel P. Bolger notes in *Savage Peace: Americans at War in the 1990s* (Novata, California, 1995), 267, "...Americans had contracted a very advanced case of hubris."

strategy. Like Bush, Clinton depended heavily on his Secretaries of State, Warren Christopher and Madeleine Albright, to keep him out of the hegemony trap.[32] The experiences, educations, and temperaments of Christopher and Albright inclined both of these advisors to pull the President and his administrations away from the exercise of American military power. Christopher was a lawyer with substantial experience in Washington as a law clerk, a Deputy Attorney General, and a Deputy Secretary of State. At State under President Carter, he had taken a strong interest in human rights.[33]

Albright was a sharp contrast with Jeane Kirkpatrick. Both had their doctorates in political science from Columbia University and both had studied abroad. But Albright's family had experienced war and anti-Semitism first hand. Forced to flee Europe, they settled in the United States, where her father became the dean of a graduate school of international studies. Like her predecessor, Albright had gained experience in the Carter administration, serving on the staff of the National Security Council. On the faculty at Georgetown, she was a talented teacher and scholar. Ambassador and then U.S. permanent representative at the UN, in 1997 she became the first female Secretary of State.[34]

Albright and Christopher tried to keep the United States in a leadership position while guiding Clinton away from using American military power.[35] Early on, the administration pulled back abruptly in Somalia and refused to become involved in the genocide in Rwanda. There was potential in the Rwandan case for organizing a joint UN command similar to the one that had defeated Iraq. But neither the United States nor its allies took any decisive action. Burned by the problems that developed in Somalia, the United States backed off while as many as a million Rwandans were slaughtered.

---

[32] Judging from Clinton's list of intelligence priorities in 1995, he was apparently also determined to avoid shadowy CIA operations in countries like Afghanistan. Steve Coll, *Ghost Wars: The Secret History of the CIA, Afghanistan, and bin Laden, from the Soviet Invasion to September 10, 2001* (New York, 2004), 361–62.

[33] Born in North Dakota and educated in California, Christopher clerked for Supreme Court Justice William O. Douglas (1949–1950), was at the Justice Department from 1967–1969, and at State from 1977–1981.

[34] She would also have been the second Jew to become Secretary of State (Kissinger was the first) had not her family converted to Catholicism to protect themselves. Like many professionals moving ahead (see Chapter 4), she later became an Episcopalian.

[35] It was apparently this aspect of the Clinton administration to which Donald Rumsfeld objected: When challenged, he said, there was a "'reflexive pullback' – caution, safety plays, even squeamishness." Later, Rumsfeld would get a chance to support a more aggressive policy. Bob Woodward, *Bush at War* (New York, 2002), 19–20.

Uncertain about its empire and the role it should play in the world, the United States was bobbing back and forth as it had periodically for the past century. The bobbing had become more erratic since the defeat in Vietnam. Discussing Rwanda, President Clinton later said, "I blew it." But that doesn't capture the full meaning of the U.S. response to genocide in Africa. If the United States was going to become the world's well-armed policeman, where and why would it enforce the law? And what would that law be? Would, for instance, all genocides be equal?

The Rwandan genocide provides an important limiting case – especially in light of the events that followed in East Europe. After one allows for the bad experience in Somalia, the logistical problems of reaching Rwanda, and the long history of ethnic murder and war between the Hutu and Tutsi ethnic groups, you are still left without a full explanation of the failure of the United States to press harder for an international response. I believe the explanation involves racism – the assumption that African lives didn't matter as much as lives in, say, Europe. Or certainly in America. There was the potential in the Rwandan case to organize through the UN an international response that might have saved many lives. But that would have required quick, forceful leadership by the United States and the United Nations. Neither responded decisively and the genocide ground to its horrible conclusion.

Bosnia and Kosovo were closer to home and didn't have a clear-cut racial element. The problems were somewhat similar but the outcomes were different. Here again came the lure to a hegemonic power confronted by a complex, age-old, ethnic struggle. This Balkan crisis was an ancient struggle with a post–Cold War twist. As communist power and authority dissolved, Yugoslavia had fallen apart. This launched a civil war between the Bosnian Serbs, mostly Christians, and the Bosnian Muslims and Croats who were seeking autonomy. The United States sympathized with those Bosnian Muslims and Croats who wanted their own country, and the U.S. Air Force was ready to bomb the Serbs who were trying to hold the country together under their control. But the Clinton team could not win the support of its European allies. Badly scarred by two world wars, hesitant to use force, and knowing that this was an ethnic quagmire, Europe opposed intervention. Forced to deal with European powers that could not be persuaded or bullied to support military involvement, the United States put the war on hold.[36]

---

[36] Bill Clinton, *My Life* (New York, 2004).

But the civil war continued. Encouraged by the fact that Slovenia and Macedonia became completely independent, the Croats and Bosnian Muslims pushed ahead to gain independence from the Serbian government under Slobodan Milosevic. In the war that followed, the Serbs were guilty of brutal ethnic cleansing. First in Croatia and then in Bosnia, men, women and children were slaughtered by an army seeking to unify the former nation under the Serbian government. Both the United Nations and the European Community (later the EU) organized conferences, but talking didn't solve the problem. The Europeans and the UN did nothing decisive to prevent the genocide.[37]

President Clinton decided not to blow this one. Frustrated by the unwillingness of the United Nations to do anything except talk, his administration finally turned to NATO to muster support for a military response. NATO wasn't designed for this purpose, but it had a unified military command that could be used if the European members were willing to take action. Under continued pressure from the United States, the European governments finally approved this major extension of NATO's mission. With the United States supplying most of the firepower, NATO started serious air attacks against the Serbian army. Having no way to defend itself against the powerful air campaign, Serbia was forced to negotiate a settlement.[38]

The Clinton administration created a venue for the peace discussions through a Dayton, Ohio conference (1995), and the Dayton Accords ended the Balkan war. Like the settlement in Iraq, the Dayton agreement was a compromise solution that left in power a brutal government guilty of genocide. Unlike the situation in Rwanda, however, the joint American-European military effort ended the killing and created the possibility that NATO would continue to play a forceful role in European affairs.

The Accords left unsettled the problem of Kosovo, which was a part of Serbia populated largely by Albanians. Once again, nationalistic aspirations broke a country apart. Once again a military struggle followed. And once again, the United States became involved. This time, however, the NATO allies were already committed and were prepared to extend their military operations. The United States led the bombing campaign that followed the breakdown of peace negotiations between the Serbs and

---

[37] Ibid.
[38] Bill Clinton provides his perspective on Bosnia in *My Life* (New York, 2004), 509–14, 534, 541, 552, 581–83, 590–91, 633, 672–76, 684–91.

the independence movement. Overwhelming air power again destroyed Serbian resistance, along with much of the country's infrastructure. At last the UN sent a peacekeeping force to take control of Kosovo. Substantially short of perfect, the resulting settlement was consistent with the previous pattern of compromise solutions in America's ongoing experiment with hegemony.[39]

Constantly lured toward unilateral military interventions, President Clinton only swerved away from the Bush policies in one crisis. This took place in the Caribbean, where the United States had been the dominant force since the late nineteenth century. In Haiti, a military coup overturned the democratically elected President Jean-Bertrand Aristide and provoked the Clinton administration to intervene, without even obtaining Congressional support. The only precedent for this type of unilateral action since 1980 was President Reagan's use of military force to overturn a coup in Grenada. Otherwise, the United States had been a good neighbor.

Upset by seeing democracy undone in Haiti, the United States called on its navy and marines to restore a legally elected government. With American forces on the way, the Haitian military leaders left the country and Aristide was returned on condition that he implement policies *approved by the United States*. The results did not encourage idealists to believe that the United States should replace the Good Neighbor Policy by a return to gunboat diplomacy.[40]

The boldest move by Clinton and Secretary Christopher required no military forces and no exercise of international political power. The George H. W. Bush administration had signed the North American Trade Agreement opening U.S. borders to trade with Canada and Mexico. Canada posed very few problems. But Mexico did. There was widespread fear that American manufacturing plants would move toward the cheap labor of Mexico – as they did. There was fear as well that the pact would increase the flow of immigrants to the United States – as it did. The number of unauthorized Mexican immigrants to the United States doubled in the 1990s. For the Democratic Party and the Clinton administration, this was a hard pill to swallow. Especially since a Republican administration had originally prepared and packaged the pill.

[39] Ibid., 848–60.

[40] According to Bill Clinton, National Security Advisor Anthony Lake commented on problems like those in Haiti, Somalia, and Bosnia, saying: "Sometimes I really miss the Cold War." Ibid., 554.

The least painful course would have been to let the treaty die. The AFL-CIO was fiercely opposed to NAFTA, and that opposition alone could easily have killed the agreement. But Clinton, Christopher, and their staffs pressed on, working to convince congressional Democrats to support the measure. This was, I believe, the greatest single act of statesmanship of the two Clinton administrations. The vision of a free-trade area stretching from Canada through Mexico was appealing but politically dangerous. Protectionist pressures were growing as America's Rust Belt states continued to lose manufacturing plants.

"Some voices," Secretary Christopher said, "are telling the American people that the way to prosper is to close our borders, to retreat behind walls of high tariffs and trade barriers." Those voices were loud and hard to ignore. But the administration rejected that advice. "We have reason to be confident of our strengths," Christopher said. "We are the number one global exporter. We have the most productive labor force. Our high technology is the envy of the world. Given an open market, our workers and companies can compete and win."[41]

Many Americans were less confident than Christopher, but NAFTA squeezed through Congress and provided a foundation for an even bolder move toward a free-trade area for the entire Western Hemisphere.[42] Once again, the administration was supporting a measure introduced by the Bush team. Looking over their shoulders at the European Union, both administrations were clearly seeking to consolidate a similar, regional trading bloc. The World Trade Organization's (WTO) vision centered on a free-trade globe and considerable progress was being made toward that goal. But political and trade consolidation was also taking place on a regional basis, and the United States was trying to keep up.

Of course Congress was less enthusiastic about the Free Trade Area of the Americas (FTAA) than the White House and State Department. A serious backlash against the FTAA and the WTO pushed the administration away from the regional plan and toward less ambitious bilateral agreements. But the issue would remain on the table after Madeleine Albright became Secretary of State and would, like the volatile Middle-Eastern situations, be passed along to the next administration.

---

[41] Warren Christopher, "U.S.-Mexican Relations and NAFTA," June 21, 1993, U.S. Department of State Dispatch.

[42] The vote was decisively positive in the Senate (61–38), but the House vote was close (234–200). In the House, the vote in Clinton's own party was 156 against and only 102 in favor of NAFTA.

Lessons

As a historian, teaching and studying America's modern development, I could see several lessons in the American experiences with empire during the last two decades of the twentieth century. Even though Americans at that point had not forgotten what happened in the 1970s, Reagan, Bush, and Clinton all pushed ahead and made progress in the search for an appropriate post-Vietnam global strategy. They were all far better than their immediate predecessors at using their professional advisers, drawing on the strengths of the State Department, and promoting policies that preserved the country's working relationships with its European and Asian allies.

There were flip-flops, which is what "searching" always involves. But all three presidents were able to provide effective leadership that drew on the technical capabilities of their advisers without losing control, as Nixon had, of policy.

Bush and Clinton adjusted very well to two fundamental shifts in America's position in the world. As the Soviet empire collapsed, the NATO nations were no longer client states beholden to U.S. power. The United States found this new situation uncomfortable during the first stages of the Balkan crisis. Gradually, however, the United States accommodated its policies to the new situation in Europe. While they did so, both administrations were repeatedly pulled toward the hegemony trap. There were always crises that seemed to call for America to use unilateral military power to create a better world. Neither Bush nor Clinton stayed completely out of the trap, but their bitter experiences in trying to reshape the internal politics of other nations turned them away from further adventures abroad. This was a hard lesson to learn. It was a lesson that could also be forgotten all too easily.

As the interventions in Somalia and Haiti demonstrated, the pull toward foreign adventures was powerful. Clinton struggled over the situation in Iraq and used American air power several times in an effort to constrain Saddam Hussein.[43] Both presidents were faced with a world in which moral problems abounded, and both had to fight off the desire to move quickly and unilaterally to create an American settlement. Both presidents worked hard to avoid abrupt, unilateral military actions of the

---

[43] Bill Clinton, *My Life*, 717, 728, 769, 771–72. By early 1998, Clinton had decided "Saddam never moved except when forced to do so" (778). After Hussein refused to keep his commitments on UN inspections, the United States and the UK launched a formidable four-day air assault (833–34).

sort that many Americans favored. They helped the country push forward in its ongoing quest for the right balance between a realism based on force and an idealism suited to American values. Their history in this regard was short of perfect, but they logged remarkable accomplishments at the end of a century that saw more lives destroyed by war than at any time in human history.

My personal "lesson" was the same one that Robert McNamara had learned. Reflecting on his own sad experiences with the Vietnam War, McNamara had concluded that America should only exercise its awesome military power when it had almost universal support for its action.[44] This was certainly the case with Bush's First Gulf War. But I remained fearful about the two-generation cycle that shapes and reshapes our social memory of events like those in Vietnam. With the passage of two generations, we forget the failures of the past. Then, our understanding of how we should conduct ourselves in the world needs to be renewed.

That needs to be done by effective, articulate leaders who have the confidence and strength of character to steer a course between the realists and the idealists. They have to deal on a day-to-day basis with the hubris that hegemony breeds in many professional experts. To do that, a president needs a good sense of history, good judgment, and a good grip on America's most important values. Leaders like that are always in short supply.

---

[44] Robert S. McNamara, "Reflections on War in the Twenty-first Century," in Charles E. Neu, ed., *After Vietnam: Legacies of a Lost War* (Baltimore, 2000), 105–29. "I believe . . . ," McNamara said, "that for the future, the United Nations charter offers a far more appropriate framework for international relations than does the doctrine of power politics" (110).

17

The American Dream, 1981 to 2001

I'm living and raising a family in a struggling city, and I won't pretend that this hasn't influenced my history of America in recent decades.[1] I feel close to this struggle every morning when I read the newspaper.[2] You may be familiar with Baltimore because of a movie or television program. If you watched *The Wire*, you probably have a mental picture of dark streets, warehouses, and crime. We have plenty of those. Baltimore is typical of the East Coast port cities that have been having severe problems for many years now, have had one or more surges of inner-city revival, and are continuing to look for ways to deal with drugs, crime, and commercial decay.

Each city has, of course, its own particular qualities and history. In Baltimore, for instance, there are several enclaves within the city where the big old houses of yesterday's urban elite have not been broken into apartments, one of the first steps toward decay. My family and I live happily on one of those urban islands, Guilford, eight minutes from my university and twelve minutes from my young daughters' school.

As you've already seen in the previous chapters, the educational system is crucial in my version of modern American history. That system,

---

[1] Although Mary Ryan's *Mysteries of Sex* gives you some guidelines for gender relations near the end of the century, and the earnest student can gather information on the cities in Rufus P. Browning, Dale Rogers Marshall, and David H. Tabb, *Racial Politics in American Cities* (White Plains, NY, 2003 edition), you are largely on your own in piecing together this part of recent American history.

[2] Given that you know my age from Chapter 1, you will understand why I continue to read two newspapers on most days, sometimes before breakfast, sometimes after dinner (which is of course related to the fact that I have two young daughters).

from kindergarten through high school and on to the universities and professional programs, produced the professional experts, the brokers, and leaders you've been reading about. It's more important to America than any other single set of institutions, including those on Wall Street or on Pennsylvania Avenue. For most Americans, the first step on the mobility staircase has been through education, and that staircase has for more than a century taken city and country kids into the professions, into the middle class, and into a better life. Their progress has been driving America's progress – and still is today.

But that educational staircase is broken in Baltimore and other cities in crisis. For a substantial part of the American population, this has deprived their children of the opportunity to move up and play the role they deserve in the American mobility drama. I've been able, barely at times, to send four daughters to a wonderful private school, Friends School, but most of the people who live in our large cities can't afford to do that. They need public education through high school and through higher education as well. They need public education that works.

The collapse of urban public education was particularly galling for African Americans because the school decay accelerated just as the civil rights movement was finally allowing them access to political power and better lives. When more and more African Americans left the agricultural South and headed into urban centers, they were squeezed into slums and their children were sent to schools that reflected the declining economies of the older manufacturing centers. In 1954, the Supreme Court rejected the "separate but equal" doctrine that had kept most black Americans in decidedly inferior schools. But now all they had in the cities was an equal opportunity to attend inferior schools that still wouldn't put them on the path to the professions. What a cruel trick history was playing on them.[3]

The Talented Tenth and the Reform Impulse

Not everyone was willing to let urban schools collapse. In the late 1980s, Kurt Schmoke set out to find an answer to the crisis of inner-city education. He was a lawyer and was everything that W.E.B. Du Bois had hoped for in the Talented Tenth, the elite who could lead African

---

[3] Thomas J. Sugrue, *The Origins of the Urban Crisis*, is particularly instructive in this regard.

Americans upward in their society.[4] A scholar-athlete, Schmoke had gone to Yale University in 1967 after graduating from one of the few good public high schools left in Baltimore. Active in student government and in community service, he continued to be a leader in New Haven and after graduating (1971), he was a Rhodes Scholar at Oxford University. Harvard Law School followed, as did a successful career in the Carter Administration and then an appointment as Assistant United States Attorney in Baltimore.

In 1987, Kurt Schmoke became the first black mayor elected in this American city and launched an effort to make Baltimore "the city that reads." Baltimore was spending almost one-third of its annual budget on education, but the results were depressing.[5] One study discovered that a quarter of a million of the system's books couldn't be accounted for, and parents in one of the schools were sending toilet paper with their kids because the supplies had run out. Facing teacher shortages in the classroom, the schools hired instructors with literacy problems and then found that four-fifths of the city's students couldn't pass the state writing test.[6]

The new mayor, who had stellar credentials for reform leadership, knew that his city had severe problems. Flight to the suburbs was cutting into the tax base and employment opportunities. Here, as elsewhere in the Rust Belt, the older manufacturing industries had been collapsing for a long time. Drugs and crime had made the public housing reforms of the 1960s an urban problem of the 1980s. Nowhere were the unanticipated consequences of LBJ's New Society more evident than in the projects.

Schmoke didn't ignore these problems, but he wisely made education reform the centerpiece of his program. Reform would be difficult, if only because the Baltimore school system was large. There were 186 public schools, well more than 100,000 students, and more than 11,000

---

[4] Richard Florida, *Cities and the Creative Class*, 38, concludes that although Baltimore has "deep reservoirs of technology and world-class universities," it is failing to grow because it is "unwilling to be sufficiently tolerant and open" and thus attractive to the creative class. Schmoke's election and efforts at reform seem to me to suggest otherwise.

[5] U.S. Bureau of the Census, *Statistical Abstract of the United States: 1991* (Washington, 1991), No. 493, Finances for 1986. The state provided aid, but political battles erupted between the wealthy counties (e.g., Montgomery) and the city. *Washington Post*, January 26, 1987, Metro, 1.

[6] *Washington Post*, July 28, 1986, Metro, 1. *New York Times*, November 24, 1985, Section 1, 50.

employees. The dropout rates were high. The test scores were low.[7] But Mayor Schmoke recognized that without educational reform, most African Americans would continue to be more concerned about the minimum wage than the path to the professions, the path he had taken.

From the very beginning, his reform plan hit two formidable roadblocks. One was the centralized, bureaucratized administration that was, as we've seen, the product of an earlier phase of reform. The changes of the progressive era, especially the professionalization of teaching and the development of centralized administrations, had improved public education in Baltimore and other cities during the early twentieth century. But as the school bureaucracies became deeply entrenched, they created a major barrier to further change. Particularly to serious change. Like the large corporations that had grown conservative about change during the American Century, the school administrations had turned in on themselves, focusing on the daily chores of using scarce resources to keep things running. Avoiding conflict was the essence of administrative self-defense. Where you sat (i.e., your job), an experienced public administrator once observed, had a great deal to do with where you stood on an issue like school reform.[8]

Reinforcement for the school administration's opposition to change came from the teachers' unions, which had evolved along lines similar to those of the bureaucracy. The unions had long provided teachers with the representation they needed in dealing with the administrative bureaucracy. By dint of their educations, experiences, and social standing, public school teachers were professionals, as were the administrators. Economically, however, teachers lived on the lower edge of the middle class in urban America. Not many could afford to live in enclaves like Guilford, the area I described a few pages ago. Issues of fringe benefits and job security were important to Baltimore's teachers, none of whom could bargain individually on those issues.

But the union sword cut both ways. The power to help teachers was also the power to block changes that might threaten the teachers or the unions. Wherever the unions achieved solid representation, creative change in the school systems slowed or stopped. Once a union joined

7 Maryland State Department of Education, *Facts about Maryland Public Education, 1985–86. Washington Post*, July 28, 1986, Metro, C1. *New York Times*, November 24, 1985, Section 1, 50.
8 Harold Seidman, *Politics, Position, and Power: The Dynamics of Federal Organization* (New York, 1980).

forces with the administrators, it took heroic measures to make significant changes in the school system. This was especially true in a city like Baltimore, where education had become a racial issue. Black teachers and administrators had fought hard for many years to win positions in the system, and reform – especially when it came from white leaders and foundations – aroused deep suspicion and opposition to change.[9]

Kurt Schmoke could not avoid a struggle against both the unions and the school administrators, a struggle he tried to avoid. His goal was noble and worthy of our respect. But he was unable to persuade either the administrators or the unions to allow the kind of deep structural changes that were needed. He was unable to break the administration-union combine, and reform soon fizzled out to a depressing conclusion.[10] He was certainly not the only big-city mayor to get a failing grade for school reform. Unfortunately, he was in that regard close to the norm.

Although Schmoke emphasized the school problem, he was not a single-issue leader. He could see, for instance, what illegal drugs were doing to Baltimore and other cities. Unlike most other mayors, however, Schmoke was honest, outspoken, and imaginative about what the United States was doing and what it needed to do about the drug trade. He called for a debate on alternatives to the "war on drugs." As he pointed out, we hadn't won the war and weren't likely to win it even though we were spending billions of dollars to stop the shipments and distribution of marijuana, heroin, and cocaine. We were filling the jails and prisons with drug users and dealers. We were losing the war but were unable to have a serious discussion of alternatives such as decriminalization.[11]

---

[9] Especially enlightening is the comparative study by Clarence Stone, Marion Orr, and Donn Worgs, "The Flight of the Bumblebee: Why Reform Is Difficult but Not Impossible," *Perspectives on Politics*, 4, 3 (September 2006), 529–46. "Baltimore," the authors conclude, "is the reform bee that did not fly" (540). The authors also conclude that "expertise and connections to sources of professional knowledge provide a valuable means for matching concrete and specific activities with a broad reform goal" (542).

[10] Following his three terms as mayor, Kurt L. Schmoke practiced law and then became Dean of the Howard University Law School. http://findarticles.com/p/articles/mi_moDXK/is_19_19/ai_94592275. See also http://biography.jrank.org/pages/2429/Xchmoke-Kurt.html.

[11] *Washington Post*, September 30, 1988. *New York Times*, November 27, 1989. See also the *National Review* discussion of "The War on Drugs Is Lost," July 1, 1996, at http://www.nationalreview.com/12feb96/drug.html. Schmoke was in two episodes of the HBO series *The Wire*, acting as a health commissioner advising on an ad hoc drug decriminalization issue.

An introductory course on economics was all you needed to understand why the war wasn't working. When the government was able to cut the supply of drugs, it raised the price on the street. The incentives to deal went up and supply usually caught up with demand fairly quickly. Given the alternative forms of employment available to young men in Baltimore and other inner cities, the immediate rewards of the drug trade outweighed the risks. But Schmoke's suggested alternative – decriminalization and treating addiction as a public-health problem – spurred moral outrage and political condemnation, neither of which provided any new solutions to this enormous social problem. Subsequent mayors turned to less challenging issues, leaving Baltimore in deep distress, concerned but uncertain what to do about the gang wars, the murder rate, the addicts, and the incredibly high percentage of young African-American males in prison. By the 1990s, more than half of the young black adults in Baltimore were "under criminal justice control."[12]

Drug use was one of the several public health issues in central cities like Baltimore. Needle sharing spread infectious diseases, including HIV/AIDS. Despite the expansion of clinics and the availability of emergency wards, health care for inner-city residents, and especially black Americans, was poor. The most telling figures were those comparing life expectancy for black and white Americans. By 1998, white males could expect to live almost seven years longer than African-American men. For women, the difference was slightly more than five years.[13] Poor prenatal care meant that African-American infants were more likely to die while being born, and low vaccination rates in the inner cities placed preschool children at risk for infectious diseases that were seldom seen in the suburbs.[14]

All of these problems were exacerbated by a new wave of immigrants from Mexico and Central America. The United States had abandoned the national-origins quota system in the 1960s, and millions of Latinos were now leaving the urban and agrarian poverty of their countries to

[12] Center on Juvenile and Criminal Justice, "The Punishing Decade: Prison and Jail Estimates at the Millennium," available at http://www.cjcj.org/pubs/punishing/punishing .html.

[13] Michael R. Haines, "Life Expectancy," in Susan B. Carter, et al., eds., *Historical Statistics of the United States*, volume 1, 441.

[14] Johns Hopkins University and the University of Maryland, *The Baltimore Immunization Study: Immunization Coverage and Causes of Under-Immunization Among Inner-City Children in Baltimore* (Baltimore, 1993). See also *New England Journal of Medicine*, 327, 25 (1992), 1794–1800. *Health Line*, February 8, 1993. *Pediatrics* 91, 1 (1993), 1–7.

try their luck in America, most often in the inner cities.[15] They suffered the same handicaps that black Americans experienced in the struggling cities. Starting at the bottom of the economic order in America's corporate economy, Latinos took low-paying, low-status jobs that blacks had formerly filled. Their reward was an opportunity for their children to get ahead, an opportunity that was marred by overloaded and underfinanced school systems like the one in Baltimore.

The Talented Tenth – a Philadelphia Story

Despite these handicaps, some inner-city African Americans still made it onto the educational path to the professions. Outside of the large, older cities like Philadelphia, in communities where education was not on life support, civil rights advances paid off for some black Americans. They paid off too in Philadelphia for those whose parents could afford to pay private school tuitions. In some cases, African-American children could also benefit from the busing that moved them into successful white schools. When busing was forced on the schools by the courts, it provoked a mighty wail of protest all over America.[16] I was a bit surprised by the intensity of the reaction because we had always had busing in tiny Princeton, Indiana.[17] The black students attended a little one-room school off to the side of town until they were ready to go to high school. Then they were bused to Evansville, about twenty-eight miles to the south. I don't recall a single protest about this in the 1940s.

Regardless of the riots and the waves of fear about changing racial relations, there were African Americans who were determined to use busing to help their children get a better education. One of them was an

[15] The national-origins quota system was eliminated in 1965 and Congress changed the law again in 1986 and 1990. In the 1980s, the number of U.S. foreign-born from Mexico and South America doubled and from Central America more than tripled.

[16] Ronald P. Formesano, *Boston against Busing: Race, Class, and Ethnicity in the 1960s and 1970s* (Chapel Hill, 1991) provides an in-depth analysis of the problem. Emmett H. Buell, Jr., with Richard A. Brisbin, Jr., *School Desegregation and Defended Neighborhooods: The Boson Controversy* (Lexington, Massachusetts, 1982), offers a survey of the issue. Malik Morrison, "An Examination of Philadelphia's School Desegregation Litigation," *Penn GSE Perspectives on Urban Education*, 3, 1, http://www.urbanedjournal.org. In August 1971, ten school buses in Pontiac, Michigan were bombed by whites protesting busing. Riots also erupted in Louisville, Kentucky. http://www.occidentaldissent.com/american-racial-history-timeline-ii/.

[17] Although the school was fairly close to our house, I didn't know it existed until my sister told me about it. As I noted before, I only knew one black person in Princeton and then only by his nickname.

elderly janitor in Philadelphia who wanted his son Ken to have the kind of formal education needed to make it into a respectable profession. Eager to get his children on the path to a better life, Otis Frazier was a fierce disciplinarian. He had learned his lessons in discipline and self-reliance as a fourteen-year-old farm boy. His father, who couldn't see any chance for him to get ahead in South Carolina, put him on a train and sent him north to find a better life in Philadelphia. Having neither family nor friends for support, he managed with great self-discipline to earn a living, to educate himself without formal schooling, and later to raise a family.[18]

When a new busing program started in the 1960s, Frazier decided quickly that his children should get on board and take advantage of the city's best schools. They might have to ride three different buses to get to the other side of the city. They might be the only African Americans in their classes. But if that's what it cost to get on the road leading upward, well, that's what would be done.[19]

Driven by his father's fierce ambition, Ken Frazier excelled in school and in sports while dealing with some tricky social problems. He was smart enough to skip a couple of grades, so he was very young as well as black, surrounded by students who were all white and two years older than him. Every day, when he returned home to the inner city, he also had to negotiate the tensions created by his progress through the white man's school. Boys of any race can be incredibly nasty, and his friends were frequently as clever as they were mean.

Although he managed to navigate successfully through those turbulent years, Ken Frazier was a high achiever without a higher purpose. He was running on autopilot, drawing energy from his father, not from the substance of what he was studying. He didn't really distinguish between the different subjects he was studying: math or history, English or science, it was all the same to him. So when he began planning to go to a university, he was an admission director's dream but he didn't really know what he wanted to do. He flirted for a time with an appointment to West Point, but the military was in ill repute during the Vietnam War. After a few hesitant steps in different directions, he ended up at Penn State in the fall of 1971.

---

[18] Otis' wife died when Ken Frazier was twelve years old.

[19] Most of the information on Kenneth Frazier was collected in an interview I did with him. See also *Minority Law Journal on the web*, http://www.americanlawyer.com/mlj/summer01/texts/frazier.html; *The Metropolitan Corporate Counsel*, http://www.metrocorpcounsel.com/current.php?artType=view&EntryNo=5337 on the Street Law program; and http://people.forbes.com/profile/Kenneth-c-frazier/52791.

At the University Park campus, this sixteen-year-old freshman started to find out what he liked as well as what he could do well. This wasn't a painless or quick process, and many of my readers can probably remember similar academic struggles. I certainly can. At first Ken was drawn toward the sciences, especially chemistry. But he soon realized that he had neither the preparation nor the talent for the math required to do science successfully. For the first time in his academic career, he had hit an obstacle he couldn't climb over. Political science became his new obsession, and this one stuck. Now he had an intellectual mission that would stay with him through the next three years and point him toward a career in law after he graduated from Penn State.

Admitted to Harvard Law School in 1975, Ken arrived in Massachusetts unaware that there were some new obstacles to clear. One was social and cultural. "Where did you prep?" he was asked, and he didn't know what "prep" meant. His experience was similar to that of W. E. B. Du Bois, the young black scholar who had realized many decades before that he could be "at Harvard, but not of Harvard." Du Bois was not alone in this regard, and neither was Ken Frazier. Looking around Harvard shortly after he arrived, Ken saw that he wasn't dressed right. He didn't own a necktie or a suit. So he headed out to Filene's Basement, where he bought a black suit that made him look like an undertaker and a ladybug necktie that made him look like a recent immigrant from Eastern Europe.

Then there were the classes and the Socratic method that had terrified generations of sweating law students. It was bad enough to be embarrassed by a mistake in the presence of a senior law professor. It was a nightmare to be humiliated in front of your classmates. Fortunately the autopilot that his father had installed kicked in and helped him master the cases that were the grounding of American law. Theories and concepts were exciting, but a good command of cases was essential to survival at the Harvard Law School. A good command of grammar, he learned, was also essential to a career at the distinguished Philadelphia law firm in which he interned during the summers. Lawyers at Drinker Biddle & Reath did *not* split infinitives, he learned.

By the time he left Harvard in 1978, Ken had a better-looking suit and the right necktie. He had lost the rough edges of the inner city, and he now felt comfortable practicing law and getting along with his colleagues and clients at Drinker Biddle & Reath in downtown Philadelphia. One of the clients was Merck & Co., Inc., a giant multinational pharmaceutical company whose legal business Ken began to master. Both Merck and the law firm were pleased to see this relationship grow stronger, and Merck began to absorb more and more of his time in the 1980s. Active in Merck's business and in public service, he soon made partner. Then, in 1992, he moved to Merck as a vice president and general counsel of one of the firm's subsidiaries. After a stint as executive vice president, heading a global human health division with some 30,000 employees, he moved up to become Merck's president and then the firm's new CEO.

Ken Frazier's path to this position was not straight or simple, but the logic of his progress was clear and straightforward. Thanks to his intelligence and determination, his father's discipline, and a controversial, court-ordered affirmative action program, he got on the twentieth-century path to a successful professional career. He stayed off the streets walked by many of the other smart, inner-city African-American kids of his generation. Philadelphia in those years was similar to other large, eastern cities, including Baltimore. Drugs and gangs drained off intelligence and organizational ability, sending to prisons or graveyards young people who could have been building professional careers instead of destroying themselves. Like Kurt Schmoke, Frazier found his way into the new cadre of black professionals who made it in spite of the collapse of inner-city public education in most of America's major urban centers.

Frazier and Schmoke were part of an important emerging black middle and upper class that was professional, upwardly mobile, and frequently suburban. These African Americans were, for the most part, sending their children to private schools and then to the colleges and universities that would train them, intellectually and socially, for their role in the talented tenth. This was a black variant on the immigrant story of the American dream. Homeownership was increasing for these black Americans, along with wealth and income. The ascent was slower, the resistance greater, and the triumph limited in ways that Irish Catholics and Hungarian Americans didn't experience. Race still mattered in America, but it helped a great deal if you had a Harvard education, an expensive suit, and the right tie.

Talented Women – the American Story

The American story was different and the results more encouraging for white women during the late years of the twentieth century. The powerful effects of their educational accomplishments – first in U.S. high schools, then in colleges and universities, finally in a broad range of professional schools – provided a base for their progress in a number of important

American institutions. They became leaders as well as important followers in public, private, and nonprofit organizations.

One woman who cracked several glass ceilings was Hannah Holborn Gray.[20] Her ascent adds a special quality to our understanding of the immigrant variant on the American dream. She began life in Heidelberg, Germany, with all the advantages and disadvantages of the daughter of academic parents. Her mother had a PhD in philology and her father was a historian of Germany, who taught at Heidelberg University and then at Deutsche Hochschule für Politik. Dismissed from his job by the Nazis, he and his Jewish wife and young daughter fled, first to Britain and then to the United States. Hannah was raised in New Haven, Connecticut, in the shadow of a father who was an eminent Yale scholar and the first immigrant president of the American Historical Association.[21]

Hannah, who might easily have been deterred by the accomplishments of her parents, excelled in school, first at Bryn Mawr College and then at Oxford and Harvard Universities. Rather boldly, she entered her father's domain by taking on European intellectual history as her major field of study. Even before receiving her PhD (1957), she got a good taste of the bitter gender bias of Ivy education. While a tutor at Harvard, she was invited to her department's fiftieth anniversary celebration. Alas, it was being held at an all-male club. After she told them she couldn't attend, one of the historians said, "Maybe that night you could go up to Radcliffe and have dinner with some of the girls."[22]

She would return to Harvard some years later, but in the meantime, Hannah married another academic and followed him to his new post at the University of Chicago. Fortunately for her and for Chicago, the university administration abandoned its nepotism rule covering husband/wife teams and appointed her to the faculty in the history department. Moving up the ranks to full professor, Hannah Holborn Gray discovered, as

[20] In the interests of transparency, I am biased by the fact that I took a course and did one of my graduate fields with her father, Hajo Holborn, a distinguished European historian at Yale University. He was tolerant of the paper-thinness of my knowledge of European diplomacy.

[21] See Georg G. Iggers, "Refugee Historians from Nazi Germany: Political Attitudes towards Democracy," Monna and Otto Weinmann Lecture Series, September 14, 2005, available at http://www.ushmm.org/research/center/publications/occasional/2006–02/paper.pdf. See also Hajo Holborn's presidential address to the American Historical Association, *American Historical Review*, 73, 3 (February 1968), 683–95.

[22] Catherine E. Shoichet, "Gray Matters," *Harvard Crimson*, 6/5/2003, at http://www.thecrimson.com/printerfriendly.aspx?ref=348218.

did the university, that she was a talented administrator as well as an accomplished scholar. She developed a reputation for being forceful in tight situations and was shortly lured away to a deanship at neighboring Northwestern University and then to Yale where she became in 1974 the university's first woman provost.

In Yale and most large universities, the provost is the counterpart of the COO, the chief operating officer, in a business. As COO at Yale, Provost Gray had to deal with the lingering animosities created by coeducation (as of 1969) and with a bitter strike by the school's cafeteria and maintenance employees. With that crisis behind her, she became a candidate for the presidency of the university and served as acting president for fourteen months (1977–1978).[23] But then she didn't get the appointment. The Yale Corporation was still digesting coeducation and was not prepared for that radical break with Yale's long history.[24]

The University of Chicago, favored either by a shorter history or by more open minds, offered Hannah Gray its presidency. When she accepted, Gray became in 1978 the first woman president of one of America's top-tier, coeducational research universities. Unable to avoid either controversy or challenging advancements, she encountered both in her sixteen years as Chicago's president. Sometimes the fights were over money – the university budget was in bad shape. Sometimes they were over symbolic choices. One of the latter involved an award to former Secretary of Defense Robert McNamara, who was still unable to clean off the stains left by his role in the Vietnam War. Hated by many professors, students, and the media, McNamara was a lightning rod that President Gray couldn't ignore. Digging in, she went ahead with the ceremony but then defused the crisis by bringing in a faculty group to discuss changes in the award process. She was a smart, tough administrator with a strong sense of what a research university could and should do, and when she retired, the University of Chicago was one of the model institutions in American higher education. Appointed to the Harvard Corporation in 1997, Hannah Holborn Gray no longer had to settle for "dinner with some of the girls."[25]

[23] The University of Chicago, Office of the President, History of the Office, http://president .uchicago.edu/history/gray.shtml.

[24] Yale appointed A. Bartlett Giamatti as president in 1978.

[25] The new President of Harvard University in 2007, Drew Gilpin Faust, also had a free choice of dining partners. The first woman to hold this post, Faust had compiled an outstanding record of accomplishment as a historian and as the founding dean of Radcliffe's Institute of Advanced Study.

Linda Buck's path into the professions and a distinguished career was more haphazard than Gray's. Buck's family included a mixed bag of Irish and Swedish immigrants who had finally found their way across the United States to Seattle, Washington. There, her father, who worked as an electrical engineer, taught his daughter how to use power tools. Her mother encouraged her not to settle for a "mediocre" career.[26]

The career was a problem. Seattle in 1965 still had public schools that were safe and were providing students with good educations, and Linda graduated from one of them, Roosevelt High School.[27] Armed with a vague liberal desire to help other people and her mother's admonition not to be mediocre, she entered the University of Washington, just a few miles from her home. Psychology seemed to be a way of helping others, and she settled down to get ready for a career as a psychotherapist. But that didn't take hold of her mind, and she began searching again. The search took her out of school. She traveled. She lived for a time on a nearby island in the Puget Sound. Wanderlust fulfilled, she returned to the University to take classes. But almost a decade passed before she discovered her path to a career. She took a course in immunology, and the lights suddenly turned on. Now she could chart her career: "I would be a biologist."

Graduating with majors both in psychology and microbiology, Buck was admitted to the graduate program at the Southwestern Medical Center (in Dallas) of the University of Texas. There she found a mentor – a young, prolific scientist who was also a talented teacher. Dr. Ellen Vitetta, who had received her own PhD in 1968, guided Linda into the world of advanced microbiology, a world in which highly precise techniques enabled scientists to study biological processes at the molecular level. By 1980, Linda Buck was an accomplished bench scientist and was able to continue her career as a postdoctoral researcher at Columbia University. She began to work with Dr. Richard Axel in neuroscience.[28] Fascinated

---

[26] See the autobiography at http://nobelprize.org/nobel_prizes/medicine/laureates/2004/buck-autobio.html.

[27] The high school was named for the Republican Roosevelt, TR, rather than President Franklin D. Roosevelt.

[28] Axel deserves his own biography. The son of a Jewish tailor in Brooklyn, New York (both of his parents were immigrants from Poland), Axel went to public schools in Crown Heights until he was selected to attend Stuyvesant High School in Manhattan. Taking the subway to school each day, he said, "I learned to sleep standing up." From there, he went to Columbia University and then to Johns Hopkins, where he received his MD. As devoted to New York as Buck is to Seattle, Axel returned to Columbia to teach and became a full professor in 1978. As he later explained, "The city is not a museum.

by the brain's diversity, she began to look for ways to go beyond the study of the simple organisms analyzed in microbiology.

A risk taker, Linda found at Columbia a scientific environment that encouraged her efforts to do work that was not "mediocre." In 1985, she had her second epiphany when she started to ponder how animals are able to smell. Here indeed she had a hold on a problem in diversity. Humans and other animals could distinguish between thousands of different smells. How did they do this? How does your family dog, which is much better at this than you are, separate one smell from another? Dogs and humans were not suited to laboratory study, but rats were. She was able to establish the gene basis for the rat's odor receptors, discovering that the animal had more than a hundred such unique receptors. She and Richard Axel published their path-breaking research in 1991.[29]

Buck pressed forward with this work over the following decade, working now in her own laboratory in the Harvard Medical School's Neurobiology Department. She was, in the language of the biosciences, "at the tip" in this particular branch of neuroscience. Shifting from rats to mice, she and her colleagues began to work back from the receptors to explain how the brain perceives different smells. She and Axel were following the same path of discovery, and their findings over the next decade were complementary. Now, Linda was able to explain how slight differences in an odor could be detected and how the differences were conveyed to the cortex of the brain.

While her laboratory and research in Boston were thriving, Buck still had the sort of deep-set longing for Seattle that can only be fully understood by natives of the Northwest Coast. Family and friends called her back, as did her partner, a fellow scientist who was now at the University of California in Berkeley. Rain notwithstanding, she decided to return to Seattle in 2002. She took a position at the Fred Hutchinson Cancer Research Center and was also affiliated with her alma mater, the University of Washington. Two years later, she and Richard Axel shared the Nobel Prize for scientific achievement in physiology and medicine. A Fellow of the National Academy of Sciences, Linda Buck's search had carried her from a public high school to the very peak of American medical science.[30] She and Richard Axel had helped us learn something new and important about being human.

It's dynamic, changing, and crazy. And I love it." http://www.cumc.columbia.edu/news/journal/journal-o/winter-2005/nobility.html.

[29] Linda Buck and Richard Axel "A Novel Multigene Family May Encode Odorant Receptors: A Molecular Basis for Odor Recognition," *Cell*, 65 (April 5, 1991), 175–87.

[30] Dr. Linda Buck 2004 Nobel Laureate, http://www.fhcre.org/researchnobel/buck/.

Two Americas and Two Dreams

As the millennium approached, it was increasingly clear that despite the success of the American Solution, there were actually two Americas, two variants on the American dream of progress. For all of those millions who could take advantage of the enormous educational system funneling people into the professions – people like Linda Buck, Hannah Holborn Gray, Ken Frazier, and Kurt Schmoke – the society was still creative, still changing rapidly, still generating opportunities for advancement.

The suburbs were thriving. Homeownership in America had by the end of the century reached almost unbelievable levels. The figures were unusual internationally and historically. There was no developed economy in the world that had so many urban people living in homes that they owned. The two giant quasi-governmental organizations, nicknamed Fannie and Freddie, which were providing the foundation for the mortgage industry were also doing very well, paying good dividends to the individuals who had purchased their securities. Professionals in America seemed to have entered an entirely new era in which economic opportunity came without any sacrifice of security.

The economy appeared to be strong enough to weather any storm. The recession of the early 1980s had pushed up unemployment to very high levels, and the stock market crash of 1987 had appeared to be seriously threatening for a time. But the United States had weathered both of these downturns without serious repercussions, and it was reasonable to assume that the same would be the case when the dot-com bubble began to burst in 2000. After all, this was the larger story of American capitalism, which had always progressed in a series of great cycles. Exuberance was as American as professional football.

Americans who could afford modern health care were doing well too. The first Clinton administration had proposed major changes in health care but had been unable to get them through Congress. The strongest argument against significant change was the evidence that Americans were living longer lives. Average life expectancy had increased to a record of almost seventy-seven years by the end of the century.[31] Medicine and the medical sciences were still experiencing substantial changes, and there was good reason to believe that these therapeutic and institutional innovations would continue. Even the deadly HIV virus seemed to have been brought under control by new medications. For middle-class, suburban

---

[31] U.S. Department of Health & Human Services, October 10, 2001, http://www.hhs.gov/news/press/2001pres/20011010.html.

Americans and their children – men and women, whites and blacks – the new millennium promised to be just as fruitful as the past one had been. Their version of the American dream was being realized.

In the hollowed-out central cities, the dreams and the day-to-day realities were different. Looking at what was happening in the early 1990s, one scholar concluded that suburbanization had "sucked the life out of the central cities...." Many were facing "a financial 'death spiral.'" Seen from Raymond A. Mohl's perspective, "Crime, violence, drugs, unemployment, poverty, and homelessness have plagued U.S. cities for too many years, tearing at the human fabric of urban life. Decades of neglect and physical decay have undermined the urban infrastructure.... Schooling, health care, social services, and environmental protection have deteriorated badly...."[32]

City planners looked increasingly to regional development as a solution, but these proposals met stout resistance from voters in the suburbs. The truth was that the slums of the inner cities were beyond the reach of the planners and their political supporters.[33] They could push the slums around with urban renewal, but they couldn't get rid of them. They could and did tear down the projects, but the people living in those decaying urban towers were not destined to move to the suburbs and buy a nice house surrounded by green grass. The "grass" that was most important in the inner cities was part of the drug trade that was the dominant commercial enterprise on the streets. The drug gangs were growing more and more contemptuous of police authority and in some cases had corrupted it. Gang cultures mocked all kinds of authority, whether it came from the police, the judges, or teachers. The schools were beleaguered and sadly, they were the only path into a better life for most of the children of the inner cities.

Quiet Problems

Quietly, other problems were developing for Americans, urban and suburban, in the last two decades of the century. The American Solution was boosting productivity, the best measure we have of the efficiency and competitiveness of the economy. This had been the heart of

---

[32] Raymond A. Mohl, "Shifting Patterns of American Urban Policy since 1900," in Arnold R. Hirsch and Raymond A. Mohl, eds., *Urban Policy in Twentieth-Century America* (New Brunswick, 1993), 1.

[33] Ibid., 7.

American growth over the previous hundred years. But curiously, most of the increased wealth stemming from productivity gains was going to the very wealthiest Americans. Working-class income had leveled off and stayed level. So too with middle-class income. But the hedge fund tycoons and the wealthiest CEOs, the financiers of American capitalism, were taking bigger and bigger pieces of the pie. That wasn't a significant problem so long as the economy was growing and unemployment was very low. But a sharply skewed distribution of income was leaving the economy increasingly vulnerable to a downturn that could potentially impact all classes of Americans.

Equally ominous were the declines in American enrollment in those colleges and universities that were essential to American science and engineering. Fortunately, the shortage was being made up by immigrants, many of whom remained in the United States after they finished their educations. But that was another quiet change that was leaving the United States vulnerable to anything that might prevent foreign students from coming to America to study. There were official concerns about this situation. But nervousness seldom leads to forceful political responses. The problem was identified and then largely ignored.

By 2001, America was vulnerable on several fronts, but one of the nation's most trusted experts, Alan Greenspan atop the Federal Reserve System, assured the country that all would be well, that the prosperity for which so many Americans had sacrificed would continue and with it the American dream. Confident in Greenspan's judgment, I headed off with my family to Italy in August 2001 to enjoy a quiet semester teaching in beautiful Florence.

18

The Creative Society in Danger

Having worked hard for many years to become a better historian, it's difficult to try to become an adequate journalist. You can't avoid doing that, however, when you start to write about current events.[1] There is no way to stay clear of the heightened emotions, the lack of accurate information, and the flood of media evaluations concerning the nation's policies and leaders.[2] The historian loses the advantage of knowing what the endgame is. The history of the Cold War certainly looked different in 2001 than it did in 1981. But given that all of the major themes of this book have come into play in the last few tumultuous years, we can't avoid this brief venture into the recent past and into the lives of some more American professionals. In an effort to compensate for the loss of perspective, I'll try to place recent events against the historical template developed in the previous chapters. Maybe that will help.

The W Factor

When George W. Bush took office in 2001, he was riding the wave of a conservative movement that had exercised substantial power in America for almost half a century. You might date the conservative era from 1946, but I believe a more decisive move to the right came with the

---

[1] Further reading in this case would include Bob Woodward's *Bush at War* (New York, 2002), *Plan of Attack* (New York, 2004); *State of Denial* (2006); and *The War Within: A Secret White House History, 2006–2008* (New York, 2008).

[2] If you're thinking that this imaginary line may have been crossed in earlier chapters, you are probably right. Odds are that you are an experienced professional and should be commended for also being a thoughtful reader.

election of President Eisenhower in 1952. After Ike, the conservative reign was disrupted by the assassination of President Kennedy and the political changes that flowed from that catastrophic event. But the nation soon veered back into conservative territory. Rhetoric aside, the United States has remained basically conservative since that time. Even the 2008 presidential election was not really fought over a liberal-conservative divide. Both of the major candidates worked hard to stay close to the middle of an American political spectrum heavily weighted toward moderation.[3]

After 1981, as we've seen, a big gap had emerged between the rhetoric and realities of conservative governance. Public spending had continued to grow and to become a larger part of the total national economy between 1981 and 1993.[4] For much of the time, tax cuts had produced predictable deficits that were funded using debt. The desire for new government services and financial support had kept conservatives from honoring Reagan's promise to "curb the size and influence of the Federal establishment." At best, conservatives had been able to slow the rate of growth in some selected parts of the federal and state governments by 1993.[5]

The two administrations of George W. Bush – the first MBA to hold that position – fit comfortably in this version of conservatism. The Bush rhetoric harkened less to Reagan than it did to Eisenhower's "Middle Way." Bush announced "a new commitment to live out our nation's promise through civility, courage, compassion and character." Alliteration aside, compassion was an important theme in the initial media image in large part because it provided a counterpoint to the harsh American Solution still being worked out in the private sector. Instead of creative destruction, the administration would with compassion confront America's "deep, persistent poverty," the "proliferation of prisons," and "children at risk." "Government," Bush said, "has great responsibilities for public safety and public health, for civil rights and common schools."[6]

Compassion along these lines turned out to be expensive. In 2003, the Bush administration and Congress added drug benefits to Medicare, with

---

[3] We will discuss the 2008 election later in this chapter.

[4] Under Clinton, government expenditures had continued to grow at about the same pace as they had during the years 1981–1991, but the entire economy was growing much faster. By 2001, the role of all government had decline from 23.05% of U.S. national income to 20%.

[5] Ballard C. Campbell, *The Growth of American Government*, 229.

[6] The speech is available at http://www.whitehouse.gov/news/print/inaugural-address. html.

an initial price tag of $395 billion. Since that time, the estimates have gone up significantly. The problems of increasing drug costs and an aging population were real. Private insurance was not filling this gap, and there were many millions who were not covered by any medical insurance.[7] As had been the case in the previous two decades, conservative ideology yielded to the realities of American democracy.

This was also the case with the government's powerful intrusion into local education through the new policy of "No Child Left Behind" (NCLB, 2002) and of standardized exams.[8] In education, most of the costs continued to be borne by local and state governments, but NCLB (or "Nickelbee") increased federal support for local education. In education as in health care, the price tag on compassion turned out to be high.

That was especially important because the White House was trying to achieve these lofty goals while also using tax cuts in an effort to rein in government spending and encourage economic growth.[9] The resulting fiscal policy was successful politically but a failure economically, as was the case during the previous two decades. The demand for services and government support was strong, the interests accustomed to federal subsidies were well organized, and the political pressure on Congress was too intense to allow the cuts in spending that the administration and its conservative economists wanted. Instead of a Chicago School solution, America continued to implement policies consistent with the economics of the late John Maynard Keynes.

In practice, it was hard to distinguish between compassionate conservatism and moderate American liberalism of the post-New Deal variety. Even though "liberalism" had become a negative political label, Americans from 1980 to the present had continued to look to government for new services and support. Instead of an epochal battle between the market and government, America unfurled a conservative banner, announced conservative goals, and marched off slightly to the left of center. The march was led by the professional experts who've played a central role in this account of modern American history. The U.S. political environment

---

7 The number of Americans, including noncitizens, not covered by any form of medical insurance is probably more than 45 million. The figures are debated, but the most reliable account is *National Health Statistics Reports*, 1 (June 19, 2008), available at http://www.cdc.gov/nchs/data/nhsr/nhsr001.pdf.
8 The exams were standardized at the state level.
9 This approach resembled the policies of the Reagan administration, which had adopted a similar fiscal strategy (as noted in Chapter 15).

at all levels was now densely packed with expertise. Many of the experts had long been ensconced in the bureaucracy. Others rode into town with each new administration. Their ranks in 2001 included a number of neoconservatives, the "neocons," who had strong ideas about domestic policies, especially those dealing with welfare and regulation. They also had strong ideas about the American empire.

The Hegemony Trap Closes

One of the important reasons that domestic policy in the Bush era didn't change more radically than it did was the administration's turn to new, more aggressive policies toward the U.S. empire. When Bush took office in January 2001, he was handed a full measure of issues carried over from the Clinton administration. But neither Clinton nor his predecessor had left the United States in the hegemony trap (on the trap, see Chapter 16). It appeared at first that the new President would also stay out. "We will build our defenses beyond challenge," Bush told Americans, "lest weakness invite challenge. We will confront weapons of mass destruction, so that a new century is spared new horrors. The enemies of liberty and our country should make no mistake: America remains engaged in the world by history and by choice, shaping a balance of power that favors freedom."[10] The policy of "shaping a balance of power" and sparing the world "new horrors" suggested that the Bush administration would use its overwhelming military power much as Clinton and Bush's father had.

One indication of President George Bush's intent was his appointment of Colin L. Powell as Secretary of State – the first African American to hold that leading position in the Cabinet. Powell's popularity was reflected in the unanimous vote his appointment received in the Senate. He quickly made his own objectives clear. In the Middle East, he would try to get out of the "cycle of violence, provocation and reaction. . . . We are deeply engaged on a daily basis," he said, "in trying to lower the level of violence and to restore a measure of trust between the two sides." Then, he hoped, they would be able "to move back to negotiations, the negotiations that are so vitally necessary to achieve a lasting peace and a permanent solution." In Iraq, "we are going to work with the United Nations and our Arab friends to revise the sanctions policy, so that it is directed exclusively at preventing Iraq from a military buildup and developing weapons of

[10] "First Inaugural Address," January 20, 2001, available on www.americanrhetoric.com/speeches/gwbfirstinaugural.htm.

mass destruction. . . . " [11] In August of 2001, Powell looked forward to "a future of loving one another, a future of friendship, a future where you can take advantage of the wonderful opportunities that the twenty-first century holds." [12]

A few weeks later, friendship and love gave way to violence. Powell and the White House were suddenly thrown into the trap when terrorist hijackers flew two commercial jets into the World Trade Center in New York City. Thousands of Americans, most of them civilians, died in the attacks that destroyed the twin towers. A similar attack on the Pentagon followed, and a fourth attack was thwarted, but the hijacked plane crashed and all its passengers died. [13]

I saw these events in kaleidoscopic style, viewed from Italy, where I was teaching and managing a small Johns Hopkins educational program. For a time, communication with the United States was almost impossible because so many people in Italy were placing long-distance calls. The circuits were overloaded. Learning finally that my family in America was safe, I could turn my attention to the safety of my charges – my wife, two young daughters, and the Hopkins graduate and undergraduate students in Florence. The U.S. State Department issued calming messages, accompanied by frightening warnings not to wear U.S. sweatshirts or go to American movies or otherwise identify yourself on the street as an American. For a few weeks, chaos and misinformation reigned. We were caught up for a time in national mourning, but then gradually everything settled down. Despite the beginnings of a new war in the Middle East, the students got back to learning Italian, and I was able to resume higher education in history.

The terror of September 11, 2001 prompted a quick and powerful military response by the United States and Britain. Support for the al-Qaeda terrorists and their leader Osama bin Laden was being provided by the Taliban regime in Afghanistan, and that was where the joint U.S.-UK bombing attacks began. [14] Ground operations followed, with the bulk of the foreign troops coming from America. Once the U.S. and allied forces

---

[11] Speech to the Arab American Institute Foundation, May 5, 2001, available at www .state.gov/secretary/former/powell/remarks/2001/2741.htm.

[12] Speech to the Seeds of Peace, August 14, 2001, available at www.state.gov/secretary/ former/powell/remarks/2001/4545.htm.

[13] The fourth plane, perhaps sent to hit the White House, crashed when the passengers attacked the hijackers.

[14] Bob Woodward of the *Washington Post* provides an exciting blow-by-blow, day-by-day account of the decision to strike in Afghanistan in *Bush at War*.

had driven the Taliban out of power, the Afghan operation became a NATO military occupation designed to stabilize a new regime.[15] To this point, at least, the Afghan phase of antiterrorism closely resembled the first Gulf War of 1990–1991: both had limited objectives, considerable international support, and the backing of the United Nations.

Then, however, the Bush administration jumped feet first into the trap. In 2003, the United States launched an attack aimed at overthrowing Iraq's brutal dictator, Saddam Hussein, and creating a government that would be friendly to U.S. goals in the region, unfriendly to Islamic terrorists, and perhaps become a peaceful, successful democracy or democratic federation.[16] Iraq was supposedly supporting al-Qaeda and was said to be developing, or perhaps had already developed, weapons of mass destruction. The evidence for these two charges appeared to be suspiciously thin. But the memory of 9/11 was strong and the powerful winds of nationalism swirled into the fold many Americans who would later regret their support for the war.[17] The U.S. Congress went along with the president, even though the administration's goals in Iraq were unrealistically ambitious. Now the international support, even from the start, was narrow.[18] The United States no longer had the backing of the United Nations. As the UN Secretary General said, "I have indicated it was not in conformity with the U.N. charter. From our point of view, from the charter point of view, it was illegal."[19]

Even more telling than the opposition of the UN's Kofi Annan was the wavering support and finally the disapproval of the one person in the administration best qualified to judge this radical course of action. Secretary of State Powell argued within the White House against an invasion.

[15] The NATO resolution, which stated that 9/11 was an attack on the treaty organization, preceded the military action, as did the UN's initial statement of a position on the terrorist attack and response.

[16] As Bob Woodward carefully notes, both Donald Rumsfeld and Paul Wolfowitz of the Department of Defense were in favor of striking at Iraq when Bush and his national security advisors were initially discussing how to respond to the 9/11 attacks. *Bush at War*, 49, 60–61, 81m, 83–84.

[17] Hillary Clinton later found it difficult to explain her 2002 vote in favor of the war in Iraq. See, for instance, http://www.huffingtonpost.com/2008/01/13/hillary-clinton-defends-2_n_81261.html?view.

[18] In addition to the United Kingdom, thirty-nine other nations initially provided some measure of support for the invasion. The bulk of the forces were, throughout, provided by Britain and America – especially the United States.

[19] *BBC News*, http://news.bbc.co.uk/go/pr/fr/-/1/hi/world/middle_east/3661134.stm. *World Press Review*, http://www.worldpress.org/specials/iraq/. *The Guardian* September 16, 2004, at http://www.commondreams.org/headlines04/0916-01.htm.

Containment, he contended, was the best approach to Saddam Hussein's regime.[20] Powell's hand was the surest, most experienced in the administration. But he lost that internal debate as President Bush turned toward more belligerent advice from Vice President Cheney, the Defense Department, and the intelligence services, including the CIA. Consensus quickly supplanted discourse. Powell resigned in 2004, and the influence of the neocon advisors sharply increased.[21]

The neocons wanted to demonstrate American power and consolidate the Middle Eastern corner of the empire. Certain of their realist mix of ideology and strategy, they won control of foreign policy in the Bush administration. Like the popular journalist Tom Friedman, the neocons thought they had the correct vision of America's role in the world. The neocons wanted to establish that role by overwhelming military force, and at first it appeared they might be right.[22] The war was short and the casualties limited.

But the postwar efforts to produce a client state that was stable, peaceful, and friendly to the United States and the United Kingdom were prolonged, deadly, and expensive. As of the publication of this book, they are still not over. No longer satisfied to support democracy by example, the United States was charting a new course, seeking "the expansion of freedom in all the world. . . . " As President Bush explained, "it is the policy of the United States to seek and support the growth of democratic movements and institutions in every nation and culture, with the ultimate goal of ending tyranny in our world. All who live in tyranny and hopelessness can know: the United States will not ignore your oppression, or excuse your oppressors. When you stand for your liberty, we will stand with you."[23]

---

[20] Associate Press, August 11, 2003, "Powell's Case for Iraq War Falls Apart 6 Months Later," at http://www.commondreams.org/cgi-bin/print.cgi?file=/headlineso3/0811–09 .htm. *CBS News*, February 4, 2004, "The Man Who Knew," at http://www.cbsnews. com/stories/2003/10/14/60II/main577975.shtml. *The Sunday Times*, July 8, 2007, at http://www.timesonline.co.uk/tol/news/world/us_americas/article2042072.ece?pring=.

[21] The early development of neoconservatism is discussed briefly in Bruce J. Schulman and Julian E. Zelizer, eds., *Rightward Bound: Making American Conservative in the 1970s* (Cambridge, 2008). For more detail, see Alan Weisman's *Prince of Darkness: Richard Perle: The Kingdom, the Power, and the End of Empire in America* (New York, 2007).

[22] Those who might think I'm being too harsh with Friedman should look again at the cover of the *New York Times Magazine* on March 28, 1999, which featured a fist painted with the American flag. This, the cover said was "What the world needs now. For globalism to work, America can't be afraid to act like the almighty superpower that it is."

[23] President Bush's second inaugural address, January 20, 2005. Available at www.npr .org/templates/story/story.php?storyId=4460172.

After years of military struggles, many Americans had decided by 2008 that this particular border of the empire could probably be abandoned – just as the United States had long ago abandoned Vietnam, and before that revolutionary China, and before that the revolution in Russia.[24] The cost was too high in dollars and lives – especially the latter. Our position in the world was weakened and the war budgets had made it impossible for the government to address other problems, including those created by the growing numbers of citizens without health care insurance.[25] Counterterrorism was also impinging on some of America's important science and engineering programs by choking off the flow of talented students to the United States.[26] As the ripples from the Iraq War spread through the society, they produced effects that would be felt for many decades. The link to American values, the idealist position, had been lost when the United States decided to launch the invasion. It could not be regained now by rhetoric about democracy and freedom.

A "true bill" on the war would also include the first significant tarnish since World War II on the reputations of the nation's military officers. As we've seen in the previous chapters, the military had produced a number of outstanding American leaders, including one president. But now, for the first time, corruption charges against military officers responsible for big-budget items in Iraq started popping up in the news. I've long contended that since 1900, military professionals were one of the few groups of Americans to achieve substantial power in society without experiencing an initial wave of corruption. My assumption was that the values instilled in the service academies and reinforced during the officers' careers were responsible for that achievement. But now, while awaiting the disposition of some of the cases, I've had to qualify that evaluation.[27]

---

[24] Jonathan Freedland, "Bush's Amazing Achievement," *New York Review of Books*, 54, 10 (June 14, 2007) probably exaggerates the extent of the "near consensus among those who study international affairs" that the invasion of Iraq is a "calamity." But the author is not far from the mark.

[25] The figure for those without health insurance was probably more than 45 million by 2007.

[26] The National Academy of Sciences, National Academy of Engineering, and the Institute of Medicine, *Rising Above the Gathering Storm: Energizing and Employing America for a Brighter Economic Future* (Washington, 2005). National Research Council of the National Academies, *International Benchmarking of U.S. Chemical Engineering Research Competitiveness* (Washington, 2007).

[27] United States Attorney Southern District of New York, "U.S. Army Officer Arrested . . . ," November 20, 2007. James Glanz, et al, "Inquiry on Graft in Iraq Focuses on U.S. Officers," *New York Times*, February 15, 2009. Courtesy of Lyric Wallwork Winik, Congressional Budget Office, "News Conference Re Contractor Costs for the War in Iraq," August 12, 2008. Senate Democratic Policy Committee. "Hearing: An

Hubris and the Market Economy – All over Again

As war in the Middle East ground ahead, the United States suffered a crippling blow at home. From the Carter administration through George W. Bush's presidency, the United States had gradually weakened the hand of government and strengthened reliance on markets.[28] Reality had fallen short of the rhetoric, as we've seen, but the direction of change in the regulatory state was clear. Like the welfare state, the regulatory state had been pared down while the U.S. economy was growing and changing in response to the combined forces of globalization and the third industrial revolution. New institutions, like hedge funds, emerged as major players in the U.S. economy. New financial instruments called derivatives became important.[29] By 2007, well over $3 trillion in derivatives and foreign exchange was being bought and sold *every day*.

Most Americans had at best a vague idea of what a derivative was or how exactly a hedge fund really made money. There was a widening intellectual gap between the professional money managers and the public. But the gap didn't seem to matter as long as the economy was growing, new jobs were being created, and mutual funds were reporting good results. The experts at the Federal Reserve and the professionals, including the so-called "quants," who were in the saddle at many of the financial institutions, were doing well for themselves and for all those Americans who had any money to invest.[30] Retirement funds were a very large and growing part of America's wealth.

These astonishing changes in the economy continued to funnel money into the bank accounts of hedge-fund managers, CEOs of multinational firms, and many other leading players in the world of finance. New York's role in the global financial turnover was exceeded only by London's.[31] Profits were immense, and the annual pay plus bonuses for the top 1

Inside View of the "Second Insurgency. How Corruption and Waste are Undermining the U.S. Mission in Iraq," September 25, 2008.

[28] Deregulation and privatization in federal, state, and local government had gradually shifted the balance from public to private authority, from government to the markets that now exercised control of these economic institutions. Regulatory neglect and inefficiency had somewhat the same impact in some cases.

[29] Derivatives are simply securities that derive their value from something else. It could be the price of oil or steel or measures of the stock market's performance. They are used frequently as "futures" to hedge against changes in the markets.

[30] The "quants," many of them economists or mathematicians, are experts who use sophisticated quantitative models to guide their investments.

[31] The British economy had made a rather surprising recovery on the basis of its ability in global finance.

percent of Americans were stunning. The distribution of income and wealth was tilted more and more toward the top, toward the wealthiest Americans.[32] The country was crawling farther and farther out on an economic limb that was getting dangerously thin.

There were several fiscal tremors that could have warned the experts about what was coming. When the hedge fund Long Term Capital Management and its Nobel Prize winners collapsed at the end of the 1990s, regulators should have started asking serious questions about the "quants" and the role of their funds in the economy. There had also been a scare when the dot-com bubble popped in 2000 and 2001. But that bad news was brushed off when the stock market recovered relatively quickly. The collapse exposed some corruption that might also have raised serious questions about the regulatory system, but those signals were ignored.[33] The next warning came from Texas, where the giant Enron Company went under and brought to light significant weaknesses in corporate governance, the nation's accounting practices, and the federal regulatory watchdogs.[34] Nor was Enron the only American corporation involved in corrupt practices. From 2001 to the present day, indictments have flowed out of grand juries in impressive spurts, all over the country. Hardly a month went by for several years without new pictures of men in pin-striped suits wearing handcuffs, taking their "perp walk" in the company of police officers and television crews.[35]

The U.S. Congress once again produced its own share of corrupt and corrupting politicians. There was a major lobbying scandal that brought down some distinguished lawmakers and tarnished the reputations of many others. The congressional Republicans made disgraceful use of the "earmark" privilege to reward constituents and financial supporters. Democrats were, of course, happy to join in this fiscal charade – with renewed vigor after they retook control of Congress in 2006.

[32] In addition to Richard B. Freeman, *America Works*, 41–57, see G. Ross Stephens, "Public Policy, Income Distribution, and Class Warfare," Berkeley Electronic Press, 2009.

[33] John Kenneth Galbraith's charming account of the "bezzle," the total amount of money embezzled at any one time, provides an appropriate analysis for some of these tawdry events. *The Great Crash, 1929* (Boston, 1954).

[34] Christopher L. Culp and Steve H. Hanke, "Empire of the Sun: An Economic Interpretation of Enron's Energy Business," *Policy Analysis*, 470 (February 20, 2003), 1–19. Paul M. Healy and Krishna G. Palepu, "The Fall of Enron," *Journal of Economic Perspectives*, 17, 2 (Spring 2003), 3–26.

[35] The reference is to a "perpetrator," one charged with a crime. These "walks" were clearly staged for TV coverage by the officers conducting the arrests. My guess is that they have had some impact on those contemplating similar crimes, but I have no evidence of this.

Were we being forced to live once again through the Gilded Age of the late nineteenth century? Yes and no. Yes, there were similarities insofar as the economy, the business system, and many of America's largest firms had once again outgrown the regulatory state. Once again, hubris was at work, convincing many corporate leaders that they were beyond the law. But in the early twenty-first century, the corporate corruption took place in a much larger national economy with a far more powerful government. New regulations and prison terms followed quickly and seemed to clear the air. Little public action of that sort had taken place in the Gilded Age.

But then, suddenly, a third major crisis roared through the nation. This one threatened to break that thin branch on which we were sitting and send America tumbling into a Great Depression like the 1930s. Now America got to see up close the other side of the flexibility coin. The same type of entrepreneurship that had produced the "high-risk securities" – that is, the junk bonds of the successful turnaround of the 1980s and 1990s – also produced the subprime mortgages and securitized mortgage packages that triggered the nation's current economic dilemma. There are plenty of leaders, experts, and institutions to blame. They include the legislators who urged Fannie Mae and Freddie Mac to push subprime mortgages and extend homeownership to millions of Americans who had not been able to buy their own homes. We should also add to the lineup the well-paid professionals who led those agencies and the even better-paid executives of the nation's banks. They followed the leader and marched their organizations toward and sometimes into bankruptcy. Their decisions were vetted by the professional risk managers who got paid to keep businesses out of trouble. What about the mortgage brokers and the individuals who put their signatures on dangerous mortgages? Yes, they get some blame too.

The result was a major recession that has spread through the global economy and left many Americans uncertain about their immediate futures. Retirement and college-savings funds took severe hits. Unemployment shot up, along with bankruptcies. This was not an unprecedented series of events. In retrospect, we can see that the United States had simply stayed on its traditional course, once again trading economic security for financial innovation.

Although the specter of the Great Depression won't go away, the contrast between 1931 (where you began reading in this history) and 2009 should be reassuring. In 2008 and 2009, the U.S. government moved far more decisively than it did in the 1930s. The government cooperated with other nations, and all were guided by leaders with a far better understanding of the economy than any of the experts in the 1930s. This didn't guarantee success. But it made it much more likely. It wasn't certain that the multibillion-dollar stimulus packages would promote recovery – a good subject for another book – but we can be certain that a more equitable distribution of income and wealth would have made the economy less vulnerable than it was by the end of the Bush presidency. One hopes the Washington experts will notice that as well.

The American Response

Have the financial crisis and the latest war on the fringes of the empire squeezed the creativity out of America? No. This is a large, complex society with a broad institutional base supporting the professions and encouraging change. Markets still clear and the turnaround specialists are still cleaning out the worst failures and sprucing up the organizations that can be saved. In the midst of great uncertainty, there are plenty of signs that this is still a creative society – one that learns from the past and continues to be flexible, a society with tremendous resources and a determination to use them to solve problems of the sort we've been discussing.

Even cities like Baltimore haven't given up, for instance, on the struggle to improve their school systems and widen the path to the middle class. Baltimore recently acquired new educational leadership from a chief executive officer with experience in the much larger system in New York City. Recognizing what had to be done to achieve significant reform, Andres Alonzo made a frontal attack on the combine that had defeated Baltimore's Mayor Schmoke. Alonzo started by introducing major changes in the school administration and in the planning time for teachers. The city teachers union screamed in protest. Drawing a line on the asphalt, the union launched a series of skirmishes over issues large and small. The union brought out big guns from the American Federation of Teachers and put people in the street chanting "Alonzo Must Go!" This is a miniature power struggle with major implications for cities like Baltimore, for African Americans, for Latinos, and especially for their children. The combine opposed to change could not have done a better job of defining their role in the urban school crisis I've been describing.[36]

---

[36] See, for instance, the *Baltimore Sun*, October 2, 10, and 18, 2007; also August 13, 2008.

Is there hope, then, for public education in a city like Baltimore? St. Louis? Chicago? New York? Boston? Los Angeles? Yes, a creative American solution is still feasible and certainly desirable. But leaders like Alonzo will have to win their battles and that struggle is likely to continue for many years. The most recent national program, No Child Left Behind, has not changed the local trench warfare required to transform these large school systems with their bureaucratic roots deeply planted in ethnic soil. In Baltimore, Andres Alonzo recently stepped up his campaign against the opponents of change. Schools that can't make it are being closed. More administrative fat is being boiled out of the system.[37] This is a war, not just a battle, so the outcome will have to wait for another history to be written.[38]

Fortunately, school reform is also getting growing support from the charter schools, which are another encouraging response to the crisis of urban public education.[39] Some charter schools fail and others don't do better than the public schools, but they still represent unusual opportunities for educators to experiment with new approaches to this crucial aspect of inner-city life. Obviously, the troubled urban systems need higher levels of innovation. Stasis equals failure.

Consider for a brief moment what has been accomplished in Baltimore and elsewhere by the KIPP schools. KIPP – that is, the Knowledge Is Power Program – is national in scope, and the schools are scattered over the entire country, from Lynn, Massachusetts, to Minneapolis, Minnesota, to San Antonio, Texas, and to San Jose and Los Angeles, California. KIPP is one of the most successful of the many recent experiments in dealing with the cultural, social, and intellectual problems of the inner cities.

KIPP is admired by many school administrators, public and private, black and white. One of them is a daughter of mine, who has her doctorate in education from Columbia University, where the KIPP idea originated.

---

[37] *Baltimore Sun*, March 11, 2009.

[38] The struggles can be followed in the pages of the *Baltimore Sun*. See, for instance, the articles on September 19; November 17; and November 18, 2010. The latter issue reported on a new, breakthrough union contract that linked evaluations of city teachers with student performance.

[39] Charter schools are either private or private/public organizations with specific charters from their cities and school districts. Because on a day-to-day basis they operate outside the urban structure of political authority, they have an opportunity to be more flexible than most public schools. From time to time, the charter schools have had to fight for their opportunity to introduce innovations. See, for instance, the editorial "Union Orders," *Wall Street Journal*, October 12, 2007, A16.

Dr. Jennifer Galambos lauds the KIPP strategy of creating a highly disciplined, middle-school environment, one in which teachers are actually available for consultation in the evenings and the school program in effect becomes an extension of the family.[40]

Dr. Galambos, who is director of Bryn Mawr Middle School in Baltimore, believes these schools work where others fail in part because of their strong emphasis on values. KIPP's students wear uniforms and get rewards for classroom achievement.[41] The goal is specific: a college or university education. To date, KIPP schools have sent almost 80 percent of their eighth-grade graduates on to higher education, a truly astonishing record of accomplishment.

The KIPP strategy has, of course, aroused controversy. The schools are "drill and skill" oriented, with a highly structured daily program that's longer than the normal public school day. The general drift of American education has been away from this sort of structure and rote learning, which makes KIPP unpopular with some educators. Many other charter schools give greater emphasis than KIPP does to community involvement. But the counterargument is powerful: KIPP has a track record. KIPP is successful in getting inner-city kids on the path to the professions. From my historical perspective, KIPP and the other charter schools are the best sign we have that this is still a creative society, still a society that hasn't given up – even on its struggling cities.

Will that last? The challenges of the nation's current financial crisis, the concerns about a rapidly growing China, and the anxiety about competition from India are all unsettling. So too is the development of a larger, more consolidated European Union that is allied with America but increasingly mindful of its own interests – interests that frequently diverge from those of the United States. Will America be able to cope with these challenges and consolidate its own free-market area in the Western Hemisphere? Will the country be able to absorb the additional millions

---

[40] Forty-eight of the fifty-seven KIPP public schools are middle schools (fifth through eighth grade). For a list of all the KIPP schools, go to http://www.kipp.org/09/schools/list.cfm. Recently, the union in Baltimore has launched a new attack on the KIPP schools, bringing their future into doubt. The war goes on.

[41] According to KIPP's publications, more than 90% of their students are either African American or Hispanic/Latino, and the overwhelming majority comes from low-income families. http://www.kipp.org/01/. Because I know her mother, I was able to interview one of the outstanding students from the KIPP school in Baltimore: Shanika Paul, who is finishing this year, has received a full scholarship to an excellent boarding school in Massachusetts, where she will continue her education next fall.

who will immigrate from Central and South America if economic consolidation of the Western Hemisphere is realized? That will depend on whether Americans, their institutions, their professionals, and their political leaders continue to be as flexible and innovative in the future as they have been in the past. If Americans can balance security and equity with their traditional tolerance for the negative aspects of creative destruction, the future remains bright. But there will be many difficult political choices to make – just as there were in the years immediately following World War II.

The Japanese are Coming

Before World War II ended, there were wild fears in Southern Indiana that Japanese airplanes were going to fly across the Pacific Ocean, pass over Los Angeles and the Rocky Mountains, and target little towns like Princeton. To prepare, the Boy Scouts covered their flashlights with red cloth and tramped around in the dark, conducting idiotic air-raid drills. Having accumulated knowledge from the many comic books that dealt with the war, the Scouts marched around in the dark and had heroic thoughts about what they would do when the enemy arrived in Princeton.

Well, it finally happened. In 1998, the Japanese arrived. But they came in peace to provide Princeton with a brand-new, billion-dollar Toyota factory. On the south side of the town, along the road that passed by my former home, Toyota built a plant that now manufactures minivans and SUVs and is the town's largest employer. Princeton, Indiana, has joined the global economy. The city's population has increased and until the recession, local businesses in the county were thriving. No longer entirely dependent upon coal mines or crops, Princeton's future looks different than it did twenty years ago, and it now looks bright. Towns like Fostoria, Ohio (which we visited in the first chapter), are still shrinking, left behind as America becomes a nation of megacities and suburbs. But as Princeton illustrates, even the smallest towns can be transformed by the powerful forces of the global economy.[42]

Not all the economic changes have been kind to Princeton. The town has followed the pattern of big cities like Detroit and experienced hollowing out as the suburbs and shopping centers expanded. New homes are being built outside of the town and many of the store fronts downtown

---

[42] *Evansville Courier Press*, June 11, 2008.

are empty. But given a choice between hollowing and shrinking, Princeton and Gibson County appear to have opted for growth in whatever form it takes. That too is a typical American solution.

Much has changed in Princeton, but the political climate remains almost as conservative as it was when I lived there. In the 2008 election, the vote in Princeton's county (Gibson) was 8,449 for John McCain and 6,455 for Barack Obama. The stunning news is that more than 6,000 people in Gibson County actually voted for an African-American president.[43] I don't know whether my former coworker at the grocery store, Caledonia, is still alive, but wherever he is, he must have been smiling. Especially when he learned that the state of Indiana broke a forty-year tradition and went for the Democratic candidate. Obama's victory in Ohio was important but more predictable. Indiana's vote was an astonishing change in a state that had once been a breeding ground for the Ku Klux Klan.

What better measure of America's capacity for creativity than the election of the nation's first black president? We began this history when the country's presidents were unconcerned about discrimination against African Americans, about lynchings, about an educational system that made it almost impossible for black Americans to get ahead. Now Barack Obama was freely and fairly elected to the nation's highest office. Given the war in the Middle East, the collapse of President Bush's support, and the devastating recession, a Democratic victory was perhaps predictable. But *not* the victory of an African American.

Obama was born in 1961, the year when another young American, John Fitzgerald Kennedy, became President. Unlike Kennedy, Obama didn't come from a wealthy family with strong political connections. But Obama was able to get on the educational path to the professions, and he excelled. His route into the professions, like his family background, was unusual, but his performance was just what we would expect from a literate high achiever. Able to transfer from Occidental College in Los Angeles to Columbia University in New York, Obama graduated in 1983 with a degree in political science. Searching for his niche, he settled into community work in Chicago. Returning to school, he entered the Harvard Law School where he was phenomenally successful and became the first African-American president of the *Law Review*. Returning to Chicago, Obama taught, practiced law, and was active in a large number of civil rights and community social work programs. His first elective position

---

[43] The numbers here are courtesy of Travis Neff, who writes for the local newspaper, the *Princeton Daily Clarion*.

(1996) was to the Illinois Senate, where he served until 2004, when he won his campaign for the U.S. Senate.

Obama's presidential victories – first in an extended primary campaign and then in the general election – were the personal triumphs of a charismatic speaker and a shrewd politician. He wisely positioned himself to seize the leading issue of the day, the nation's economic turmoil, and was able to fend off charges that his policies would pull the government sharply to the left, out of the moderate middle way. Voters were less concerned about his race and his questionable association with a radical black pastor than they were with his obvious interest in helping them cope with economic insecurity.

As important for this history as Barack Obama's personal victory was the social accomplishment, the triumph for American democracy, achieved in the 2008 election. It had been only a few decades since African-American leaders had been honored to meet with President Eisenhower in the White House. Now, in January 2009, a black man was inaugurated as the forty-fourth President of the United States. The social transformation that had been the dream of W. E. B. DuBois and Martin Luther King, Jr. hadn't become the reality of the twenty-first century, but Obama's election was a significant benchmark of progress. And it's important to recognize that Obama heads a phalanx of talented women and minorities that are changing politics in America. Look around and you can see what Governor Bill Richardson (Hispanic American) has accomplished in New Mexico, what women like Governor Chris Greggoire (Washington) are doing to change American politics, what Mayor Antonio Villaraigosa (Hispanic American) has done in Los Angeles, and what Governor Piyush "Bobby" Jindal (Indian American) is doing in Louisiana.

A twenty-first-century, expanded form of the talented tenth has arrived in a manner that Du Bois could never have imagined. They're charting a new course, one suggesting that America will eventually provide true equality for all of the nation's ethnic minorities and for women as well as men. This was the promise of Obama's inauguration and the appropriate symbol of a century of progress. For a few days, at least, Americans could look away from the nation's economic crisis and enjoy the euphoria of the election.

In office, Obama is confronted by the four problems we've discussed in these pages. He has to help the nation solve its current financial problems without destroying its ability to remain the world's most creative and efficient economy. The struggle to ensure equity and security for the

American people is far from over, and that ongoing process is taking place in a global economy that places ever greater emphasis on efficiency and innovation. In foreign affairs, President Obama will have to establish a new balance between realism and idealism without endangering America's national security. He will be tempted, as all of our modern leaders have been, to ignore the country's democratic values. There will be advisors who promote clandestine operations in an effort to avoid public criticism and debate. The President and his advisors will need to rethink the U.S. empire, both its ends as well as its means.

The fourth problem isn't on the first page of the new president's agenda. But from the perspective of this history, his greatest challenge may involve finding new and successful ways to help the struggling cities where most of us now live. Many of the urban problems, especially the problems in education, can only be solved through local and state governments and through private, creative initiatives like the KIPP schools. But local innovators will need the leadership and support of President Barack Obama, who will certainly want to ensure that women and minority children will all have the opportunity to follow his path to success.

Acknowledgments

A proper acknowledgement would include the names of all my university students, undergraduate and graduate, from Rice, Rutgers, Yale, and Johns Hopkins. To do the job correctly, I would also have to list all of the colleagues who have helped me change my perspectives on American history, colleagues here and abroad, colleagues in the programs where I have held fellowships, and all those who have presented papers in the seminars at Johns Hopkins since the 1960s. Clearly I can't do that even if my editor would allow it. So this general statement of thanks will have to suffice.

My family deserves a great deal of credit too, and with that in mind, I've dedicated this book to my four daughters: Denise, Jennifer, Katherine, and Emma. They put up with a great deal while I was researching and writing this history, and they contributed more ideas than they will ever know to the finished product.

There would not have been a product if I didn't have a talented editor at Cambridge University Press. Frank Smith has worked with me, my students, and academic colleagues on many books, all of which he has improved as they moved through the editorial process. His good judgment and experience came into play as the book was being written, published, and marketed. He and fellow historian Angus Burgin kept me from adding an Epilogue on the years 2009–2010 that would, I could finally see, have quickly dated this account. At Cambridge, Emily Spangler and Eric Crahan presided over the publication process and I am indebted to them for their skillful and prompt efforts on my behalf. Cathy Felgar guided the manuscript through production, and I would like to thank her, her colleagues, and Kenneth Karpinski (Aptara, Inc.) for their vigorous efforts to get this book published.

Over the years, I benefitted by having a number of excellent research associates. They included Jill Friedman, Amanda Herbert, Patti Li, and Jessica Ziparo. All of them gave me editorial advice as well as research assistance, and I owe them large debts for their energy, intelligence, and, above all, their good judgment.

Along the path toward publication, I received considerable financial support and encouragement. At the Library of Congress, I held The Cary and Ann Maguire Chair in Ethics and American History in 2006, when I was launching this study. The John W. Kluge Center was a great place to work, and I made good use of the Library's unrivaled resources. I benefitted from the kindness and support of the several members of the Center's staff and the other participants in the program. The Guggenheim Foundation extended me a Fellowship (2006–2007) that came at a crucial point in my effort to sweep through the entire twentieth century in these historical essays. I hope the Foundation and the Center will find the finished work worthy of their backing.

Throughout my research and writing, the Johns Hopkins History Department provided me with a setting that encourages scholarship without imposing any limits on historical inquiry. Gaby Spiegel and Bill Rowe were supportive Chairs, and I also thank Deans Adam Falk and Katherine S. Newman for their tolerance and help. I was able to present some of my early chapters to "The Seminar" at Hopkins. A vigorous response by the participants left me with a number of ideas that helped me improve the book. In the History Department, I enjoyed the support of an excellent staff that includes Lisa Enders, Jennifer Rodriguez, Jennifer Stanfield, and Megan Zeller. Clayton Haywood and Lisa Nawrot provided computer assistance that could be understood by a mere professor of history.

A few of my former colleagues and students crept into my footnotes, and several of them participating in bringing out a volume on *The Challenge of Remaining Innovative: Insights from Twentieth-Century American Business*, edited by Sally H. Clarke, Naomi R. Lamoreaux, and Steven W. Usselman. I learned a great deal from those essays as I was finishing my analysis of American creativity. None of my friends, family members, editors, or colleagues carry any responsibility for my conclusions about American history, but I hope they will understand how indebted I am to all of them for their support.

Index